The Responsive Public Library Collection

THE RESPONSIVE
PUBLIC LIBRARY COLLECTION
How to Develop and Market It

Sharon L. Baker
University of Iowa

1993
LIBRARIES UNLIMITED, INC.
Englewood, Colorado

To Barb and Esther

LIBRARIES UNLIMITED, INC.
P.O. Box 6633
Englewood, CO 80155-6633

Library of Congress Cataloging-in-Publication Data

Baker, Sharon L.
  The responsive public library collection : how to develop and market it / by Sharon L. Baker.
    xi, 330 p. 17x25 cm.
    Includes bibliographical references and index.
    ISBN 0-87287-911-9
    1. Libraries and community--United States.   2. Public libraries--United States--Marketing.   3. Public libraries--Collection development--United States.   I. Title.
  Z716.4.B25   1993
  027.473068'8--dc20   92-40997
                                                                CIP

Contents

Acknowledgments

Over the years, a number of people have contributed greatly to my understanding of the subject of marketing, collection development and evaluation, and public libraries. My deepest appreciation goes to Esther Bierbaum, who taught me the importance of exploring a subject in depth, cast a thoughtful, critical eye on the chapters here, and listened patiently to my developing thoughts on the subject; Lolly Eggers, who taught me to pay attention to practical realities as well as theoretical concerns, critiqued my manuscript from that perspective, and gave feedback on a number of marketing techniques that I recommended that her public library use; Sarah Ann Long, who taught me, by example, the importance of marketing library services in general; and Herbert Goldhor, who taught me how to think critically and to carefully consider research in the field.

I also wish to thank several individuals who provided various types of support at the University of Iowa's School of Library and Information Science: Carl Orgren, who arranged for me to have time to finish this book and provided graduate assistant support; Leandra Sunseri, who helped track down pertinent, concrete examples to illustrate the theoretical concepts mentioned here; Jan Zauha and Dawn Story, who retrieved and verified numerous citations; Pat Kondora, who typed this manuscript; and Joyce Hartford and Herb Snyder, who patiently listened to all my stories.

Introduction

Marketing was designed for organizations in trouble. And many of today's public libraries are in trouble. During the past 15 years, patron expectations about the types of services and collections that libraries can offer have risen greatly. Public libraries could once get by with providing books, magazines, newspapers, and a few records and films for their patrons. Now patrons are demanding books-on-tape, compact disks, videotapes, computer software, machine-readable data files, and other media, in addition to the more traditional fare.[1] But although user expectations have risen, funding levels have not kept pace with the rate of inflation or with even higher increases in the costs of library materials. The result has often been cuts rather than expansions in services and collections (Quinn and Rogers, 1992; Curley, 1990; Sherlock, 1990).

This has produced underfunded, understaffed libraries that often have collections and services that are of less than optimal quality. For years, librarians have been told that they are providing "half-right" reference services.[2] Now studies are showing that the average public library fills only 50 percent to 65 percent of patron requests for specific items at the time these requests are made.[3]

Van House has noted that "[p]ublic library use is voluntary. The library makes itself available and attractive, but in the end the individual decides whether or not to use it" (1983, 365). This raises the question: Why should individuals decide to use libraries that meet only half their needs? The answer, of course, is that they should not. After all, the residents of the communities that public libraries serve are rational and intelligent people who are able to make comparisons between services that fulfill their requirements and those that do not. If community residents can meet their needs for recreational, informational, and educational materials through other sources (bookstores, book clubs, subscription services, video rental outlets, electronic database providers, and the like), why should they support the library—with either their patronage or their tax dollars?

On the other hand, if public librarians redesign services and collections so that patrons can find what they need, libraries should be able to obtain long-term support—in the form of usage and funding—so that they can remain viable in a changing world. Marketing can help librarians accomplish this task, because, by definition, marketing is "the analysis, planning, implementation, and control of carefully formulated programs designed to ... achieve organizational objectives" (Kotler, 1982, 6).

1

Marketing, as it relates to collection management in public libraries, requires the analysis, planning, implementation, and control of programs designed to provide community residents with the items they want when these are requested. In other words, marketing public library collections means designing the collection in response to the needs and desires of those whom the library serves. Librarians with a marketing philosophy focus on *patron needs*, even if fulfilling some of these needs (e.g., providing light reading, such as Harlequin novels) makes the librarians uncomfortable. Marketing-oriented librarians will also use effective pricing, communication, and distribution techniques to reduce patron costs of using the collection, to increase patron awareness of the collection's contents, and to motivate patrons to use these materials.

As Kies (1987) has carefully documented, the library profession's interest in marketing activities goes back to the late 1800s. For example, in 1876, Samuel Swet Green suggested that librarians should determine user needs before choosing works for the collection. In 1893, the Pawtuxet Valley (Rhode Island) Public Library promoted its new acquisitions on lists posted in various public locations around town. In 1895, the St. Louis Public Library wrote to parents urging them to bring their children to the library during the summer months when school was closed. And the following year John Cotton Dana used his position as American Library Association president to advocate the use of a variety of promotion techniques in libraries.

Indeed, over the years librarians have often "instinctively exhibited the sensitivity, responsiveness, and flexibility that are [the hallmarks of marketing]" (Wood, 1988, xiii). But most librarians have performed marketing activities on a piecemeal basis—conducting a few user studies here, promoting a few aspects of their collection there. They did not begin to think seriously about adopting a comprehensive and fully integrated approach to marketing until the mid-1970s, when the effects of rising inflation substantially eroded the minimum budgets they already had (Tucci, 1988; Wasserman and Ford, 1980). Even then, some library leaders felt that marketing was a fad—one that they hoped would pass quickly.[4]

Shapiro (1980) says public libraries have failed to establish comprehensive marketing programs for a number of reasons. One is their reluctance to adopt "commercial" activities. This reluctance is partly explained by the fact that many commercial marketers use slick, hard-sell tactics, which could certainly cheapen the image of the library as an institution capable of improving the quality of life. But what some librarians have failed to realize is that the techniques used to market a product are up to institutional leaders. And very few leaders in the library field advocate using hard-sell tactics. In fact, more appear to err by underpromoting their collections, believing that good quality resources will "sell themselves," rather than overpromoting them.

A second reason for neglecting marketing is the difficulty that top library administrators face in measuring the effectiveness of marketing efforts, because public libraries lack bottom-line, profit or loss figures. Although some librarians have suggested that circulation figures can serve as a total substitute for profit figures, more would agree that this type of quantitative figure is only one means of measuring success. This does not imply that public libraries should avoid marketing their wares, however; rather, they should consider developing, then routinely using, other, more varied means of measuring the success of their marketing efforts.

A third difficulty is the fact that library administrators often have unrealistic expectations about what can be accomplished by marketing programs. This is particularly true because such programs often lack enough specially trained staff members to effectively administer them. For example, Wylie and Slovacek (1984) found that less than one-third of the marketing programs in public and academic libraries are run by people who have had formal training in marketing or public relations. And only 19 percent of the libraries that had marketing programs had developed formal plans to guide the operations of these.

Public librarians themselves have suggested a fourth reason why they are neglecting marketing: they lack the money, time, and staff to conduct such efforts. As Vavrek (1988) notes, there is a certain irony in this statement: staff at these libraries do not have the time to determine the most effective and efficient means of serving the community because they are too busy trying to be all things to all community residents. Baker and Lancaster (1991) and Baker (1987) have also noted the lack of foresight shown by those who concentrate on satisfying immediate needs rather than comprehensively evaluating existing resources and services, then developing effective library programs that will work over both the short term and the long.

Today, there is mounting evidence that marketing, with its emphasis on meeting user needs and on adopting an overall systematic plan to meet library objectives, can help libraries operate more efficiently, provide collections and services that will better satisfy patrons, and attract more resources, be they users, supporters, or funding dollars. Consider the case of Pine Mountain (Georgia) Regional Library System. In 1986, this system, like many rural libraries, provided a minimum level of service and was short on both funding and staff. The library decided to practice marketing, using the procedures spelled out in *Planning and Role Setting for Public Libraries: A Manual of Options and Procedures* (McClure and others, 1987). Staff gathered data on the people they served, developed a comprehensive plan to focus the library's efforts on providing the popular and educational materials that were most desired by community residents, carried out the activities specified in the plan, and evaluated the success of these. The results were dramatic: library staff became more responsive to community needs, made more effective decisions, improved their communication with community residents and funding officials, and obtained a 91 percent funding increase over a three-year period (Hopper, 1991).

The growing number of articles and research studies that have been published in the last decade indicates an ever increasing interest in marketing library services.[5] The literature has evolved from popular and review articles discussing basic marketing concepts in the early 1980s to works discussing the application of marketing segmentation and other advanced techniques beginning in the mid-1980s (Tucci, 1988). The library press has published special issues of a number of journals and more than a dozen full-length books on the topic. And the Public Library Association, through the work of the Marketing Public Library Services Section and through individual publications like *Planning and Role Setting for Public Libraries: A Manual of Options and Procedures* (McClure and others, 1987), is actively promoting marketing throughout the profession.[6] This "fad" appears to be here to stay.

This book grew out of my own recognition of three factors:

1. Few authors have described, in any detail, how marketing principles can be applied to collection development. Although a number of recent, thoughtful works on marketing exist, most discuss how marketing can improve the overall ability of a library to meet patron needs, improve satisfaction rates, and increase funding, rather than focusing on collection-related issues.[7]

2. Few published works discuss theoretical aspects of collection development in public libraries. For example, when Kohl (1988) reviewed research that had been published in 33 core North American library journals from 1960 through 1983, he uncovered only 14 articles that concentrated on that topic.

3. Many librarians want to learn more about this topic. One recent study showed, for example, that more than half the directors of public libraries serving populations of 100,000 or more felt that their staff members wanted and would benefit from continuing education efforts that addressed collection development practices (Wall, 1989).

This book attempts to address these issues by providing a basic introduction to the topic of marketing public library collections. Each chapter spells out questions that librarians need to ask themselves or discusses principles that they should consider when developing collections that are responsive to the needs of current patrons and of the community as a whole. Research studies and practical examples are included to illustrate various points. No attempt has been made to be comprehensive. Rather, the book was designed to present a broad overview of the topic, referring readers to more specialized works when these are appropriate and available.

Chapter 2 introduces some of the theoretical principles that underlie the book: what marketing is; how redesigning a library's products and its pricing, distribution, and promotion practices can help increase patron demand for materials; and what types of orientations libraries can exhibit toward marketing. It also recommends that public libraries adopt a societal-marketing orientation.

Two marketing trends that are profoundly affecting collection management in public libraries are the focus of chapter 3. The first is the move away from mass marketing—in which the public library tries to be all things to all people—toward differentiated marketing. The latter requires that a public library conduct an in-depth community analysis to determine what library services are needed; write a mission statement that specifies a few roles (e.g., *popular materials center* or *community information center*) that will meet a majority of user needs; and concentrate the bulk of its collection development resources on fostering the roles it has chosen to emphasize. It often does this by designing its collection and services to meet the needs of specific target markets—small homogeneous groups of potential patrons with common information needs. The second trend is the growing recognition that collection management should occur as an integrated, three-step cycle that involves comprehensive evaluation of the existing collection and of unmet patron requirements for materials, selection of materials to fill the needs documented in that evaluation, and active, systematic promotion of materials to patrons.

Chapter 4 discusses some broad questions that public librarians need to ask themselves when considering decisions relating to the library's products—that is, the items in the collection. These questions include the following: What segments of the community use the library collection? What elements do individual users consider when making selections in libraries? What mix of products will best meet user needs? And how does the life cycle of a particular product affect the level of demand for it?

Chapter 5 spells out some of the costs that patrons must bear in using the collection, like the cost of traveling to the library, of searching the catalog, of standing in line to check out materials, of filing reserve or interlibrary loan requests, and so forth. Also discussed are four basic pricing objectives that a library may choose: maximizing use, recovering costs, maximizing profit, and discouraging use. A final focus is on factors that librarians should consider when setting pricing objectives and considering price changes.

Issues relating to place (that is, how the items in the collection are distributed to library patrons) are discussed in chapter 6. Relevant sections concentrate on factors that should be considered when determining the types of collection distribution outlets (e.g., branch libraries, deposit collections) that a library system can use; the distribution of items among these outlets; the kinds of works within a single facility that librarians might wish to house in separate collections, rather than integrating among materials in the regular stacks; and the methods that librarians can use to lay out a building's interior for maximum distribution effectiveness.

Chapter 7 describes various questions that librarians can ask themselves when making promotion decisions—decisions that relate to informing target markets of the costs and benefits of using library resources. What target market is the library trying to reach with a particular promotion effort? What type of response is being sought from the target market? What type of message will the library try to convey to the target market? What techniques can libraries use to promote their products? How often should promotion occur? And how will the library evaluate the results of its promotion effort?

The eighth chapter recommends that public libraries put into place a product-analysis approach to collection evaluation that involves four separate tasks: identifying currently owned items that are heavily used; identifying currently owned items that are lightly used or not used; identifying items that are not in the collection but are desired by patrons or potential patrons; and identifying other barriers that inhibit use of the collection. The chapter explains why libraries should consider performing these tasks and describes specific evaluation techniques and procedures that can be followed to accomplish these tasks.

Major steps that a public library can take to establish marketing-based selection practices throughout the entire system are outlined in chapter 9. These include the following: writing a collection development policy that indicates how the roles a library has chosen to emphasize will influence collection development efforts; reviewing materials budget allocations to ensure that these are consistent with what the library is trying to accomplish; establishing a centralized selection program to do formula-based purchasing; and asking the library's professional selectors to review the objective data that have been collected about the past and present use of the collection, then follow a series of marketing-based principles when making selection decisions.

Chapter 10 focuses on techniques that libraries typically use to promote their collections, including point-of-purchase displays, display shelving, book lists, booktalks, reference and readers' advisory services, fiction and reader interest categorization, and collection-related events. Specific questions that are addressed include the following: What aspects of the collection can be promoted? What factors should guide librarians making promotion decisions? And what internal and external promotion strategies are most effective in increasing use or user awareness of the collection?

The final chapter describes how library leaders can work to establish a climate in which a change to marketing-oriented collection development principles can be made. It discusses steps that the library can take to train staff members in basic marketing concepts; devise a plan that will list marketing goals and objectives, then spell out practical activities to help translate these into reality; provide sufficient resources to implement the plan; evaluate the success of the plan and make changes as a result of evaluation findings; adopt various other techniques to reinforce staff awareness of marketing concepts on a regular basis; and be sensitive to issues relating to resistance to change.

Notes

[1]Wortman (1989) provides a good overview of the various kinds of media that patrons are demanding.

[2]See, for example, Stephan and others (1988) and Crowley (1985).

[3]See, for example, Gajerski (1989) and Kuraim (1983).

[4]See, for example, Berry and others (1974).

[5]An annotated guide by Norman (1989) lists 114 published works about marketing in libraries from 1981 to 1989.

[6]For information on the Marketing Public Library Services Section, see the "Section News" column in each issue of the journal *Public Libraries*.

[7]See, for example, Leerburger (1989), Kies (1987), and Weingand (1987).

References

Baker, Sharon L. "The Use of *Output Measures for Public Libraries* in North Carolina Public Libraries." University of Iowa School of Library and Information Science, Iowa City, 1987. ERIC ED288538.

Baker, Sharon L., and F. Wilfrid Lancaster. *Measurement and Evaluation of Library Services*. 2d ed. Arlington, Va.: Information Resources Press, 1991.

Berry, John, Shirley Havens, and Karl Nyren. "Editorial: The Selling of the Library." *Library Journal* 99, no. 2 (15 January 1974): 85.

Crowley, Terry. "Half-Right Reference: Is It True?" *RQ* 25, no. 1 (Fall 1985): 59-68.

Curley, Arthur. "Funding for Public Libraries in the 1990s." *Library Journal* 115, no. 1 (January 1990): 65-67.

Gajerski, B. "Edmonton Public Library: 1989 User Survey." Edmonton Public Library, Edmonton, Alberta, 1989. ERIC ED327184.

Hopper, Lyn. "Planning Pays for the Small, the Poor, and the Busy: An Exhortation and a Bibliography." *Public Libraries* 30, no. 1 (January-February 1991): 21-24.

Kies, Cosette N. *Marketing and Public Relations for Libraries*. Metuchen, N.J.: Scarecrow Press, 1987.

Kohl, David F. "Collection Development: An Overview of the Research." *Collection Management* 10, no. 3 (Fall 1988): 1-13.

Kotler, Philip. *Marketing for Nonprofit Organizations*. 2d ed. Englewood Cliffs, N.J.: Prentice-Hall, 1982.

Kuraim, Faraj Mohamed. "The Principal Factors Causing Reader Frustration in a Public Library." Ph.D. diss., Case Western Reserve University, 1983.

Leerburger, Benedict A. *Promoting and Marketing the Library*. Boston: G. K. Hall, 1989.

McClure, Charles R., Amy Owen, Douglas L. Zweizig, Mary Jo Lynch, and Nancy A. Van House. *Planning and Role Setting for Public Libraries: A Manual of Options and Procedures*. Chicago: American Library Association, 1987.

Norman, O. Gene. "Marketing Library and Information Services: An Annotated Guide to Recent Trends and Developments." *Reference Services Review* 17, no. 1 (Spring 1989): 43-64.

Quinn, Judy, and Michael Rogers. "News—Library Budgets Survey '91: Hard Times Continue." *Library Journal* 117, no. 1 (January 1992): 14-18, 20, 22, 26, 28.

Shapiro, Stanley J. "Marketing and the Information Professional." *Special Libraries* 71, no. 11 (November 1980): 469-74.

Sherlock, Katy. "Public Library Circulation, Expenditures Edge Upward." *American Libraries* 21, no. 8 (September 1990): 740.

Stephan, Sandy, Ralph Gers, Lillie Seward, Nancy Bolin, and Jim Partridge. "Reference Breakthrough in Maryland." *Public Libraries* 27, no. 4 (Winter 1988): 202-3.

Tucci, Valerie K. "Information Marketing for Libraries." In *Annual Review of Information Science and Technology*, vol. 23, ed. Martha E. Williams, 59-81. New York: Elsevier Science, 1988.

Van House, Nancy A. "A Time Allocation Theory of Public Library Use." *Library and Information Science Research* 5, no. 4 (Winter 1983): 365-84.

Vavrek, Bernard. "The Public Library at Crisis: Is Marketing the Answer?" *North Carolina Libraries* 46, no. 3 (Fall 1988): 142-47.

Wall, Thomas B. "Metropolitan Library Section's Professional Needs Survey." *Public Libraries* 28, no. 3 (May-June 1989): 182-87.

Wasserman, Paul, and Gary T. Ford. "Marketing and Library Research: What the Library Manager Should Learn." *Journal of Library Administration* 1, no. 1 (Spring 1980): 19-29.

Weingand, Darlene E. *Marketing/Planning Library and Information Services*. Littleton, Colo.: Libraries Unlimited, 1987.

Wortman, William. *Collection Management: Background and Principles*. Chicago: American Library Association, 1989.

Wood, Elizabeth J. *Strategic Marketing for Libraries: A Handbook*. Westport, Conn.: Greenwood Press, 1988.

Wylie, Frank W., and Simeon P. Slovacek. "PR Evaluation: Myth, Option, or Necessity." *Public Relations Review* 10, no. 2 (Summer 1984): 22-27.

Marketing, the Marketing Mix, and Marketing Orientations

2

Philip Kotler, one of the nation's leading marketing experts, has defined marketing as "the analysis, planning, implementation, and control of carefully formulated programs designed to bring about voluntary exchanges of values with target markets for the purpose of achieving organizational objectives. It relies heavily on designing the organization's offering in terms of the target markets' needs and desires, and on using effective pricing, communication, and distribution to inform, motivate, and service the markets" (1982, 6). Each of the elements contained in this definition relates to the concept of building responsive library collections.

The words "analysis, planning, implementation, and control" illustrate the connection between marketing and planning in general, one that a number of authors in the field have spelled out in some detail.[1] During the last two decades, public libraries have increased their reliance on formal planning processes. Techniques like those spelled out in *A Planning Process for Public Libraries* (Palmour, Bellassai, and DeWath, 1980) and in *Planning and Role Setting for Public Libraries: A Manual of Options and Procedures* (McClure and others, 1987) can and have helped librarians to evaluate their services more systematically and to make plans for improvement.

But librarians can conduct evaluation and planning activities on a more specific level, concentrating on the collection itself rather than the broader smorgasbord of all library services. Thus, one aspect of marketing public library collections involves gathering current, objective data to see the extent to which the collection has "worked" in the past, developing better purchasing strategies to overcome problems identified during the evaluation stage, carrying out those strategies, and monitoring results to see the effects of the changes.

The phrase "carefully formulated programs" implies that marketers should rely on well-thought-out programs when making decisions that affect collection development rather than on off-the-cuff ideas of what might work and what might not. Profit-making organizations often conduct careful experiments before introducing new products, something that few libraries can afford to do (Baker, 1989). However, librarians can read the research on marketing and collection development that has been done both by libraries and by their competitors (e.g., bookstores and publishers).[2] Librarians can also carefully study their own successes and failures, then weigh the advantages and disadvantages of making certain types of selection choices before actually spending any money.

The notion of "bring[ing] about voluntary exchanges of values" is one that may be new to some. Many public librarians have been leery of marketing because they think it relies on the use of manipulative selling techniques (the kind that used-car salesmen stereotypically practice) that may not provide patrons with what they want and so cause dissatisfaction with library services over time. But the true marketer recognizes that it is human for patrons to take and then to repeat those actions that are in their best interests. The true marketer, therefore, tries to design a product, in this case a collection of print and nonprint materials, that will provide patrons with so many benefits that they will use the library because they want to and will even give the library something in return. In fact, Dragon (1983) suggests that it may be useful for librarians to think of their patrons as persons who have the potential to award prizes to the library if they find its products useful. The prizes may take various forms, including more patron attention, greater use of its collections and services, and better financial support.

The next phrase, "with target markets," is particularly relevant to public libraries. Although it may seem that the process of targeting calls for the library to segment its market into manageable pieces (for example, the illiterate, fiction readers, retirees, videotape users, preschoolers), a better approach is to collect information about the residents libraries are funded to serve and let this information dictate which target markets should be pursued. In other words, librarians should not segment the market; they should look for already existing segments of the market to pursue. Librarians are better off choosing to serve fewer target groups, because they cannot, with current levels of staff and funding, meet the demands of everyone without further diluting the quality of library services.[3] The ability of a collection to meet patron needs can also be diluted when resources are spread too thinly. For example, Kuraim's (1983) study indicates that the biggest reason that public libraries are meeting only about half of patron demands for specific materials is that libraries are trying to provide a very wide range of titles, many of which are little used, while failing to duplicate classic and popular materials in the quantities needed to meet patron demands.

The words "for the purpose of achieving organizational objectives" need little explanation. Ideally, a library that develops and implements the kind of thoughtful, consistent plan discussed so far will be able to meet its collection management objectives.

The principle of "rel[ying] heavily on designing the organization's offering in terms of the target markets' needs and desires" is one of the more critical aspects of marketing. This principle suggests that librarians should examine, on a regular basis, who their users are and what they need.[4] Librarians should also be professional enough both to listen to the needs of these users and to redesign the collection in terms of those needs, even when the needs (for example, for Danielle Steel novels) do not reflect the librarians' personal tastes. Librarians cannot expect to increase the probability that an exchange will occur unless they design their collections to be more responsive to user needs.

The final phrase, "using effective pricing, communication, and distribution to inform, motivate, and service the markets," refers to the fact that marketing employs these tactics to reduce patron costs of using the collection and to inform and motivate patrons to use library resources.

It is relatively easy to see, after reviewing aspects of Kotler's definition, that marketing has a ready application to collection development.

The Marketing Mix: How the Four P's Affect Collection Development in Public Libraries

Librarians who want to develop responsive public library collections need to consider what marketers call "The Four P's." These are four broad factors that influence customer demand: product, price, place, and promotion. Ideally, librarians should mix these four components in a way that will increase the likelihood that a patron will use and be satisfied with the library's collection. That is, librarians who want to market their collections need to do the following on a regular and continuing basis:

1. Examine the short-term demands of prospective patrons and the long-term requirements of the communities they serve and design a product, in this case the overall library collection, that will meet these needs.

2. Set the price of using the collection as low as is feasible, given the constraints placed on the library by its current budget and staff.

3. Design a place or distribution system that will allow patrons to obtain needed items in the collection quickly and conveniently.

4. Promote the collection's availability, advantages, and costs to patrons.

In other words, a responsive public library purchases needed items for the collection, makes patrons aware of these items, and delivers them, at the lowest feasible cost to patrons, at the time that they are desired. Chapters 4, 5, 6, and 7 explain basic concepts relating to the four P's.

What Types of Orientations Can Libraries Exhibit Toward Marketing?

Although many public libraries have readily adopted some marketing techniques (e.g., promotion of services), few are truly "marketing oriented" (Vavrek, 1988; Kotler, 1982). This is because they tend to focus on production, product, or sales rather than on meeting customer needs and desires. Listed below are five different types of orientations that organizations can adopt.

A Production Orientation

An organization with a production orientation feels that its major task is to efficiently produce or distribute its goods or services (Kotler, 1982). Although most would agree that libraries should be able to distribute the materials in their collections quickly and efficiently to patrons, librarians with a production orientation value efficiency more than they value patron convenience or satisfaction.

Let me illustrate this with a personal example. Some years ago, I visited an undergraduate library at a major midwestern university to browse for books on interior design.[5] I discovered that all books on this topic were shelved in a compact storage area that could be opened only by staff. Upon further inquiry, I was told that the shelving system was opened only once per hour and that I would have to list the titles and call numbers of all the books I wanted so that a clerk could enter the closed stacks area and retrieve them. I explained that I just wanted to browse until I found something interesting but was informed that this would not be allowed. When I expressed concern that my needs were not being met, I was told that the university had adopted compact shelving to store its collection more efficiently and that sometimes the needs of individual patrons had to be sacrificed as a result. Because I did not want to deal with the hassles imposed by this library system, I left without retrieving any books. As this example illustrates, although libraries should be interested in increasing their efficiency, they need to realize that adhering to a strict production orientation—which emphasizes efficiency at the expense of service—can decrease, rather than increase, patron use and satisfaction levels.

A Sales Orientation

An organization with a sales orientation feels that its major task is to stimulate the interest of potential consumers in the organization's existing products and services (Kotler, 1982). The organization assumes that the customer is failing to demand its products because of a lack of awareness, rather than because the product doesn't meet the customer's needs in some major way (for example, its focus, design, quality, or cost is wrong for the customer). Therefore, the organization tries to educate the public about the value of its products.

Certainly, promotion can be a key to increasing use of library collections. Indeed, as Rice says, the idea behind a good publicity campaign is "to present the case for the merits of a cause or an institution so cogently, so winningly, so irresistibly, that the hearts and minds of men will be captured" (1972, 3-4). But although promotional techniques may entice library patrons into trying services they haven't used before, the techniques need to be coupled with efforts to redesign those products to meet patron needs. Otherwise, patrons may be dissatisfied with the products and fail to become repeat users. They may also question the library's credibility and distrust any future messages it generates (Corrick, 1983).

The failure to redesign library collections and services in light of patron needs before promoting them may explain, at least in part, why use of library products and services may increase drastically when they are promoted but fall off rapidly when the promotion stops. For example, Owens (1987) conducted an experiment to determine the most effective means of publicizing a library-based information and referral service in a predominantly rural area. She publicized the service in a variety of ways: through public service announcements on the radio and cable television stations, advertisements and feature articles in area newspapers, brochures and posters distributed in the community, and contacts with local social service agencies. Although the number of information and referral calls to this public library increased by tenfold during the initial days of a four-week publicity blitz, they fell to pre-publicity levels within six weeks after the campaign ended. In other words, advertising and sales techniques, when used by themselves, may not significantly increase patron use of a library's services or collections over time.

A Product Orientation

An organization with a product orientation feels that its major task is to generate products that are in some way "good" for the public (Kotler, 1982). This type of organization loves its product so much that it may not be willing to listen to what its customers want or need. The organization focuses on producing a "quality" product rather than one that is "fit for the customer's purpose" (Van Loo, 1984).

In collection development, a product orientation is shown by those who argue that the library should limit itself to providing only items of high quality. Merritt has described this as the "give-them-what-they-should-have" theory of book selection, a theory that "posits the public library as an educational institution containing books that provide inspiration, information, and recreation, with insistence that even the last mentioned should embody some measure of creative imagination. The collection should include only those books which one way or another tend toward the development and enrichment of life" (1979, 19).

A product orientation has been around since the earliest days of public libraries. For example, a librarian writing in 1903 suggested that librarians should improve patrons' reading tastes by removing all materials of poor quality from the collection, substituting high-quality ones, and habituating readers to using the latter by emphasizing typographic attractiveness and prominent display of titles (Bloom, 1976). Other librarians used the two-book system to wean readers away from the "frivolous" activity of fiction reading. They allowed patrons to check out two, rather than one, book at a time if the second was nonfiction (Ross, 1991). Still other librarians placed fiction in a ribbon arrangement "on one shelf around the room, with non-fiction classes above and below it, the expectation being that many users who read only fiction [would] in this way be attracted to non-fiction books and begin to withdraw and read them" (Bostwick, 1929, 195-96).

Advocates say focusing entirely on "quality" book selection helps the library accomplish its educational mission in at least three ways (Berry, 1990, 1979; Bob, 1982; Dessauer, 1980; Kister, 1971). First, the library provides works of permanent value, thus introducing patrons to the delights of "good" literature and the intricacies of a variety of nonfiction topics. Second, the library provides quality materials for a wide range of people. This encourages development of diverse points of view and a general public commitment to intellectual freedom, a basic tenet of the democratic ideal. And third, the library serves as a depository of civilization that will preserve knowledge for the future.

Many of the arguments that quality advocates use are very appealing. For example, most librarians would agree with Bob's statement that "[l]ibraries have a responsibility to ideas, to nurturing, sustaining, preserving, and making readily available the intellectual capital of our society to anyone who may want or need it, now or in the future" (1982, 1710).

But librarians with a product orientation may be extreme in their insistence that lower quality works should be excluded from or greatly de-emphasized in the collection, even if patrons want them. For example, Bob has suggested that public librarians consider demand for a popular but poor quality item in the following way:

> A new novel comes along by a well known hack. It is real crap and everyone knows it. But unfortunately, like all really consummate crap, it is extremely well advertised. Moreover, the book's cover will display bare-assed Bertha's big boobs *in puris naturalibus*. In a word, it is a sure seller. The library is faced with the usual dilemma: "Should we buy it?" ... [Let's suppose] that library "A" practiced the proper principles of non-selection. What would it do...? It might, if it were terribly courageous, issue a list called, "Books We Didn't Buy and Why." And every time a patron asked for "Bertha," it would give the patron an annotated list that might read:
>
>> "Bertha's biggies were universally panned by critics. The book is formula fiction at its worst. Our library is facing a budget crunch and so we feel that your tax money should not be wasted. To spend $10 on this, or even $6 at discount, would be a sin worse than any committed by Bertha. When this book comes out in paperback at 25% of the hardcover price, then we might buy it. Meanwhile, don't hold your breath. After all, what is the rush? Jerqueline Paisan has been writing essentially the same novel for 25 years. She just changes the titles and the names of the characters. Read one of her old ones while you're waiting. After all, why do you have to read the same book that everyone else is reading? Try being an individual. When was the last time you read (if ever) 'Anna Karenina' or _____ (fill in with other possible titles.)"
>
> What a breath of fresh air to read an honest annotation for a change! (1976, 1, 6)

The above example illustrates why proponents of quality selection are often accused of elitism. In this type of product-oriented selection, librarians may impose their preferences and judgments on others, thus interfering with the rights of patrons to choose materials to fit their own needs. Critics of quality selection say that the elitist collections that result are far above the tastes and needs of the average reader. They add that this selection bias has caused most public libraries to be used by a small segment of the total population, a segment that is predominantly white, middle-class, well-educated, and female (Hole, 1990; Moran, 1985; Dragon and Leisner, 1983; Hirsch, 1979).

The selection of materials based only on quality has a second flaw: it presumes that librarians recognize quality when they see it. This may or may not be true. Although several studies have shown that librarians who have received instruction in selection as part of a master's program in library science do in fact select "higher quality" items than their nondegreed counterparts, many of the selectors in the nation's small and medium-sized libraries do not have such training (Turow, 1978; Bendix and Pennypacker, 1967; McCrossan, 1966). Moreover, these research studies are themselves suspect, because they use rather subjective standards to define quality.

Currently, many schools of library and information science appear to be encouraging a product orientation. For example, when Moran studied collection development practices in more than 100 library schools in the United States, she found that "a large part of the student's time in collection development courses and courses on specific literatures is spent in learning how to assemble the best collection of materials—how to apply objective standards to select the highest quality materials, what reviews to consult, and how to establish bibliographic control of the material" (1985, 27). In contrast, only 12 schools had courses in which concepts related to "popular" materials were taught. If today's librarians are to develop true marketing orientations, this pattern should be changed.

Another kind of product orientation relates not to the quality of individual works but rather to the usefulness of library collections as a whole. Librarians tend to believe that everyone could benefit from having access to library materials. However, a growing number of studies suggest that some people just aren't interested in the products that libraries offer.

For example, when Madden (1979a, 1979b) analyzed information from a nationwide study of life-styles, he discovered a strong relationship between library use and an active life-style and drew some very interesting conclusions:

1. Nonusers have horizons that tend to stop at their front doorsteps. Their values are highly conservative and patriotic. As a group, they are less educated, watch a great deal of television, have few outside activities other than necessary ones like working, going to the dentist, or grocery shopping, and dislike change in general. The female nonuser, who generally is not interested in enlarging her everyday activities, is an unlikely candidate for a library outreach program. Although some male nonusers could be reached through a very extensively publicized home improvement and automobile repair collection, most will never become regular library users.

2. Moderate library users are much more active. Ninety percent are high school graduates; many have attended college. They are less conservative than nonusers but still believe in more traditional sex roles (male as provider, female as nurturer). The library can attract these people by providing items of direct relevance to their rather tangible interests, like works relating to their home and jobs, to child raising, and to leisure interests.

3. Heavy users are generally active and very involved in life. They enjoy reading, taking courses, participating in sports, and traveling. They are fairly liberal in their ideas, including those relating to sex roles. Most have had some college course work. These people are natural library users who account for about 80 percent of total library use.

Madden's findings, which indicate that libraries may fail to convert nonusers to users, are not isolated ones. For example, a survey conducted by the Enoch Pratt Free Library in Baltimore, Maryland, discovered that 43 percent of its nonusers said nothing the library could do would attract them. Two of the major reasons for nonuse were "read few or no books" and "just don't go/need to go" (Results, 1987).

Although some public librarians are still arguing that developing high quality collections will increase demand among community residents, there is little evidence that adopting this type of product orientation has raised overall levels of patron use or satisfaction with the collection.

A Marketing Orientation

An organization with a marketing orientation feels that its major task is a multifaceted one: to systematically study customer needs, wants, preferences, and satisfaction levels; to redesign all elements of its products that are not satisfactory; to appropriately price and distribute these products; and to communicate their value to customers (Kotler, 1982). A marketing orientation recognizes the value of increasing production efficiency, of producing quality products, and of stimulating the consumer's interest in the organization's products and services, but not at the cost of user needs.

In collection development terms, a marketing orientation is revealed in a strong emphasis on patron demand. As Merritt notes, the demand or give-them-what-they-want theory of collection development "sees the public library as a democratic institution, supported by taxes paid by the whole community, each member of which has an equal right to find what he wishes to read in the library collection" (1964, 19). Although many give McColvin (1925) credit for developing the demand theory in some detail, others before him had considered the topic. Charles Cutter was one of the more outspoken of these pioneers. In an address to the Western Massachusetts Library Club in 1901, he posed the query "Should libraries buy only the best books or the best books that people will read?" then argued that

> [t]he question answers itself; there is no real opposition between its parts. Of course, we are to buy the best books, and if we have limited funds we can buy no others, or equally we shall not get all of the best. But equally, of course, this means the best books for the particular library in question, and that is the same as the best books that its people will use; for an unused book is not even good. Not the best books for the librarian, nor for the book committee, nor for the self-elected book committee outside of the library, nor for the shelves (to keep them warm by never leaving them); but the best books to satisfy the just demands of our clients for amusement and knowledge and mental stimulus and spiritual inspiration. The library should be a practical thing to be used, not an ideal to be admired." (1901, 101)

Proponents of a strict marketing orientation say libraries that emphasize user demand will meet patron needs and wants more successfully and gain higher overall use and a broader-based clientele. The experiences of some libraries support this view. Libraries that have claimed higher circulation rates after implementing marketing techniques like demand-oriented buying and merchandising include the Baltimore County (Maryland) Public Library (Davis, 1979), the Logan Square Branch of the Chicago Public Library (Ballard, 1981), and the Dallas Public Library (Green, 1981). The Queens Borough (New York) Public Library says its circulation doubled in seven years due to its emphasis on user demand (Sivulich, 1989). And when service hours were substantially reduced at the Brooklyn (New York) Public Library, marketing practices slowed down the expected decline in circulation (Martinez-Rivera, 1987).

There is also evidence to support the fact that marketing may lead to a broader base of users. For example, D'Elia and Rodger (1987) found that there are no significant differences among the average numbers of materials checked out by individual patrons at various libraries. These authors suggest that circulation per capita may thus indirectly measure the percentage of community residents that actually uses a library. That is, libraries that have higher circulation per capita figures may be drawing more *different* people into the library.

The question then becomes: Do demand-oriented libraries have higher circulation per capita rates than the average library? Several studies have examined these rates for a sample of public libraries nationwide. For example, Zweizig (1985) found that 93 single outlet public libraries across the country, serving populations ranging from 1,300 to 155,000 persons, reported an average circulation per capita rate of 5.8. And data collected by the Public Library Association revealed an average circulation per capita rate of 7.1 for 522 public libraries of all sizes nationwide.[6] Although no large-scale, definitive studies have explored the issue, a scanning of raw data from some libraries that claim to be demand-oriented shows that their circulation per capita rates are generally much higher than that of the average public library. For example, the Baltimore County (Maryland) Public Library has a circulation per capita rate of 18.3 (Public Library Association, 1991). Future studies should verify whether the average circulation per capita rate of demand-oriented libraries is significantly higher than that of non-demand-oriented institutions. If so, libraries will have further evidence to support the principle that buying items that patrons want will eventually attract more users, including users from the fringe market.

The Baltimore County Public Library (BCPL) is well-known for its marketing orientation, in part because of the crusading spirit of its director, Charles Robinson.[7] At BCPL, a central selection staff of four professional librarians, assisted by a committee of librarians drawn from the total system, predicts user demand by monitoring publishing trends, including the promotion particular titles are receiving in the print and electronic news media. Only after they establish potential use of a title will they consider it for purchase. As the head of materials selection at BCPL has noted, anticipated blockbusters by such popular authors as Sidney Sheldon and Danielle Steel are purchased in enormous quantities (literally hundreds of copies) without considering the quality of the works (Wisotzki, 1989).

Collection development is carried further at BCPL by monitoring use of individual titles after purchase. Stock turnover rates (the ratio of circulation to volumes owned) are established for each Dewey Decimal section and are employed as rough weeding guidelines for discarding individual titles. Some items are kept even if they have not circulated well; however, these are limited to items with projected in-house use, items with seasonal demand, or items that are the sole source covering a subject area (Engel, 1982). And BCPL's goal is to hold these little-used titles to five percent of the total collection (Davis, 1979).

Although predicting use is not easy for titles that are neither esoteric nor of blockbuster potential, a fall 1981 survey showed that BCPL met user demands for 86 percent to 97 percent of specific known-title requests (Engel, 1982). The accessibility rate at most public libraries appears to be much lower. For example, 52 percent of patrons at the Edmonton (Alberta) Public Library frequently found that the books they sought were missing from the shelves, generally because they were already checked out to another borrower (Gajerski, 1989). One author who examined a number of availability studies concluded that the average public library in the United States met only half its users' demands for known items (Kuraim, 1983).

In addition to analyzing the needs of their target markets and purchasing large quantities of popular materials to guarantee that patrons' demands will be met, Baltimore County has adopted other marketing techniques. For example, it places branch libraries in high traffic centers like shopping malls and merchandises its wares using promotional techniques that have been more commonly adopted by retail book stores than by public libraries.

Many people have criticized libraries like BCPL that use patron demand as a primary selection criterion. Demand advocates are charged with becoming today's "elitist authoritarians" who serve only middle-class popular fiction readers (Spiegler, 1980), equate circulation counts with the library's goals (Dessauer, 1980), surrender responsibility for book selection to the publishers' publicity experts who create demand (Bob, 1982), and contribute to a widespread decline in collection quality.[8]

A Societal-Marketing Orientation

The debate over whether public libraries should purchase works of high quality or buy items that will meet patron demand has, of course, not yet been resolved.[9] But many librarians would agree with Cutter that libraries should provide materials that will satisfy the demands of their clients whether it be for amusement or knowledge or mental stimulus or spiritual inspiration. This observation is supported by a recent study of public library directors in Illinois, who were asked whether they agreed or disagreed with 17 statements that reflected the quality-versus-demand debate. As figure 2.1 shows, although a demand-driven philosophy is favored by most of the directors, more than 75 percent also felt that libraries should provide books of high quality and enduring value and should collect classic books and encourage patrons to read these (Hamilton and Weech, 1988, 1987).

75% or More of the Directors Agreed with These Statements:

A library's primary goal should be user satisfaction.

The focus of the library's collection should be on the actual utility of the collection to its current users.

The first consideration should always be whether a book is likely to be of interest to the library's patrons.

User demand should be the primary criterion for buying books.

Libraries should consider buying multiple copies of materials in heavy demand.

A library should buy more books in a high-demand area (such as romance or biography) than in an area in which there is little interest.

Good service should be provided to patrons who favor best-sellers, mysteries, romances, and other popular literature.

Libraries should concentrate on providing copies of books of high quality and enduring value.

Libraries should collect classic books to encourage patrons to read such books.

50% to 74% of the Directors Agreed with These Statements:

Standards of quality or literary merit should not be imposed; the simple fact that the user desires the material should be sufficient for the material to be considered for purchase.

Libraries should purchase books on best-seller lists, even if they don't meet the library's selection criteria.

Every library should offer a wide variety of materials, both those hailed as the best of their kind and the worst.

Many commercial merchandising techniques, such as those used in bookstores, can be used in public libraries.

Fewer than 50% of the Directors Agreed with These Statements:

Libraries should purchase enough copies of best-sellers to ensure that patrons do not have to wait for the books.

Libraries should be more interested in giving people the classics, instead of what they want.

Libraries should select books that patrons ought to read.

A library collection should be considered a resource; actual demand and use are secondary.

Reprinted, in modified form, with permission from Hamilton and Weech (1988, 33-34).

Fig. 2.1. Attitudes about the quality-versus-demand debate among public library directors in Illinois.

These data suggest that public librarians may be moving beyond both a strict product orientation, in which librarians limit themselves to dictating public taste, and a strict market orientation, in which they limit themselves to interpreting public taste. Such a move is more typical among nonprofit than for-profit organizations, because the former face two problems in committing themselves to satisfying customer needs and wants:

> First, customers may have wants that are not proper to satisfy, either because they go against society's interests (such as buying handguns) or against the consumers' long-run interests (such as cigarette smoking). Second, customers may have needs which they do not recognize (such as the need for a quality education) that a nonprofit organization may want to press on the consumer for his/her good, even though it may be costly to do. A growing number of marketers see their responsibility to take four factors into account in their marketing decision making: consumer needs, consumer wants, consumer interests, and society's interests. (Kotler, 1982, 23)

Thus, Kotler has added a fifth orientation, one that is more palatable to many librarians. An organization with a societal-marketing orientation feels that its main task is to identify the needs and wants of its customers and to adapt the organization to delivering satisfactions that preserve or enhance the customers' *and* society's well-being (Kotler, 1982, 23).

The public library's responsibility toward society as a whole has been repeatedly discussed by both individual librarians and organizations such as the Public Library Association. Ten years ago, PLA stated that "[f]ree access to ideas and information, a prerequisite to the existence of a responsible citizenship, is as fundamental to America as are the principles of freedom and equality and individual rights. This access is also fundamental to our social, political and cultural systems.... Access to information and the recorded wisdom and experience of others has long been held a requirement for achieving personal equality, and for improving the quality of life and thought in the daily activities and relationships of individuals" (Public Library Association, 1982, 1). Indeed, municipalities, counties, and regions generally fund public libraries with this goal partially in mind. However, these funding bodies also want the library to be responsive to the information demands that residents are making.

Librarians with a societal-marketing orientation try to balance the immediate demands of their patrons with the long-term needs of society. They might, for example, decide to devote a good portion of their materials budgets to popular recreational materials, while simultaneously buying and systematically promoting quality items to meet patron needs for education and enlightenment. A number of public libraries are striving to achieve such a balance—meeting short-term user demands and long-term societal interests. For example, many libraries designate a portion of their budgets to purchase best-sellers and other high-demand titles expected to circulate well at branch libraries, while buying specialized and quality materials for the main library collection.[10]

Conclusion

This book makes the assumption that a societal-marketing orientation is an appropriate one for public libraries to adopt. The collection development practices and principles set forth here are based on this assumption. After all, public libraries are funded by governmental agencies in order to improve the quality of life for community residents. Thus, part of the mandate for library services is to improve society as a whole. But librarians should resist improving society solely in the way that they, the librarians, feel it should be improved; indeed, this constitutes a subtle form of discrimination. To avoid this, librarians should also pay attention to the types of materials that their patrons, who may have very different views from the librarians, want the library to provide.

Notes

[1]See, for example, Weingand (1987).

[2]In one study on decision making, McClure and Samuels (1985) found that librarians often fail to read research findings even when a topic has been well studied; instead, they rely on personal opinion as a major source of evidence when making decisions.

[3]This point was made particularly well in an article by Martin (1983) and, as discussed later in this chapter, is the premise on which *Planning and Role Setting for Public Libraries: A Manual of Options and Procedures* (McClure and others, 1987) is based.

[4]There is growing evidence that librarians are becoming more interested in doing this. For example, Illinois public library directors rated the question "Who are my users and what are their information needs?" as one of the most important research questions for their individual libraries and the state as a whole to address (Estabrook and Albritton, 1991).

[5]I have chosen, throughout this book, to identify individual libraries when they are providing good service, when I have obtained permission to use their names, or when information on the library's practice has been published elsewhere. I will refer to other libraries by size and general geographic location only.

[6]This figure was calculated from raw data presented in Public Library Association (1991, 94-97).

[7]This spirit is expressed quite well in Robinson (1984).

[8]To date, however, there is no evidence to corroborate the belief that overall collection quality is lower in libraries with a marketing- or demand-orientation than it is in those with a product- or quality-orientation. See, for example, Baker (1984).

[9]Librarians are not the only ones who continue to hash and rehash the quality-versus-demand debate. See, for example, Radway's (1988) description of the debate that goes on among the editors responsible for choosing the titles that the Book-of-the-Month Club will feature.

[10]See, for example, Tucson (1982).

References

Baker, Sharon L. "Does the Use of a Demand-Oriented Selection Policy Reduce Overall Collection Quality? A Review of the Evidence." *Public Library Quarterly* 5, no. 3 (Fall 1984): 29-49.

———. "Problem Solving Through Experimental Research: The Need for Better Controls." *Library Trends* 38, no. 2 (Fall 1989): 204-14.

Ballard, Thomas H. "Logan Square Experimental Book Branch." *Illinois Libraries* 63, no. 8 (October 1981): 583-86.

Bendix, Dorothy, and Arabelle Pennypacker. "Curriculum: Book Selection." *Drexel Library Quarterly* 3, no. 1 (January 1967): 72-83.

Berry, John. "Leaning Toward 'Quality'." *Library Journal* 104, no. 17 (1 October 1979): 2013; reprinted in *Library Journal* 115, no. 11 (15 June 1990): 76.

Bloom, Herbert. "Adult Services: 'The Book That Leads You On.' " *Library Trends* 25, no. 1 (July 1976): 379-98.

Bob, Murray. "The Case for Quality Book Selection." *Library Journal* 107, no. 16 (15 September 1982): 1707-10.

———. "Principles of Library Non-Selection." *NYLA Bulletin* 24, no. 5 (May 1976): 1, 6.

Bostwick, Arthur E. *The American Public Library*. 4th ed. New York: Appleton, 1929.

Corrick, Annabelle. "Marketing as Applied Through Publishing: Converting Theory to Practice." *College and Research Libraries* 44, no. 1 (January 1983): 38-45.

Cutter, Charles A. "Should Libraries Buy Only the Best Books or the Best Books that People Will Read?" *Library Journal* 26, no. 2 (February 1901): 70-72.

Davis, Kenneth C. "The Selling of the Library: Baltimore County System Challenges Assumptions About Library's Role." *Publishers Weekly* 216, no. 7 (13 August 1979): 26-28.

D'Elia, George Patrick Michael, and Eleanor Jo Rodger. "Comparative Assessment of Patrons' Uses and Evaluations Across Public Libraries Within a System: A Replication." *Library and Information Science Research* 9, no. 1 (January-March 1987): 5-20.

Dessauer, John P. "Are Libraries Failing Their Patrons?" *Publishers Weekly* 217, no. 2 (18 January 1980): 67-68.

Dragon, Andrea C. "The Marketing of Public Library Services." *Drexel Library Quarterly* 19, no. 2 (Spring 1983): 117-32.

Dragon, Andrea C., and Tony Leisner. "The ABCs of Implementing Library Marketing." *Journal of Library Administration* 4, no. 4 (Winter 1983): 33-47.

Engel, Debra. "Putting the Public First: The Baltimore County Approach to Collection Development." *Catholic Library World* 54, no. 3 (October 1982): 122-26.

Estabrook, Leigh, and Rose Albritton. "A Research Agenda for Illinois Public Libraries." *Illinois Libraries* 73, no. 1 (January 1991): 123-34.

Gajerski, B. "Edmonton Public Library: 1989 User Survey." Edmonton Public Library, Edmonton, Alberta, 1989. ERIC ED327184.

Green, Sylvie. "Merchandising Techniques and Libraries." *School Library Journal* 28, no. 1 (September 1981): 35-39.

Hamilton, Patricia A., and Terry L. Weech. "The Development and Testing of an Instrument to Measure Attitudes Toward the Quality vs. Demand Debate in Collection Management." *Collection Management* 10, no. 3-4 (1988): 27-42.

_____. "Give 'Em What They Want or Give 'Em What They Should Have?" *Illinois Libraries* 69, no. 4 (April 1987): 284-89.

Hirsch, Jane. Comment made during panel discussion at Lancaster, Pennsylvania, on October 3, 1979. Quoted in: Nyren, Judy. "Library/Bookstore Syndrome Eyed in Lancaster." *Library Journal* 104, no. 21 (1 December 1979): 2512-14.

Hole, Carol. "Click! The Feminization of the Public Library." *American Libraries* 21, no. 11 (December 1990): 1076-79.

Kister, Kenneth. "Let's Add Diversity." *Library Journal* 96, no. 16 (15 September 1971): 2745.

Kotler, Philip. *Marketing for Nonprofit Organizations.* 2d ed. Englewood Cliffs, N.J.: Prentice-Hall, 1982.

Kuraim, Faraj Mohamed. "The Principal Factors Causing Reader Frustration in a Public Library." Ph.D. diss., Case Western Reserve University, 1983.

Madden, Michael. "Library User/Nonuser Lifestyles." *American Libraries* 10, no. 2 (February 1979a): 78-81.

_____. "Lifestyles of Library Users and Nonusers." *Occasional Paper* (of the University of Illinois Graduate School of Library Science), no. 137 (February 1979b): 1-44.

Martin, Lowell A. "Public Libraries: Middle Age Crisis or Old Age?" *Library Journal* 108, no. 1 (1 January 1983): 17-22.

Martinez-Rivera, Ivette. "Impact of Merchandising on Library Circulation." Student paper, photocopied, Pratt Institute, School of Information and Library Science, 1987.

McClure, Charles R., Amy Owen, Douglas L. Zweizig, Mary Jo Lynch, and Nancy Van House. *Planning and Role Setting for Public Libraries: A Manual of Options and Procedures.* Chicago: American Library Association, 1987.

McClure, Charles R., and Alan R. Samuels. "Factors Affecting the Use of Information for Academic Library Decision Making." *College and Research Libraries* 46, no. 6 (November 1985): 483-98.

McColvin, Lionel Roy. *The Theory of Book Selection for Public Libraries.* London: Grafton and Company, 1925.

McCrossan, John A. *Library Science Education and Its Relationship to Competence in Adult Book Selection in Public Libraries.* Ph.D. diss., University of Illinois, 1966.

Merritt, Leroy Charles. "Book Selection and Intellectual Freedom." In *Background Readings in Building Library Collections*, 2d ed., ed. Phyllis Van Orden and Edith B. Phillips, 19-28. Metuchen, N.J.: Scarecrow Press, 1979.

_____. "Editorial." *ALA Newsletter on Intellectual Freedom* 13, no. 5 (September 1964): 71-72.

Moran, Barbara B. "Popular Culture and Library Education." *Journal of Education for Library and Information Science* 26, no. 1 (Summer 1985): 25-32.

Owens, Jo Ann B. "A Study of Methods Used to Publicize I & R Services in Public Libraries." Master's project, University of North Carolina, Department of Library Science and Instructional Technology, 1987.

Palmour, Vernon E., Marcia C. Bellassai, and Nancy V. DeWath. *A Planning Process for Public Libraries*. Chicago: American Library Association, 1980.

Public Library Association. *Public Library Data Service Statistical Report '91*. Chicago: Public Library Association, 1991.

_____. *The Public Library: Democracy's Resource. A Statement of Principles*. Chicago: American Library Association, 1982.

Radway, Janice. "The Book-of-the-Month Club and the General Reader: On the Uses of 'Serious' Fiction." *Critical Inquiry* 14, no. 3 (Spring 1988): 516-38.

"Results of Pratt Market Study Show Nonusers Not Willing to Try." *Library Journal* 112, no. 13 (August 1987): 18.

Rice, Betty. *Public Relations for Public Libraries*. New York: H. W. Wilson, 1972.

Robinson, Charles W. "Management Techniques and Service Philosophy: Their Impact on Collection Development." *Iowa Library Quarterly* 22, no. 1 (Winter 1984): 12-22.

Ross, Catherine Sheldrick. "Readers' Advisory Services: New Directions." *RQ* 30, no. 4 (Summer 1991): 503-18.

Sivulich, Kenneth G. "How We Run the Queens Library Good: And Doubled Circulation in Seven Years." *Library Journal* 114, no. 3 (15 February 1989): 123-27.

Spiegler, Jerry. "BCPL: Road to Extinction." *Library Journal* 105, no. 1 (1 January 1980): 2.

"Tucson Makes Client Demand Central to Collection Development." *Library Journal* 107, no. 6 (15 March 1982): 586.

Turow, Joseph. "The Impact of Differing Orientations of Librarians on the Process of Children's Book Selection: A Case Study of Library Tensions." *Library Quarterly* 48, no. 3 (July 1978): 276-92.

Van Loo, John. "Marketing the Library Service: Lessons from the Commercial Sector." *Health Libraries Review* 1, no. 1 (March 1984): 36-47.

Vavrek, Bernard. "The Public Library at Crisis: Is Marketing the Answer?" *North Carolina Libraries* 46, no. 3 (Fall 1988): 142-47.

Weingand, Darlene E. *Marketing/Planning Library and Information Services*. Littleton, Colo.: Libraries Unlimited, 1987.

Wisotzki, Lila. "Duplicate, Circulate: Demand Buying." Paper presented at the Public Library Association's Collection Development Conference, Chicago, 19 March 1989.

Zweizig, Douglas L. "Any Number Can Play: The First National Report of Output Measures Data." *Public Libraries* 24, no. 2 (Summer 1985): 50-53.

The Relationship Among Marketing, Role Setting, and Collection Development in Public Libraries

3

In order to explain fully the relationship among marketing, role setting, and collection development in public libraries,[1] librarians need to understand two more concepts: mass or undifferentiated marketing and differentiated marketing.

Mathews (1983a) argues that librarians have traditionally practiced mass marketing by assuming that all people have similar or identical needs for library materials and that the public library can meet these needs in rather similar ways. For instance, many public librarians have assumed that everyone has a need to be educated, enlightened, and entertained by the types of materials that public libraries have traditionally contained. Differentiated marketing, on the other hand, assumes that different classes of users have different needs and wants and, therefore, seek different benefits from using the library.

Mass Marketing: A Public Library Tradition and Problem

The mass marketing focus of public libraries has typically been revealed in mission statements that libraries have adopted—statements that describe the service philosophy under which each library operates. A mission statement is meant to serve two major purposes. First, it should give staff a shared sense of the direction in which the library is moving; this presumably helps employees work toward common aims. Second, it should help the library allocate resources by defining the boundaries of library services; any service outside these should not be funded.

Writing such a mission statement is not too difficult in the case of academic libraries, school libraries, and special libraries, because the purpose of these libraries is limited by the well-defined client groups they serve. Consider, for example, the mission statement of one high school library in the Midwest: "To provide, within the limits of our budget, a collection of print and non-print media (and the associated equipment) to meet the instructional needs of teachers and students. If extra income is obtained, to provide supplementary materials for student recreation and enrichment." This mission statement clearly indicates what the library's primary and secondary purposes are and, in so doing, provides clear direction to the media specialists who work in this school. This should help them make better decisions about what services to offer, what materials to buy, and what priorities to give to different kinds of patron needs.

Public librarians, who serve a more diverse clientele than academic, special, and school librarians, have found it harder to write such focused mission statements. For many years, the following mission statement was typical of those found in many public libraries: "To meet the informational, recreational, and educational needs of all community residents." This and similar mission statements suggest that many public libraries were practicing mass marketing—that is, trying to be all things to all people.

This attitude was not just reflected in local libraries; it was common at the national level as well. For example, the Public Library Association's "Mission Statement for Public Libraries" (1977) suggested that public libraries ideally should perform a very long list of duties. Each of these duties was very broad and would require an almost unlimited amount of money and staff time. For instance, one of these tasks was collecting and translating the human record on all intellectual levels into many different print and nonprint packages. Another was organizing this human record so that it could be accessed from many directions and so that both the facts and the wisdom in the record could be retrieved. Unfortunately, many of these tasks were and are impossible given the current (or even potential) level of resources with which public libraries operate today.

Some librarians have recognized for years that public libraries needed to become more realistic about what they could effectively accomplish and to stretch available resources by providing fewer services, of higher quality, to specially targeted groups of users. But as Watts and Samuels (1984) have noted, many of those urging public libraries to prioritize services possessed a "strong reductionist orientation" that made them promote, with almost "messianic devotion," that all public libraries should adopt the same major role. What's more, the librarians often promoted service philosophies that expressed their own values rather than ones that would meet the needs of the residents of the communities they served (Dragon, 1983).

The result of this evangelical fervor for promoting a single and often value-laden role for public libraries has been controversy, not productive action, because it has been impossible for librarians to agree which role should take precedence. Berelson (1949), for example, provoked a great outcry when he recommended, after reviewing findings of the series of studies known as the Public Library Inquiry, that public libraries should concentrate on serving the needs of the opinion leaders in the community rather than on serving the needs of all. During the sixties and seventies, many librarians opposed this suggestion and preached the doctrine that public libraries should concentrate instead on reaching out to the poor, the elderly, the handicapped, and other nonusers (Weibel, 1982). When *A Nation at Risk* (National Commission on Excellence in Education, 1983) appeared, with documentation of and suggestions for overhauling the nation's "failing" educational system, various authors reaffirmed the library's role as an educational institution.[2]

The situation was further complicated by the fact that even authors who agreed on a specific role often disagreed about how it should be accomplished. For example, both Rawlinson (1990, 1981) and Bob (1982) stated that the library's primary function is to provide materials for patron use. However, Rawlinson suggested that librarians should focus on meeting public demand for best-sellers and other popular books, while Bob rejected this as "promoting fast-food chains of the mind" and advocated providing high-quality titles instead.

Even as the controversy raged, however, a number of converging problems convinced public library leaders that they needed to quit haggling and find a realistic and cost-effective solution to meeting user needs. These problems included the budget-eroding effects of rising inflation coupled with stable tax revenues, increased demands by governmental funding bodies for library services that were both inexpensive and well used, an expanding population of increasingly sophisticated users who were asking libraries to provide a wide range of materials in many different formats, and a growing realization that spreading existing resources too thin had resulted in inadequate performance levels in most public libraries (Martin, 1983). To solve these problems, library leaders began to promote a true differentiated marketing approach, one that concentrated on developing service philosophies based on a systematic, thoughtful examination of the actual and potential needs that community residents had for library services and the use they made of them.

The Solution: Using Differentiated Marketing to Establish Role Priorities

The first part of the solution was set in place with the publication of *A Planning Process for Public Libraries* (Palmour, Bellassai, and DeWath, 1980) and its companion manual *Output Measures for Public Libraries* (Zweizig and Rodger, 1982). These books did not suggest that public libraries be all things to all people. Nor did they promote a single role for all public libraries to adopt. Instead, the manuals specified procedures that could be used to make an individual library more responsive to the needs of the community it served. Although librarians have tended to refer to these two manuals as "planning documents," they can actually be thought of as tools designed to help librarians conduct what are known as marketing audits. During such an audit, the librarian asks fundamental questions about the individuals and groups served and about the library's existing products, resource levels, mission, and possible competitors (Condous, 1983).

These two "planning" manuals addressed these issues, asking librarians to analyze — and in some depth — the needs of community residents for the types of collections and services that the library offers, the alternative sources that residents could use to meet these needs (e.g., bookstores or video outlets), and the types and levels of library use. The manuals then directed librarians to examine existing library resources and to redesign collections and services to meet community needs.

Two more current refinements of these documents, now being used in many public libraries, have reinforced the marketing principles spelled out in the earlier manuals.[3] The first is the second edition of *Output Measures for Public Libraries* (Van House and others, 1987), which includes more comprehensive directions for collecting the 12 measures of library use shown in figure 3.1.

LIBRARY USE
These measures reflect the extent to which the library is used by its community.

Annual Library Visits per Capita is the average number of library visits during the year per person in the area served. It reflects the library's walk-in use, adjusted for the population served.

Registration as a Percentage of Population is the proportion of the people in the area served who are currently registered as library users. Although registration does not necessarily reflect use, the measure reflects the proportion of the people who are potential library users who have indicated an intention to use the library.

MATERIALS USE
Libraries provide materials in many different formats for use inside and outside the library.

Circulation per Capita is the annual circulation outside the library of materials of all types per person in the legal service area.

In-Library Materials Use per Capita is the annual number of materials of all types used within the library per person in the area served.

Turnover Rate measures the intensity of use of the collection. It is the average annual circulation per physical item held.

MATERIALS ACCESS
Library users need to be able to find what they are looking for. The first three of these are Materials Availability Measures, reflecting the extent to which users succeed in finding the materials that they need during their visit. The fourth Materials Access measure indicates how long people wait for materials not available at the time of their visit.

Title Fill Rate is the proportion of specific titles sought that were found during the user's visit. It is not the proportion of users who were successful, because one user may have looked for more than one title; it is the proportion of the searches that were successful.

Subject and Author Fill Rate is the proportion of searches for materials on a subject or by an author that were filled during the user's visit.

Browsers' Fill Rate is the proportion of users who were browsing, rather than looking for something specific, who found something useful.

Document Delivery measures the time that a user waits for materials not immediately available, including reserves and interlibrary loans. It is expressed as the percent of requests filled within 7, 14, and 30 days, and over 30 days.

REFERENCE SERVICES
Reference service consists of helping clients use information resources inside and outside the library and providing personalized answers to questions.

Reference Transactions per Capita is the annual number of reference questions asked per person in the area served.

Reference Completion Rate is the staff's estimate of the proportion of reference questions asked that were completed on the day they were asked.

PROGRAMMING
Libraries provide programs to inform, educate, and entertain their clients and to promote library use.

Program Attendance per Capita is the annual number of people attending programs per person in the area served.

Reprinted with permission from Van House and others (1987, 3-4).

Fig. 3.1. Measures of library use mentioned in *Output Measures for Public Libraries*.

The second *Planning and Role Setting for Public Libraries* (McClure and others, 1987) describes procedures for collecting in-depth, factual information about the community and the library. The library gathers information about the residents served (e.g., their age, income, and educational levels), their households (e.g., size and race), and the community itself (e.g., the composition of its labor force, its media, and its school systems), as well as data about the size and scope of the library's collection, staff, financial resources, facilities, and the output measures mentioned above. A planning team—generally composed of library staff, trustees, and community representatives—determines, based on the information gathered about community needs, which of eight common roles the library should serve. The team then practices differentiated marketing when it designs a long-range plan specifying one or two primary roles on which the bulk of the library's resources will be spent.

Role identification is important because the roles that a public library chooses for itself directly affect its collection management efforts. For example, a library that has designated itself a *popular materials center* would collect current and popular materials in a variety of formats wanted by the community, such as best-sellers, other books on "hot subjects," videotapes, books on tape, and compact disks. The librarians would review current publishing trends and keep themselves informed of the promotion efforts that publishers make to sell particular titles, since these are the titles that public library patrons will want. These librarians would not try to build a highly diverse collection but would concentrate instead on purchasing the most wanted materials in sufficient quantities to meet immediate public demand, on maintaining a very current collection, and on regularly purging titles for which demand has faded.

Seven of the eight roles outlined in *Planning and Role Setting for Public Libraries* have implications for collection management. Figure 3.2 lists these roles and describes the collections that might result from focusing on them. These roles are not the only ones a library could adopt; they are simply the most common ones. A public library might choose some other role, such as serving as a school library in a sparsely populated rural area.

Libraries that follow a societal-marketing orientation should choose, as primary, those roles that best serve the short- and long-term needs of their individual communities. In the most recent *Public Library Data Service Statistical Report* (Public Library Association, 1991), the role chosen most often as a primary or secondary role was *popular materials center*. As figure 3.3 (on page 34) shows, *reference library* and *preschoolers' (or children's) door to learning* were also chosen as primary or secondary roles by more than half of the libraries reporting data. Again, the assumption being made here is that public libraries that focus the bulk of their resources on performing a few roles effectively will be better able to meet the educational, informational, and recreational needs of a majority of community residents.

(Text continues on page 35.)

Popular Materials Center
The library serves as a popular bookstore. The collection includes current and popular materials in a variety of formats wanted by the community (like best-sellers, other books on "hot" subjects, videotapes, books-on-tape, and compact disks). The library purchases the most wanted materials in sufficient quantities to meet immediate public demand. A substantial portion of the collection has been published within the last five years.

Community Information Center
The library serves as a clearinghouse for current information about the community. In addition to regular reference materials, the collection contains locally developed files with data on community agencies, clubs, and interest groups. The library has extensive vertical files on issues of current public interest and subscribes to local newspapers and the newsletters of local agencies and organizations. The library uses on-line services to supplement local information resources.

Formal Education Support Center
The library assists students in meeting educational objectives established in formal programs of study at elementary and secondary schools, academic institutions, technical schools, or other training programs. The collection contains materials in a variety of formats appropriate to the educational level(s) supported and relevant to the topics being studied. Resources include reference materials, periodicals, abstracting and indexing services, on-line databases, and access to interlibrary loan. The library may make a special effort to acquire materials listed as supplemental sources in textbooks used by local education providers.

Independent Learning Center
The library assists individuals of all ages who are pursuing a sustained program of learning independent of any formal educational program. The collection has a wide range of circulating subject materials relevant to the interests of independent learners of all ages. The materials are provided in a variety of formats and geared to varying levels of ability. Some libraries may develop extensive collections of audiocassettes or videocassettes on popular self-help topics such as health issues, investment planning, home repair, foreign languages, and psychology.

Preschoolers' Door to Learning*
The library encourages young children to develop an interest in reading and learning through services for children and for parents and children together. The collection has a variety of materials and formats for preschoolers and for adults working with young children. Some libraries provide computers, audiovisual formats, educational toys, and games to help children expand their imaginations and develop motor and sensory skills. Popular titles are available in multiple copies.

(Fig. 3.2 continues on page 33.)

Fig. 3.2. Suggested roles and their implications for collection development.

Reference Library
The library actively provides timely, accurate, and useful information for community residents in their pursuit of job-related and personal interests. The collection emphasizes informational materials to support individual, business, government, and community interests. Materials are available for all ages and reading levels. The reference collection is extensive and includes such materials as indexes, atlases, encyclopedias, handbooks, and directories. The library makes heavy use of electronic databases and has a large current periodicals collection. The library may maintain subscriptions to special indexing and abstracting services and keep files on area businesses. Development of local history archives and collecting local documents, memorabilia, and photographs may also be emphasized.

Research Center
The library assists scholars and researchers to conduct in-depth studies, investigate specific areas of knowledge, and create new knowledge. The collection has a large number of titles; extensive serials holdings; microform materials and equipment; a wide array of printed and electronic abstracting, indexing, and database services; and may include archival and manuscript materials. A high percentage of the collection in subject areas pertaining to the library's research specialties contains material that is scholarly, theoretical, or technical in nature.

Community Activities Center
The library is a central focus point for community activities, meetings, and services. The collection is not emphasized in this role.

*Many public libraries have changed this role to *Children's Door to Learning* to reflect the reality that most public libraries have separate collections and services that are designed to be used by children of all ages.

Reprinted, in modified form, with permission from McClure and others (1987, 32-39).

Role Specified*	Percentage of Libraries Choosing as a Primary Role	Percentage of Libraries Choosing as a Secondary Role	Percentage of Libraries Not Emphasizing This Role
Popular Materials Center	77.2%	16.2%	6.6%
Reference Library	55.7%	24.6%	19.7%
Preschoolers' Door to Learning**	25.4%	47.8%	26.8%
Independent Learning Center	15.8%	25.9%	58.3%
Community Information Center	11.8%	13.6%	74.6%
Formal Education Support Center	6.1%	27.2%	66.7%
Community Activities Center	2.6%	9.7%	87.7%
Research Center	2.6%	1.3%	96.1%

*The number of libraries reporting role choices was 228.

**Many public libraries have changed this role to *Children's Door to Learning* to reflect the reality that most public libraries have separate collections and services that are designed to be used by children of all ages.

Exhibit compiled from information given in Public Library Association (1991, 77-93).

Fig. 3.3. Percentage of public libraries choosing each of the eight roles specified in *Planning and Role Setting for Public Libraries*.

Librarians should remember to approach role selection cautiously for at least three reasons. First, librarians need to ensure that they are not introducing bias by selecting the roles that reflect staff members' personal values, rather than the roles that will best serve patrons. One way to circumvent this problem is to have patrons participate in the role setting process. As D'Elia and others (1991) note, the St. Paul (Minnesota) Public Library (SPPL) did this in a two-step process. First, it asked various groups of community stakeholders—adults, students, teachers, and representatives of downtown institutions—to list services that they or their constituencies either used, considered to be strong, felt could be improved, or were not currently offered but should be. These responses and those from interviews with SPPL staff and with library leaders in the metropolitan area were used to design a survey that was answered by more than 1,000 SPPL patrons. This survey clustered various library services under the eight roles and asked patrons to indicate which they felt were most important.

Librarians should also be careful about selecting too many roles, because this will cause resources to be spread too thinly. Rather they should choose a few roles that will meet the needs of large segments of the population. As figure 3.4 shows, McClure and others (1987) recommend that libraries spend 40 percent to 50 percent of their resources on one to two primary roles and another 30 percent to 40 percent on one or two secondary roles. Libraries should try to meet all remaining user needs out of the other 20 percent of their budgets or by linking users to other libraries.

Level of Priority	Large Libraries or Libraries with Extensive Resources	Small Libraries or Libraries with Moderate Resources	Effort/ Commitment Level
Primary	1-2 Roles	1 Role	40%-50%
Secondary	1-2 Roles	1-2 Roles	30%-40%
Maintenance Level	Remainder of Library Roles and Activities	Remainder of Library Roles and Activities	20%

Reprinted with permission from McClure and others (1987, 43).

Fig. 3.4. Recommended number of role priorities.

Librarians also need to be sure that, once they have chosen which roles to emphasize, they stick to that decision. Although a library may say that it will concentrate on one to two roles, it may not always follow through with this commitment when allocating or spending its resources. In order for marketing-based collection development to work, librarians will have to learn to say "no" when a request for materials falls outside the scope of what the collection should cover.

Saying "no" is made easier if the library has reflected the roles it has chosen in its mission statement. A mission statement based on this type of differentiated marketing should be tightly focused. For example, the Everett (Washington) Public Library, which chose *popular materials center* as its primary role, has adopted the following mission statement: "To make readily available the most wanted library materials to all those who use the library, to serve as an access point for any needed information, and to provide the services at an affordable cost." This mission statement is "good" (whether or not one agrees with the philosophy espoused) because it is so specific that it helps the librarian make choices about the types of services and collections that should be offered. Using this mission statement, a librarian could make clear selection decisions if patrons requested any of the following items:

- a dissertation discussing the hair imagery used in the poems of Elizabeth Barrett Browning

- a high quality work written by an unknown first novelist and put out by a university press

- Saul Bellow's latest book (past titles moderately used)

- a manual that tells how to repair Kaypro IIE computers, a model that is no longer made and about which no other patron has requested information

- a novel in the Silhouette Special Edition series, which is highly popular among current patrons

- another copy of *Great Expectations* (the current ones are always off the shelf)

- a new edition of the popular job-hunting manual *What Color Is Your Parachute?*

- a history of the Druid faith

- a popular psychology work

The same librarian would find it much more difficult to determine which of these same items should be purchased and which should not if the library's mission statement simply said: "The library will meet the informational, recreational, and educational needs of all community residents."

Subdividing the Market Further Through Market Segmentation

The process of role setting defines a few very broad markets that public libraries will pursue, from researchers to users of popular items. However, most libraries will want to subdivide or segment their audiences into smaller target markets and to study these in more depth. A target market is a relatively homogeneous group of potential patrons whom the library wishes to serve—like students who come to the library seeking help with homework. Such patrons share common characteristics (e.g., motivations and needs) that are related to differences in the ways that they will use library products and services and that can be used to predict user behavior.

There are a number of reasons why libraries should consider using market segmentation. The first is that segmentation is cost-effective. A library will generally find it less expensive to design services and collections for a relatively small number of user groups that share common characteristics than for thousands of unique individuals. Segmentation can also raise service quality, because it requires analysis of target markets in some depth—an analysis that encourages a better understanding of patron requirements. This understanding can help librarians build collections that will be better able to meet user needs. Segmenting the market can also help librarians design better promotion campaigns, because they will have more insight into, and can thus share more effectively, the benefits that various target markets can receive from using the library's collection. Segmentation can even, as Wood (1988) has noted, provide information that will help librarians choose appropriate promotional techniques, write copy, and schedule advertising time for various target markets.

Because libraries are interested in predicting use of their resources by the target market, they will want to define various market segments by

1.   listing characteristics of community residents that might affect use;

2.   determining the size and composition of groups that possess those characteristics; then

3.   noting the collection-related needs of each group, as well as the benefits they might receive from using the library's collection.

Although markets can be segmented using any characteristic that identifies or defines actual or potential customers, librarians may find it most convenient to think in terms of four broad groups of factors that affect use of a library's collection. The first are *demographic characteristics*. Factors that have been consistently associated with varying levels of use in public libraries are age, sex, income level, ethnic background, occupation, and educational level.

Some *geographic characteristics* are also related to the extent of a person's library use. The most relevant are the ability to travel (by foot or vehicle) to a library facility, the distance that must be traveled, and the residential or nonresidential status of the potential patron.

Behavioral characteristics are those that describe the extent and type of a patron's past use—of the library in general or of specific collections and services within it. D'Elia (1981), for example, divides public library users into six target markets: people who only borrow books, people who only use materials in-house, people who use the library lightly (that is, who occasionally use materials in-house or borrow them but do not make a habit of library use), heavy users, hard-core nonusers, and potential users. Massey (1976) uses five market groupings: the searchers, who are oriented toward completing a specific project; the toilers, who routinely need specific information or materials; the escapists, who want new materials to feed personal fantasies; the uninformed, who are infrequent users, are unfamiliar with library services, and are often intimidated by library staff; and the lonely hearts, who are seeking social contact.

Segmentation according to *psychographic characteristics* is a concept that is less familiar to many librarians. Such segmentation occurs on the basis of socio-economic class, life-style, personality, interests, and opinions. For example, marketers in the business sector have targeted a group called DINKS—couples who have double incomes and no kids and who have certain likes and dislikes. Libraries may find it particularly useful to segment their markets by family and life cycle characteristics. Consider, for example, the different collection-related needs that might be experienced by single-parent families with small children, dual-parent families with teenagers, and couples whose children are in their twenties.

Once relevant characteristics of potential target markets are listed, the library will need to determine the size and composition of each group. This information can be readily obtained from census records, from user studies, and from the data the library gathered during the community-analysis stage of the role-setting process.

With this information in hand, those who are responsible for collection development should find it fairly easy to list the collection-related needs of each target market. It may, however, be more difficult to list the benefits. In part, this is because patron perceptions of benefits may be different from those of library staff. Mathews (1983) discusses this problem in the context of library programs in general: "The story hour may be viewed by the library as a program for children but perceived as an hour of free babysitting by the mothers. Having several copies of best sellers may be viewed by staff as a benefit to users, but being put on a long reserve list (because the copies are always out) could be perceived by the user as a nonbenefit, since it is inconvenient to wait several days or weeks for the wanted item" (1983b, 9). But it is also difficult to list benefits that are either complex or abstract. For example, people often have difficulty describing the benefits they receive from a favorite book, which may range from "pleasurable feelings" to "in-depth insight into someone else's character" to "a chance to stretch my mind." Librarians should, nevertheless, attempt to list the generic benefits that patrons receive, because these can help the library design its collection to meet user needs.

At this point, a library will need to decide how many market segments it can feasibly serve and which of those listed should be targeted in its marketing efforts. Five different factors will influence this decision.

The first is the *diversity* of the target markets that have been identified. Because marketing strategies are more effective when they are highly focused, an ideal target market is one that contains persons with common interests and preferences who have similar needs that the library can fill. A library will find it easier to devise effective marketing strategies to reach those who teach English in area high schools and junior high schools than it will to devise one for persons who have little more in common than the color of their hair.

The *size* of the target market is also important. A library will not find it fiscally viable to devise separate marketing strategies for groups of 10 newly arrived Polish immigrants, 15 Chinese students, 20 Central American exiles, etcetera. It could, however, combine target groups that are too small to serve economically by identifying characteristics or interests common to each. For example, it could develop a marketing program to reach 500 newly arrived foreign-born residents who share the need for information about English as a second language, local laws and customs, and procedures for becoming a citizen.

Librarians will also need to consider the *viability* of reaching the target market in an efficient and economical fashion. Two major factors will affect viability. The first is the extent and type of existing resources that a library can devote to reaching a particular target market. At the very least, a library should have a collection capable of serving a particular target market and staff who are knowledgeable about the needs of that market.

Another important viability factor is the willingness of the target market to be served by the library. Although a public library will not want to ignore any group of community residents, it should concentrate the bulk of its marketing efforts on target markets that are likely to respond. Primary markets will include groups of patrons who can afford the time and monetary costs associated with using the library and who perceive that they receive benefits from this use. Secondary markets, which can be targeted when and if resources allow, will generally include "individuals who are thought of not so much as potential users, but as those who will help get the word out to others and perhaps provide support for new programs and services" (Kies, 1987, 47).

Role choice should also be considered when making decisions on which target markets should be pursued. A library that has chosen the roles of *preschoolers' (or children's) door to learning* or *reference library* will want to concentrate its efforts on target markets that support these roles—for example, students and teachers in area preschools and people who use the reference collection to seek career-development information. The library will, of course, serve users whose needs do not fall within one of the roles it has chosen to focus on; however, it may not pursue these users as diligently.

A library should also consider whether there are either *humanitarian or public relations advantages* of choosing one target market over others under consideration. A library may, for example, decide to serve target markets who would otherwise have little access to library services—like residents of area nursing homes and families who live in domestic violence shelters. It could also decide to emphasize services to area business people, to aid its funding body in fostering economic development.

Libraries will, of course, inevitably make mistakes when they identify target markets and design strategies to try to reach them. Some of the mistakes will be caused by a library's trying to accomplish too much too fast, rather than devising an achievable program to develop and market its collections. Others may result from the library's failure to realize that the size and composition of target markets can change over time for a variety of social, political, or economic reasons. A downturn in the economy, for example, may increase the number of unemployed persons that the library serves. Rather than abandoning their marketing efforts, however, libraries should concentrate on setting realistic goals and scrutinizing potential changes in target markets frequently to ensure that marketing plans remain viable over time.

Libraries also need to realize that market segmentation is inappropriate in a few situations. The first is when a user has needs that are so specialized that he does not fall into a particular market segment. For example, a library that has chosen the role of *research center* may be used by persons with in-depth requests for information in a very specialized subject field—information that few other individuals would request. But segmentation is also inappropriate in the case where a change in library products or services has the potential to affect all of its users—like longer hours of operation.

Although no one is yet conducting research to measure the changes that are occurring in collection management efforts as a result of differentiated marketing and the kind of focused role setting and market segmentation that it entails, one would logically expect that libraries that concentrate their resources on carefully chosen areas for collection management will, in the short term, increase the likelihood of meeting patron needs in those areas and raising the level of patron satisfaction. These results should lead, in the long term, to increased use by and levels of support among community residents. If the library documents its improved performance carefully, it should be able to garner the support of governmental officials and obtain increased funding.

Marketing and Traditional Patterns of Collection Development

Until the mid-1980s, most public librarians were performing three tasks when developing their collections, generally in the following order: selection, promotion, and evaluation. Librarians have generally stressed the first: *selection*. In part, this is because it is the aspect of collection development with which they are most familiar, since it is so strongly emphasized in library school (Moran, 1985).

But librarians also stress selection because it is fun. After all, librarians know before anyone else which of their favorite authors are coming out with new works. They can leaf through the boxes of new books in publishers' booths or in their own libraries and can be captured by an engaging phrase, an interesting fact, or a value-laden sentence. And they can find out what people are reading, viewing, or listening to. In fact, many librarians engage patrons in conversation at the reference and circulation desks and in the stacks to help guide their selection efforts.

The difficulty, however, is that librarians sometimes collect data to aid with selection efforts in a fairly informal fashion. For example, they collect data when they have time (that valuable and elusive commodity) to do it and tend to do it less often when they get busy with other things. Librarians also have the human tendency of emphasizing the form of data collection they find most interesting. The person who likes to talk with people about their reading interests may stress this form of data collection; the one who likes to analyze statistical data about which materials and collections are used may tend to concentrate on that. In other words, librarians can sometimes introduce bias into their selection efforts rather than performing a totally rational or systematic analysis of patron needs for materials (Bryant, 1987).

The second task that public librarians have undertaken is *promotion* of the collection. They mention new books in newspaper listings, construct colorful displays of materials within the building, try to think of phrases to use for booktalks that will excite their listeners, and use a variety of other techniques to inform patrons what materials are available.

But librarians have not always followed the most systematic plan to promote specific items or types of materials; they have sometimes relied instead on informal observation, intuition, or personal preference when determining which materials to promote. Obviously, the success of these practices will vary, because subjects that interest the librarian may fail to interest very many other people.

Another problem with past promotion efforts has been that librarians haven't always had time to measure the effectiveness of their promotion techniques. Such measurement is important because not all promotion efforts are successful. For example, Auld (1978) showed that use of books promoted on cable television did not increase significantly. This is not too surprising, because research has shown that promotion aids only work when they are easy for the patron to use.[4] Stop for a moment and think of all the things that have to happen in order for cable television promotion to increase use. The patron must subscribe to cable television, watch the program on which a book is promoted at the exact time that the book is promoted, jot down the desired title, visit the library (with the name of the title in hand), and locate the book on the shelf. This last assumes that the book is in and is shelved properly and that the patron can find it. If any one of these things does not happen, the book will remain unused. Because obtaining a book that has been promoted on cable television requires a fairly large expenditure of effort by the patron, it is not surprising that this method of promotion does not increase use significantly. Therefore, librarians should consider replacing such techniques with promotion strategies that have been proven to work.

The final collection development task librarians have performed is *collection evaluation*. In most public libraries, formal collection evaluation efforts have occurred as time permits. Because libraries are so short staffed, evaluation is often done infrequently, irregularly, or on a piecemeal basis. When collections grow too large to fit their allocated shelves, librarians will "evaluate" individual titles. If an item hasn't circulated at least X times in X years and if it isn't a "good" work (e.g., if it isn't listed in one of the standard bibliographies in the field such as *Public Library Catalog* or *Fiction Catalog*), it is weeded. Librarians have also done collection evaluation for purposes of inventory control, when they want to know which and how many items are missing. This type of evaluation occurs even less frequently—generally less than once every 10 years.[5]

Librarians have performed these three collection management tasks in good faith. Unfortunately, they have generally performed them as isolated exercises rather than as an integrated program of interrelated tasks. That is, collection management efforts in many public libraries have not always been carefully formulated programs involving analysis, planning, implementation, and control; they have not always relied heavily on designing the collection in terms of user needs and desires; and they have not always concentrated on effective pricing, communication, and distribution strategies to entice users. In other words, the collection development efforts of many libraries have not been characterized by an integrated marketing plan.

The result, although unintended, has been that the patron is often unable to obtain the item he wants at the time that he wants it. For example, one study examined the percentage of patrons who could find items they were seeking in a number of public libraries nationwide. Although, on the average, the libraries owned at least one copy of 90 percent of the titles sought, only 50 percent of the desired works were immediately available for patron use, usually because desired titles were checked out. Although selectors in these public libraries were choosing appropriate titles, they failed to purchase enough copies of these titles to meet patron demand (Kuraim, 1983).

Results of this study also show that librarians have sometimes failed to integrate promotion efforts with selection or evaluation. Librarians could have used the knowledge that most patrons were competing for the same titles and ignoring other available items if they had taken the time to understand why this happened. Research has shown that only 20 percent of the average library collection accounts for the bulk of its circulation. The other 80 percent is unused or lightly used.[6] But less popular books are not lower in quality;[7] after all, librarians select them using the same standard criteria as the more popular items. One major reason why some books circulate less is that they are not being heavily promoted by publishers, the media, librarians, or anyone else. Patrons are unaware of the merits of these particular items, so they are "lost" on the library shelves. These works are among those that would benefit from in-library promotion.

The finding of various researchers that public libraries are meeting only 50 to 65 percent of patron demands for specific items is making the library profession realize that collection management tasks could be performed more effectively if they were part of a systematic marketing plan. That is, librarians should focus their efforts on designing comprehensive and rational collection management programs that involve analysis, planning, implementation, and control in an effort to meet immediate patron needs for specific materials.

A true societal-marketing-oriented approach to collection evaluation would not follow the pattern just described—of selection based upon an informal identification of patron needs, followed by promotion efforts that may not have been evaluated to see whether they are effective, followed by infrequent or irregular collection evaluation efforts. Rather, it would require that librarians take some of the selection, promotion, and evaluation techniques that they are already using and others that have been reported in the literature and apply them in a regular and systematic fashion.

This book recommends that librarians perform the collection development tasks of selection, promotion, and evaluation in an integrated manner, in a specific order, and on a continuing, cyclical basis. Librarians should begin by evaluating their collections, not in a informal fashion when time allows, but in a continuing and comprehensive manner that identifies consistent patterns of collection use and nonuse.

The second step would be selection. But this time when librarians select materials, they will not be making their choices based on perceptions of what patrons want. Instead, librarians will have in front of them a variety of data: about use and nonuse of specific genre or subject areas of the collection; about use and nonuse of items by particular authors, of particular formats, and at particular locations; and about items wanted but not owned. Armed with this information and with their own knowledge of standard selection criteria, librarians should be able to make more effective collection development decisions.

The final step in the collection management process would be promotion—but promotion done only after librarians had identified

1. those works that would most benefit from promotion; and

2. those promotion techniques that are most effective in increasing patron awareness and use of materials.

The change recommended here, in the way collection management should be viewed in libraries, sounds fairly subtle but is actually a visionary or transformational one. Those libraries that have made the collection development process more systematic and integrated have found that both use and user satisfaction have risen sharply. These increases can make public libraries more viable over time by enabling them to better meet community needs and to gain appropriate levels of funding.

Chapters 4, 5, 6, and 7 describe the four elements in the marketing mix: product, price, place, and promotion. Reviewing these before carrying out the three collection development tasks should help librarians gain additional insights into how to build, distribute, and promote collections that are truly more responsive to the needs of library patrons, in both the short term and the long.

Notes

[1] The ideas presented in this chapter are an expansion of those discussed in Baker (1992).

[2] See, for example, Zweizig (1984).

[3] Note that these documents are being used more in libraries that serve medium-sized and larger communities and that are staffed by at least one professional librarian. In fact, Vavrek (1989) found, in a survey of more than 300 small libraries, that only 22 percent had conducted a community analysis during the last five years and only 23 percent had a multiyear plan.

[4] See, for example, Baker (1986).

[5] One author has even argued that many librarians—in lieu of evaluating, weeding, or taking inventory of their collections—actually expand their buildings, creating what he refers to as collections filled with a high percentage of works "that haven't circulated (recently), have never appeared on any recommended lists, and are not by authors whose works are important to retain" (Beckerman, 1986, 30).

[6] Trueswell (1966) was one of the first to document that 80 percent of the use came from 20 percent of the collection in libraries at Northwestern University, the University of Massachusetts, and Holyoke College. However, the 80/20 rule has been found to be valid in all types of libraries. See, for example, more recent studies by Goldblatt (1986) and Hardesty (1981).

[7] See, for example, Goldhor (1981a, 1981b, 1959).

References

Auld, Lawrence W. S. "The Effect on Public Library Circulation of Advertising via Cable Television." Ph.D. diss., University of Illinois at Urbana-Champaign, 1978.

Baker, Sharon L. "Public Libraries." In *Collection Management: A New Treatise*, 2d ed., ed. Charles Osburn and Ross Atkinson, 395-416. Greenwich, Conn.: JAI Press, 1992.

_____. "Overload, Browsers, and Selections." *Library and Information Science Research* 8, no. 4 (October-December 1986): 315-29.

Beckerman, Edwin Paul. "Administrator's Viewpoint: Housing Library Collections." *Collection Building* 8, no. 3 (1986): 29-30.

Berelson, Bernard. *The Library's Public*. New York: Columbia University Press, 1949.

Bob, Murray. "The Case for Quality Book Selection." *Library Journal* 107, no. 16 (15 September 1982): 1707-10.

Bryant, Bonita. "The Organizational Structure of Collection Development." *Library Resources and Technical Services* 31, no. 2 (April-June 1987): 111-22.

Condous, Crystal. "Non-Profit Marketing—Libraries' Future?" *Aslib Proceedings* 35, no. 10 (October 1983): 407-17.

D'Elia, George. "A Descriptive Market Segmentation Model of the Adult Members of the Public Library's Community." In *Beyond PR—Marketing for Libraries: LJ Special Report 18*, ed. Joseph Eisner, 37-42. New York: Library Journal, 1981.

D'Elia, George, Eleanor Jo Rodger, and Carole Williams. "Involving Patrons in the Role-Setting Process." *Public Libraries* 30, no. 6 (November-December, 1991): 338-45.

Dragon, Andrea C. "Marketing and the Public Library." *Public Library Quarterly* 4, no. 4 (Winter 1983): 37-46.

Goldblatt, Margaret A. "Current Legal Periodicals: A Use Study." *Law Library Journal* 78, no. 1 (Winter 1986): 56-72.

Goldhor, Herbert. "Are the Best Books the Most Read?" *Library Quarterly* 29, no. 4 (October 1959): 251-55.

_____. "Evaluation of a Sample of Adult Books in the Kingston and St. Andrew Parish Library of Jamaica." University of Illinois, Graduate School of Library Science, 1981a. ERIC ED201334.

_____. "A Report on an Application of the Inductive Method of Evaluation of Public Library Books." *Libri* 31, no. 2 (August 1981b): 121-29.

Hardesty, Larry. "Use of Library Materials at a Small Liberal Arts College." *Library Research* 3, no. 1 (Fall 1981): 261-82.

Kies, Cosette. *Marketing and Public Relations for Libraries*. Metuchen, N.J.: Scarecrow Press, 1987.

Kuraim, Faraj Mohamed. "The Principal Factors Causing Reader Frustration in a Public Library." Ph.D. diss., Case Western Reserve University, 1983.

McClure, Charles R., Amy Owen, Douglas L. Zweizig, Mary Jo Lynch, and Nancy Van House. *Planning and Role Setting for Public Libraries: A Manual of Options and Procedures*. Chicago: American Library Association, 1987.

Martin, Lowell A. "Public Libraries: Middle Age Crisis or Old Age?" *Library Journal* 108, no. 1 (1 January 1983): 17-22.

Massey, Morris. "Market Analysis and Audience Research for Libraries." *Library Trends* 24, no. 3 (January 1976): 473-91.

Mathews, Anne J. "Library Market Segmentation: An Effective Approach for Meeting Client Needs." *Journal of Library Administration* 4, no. 4 (Winter 1983a): 19-31.

_____. "Public Relations in Context: Marketing the Library." In *Persuasive Public Relations for Libraries*, ed. Kathleen Kelly Rummel and Esther Perica, 3-13. Chicago: American Library Association, 1983b.

Moran, Barbara B. "Popular Culture and Library Education." *Journal of Education for Library and Information Science* 26, no. 1 (Summer 1985): 25-32.

National Commission on Excellence in Education. *A Nation at Risk: The Imperative for Educational Reform*. Washington, D.C.: Government Printing Office, 1983.

Palmour, Vernon E., Marcia C. Bellassai, and Nancy V. DeWath. *A Planning Process for Public Libraries*. Chicago: American Library Association, 1980.

Public Library Association. "A Mission Statement for Public Libraries." *American Libraries* 8, no. 11 (December 1977): 615-20.

_____. *Public Library Data Service Statistical Report '91*. Chicago: Public Library Association, 1991.

Rawlinson, Nora. "Give 'Em What They Want." *Library Journal* 106 (15 November 1981): 2188-90; reprinted in *Library Journal* 115, no. 11 (15 June 1990): 77-79.

Trueswell, Richard W. "Determining the Optimal Number of Volumes for a Library's Core Collection." *Libri* 16, no. 1 (1966): 49-60.

Van House, Nancy A., Mary Jo Lynch, Charles R. McClure, Douglas L. Zweizig, and Eleanor Jo Rodger. *Output Measures for Public Libraries*. 2d ed. Chicago: American Library Association, 1987.

Vavrek, Bernard. "The Rural Library: Some Recent Research." *Rural Libraries* 9, no. 2 (1989): 85-95.

Watts, E. Spencer, and Alan R. Samuels. "What Business Are We In? Perceptions of the Roles and Purposes of the Public Library as Reflected in Professional Literature." *Public Libraries* 23, no. 4 (Winter 1984): 130-34.

Weibel, Kathleen. *The Evaluation of Library Outreach 1960-1975 and Its Effect on Reader Services: Some Considerations*. Champaign: Graduate School of Library and Information Science, University of Illinois at Urbana-Champaign, 1982.

Wood, Elizabeth J. *Strategic Marketing for Libraries: A Handbook*. Westport, Conn.: Greenwood Press, 1988.

Zweizig, Douglas L. "Lifelong Learning and the Library: The Public Library Response to *A Nation at Risk*." *Public Libraries* 23, no. 3 (Fall 1984): 70-75.

Zweizig, Douglas L., and Eleanor Jo Rodger. *Output Measures for Public Libraries: A Manual of Standardized Procedures*. Chicago: American Library Association, 1982.

Product Decisions 4

Even a good product may, over time, become obsolete. This means that nonprofit organizations, like profit-making ones, should examine each of their products on a regular basis to make sure it still meets consumer needs. One of the largest products that a public library has is its collection. If the collection is dated or does not meet user needs, community residents may turn to other sources to obtain the information they require.

Ideally, librarians will consider four important questions as they evaluate their collections and redesign them to better meet user needs:

1. What segments of the community use the collection?

2. What elements do individual users consider when making selections?

3. What mix of products (that is, items in the collection) will best meet user needs?

4. How does the life cycle of a particular product affect the level of demand for it?

Each of these questions is discussed below.

What Segments of the Community Use the Library?

Over the years, literally hundreds of local, statewide, regional, and national studies have been conducted to determine who uses public libraries and why. Many researchers have tried to document the percentage of nonusers of public libraries. Past studies have shown that this figure varies greatly from library to library, depending on local factors like the educational level of community residents. For example, the Iowa City (Iowa) Public Library, which serves one of the most highly educated communities in the United States, notes that 75 percent of the population it serves possesses current and valid library cards.

There are, however, no recent national studies that have documented the average percentage of users and nonusers in public libraries of various sizes. One national study did find that the percentage of community residents who possess borrowers' cards ranges from 72 percent in libraries that serve under 2,500 residents to 36 percent in libraries that serve more than 1 million persons (Public Library Association, 1991). As figure 4.1 shows, the relationship between registration and a library's size is an inverse one. That is, the percentage of registered borrowers decreases as a library's size increases.

Size of Population Served	Registration as a Percentage of the Population (Mean)*
Over 1,000,000	35.6%
500,000 to 999,999	49.7%
250,000 to 499,999	39.1%
100,000 to 249,999	46.6%
50,000 to 99,999	51.0%
25,000 to 49,999	54.9%
10,000 to 24,999	61.3%
5,000 to 9,999	55.7%
2,500 to 4,999	51.9%
Under 2,500	72.0%

*Libraries were instructed to report this figure only if they had purged invalid registrations at least once within the last three years.

Table derived from figures reported in Public Library Association (1991, 53-56).

Fig. 4.1. Average percentage of population in U.S. public libraries who are registered to borrow materials from the public library.

Because this difference is a significant one, librarians need to examine reasons behind it. Obviously, if a library does not regularly update its registration files, it will contain some inaccuracies, like the names of patrons who have died or moved away. Also, the correlation between registration and library use is a fairly loose one, because not all those who use the library are registered borrowers and not all registered borrowers actually use the library. However, neither of these factors fully explains why registration rates differ so much between large and small libraries.

Another possible explanation is that the cost of using small libraries is substantially lower than the cost of using larger libraries. That is, small libraries may be providing facilities that are closer to patrons' homes, collections that are more closely tailored to meet the needs of patrons, and more personalized services. Although little research to date has focused in an in-depth fashion on the quality of service in libraries of various sizes, librarians should determine ways that they can reduce the costs of using their collections, a subject explained in more detail throughout this book.

The lack of recent, accurate national studies of who uses libraries and why is unfortunate. But a review of older national studies and studies conducted at the local, state, and regional levels indicates that four broad-based factors have been consistently found to be related to a person's overall level of library use. These are a general desire to learn about the world, the desire to learn via books and other media rather than in some other fashion, familiarity with libraries in general, and the perception that using the library and its collections is convenient. Each is discussed below.

A General Desire to Learn About the World, Often Indicated in Level of Activity Outside the Home

Cognitive psychologists, who study how people think and make decisions, have repeatedly documented that some people are simply less interested in actively learning, changing, or growing. These people are content to repeat the same experiences over and over. Many nonusers of the library appear to fall into this group. For example, when Madden (1979a, 1979b) reviewed a national marketing study to obtain pictures of the life-styles of nonusers, he concluded that they disliked change in general, were highly conservative, watched a great deal of television, had few activities outside the home, and were significantly less educated than library users.[1] These people did not possess a general desire to learn about the world; their horizons seemed to stop at their front doors. In contrast, regular library users actively sought new experiences. They were particularly interested in improving themselves, their careers, and their homes.

Madden's conclusions are supported by a number of other studies. For example, Zweizig (1973) found that the extent to which a person was dogmatic correlated negatively with library use, and the level of community involvement and desire to learn about the world through book reading, newspaper use, and education correlated positively. Other studies that have substantiated Madden's claims include those of Willits and Willits (1991), NEA (1989), Zill and Winglee (1989), Lange (1987/1988), and Bolton (1982).

A Desire to Learn About the World Through Books and Other Media

Some people prefer to learn through experience. Others, generally due to the influence of parents, teachers, or significant others, have formed the regular habit of learning by reading, listening to audiotapes, watching videotapes, and using other media that libraries carry. Obviously, the type of learning people choose often depends on the type of task to be done; I learned to chop kindling by watching a friend do it, then trying it, rather than reading about it. However, in general, library users like to learn by reading books or using various forms of electronic media.[2]

Most library users say their parents enjoyed reading themselves and read to them when they were small. These activities help to create an atmosphere in which the reading-learning preference can grow.[3] The American school system, which stresses learning by using books and other media, helps reinforce this as well. In fact, studies have consistently shown that those who enjoy school and attain a high educational level as they grow older are the heaviest users of all types of libraries.[4]

Familiarity with Libraries in General

But not all learners and readers are library users. Rather, the people most likely to use the public library are those who, because of their family or school environment, have acquired the habit of library use. For example, Powell and others (1984) found that regular library patrons generally had access to and began using public or school libraries during their preschool or elementary school days and visited the library with a parent 10 or more times per year as a child. More recently, Lange (1987/1988) found that adults who had had frequent, positive childhood library experiences used the public library more often than adults who had never used the library as a child or who had used it infrequently. In other words, familiarity with library services breeds use.

The literature shows a number of reasons why this is generally true. First, familiarity lessens a patron's fear of the unknown. And fear has been shown to be one of two primary emotions that the average patron experiences upon entering a library.[5] In fact, library anxiety (and information anxiety in general) may be as common among the general public as math anxiety.[6] But, like most anxieties, library anxiety decreases with exposure. That is, anxiety decreases as patrons become more familiar with libraries in general or with one library in particular. The anxiety levels of most patrons decline over time, as they explore a given library on their own. However, libraries can help lessen patron fears by hiring friendly and approachable staff members, giving building tours so patrons will know where each collection and service is located, and teaching individuals to use the catalog and various other tools that give access to the collection.[7]

The other primary emotion that patrons experience upon entering a library is frustration.[8] But frustration levels are also lessened by familiarity. This is because most of the frustration is caused by the fact that patrons are often overwhelmed and confused by the size of the collection and the complexity of the various catalogs and indexes.[9] If patrons persist in spite of their frustration, their knowledge of a particular library system and of library procedures in general will increase over time, causing frustration levels to fall. That is, the more familiar patrons become with the library's collection and retrieval systems, the more likely they are to improve their skills and to find the information they need within the library.[10] The higher satisfaction that results can lead to increased use.

Finally, as patron familiarity with a library increases, knowledge of the benefits of using that particular library rises. This explains why various studies have found that once patrons have used services that are new to them (like the reserve or interlibrary loan systems), they are likely to continue using them. That is, familiarity with and successful use of library services breeds further use of those services.

A Perception That Using the Library and Its Collections Is Convenient

But even people who like to read and who generally like libraries may not use a particular library if they perceive it is inaccessible or inconvenient for them.[11] In fact, Childers and Van House (1989) discovered that patrons felt libraries would be much more effective if they paid attention to factors that would reduce the patron's costs, in terms of time and aggravation. Patrons wanted libraries to provide easily accessible locations, adequate free parking, convenient hours of operation, guidance in using the facilities, quick service, and ready availability of a wide range of materials and services.

Use of the collection itself is often affected by whether patrons can obtain materials at the time they need them. Obviously, the average public library cannot afford to purchase everything that is published. However, various authors have suggested some librarians are guilty of purchasing the kinds of materials they themselves enjoy rather than those that appeal to the public. For instance, Hole (1990) has argued that many males don't use the public library because it emphasizes "female-oriented" books like romance novels and cookbooks. This is true even when books on the subject are fairly technical or specialized, like a book on cooking with flowers. Hole says that many public libraries fail to provide enough "male-oriented" books, like hard-core adventure fiction, technical books on electrical repair, or detailed works about the hard sciences.

Other public libraries buy the types of items wanted but fail to make sure they are available when they are requested. For example, libraries may not

1. order and process new items quickly;

2. provide enough duplicates of popular classic and current works so that at least one copy is always available for checkout; or

3. ensure that returned books are reshelved quickly.

These and other convenience factors may explain, at least in part, why some potential patrons don't use library collections.

A Marketing Perspective on Public Library Use

These four patterns related to who uses the public library have been presented to this point from a library rather than a marketing perspective. But considering the latter perspective can give librarians a richer understanding of these concepts. Marketers for commercial firms commonly divide potential users of their products (in this case, the residents that public libraries serve) into three broad segments: the core market, the fringe market, and hard-core nonusers.

People in the core market are those who are generally loyal to the product. These are the library's regular users: those who like to read and use other library materials, who have developed the library habit, and who have found that libraries are generally more convenient to use than other information sources. In the past, librarians have sometimes assumed that patrons remain loyal because libraries are meeting a high percentage of their needs for educational, recreational, or informational materials. However, as noted earlier, studies are starting to show that public libraries meet only 50 to 60 percent of immediate patron needs for materials.

Why then does this core market continue to use public libraries? Bierbaum (1991) explains this with a simple equation:

$$Satisfaction - Cost > 0$$

Patrons use public libraries when they perceive that the satisfaction they receive outweighs the cost of the use. Consider, for example, the avid reader who uses the public library because he cannot afford to buy all the items he wants to peruse. On a particular day, this man visits the library looking for two books. He is very satisfied when the first is on the shelf but is irritated when he learns that the library has purchased only one copy of the other, a popular work, and that he will have to wait several months to obtain it through the reserve system. Although he complains about the wait, he continues to use the library since he cannot feed his reading habit as cheaply elsewhere. In this case, his loyalty is motivated by economic reasons.[12] All of the people in the library's core market, whether they are motivated by economic or other reasons, have decided that the benefits of using the library outweigh the costs.

In fact, Van House (1983) has suggested that middle-class patrons are most likely to use the library because the cost of such use is too high for both the poor and the rich. The poor, who are often poorly educated and lack a tradition of library use, tend to find the typical library frustrating as well as inconvenient to use. Generally they will choose another source of information, such as asking a friend, or will do without the information entirely. Those who are relatively well off find it easier to purchase the information they need (e.g., through bookstores and fee-based information services) rather than bear the personal inconvenience of visiting the library. In contrast, middle-class patrons tend to be well educated, to have been exposed to libraries enough to understand how to use libraries and to see the benefits of such use, and to have too little discretionary income to purchase the information they need. For this group, the satisfaction derived from library use tends to outweigh the costs.

The fringe market is made up of potential users: those who possess the characteristics of patrons (that is, who have a general desire to learn about the world through books and other media) but who don't generally use the public library. Several studies have found that this is not because they are unaware of public library services.[13] Rather, they tend to obtain their reading, listening, and viewing materials from other sources because they perceive that the cost of using the library outweighs the benefits.

As mentioned earlier, this perception may occur for many different reasons. For example, some residents may not have been introduced to the benefits of using the library by parents, teachers, friends, or even librarians. Other residents may have used the library on occasion but may not have gained enough familiarity with its systems to feel comfortable using it on a regular basis. Other people may have failed to find the materials they wanted at the times these were desired. And still others may have found that the personal costs (in money, time, or hassle factors) of using the library were too high. The last is particularly relevant in light of studies that show that some potential users are so busy that they have little free time in which to use the library. The *Edmonton Public*

Library User Survey (1976) found, for example, that 31 percent of those who did not use its library were simply "too busy" to do so.

The last potential consumer market consists of hard-core nonusers—those who have little or no interest in the product offered.[14] These people are unlikely to buy the product no matter how desirable and convenient it is. Consider, for a moment, the example of a diaper manufacturer whose hard-core nonusers are people who have no small children. Because these people have no immediate need for the product, they are unlikely to buy a box of disposable diapers, even if the manufacturer redesigns the diapers so that they fit better, cost less, use recyclable materials, and so forth.

The hard-core nonusers of the public library are generally those who feel they do not need its services or collections—the ones who do not want to broaden their horizons, learn about the world in general, or use libraries. For example, 43 percent of the residents served by the Enoch Pratt Public Library fell into the hard-core nonuser category when they admitted that nothing the library could do would persuade them to use it. Two common reasons for their nonuse were "read few or no books" and "just don't need to go" (Results, 1987).

Ideally, librarians would like to serve each of these groups—the core market, the fringe market, and the hard-core nonusers—because all are residents of the communities they serve. But the reality is that both publishing and personnel costs are increasing at a rate far faster than the budgets of most public libraries. Because this is the case, librarians need to concentrate on cost-effective ways of making their collections more responsive. That is, they need to choose methods that have the highest chance of success for the least possible cost.

The most efficient way to do this is to concentrate the bulk of library resources on serving those two broad groups that are likely to give libraries the greatest return for their money: the core and fringe markets. It costs less to serve these groups because they already use the types of materials libraries contain.

Public libraries should not, of course, ignore their third potential market: the hard-core nonusers. Librarians should continue to promote their collections to all community residents and to serve all those who come to the library or contact the library for service. However, librarians need to face the reality that it requires many more resources than libraries currently have to try to convert hard-core nonusers to patrons, since hard-core nonusers, by definition, don't want to use the items in library collections.[15]

What Elements Do Individual Users Consider When Making Selections?

It is useful to distinguish between a core product and a tangible product. A core product is what the consumer is really seeking. In the case of library patrons, the product is often something intangible. Library patrons may be seeking entertainment, scientific wisdom, or spiritual satisfaction. Librarians do not fill these needs directly by dancing on their desks, teaching classes in nuclear physics, or conducting prayer meetings. Rather librarians try to provide patrons with tangible products—books, videotapes, records, and the like—that contain words, sounds, or pictures that will meet user requirements. The more librarians have studied the needs of their patrons, the more likely this hope will be realized.

Each tangible product in the library's collection has various characteristics that affect whether a patron will choose it. The characteristics that most affect use of the items that public libraries house appear to be: subject, genre, quality, style, reading level, currency, language, format, attractiveness of packaging, and awareness of the author or title of a work.[16]

Subject

Librarians can get some ideas of the very broad subjects in which patrons are interested by examining studies that publishers and distributors of other media conduct on a periodic basis. For example, each edition of *The Bowker Annual: Library and Book Trade Almanac* carries information about the number of works published in different subject areas for four different formats: hardcover books, mass market paperbacks, trade publications, and CD-ROMs. These reports provide a general indication of the demand for works on particular subjects. Similar reports are commissioned and published on an irregular basis by publishers and other media distributors. Figure 4.2 gives the findings of one such study.

Type of Nonfiction	Percentage
Reference/Instruction/Computer	18%
Autobiography/Biography	15%
History	14%
Religious	9%
Health/Diet/Exercise	9%
Leisure	8%
Home and Garden/How-To	6%
Cookbook	5%
Investment/Economics/Income Tax	3%
Children's	3%
Other	7%
Don't Know	3%

Reprinted, in modified form, with permission from Gallup Organization (1988, 167).

Fig. 4.2. Types of nonfiction books purchased in U.S. bookstores in 1987.

Studies like these are best at providing a broad overview of the subjects in which people are interested. So are studies that compare the subject interests of one general type of library patron to another. For example, Willits and Willits (1991) surveyed a broad base of rural and urban library users on their reading preferences. They found that rural patrons were far more likely to want works on gardening, crafts, and religion than urban dwellers. In contrast, urban dwellers were more likely to read classic works of fiction and nonfiction than those living in rural areas.

The popularity of certain subjects will, of course, vary from library to library, depending on factors like the sex, age, educational level, and interests of the audience served. A library in a town on the North Carolina coast should have a higher demand for works on boating than a library in Washington's Yakima desert; one in the midst of the North Dakota plains should have a stronger demand for agricultural works than an inner-city branch library in Chicago. Libraries can, of course, conduct their own studies to see which subject areas their patrons prefer, a topic that will be discussed in more depth in chapter 8.

But several subject-oriented patterns of use recur in library after library. One of the most important is that the broad subject interests of patrons change slowly over time. If a subject has been heavily used in a particular library in the past, it is likely to be heavily used in the future. The opposite is also true: subjects that have received little use in the past are likely to receive little use in the future. This means that individual libraries can, by studying the use of items in their collections, predict general trends of future use, then make selections that mirror this.

A second pattern is that nonfiction works that discuss subjects that many people are aware of or have to deal with in their everyday lives are generally used more than works that do not. Consider, for example, the immense popularity of a large variety of books that focus on coping skills. Works that tell patrons how to prepare income tax returns, be good parents, fix their cars, get along with their bosses, or improve their marriages are used much more extensively than works that discuss the varieties of ducks that live in North America, Brazilian flora, DNA, or tattoo art. When students in my collection development class analyzed nonfiction items that appeared on best-selling lists, they discovered that works of popular psychology, health and fitness, and cooking appeared time and time again. Other popular items were those that dealt with people and events that appeared in the daily news — from autobiographies and biographies to books discussing current politics to humorous portraits of contemporary American life.

A third pattern common among public libraries is that, in general, nonfiction works that provide a broad overview of a subject area have a larger potential audience than works that focus on a narrow aspect of the same subject. If, for example, a library buys two recent cookbooks of equivalent quality, it should expect the one that covers appetizers, soups, main courses, and desserts to receive more use than the one that focuses solely on soups. And a collective biography of lesser-known Greek philosophers should receive more use than a biography that focuses on only one of those philosophers.

These patterns are evident among non-book materials as well. For example, when staff members at the Metropolitan Library System in Oklahoma City, Oklahoma, monitored use of magazines at 11 full-service branches, they found the three most popular were works of general interest: *People, Time*, and *Newsweek*. Other magazines that received high levels of use were general approaches to topics of broad interest to the community, like *Better Homes and Gardens, Popular Mechanics*, and *Scientific American*. Prominent among the significant number of magazines that received no use were highly technical and special interest magazines (Little, 1990).

Genre

A large proportion of fiction readers (and viewers and listeners) are influenced in their selection by the genre of the work. For example, in one of the more comprehensive studies on factors influencing patron selection in public libraries, Spiller (1980) found that 67 percent of those seeking fiction in five British libraries generally sought novels of a particular type. Most of these readers wanted the library to categorize its fiction by genre, so they could easily choose the type of book they wanted.

Again, librarians can gain an understanding of the kinds of fiction their patrons like by examining studies conducted by publishers or distributors of audiovisual materials that reveal what the general public is purchasing. For example, and as figure 4.3 shows, the Gallup Organization (1988) has determined the extent to which various genres are purchased in bookstores. The same study had other in-depth findings on the subgenres that patrons preferred. For example, the favorite types of mysteries were, in order of preference, adventure stories, detective mysteries, spy/political intrigue books, crime mysteries, solve-it-yourself mysteries, and police procedurals. Libraries can also analyze use of their own fiction collections and can survey patrons to determine the kinds of fiction they prefer, a topic that will be discussed further in chapter 8.

Type of Fiction	Percentage
Mystery/Spy/Suspense	17%
Romance	15%
Children's	13%
Action/Adventure/War	11%
Popular fiction	10%
Historical	9%
Science fiction	9%
Occult/Supernatural	4%
Humor	3%
Western	3%
Other	3%
Don't know	3%

Reprinted, in modified form, with permission from the Gallup Organization (1988, 119).

Fig. 4.3. Types of fiction books purchased in U.S. bookstores in 1987.

Quality

A third characteristic of a tangible product, quality, is, of course, a term with which librarians are familiar. Many definitions of quality exist. Consider, for example, Mann's (1971) definitions of quality fiction as writing that challenges the reader's attitudes and beliefs, and recreational fiction as writing that reinforces the reader's attitudes and beliefs. But the library profession has generally defined quality as the degree of aesthetic or artistic excellence that an item possesses. Selectors who believe in "quality" selection advocate purchasing titles that are thoughtful or insightful, cover significant subjects, present facts accurately and comprehensively, are written clearly, or possess literary merit (Gorman and Howes, 1989; G. Evans, 1987; Curley and Broderick, 1985).

These criteria reflect the standard definitions of the term "quality" that are taught in most library schools. However, when I asked students in a beginning collection development class to define the term, their responses were more varied. Among the definitions they gave of a quality title were the following:

- "one that answers the questions that I have"

- "a book that has lots of facts and figures"

- "a work of pure imagination—I hate being interrupted by facts"

- "an item that gives a good sense of place without getting bogged down in picky technical details"

- "a book that makes me laugh"

- "something that has an intricate plot"

- "one, like something by Barbara Pym, that has little plot but fascinating characters"

- "one that has characters that I like and can relate to"

- "a work that makes me think"

- "a fast read when I'm tired"

- "a book that reveals that the author has values similar to mine"

- "a fast-paced title with lots of action"

- "something that eases my spirit"

These student definitions have a wider range than many library definitions of quality. As such, the former are more akin to those provided in standard dictionaries. Although the dictionaries give "excellence" as one meaning for quality, they also list a number of others, including any of the features that makes an item what it is; its characteristic elements or attributes; its basic nature, character, or kind. These broader definitions more accurately reflect the reality that, although some patrons care a great deal about the aesthetic or artistic quality of library materials, others care more about whether a particular book is "a good fit." That is, they want a given book to meet their specific needs at a given time.[17]

A number of authors have addressed this issue in recent years. For example, Genco (1988) has argued that children have a number of psychological needs that can be met by mass market books, which often offer less complicated views of the world. These include the need for security, the need to belong, the need to love and be loved, the need to achieve, and the need for change, as well as the need for aesthetic satisfaction. Obviously, adults have the same needs, which can often be satisfied by works that some librarians would not consider "of high quality."

More recently, Ross (1991) conducted a series of in-depth interviews to determine how people choose books. She found that an important factor in choice was the amount of stimulation that readers desired at any given moment. Generally, when people's lives were hectic, they limited their outside activities to those that were more familiar. During these times, they often read works about familiar subjects, read genre titles that followed predictable formulas, or reread titles by their favorite authors. In contrast, when people's lives were calmer, they were more likely to reach for something different: works that were intellectually challenging, that explored new topics, or that shed new light on familiar subjects.

These studies and others have found that people use libraries because libraries provide books and other forms of media that can help them satisfy various kinds of needs — for entertainment and escape as well as for information and enlightenment.[18] Librarians should, therefore, build collections that will meet a broad spectrum of patron needs over time. That is, they should provide a variety of works so that patrons can find items that will fit their particular needs at any given time. This practice is in keeping with the societal-marketing orientation recommended in this book.

Style

A product's style refers to its distinctive look, feel, or tone. For example, a self-help book and a textbook, even when they cover the same topic, generally have very different styles. So do works by different authors.

Many patrons look for works that have a style that fits their needs or interests. A number of years ago, I saw a librarian trying to help two men who were browsing among the books that dealt with restoring vintage cars. One ended up choosing a text-like book, because he wanted "to find out a lot about the subject in general." The other chose a self-help book with many color photographs of the restoration process; he had purchased an old car and wanted practical information to help him return the car to its previous glory.

Spiller (1980) found that stylistic concerns were particularly important among those who were searching for works of fiction. Patrons tried to increase the likelihood that they would find a good match stylistically in a number of ways. For example, 88 percent of those looking for fiction titles read the blurb on the book or reviews that were printed on the back cover; 33 percent examined the text itself. These readers were primarily interested in finding books with "a good plot," "interesting characters," and "a style that did not grate," although the individual definitions of these characteristics varied greatly from patron to patron.

Most of the studies on style have limited themselves to providing a broad overview of the kinds of items that patrons desire. For example, the Gallup Organization (1988) found that 47 percent of male mystery readers enjoyed hard-boiled detective stories, but only 14 percent of the women readers did. In contrast, 49 percent of female mystery readers wanted a romantic mystery; only 13 percent of males liked this type.

In recent years, however, librarians, scholars of popular culture, teachers, and psychologists have begun to explore reasons why people choose certain styles of reading. Elsewhere, for example, I argue that an understanding of personality type can help readers' advisers recommend books that their patrons will like to read (Baker, 1992). A mystery reader who is highly concrete and literal may prefer the work of Ed McBain, who, as the following quotation illustrates, tends to write in highly concrete terms: "He was a white man—in his early fifties, Carella guessed—wearing blue slacks, a lime green T-shirt and a dark blue cardigan sweater. No shoes. His hands were bound behind his back with a twisted wire hanger. The T-shirt had been slashed to ribbons. There were stab wounds on his chest and his throat and his hands and his arms. One ear dangled loose from the right side of his head where it had been partially severed" (McBain, 1980, 7). In contrast, a person who is highly intuitive or figurative may like works that require reading between the lines. This type of writing appears in the following passage, where cleric detective Father Brown discusses a queer, crooked Oriental knife, inlaid with brilliant stones and metals.

> "The colors are very beautiful. But it's the wrong shape."
> "What for?" asked Flambeau, staring.
> "For anything. It's the wrong shape in the abstract. Don't you ever feel that about Eastern art? The colors are intoxicatingly lovely; but the shapes are mean and bad—deliberately mean and bad. I have seen wicked things in a Turkish carpet." (Chesterton, 1911, 178)

Because only a few other authors have explored underlying reasons why patrons prefer works of a certain style, the findings in this area are still tentative.[19] But librarians generally agree that patrons consider style when choosing works.

Reading Level

Most experts agree that some works are more difficult to understand than others. Works that contain involved sentence structures, complicated vocabularies, complex ideas, or highly technical data are likely to appeal to a smaller audience. Works that are written more simply, mix text with colorful graphics or photos, or cover fewer ideas at one time will generally have a broader appeal.

A number of studies illustrate these concepts. In one, a psychologist named Nell (1988) asked 129 university students to read 30 abstracts (with no designations as to author or title) and choose those with which they would be most and least likely to relax. Forty-four librarians read the same abstracts and placed them in order by their expected use. Both students and librarians ranked works in a consistent order, with easy-to-read works of best-selling and genre fiction first, more complicated narratives in the middle, and hard-to-read expository works of nonfiction last. In a similar vein, Spiller (1980) found that recreational (genre) fiction was borrowed three times as often as serious fiction (that is, works complicated in ideas, vocabulary, or tone) in five British public libraries.

Currency

The currency of a work has also been shown to affect its use. This is particularly true for subject areas of the collection where there are recent innovations or fast changes (e.g., works covering computer technology, tax laws, or recent political changes). This fact has caused some libraries, like the Orange (New Jersey) Public Library (OPL) to amend the standard library practice of filing catalog cards alphabetically by author under each subject heading. OPL files them by date of publication instead, placing the most recently published works at the front—a practice that a majority of patrons appreciate.

Note that, although many patrons choosing fiction want to read the latest works by their favorite authors, they are slightly more content than are nonfiction readers to browse among older works to find something that will appeal to them. Patrons do, however, avoid fiction that strikes them as old-fashioned. They also avoid older works that seem, to current readers, offensive in their portrayal of social mores—like works that stereotypically portray women and girls as pretty but empty-headed followers of men.

Language

Although few studies have been conducted in public libraries, studies in libraries of other types have consistently shown that materials written in the primary language(s) spoken in the geographic area in which the library is located will circulate significantly more than materials written in other languages.[20] Most public libraries in the United States have accepted the fact that the audience for secondary languages is rather small and purchase few foreign language materials.

However, public libraries that serve geographic areas where there are high concentrations of native speakers of a foreign language are buying non-English-language works for these prospective patrons. For example, the Houston Public Library developed a collection of recordings of children's folktales, nursery rhymes, and poetry in Spanish to meet the needs of a sizable Hispanic population (Zwick, 1989). And the Denver Public Library expanded its collection of Vietnamese materials and conducted workshops to train staff members to help Denver's growing Vietnamese community make full use of the library's collections and services (Denver, 1988).

Format

Format is yet another characteristic that affects the level of use of products in the collection. The hardcover book is still, of course, the "normal" format in libraries, although libraries are purchasing more paperbacks than in the past. In spite of some well-publicized resistance to nonprint formats,[21] videotapes and compact disks are among the most heavily requested items. In fact, some libraries claim that many former nonusers began using the library to obtain videotapes, became more familiar with the benefits of library services in general, and now borrow other items in the collection.[22] At the same time, the use of other, often technologically dated formats (e.g., 8mm films, film loops, and phonograph records) is declining.

Often libraries choose to go after a target market by selecting formats that would appeal to it. This tactic was used by the Poplar Creek and Bartlett public library districts in Illinois, which worked together to obtain a Library Services and Construction Act (LSCA) grant to purchase collections of large-print books, books-on-tape, and videotapes for senior citizens who might have difficulty reading the print in standard-size books (Kiefer, 1987). Other tactics that public libraries have used are purchasing paperbacks and comic books to attract young adults and books-on-tape to attract people who travel frequently by car.

Attractiveness of the Packaging

Book publishers and distributors of audiovisual products have known for many years that good packaging can make the difference between mediocre and good sales of the product, because the cover entices the reader to pick up the work. This principle is illustrated by the results that Vintage obtained when it redesigned the covers of its classic fiction titles. Vintage distributors placed books with the newer, brighter, more sophisticated covers beside the older versions of the same works in several bookstores. Although the price of books with the new covers was significantly higher than that of the same books with the old covers, the new works outsold the old by as much as a three-to-one ratio (Youman, 1989).

Results like this explain why publishers and distributors constantly try to come up with new ways to enhance the packages in which their products are sold. Some publishers use packaging gimmicks to do this. For example, Warner Books published a political novel that featured a transparent light-red film "window," shaped like a sniper's gunsight, which focused on the head of the victim seen through the transparent die-cut (Frank, 1989). Horror publishers have increasingly used holograms on the covers of their books; the holograms feature, in their dormant state, normal people who change to monsters when the books are moved (Frank, 1988).

Other manufacturers hire illustrators who are particularly good at capturing a look that will sell. Elaine Duillo has painted steamy covers for more than 500 romance novels (Neill and Cagle, 1989). And Michael Phelan has illustrated many science fiction novels in a movie-poster style (Sherman, 1984).

Still other publishers target covers to appeal to special markets. Chevannes and Garrard (1987) note that covers designed for a British market are too weak, gentle, and pretty to do well in the United States. In contrast, American covers are perceived by the British as being overly bold, graphic, and coarse. Publishers have often developed different covers for their two major markets: bookstores and schools/libraries. The former are generally flashy; the latter emphasize the thoughtful, literary look (D. Evans, 1987). Publishers also use different covers for different segments of the book-buying population. For example, Fawcett designed covers of *Gone to Soldiers*, by feminist writer Marge Piercy, for nine different audiences. Among these were male readers, feminists, "traditional women," war buffs, and romantics (Paperback, 1988).

Packaging innovations are not limited to covers for mass market paperbacks for an adult audience. Publishers of children's and young adult titles are using more fantastic cover images for kids who are raised on MTV, as well as timely, realistic covers that emphasize mood and character (Frank, 1990). Publishers are also paying attention to cover design for trade books, and distributors of other audiovisual materials are following suit.

As one might expect, package designs influence patron selections in libraries in the same way that they influence customer selection in bookstores and other media outlets. For example, Spiller (1980) found that 31 percent of fiction readers in five British public libraries were influenced in their selections by the book's cover.

Libraries should take advantage of the fact that publishers and distributors are designing packages to stimulate demand by offering materials in their original packages, whenever possible. Of course, a library may occasionally want to repackage a product. This may occur when the original package is damaged (as in the case of a book that needs rebinding) or when there is a special need to control a product for security reasons. Even in these cases, it is to the library's advantage to use as much of the original packaging as it can. For example, workers at the King County (Washington) Public Library trim the boxes that new videotapes come in, slip them into clear plastic cases so the original covers can still be seen, then display the cases. The tapes themselves are housed at the checkout desk to deter theft (Julien, 1985).

Awareness of the Author and Title

The patron's awareness of a particular work is one of the largest influences on whether he will choose it in a library. Several factors may affect the level of patron awareness. One of these is name recognition of the author. For example, Spiller (1980) found that 54 percent of those seeking fiction either actively sought works by a particular author or, while browsing, recognized an author as one they had heard of and were interested in reading.[23] Studies have shown that media users in general are willing to try works by new authors;[24] however, they often fail to do so because they are unaware of the merits of a particular writer. This explains why an author generally builds up name recognition over time, although awareness is also high of works by first-time authors who are famous for other reasons, like Lee Iacocca and David Stockman. In other cases, a patron may be more familiar with a title than with an author. This happened with Scott Turow's first novel, *Presumed Innocent*, which was made into a movie. In still other cases, patrons may be more familiar with the name of a series than that of an author in that series. For example, public library patrons often request romances from the Silhouette Special Edition series or videotapes from the "Masterpiece Theatre" series.

The degree and type of publicity that an item receives in the media directly affects the likelihood that patrons will hear about that item and want to read, listen to, or view it. Works that are prominently featured — in newspaper and magazine reviews, advertisements, television and radio talk-show spots, bookstore signings, and the like — are likely to be in high demand among library patrons.

Although most promotion efforts are formally sponsored by publishers and distributors of print and nonprint materials, serendipity can also play a role in generating demand. A few years ago, an unknown author named Tom Clancy published, through the Naval Institute, an obscure technological thriller called *The Hunt for Red October*. Then President Ronald Reagan, who was given a copy of the book by a friend, mentioned the work in a news conference. The story was picked up by a national news magazine, which featured Clancy's book in some depth, then by the media in general. Within one month, Clancy became a best-selling author.

The notion that promotion in the general media greatly affects the patron's likelihood of hearing about and then wanting a particular item helps explain, in part, why older titles are not as heavily used as newer ones. In the past, a number of researchers have shown that works in the social sciences and sciences circulate less as they grow older.[25] Some librarians have felt that this is largely due to the fact that some of the factual information becomes obsolete. However, the circulation of many works in the humanities, which often contain less information of a factual nature, and the circulation of fiction titles also tend to decline fairly quickly, generally within three to five years after publication and purchase.[26] This decline is, at least in part, due to the fact that publicity for these titles decreases significantly during that time.

Another type of promotion, which is often more low-key in the short run but may have long-term effects, is word-of-mouth referral. Members of the general public who are enamored with certain works will promote them among friends, family members, and colleagues. This is what happened with two books that have graced trade best-seller lists for years: Richard Bolles' *What Color Is Your Parachute?* and M. Scott Peck's *The Road Less Traveled*. And classic titles, from Charles Darwin's *Voyage of the Beagle* to J. R. R. Tolkien's *Lord of the Rings* trilogy, remain popular because they keep getting word-of-mouth referral.

Use of items that are promoted within the library — through book lists, displays, positioning in prominent locations, and the like — also tends to be higher. For example, studies have revealed higher use among books displayed near the library's door, near the circulation desk, or on eye-level shelves.[27]

Other Factors Influencing Book Choice

Obviously, many other factors can influence book choice, although often to a lesser degree. For example, when Spiller (1980) surveyed 500 readers in five British public libraries, he found that less than 1 percent said each of the following factors influenced their selection of fiction: size of print, design of typeface, length of the book, sex of the author (many men did not want to read works written by women!), and number of date due stamps in the book (that is, its popularity with other patrons).

What Mix of Products (Items in the Collection) Will Best Meet User Needs?

To maximize use and user satisfaction, libraries need to make informed decisions about product items, product lines, and product mixes of their various collections.

A product item is an individual work within the library's collection. A paperback copy of *David Copperfield* is a product item. So is a cassette tape of *The One-Minute Manager* or a compact disk that features Bach played on the pedal harpsichord.

A product line is a group of product items that are closely related to each other, generally because they function in a similar manner. Some product lines within a library include all works in a particular format, all works on a particular subject, all works in a particular genre, all works with the same title (regardless of format), or all works by the same author.

A product mix is the entire set of product lines and items that a particular library offers to its patrons. Note that product mixes often vary from branch to branch of the same library system.

Public librarians who are trying to develop a responsive collection will periodically review their product mix. That is, they will evaluate the usefulness to individual patrons and society of all product items and lines and make decisions about these. Librarians can do this by

1. identifying products that are heavily used;

2. identifying products that are not used; and

3. identifying products that are desired by patrons or potential patrons but are not in the collection.

Each is discussed briefly below and in more detail in chapter 8.

Identifying Products That Are Heavily Used by Patrons

Whenever possible, librarians will want to duplicate or in some other way increase access to product items that are in such demand that patrons have trouble obtaining them, like best-selling titles and frequently requested classic works. Librarians will also wish to identify and expand popular product lines, so that sufficient quantities will exist to meet the needs of regular users.

Identifying Products That Are Not Used by Patrons

Librarians will want to discontinue product lines that are not being used (e.g., 8mm films) to free resources to expand or add product items and lines that users want. They will also want to weed product items that have lost their relevance and have little likelihood of getting it back (e.g., a 1962 book on space exploration). However, like other agencies that operate under a societal-marketing orientation, libraries may keep other little-used products if they appear to have some long-term value to the community. For example, public librarians in Illinois may choose to keep fiction titles by Illinois authors, even if they have not circulated well. However, librarians should not let these products sit on the shelves; they should promote them on a continuous basis to make patrons aware of the benefits of using these titles.

Identifying Products That Are Desired by Patrons or Potential Patrons But Are Not in the Collection

By adding these products, librarians may increase user satisfaction with the collection. A side benefit is that overall use may also rise. For example, when Dorrell (1980) added comic books to a public junior high school library, user satisfaction rose, circulation of other materials increased by 30 percent, and the number of students visiting the library jumped an astonishing 82 percent.

How Does the Life Cycle of a Product Affect Its Level of Demand?

Most stores carry a few product items or lines that it considers staples, which continue to sell well over time. In a grocery store, these are items like milk and bread. In a public library, these items are likely to be classic works or works on ever-popular topics like cooking. But the majority of products in a library are not staples; they are items with a finite life span. These products go through several distinct stages in their life cycle before suffering an eventual decline in demand.

Use of a product is generally slow in the introductory stage for a variety of reasons. One is the reluctance of some consumers to accept a new product until they have studied its advantages and disadvantages. Consider, for example, the number of patrons who seek the works of familiar authors, whom they already know they like, before browsing among the works of other authors (Spiller, 1980).

Demand may also rise slowly in the introductory stage because of delays in distribution or because of consumer reluctance to buy new products until technical problems in production have been resolved. For example, a number of consumers waited to buy a videotape player (and hence to borrow library video-tapes) until manufacturers chose VHS over Beta as the industry standard.

Typically, a few people who are open to trying new products keep demand for the product afloat during this stage. But libraries can also take steps to build product awareness. For example, a number of libraries promote new items on some type of display. New items featured in this way circulate significantly more than new items that are interfiled with the regular collection.[28]

Once word about the good points of the product begins to spread rapidly, the product enters its growth stage. Libraries can best meet the quickly increasing demand by offering the product in various formats (paperback, hardback, large-print, books-on-tape) and by rapidly distributing the product to as many library locations as possible to ensure that it is readily accessible.

When a product reaches the maturity stage, demand will wane because many consumers have already used it. One common way of ensuring that demand remains at a level that will justify keeping the product on the shelf is to promote the product more heavily. This is what the Davidson County (North Carolina) Public Library did when it promoted, via book lists distributed to patrons, older books whose use had waned; circulation of these works increased by 220 percent (Parrish, 1986). Another way to keep demand from declining is to reduce the cost of the item. For example, libraries with rental collections of videotapes might follow the lead of retail video stores by charging less for older videotapes. Unless mature products are revitalized, their use will lag.

The decline stage is characterized by a strong decrease in demand. Technological innovations may cause the decline; witness the decrease in the demand for record albums now that more community residents have purchased compact disk players. A decline may also be due to changes in style or tastes, as with older books on interior decoration. The library's task, during this stage, is to eliminate products and services that have become unacceptable to users, by either weeding dated items or eliminating entire product lines that are not being used (e.g., film loops and 8mm films).

Some product lines in libraries have fairly long life cycles. For example, it is likely that the demand for certain formats (e.g., books and magazines), subject areas (e.g., cookbooks and resume guides), genre areas (e.g., romance fiction and mysteries), and well-known authors (e.g., James Michener and Dick Francis) will remain in the growth or maturity stage and thus will continue to meet user needs for a number of years.

Other product lines have somewhat shorter life cycles because they are replaced by lines that are newer, more convenient, or more fashionable. For example, the popularity of "old-fashioned" authors, like Emilie Loring and Zane Grey, and of dated subjects, like commune living, is also falling.

Not all products follow the standard life cycle described above. In a few cases, a mature product will gain new life. Often this is due to some type of promotion. For example, librarians have seen the use of many "mature" books rise when they are made into television shows or movies.

Other products alternate periods of relatively high use with relatively low use. The most obvious example is that of seasonal works—from stories about Christmas, Easter, and Thanksgiving to works on cross-country skiing, sailing, and mushroom gathering.

This pattern of use is also common among works in demand for school assignments. For example, the Orange (New Jersey) Public Library, which serves a largely African-American population, has multiple copies of a number of black history works. Demand for these items is sluggish but steady most of the year but explodes during Black History Month, when school teachers regularly assign projects that require use of these works.

Products may also have faddish, or very rapid, life cycles. That is, the products attract quick market attention and are adopted with great vigor, but interest declines rapidly. Consider, for example, the circulation of exposé books like *Nancy Reagan: The Unauthorized Biography* by Kitty Kelley. Public libraries that want to meet immediate patron demand for faddish books can purchase them in multiple copies or obtain multiple copies on a lease-purchase plan from vendors like Baker and Taylor. However, libraries will not generally find it worthwhile to promote these titles once demand wanes.

Conclusion

The product decisions libraries make are important ones, because they have the potential to affect patron satisfaction and levels of use in the short term and communitywide support of the library in the long term. Librarians should make these decisions thoughtfully, rather than impulsively, considering the basic principles spelled out here and the more specific guidelines for product analysis that are discussed in chapter 8.

Notes

[1]Madden's work is described more fully in chapter 2.

[2]See, for example, Gallup (1978) and Zweizig (1973).

[3]See, for example, Duncan and Goggin (1982).

[4]See, for example, Wittig (1991), Willits and Willits (1991), and Lange (1987/1988).

[5]See, for example, Mellon (1988, 1986).

[6]Wurman's 1989 book *Information Anxiety* is useful in helping librarians understand the psychological context of this problem, although it does not mention libraries per se.

[7]Kaehr (1989) has convincingly argued that many adults would benefit from formal bibliographic instruction programs in public libraries.

[8]See, for example, Totterdell and Bird (1976).

[9]See, for example, Ross (1991) and Baker (1986b).

[10]This finding parallels one that shows that the more familiar the average reference librarian is with the resources in the collection, the more accurate he will be in answering reference questions. See, for example, Halldorsson and Murfin (1977).

[11]See, for example, Van House (1983) and D'Elia (1980).

[12]In fact, a study by Roy (1984) showed a high correlation between heavy reading (10 or more books per year) and library use. This suggests that many heavy readers may be motivated to use the public library because they can't afford to buy all the books they want to read.

[13]See, for example, D'Elia (1980).

[14]D'Elia (1980) was one of the first to apply the term "hard-core nonusers" in a public library setting.

[15]Moreover, there is an ethical question involved in trying to serve these people. It is one thing for librarians to try to persuade people that learning and libraries are good for individuals and society. It is quite another for librarians to impose their own beliefs on others.

[16]The information presented in the following sections is based on research findings. The reader who desires a nonresearch-oriented, more humorous slant on the issue should refer to Katz (1990).

[17]This explains, incidentally, why Goldhor (1959, 1981a, 1981b) found, in studies conducted 20 years apart in locales as diverse as Indiana and Jamaica, that there was no significant correlation between circulation and the quality of books as measured on an objective scale.

[18]A number of other works have addressed reading from this psychological perspective. Some of the more interesting are those by Gold (1990), Sabine and Sabine (1983), and Holland (1975).

[19]Other authors who discuss stylistic concerns in an interesting fashion include Roberts (1990), Saricks and Brown (1989), and Cawelti (1976).

[20]See, for example, Britten and Webster (1992).

[21]See, for example, Manley's (1990) claim that librarians are making a dire mistake when they stock and circulate videocassettes.

[22]See, for example, Robinson (1987).

[23]The same study also found that many of those who browsed, rather than looked for books by a particular author, either couldn't remember the names of authors or were unaware of what had been published.

[24]For example, the Gallup Organization (1985) found that 6 in 10 book buyers say it is not true that they rarely buy books by an unfamiliar author. Those most likely to try new authors are heavy book buyers and the college educated.

[25]See, for example, Van Styvendaele (1981).

[26]See, for example, Griscom (1983) and Hardesty (1981).

[27]See, for example, Baker (1986a), Shaw (1938), and Carnovsky (1933).

[28]See, for example, Mueller (1965).

References

Baker, Sharon L. "The Display Phenomenon: An Exploration into Factors Causing the Increased Circulation of Displayed Books." *Library Quarterly* 56, no. 3 (July 1986a): 237-57.

_____. "Overload, Browsers, and Selection." *Library and Information Science Research* 8, no. 4 (October-December 1986b): 315-29.

_____. (In press.) "What Patrons Read and Why: The Link Between Personality and Reading." In *Research Issues in Public Librarianship: Trends for the Future*, ed. Joy M. Greiner. Westport, Conn.: Greenwood Press, 1993.

Bierbaum, Esther G. Series of personal conversations held at the University of Iowa, School of Library and Information Science, during 1991.

Bolton, W. Theodore. "Life Style Research." *Library Journal* 107, no. 10 (15 May 1982): 963-68.

Britten, William A., and Judith D. Webster. "Comparing Characteristics of Highly Circulated Titles for Demand-Driven Collection Development." *College and Research Libraries* 53, no. 3 (May 1992): 239-48.

Carnovsky, Leon. "The Dormitory Library: An Experiment in Stimulating Reading." *Library Quarterly* 3, no. 1 (January 1933): 37-65.

Cawelti, John G. *Adventure, Mystery, and Romance: Formula Stories as Art and Popular Culture*. Chicago: University of Chicago Press, 1976.

Chesterton, G. K. *The Innocence of Father Brown*. New York: John Lane, 1911.

Chevannes, Paul, and Leslie Garrard. "Cross-Cultural Covers." *Publishers Weekly* 232, no. 22 (27 November 1987): 37-40.

Childers, Thomas, and Nancy A. Van House. *The Public Library Effectiveness Study: Final Report*. Philadelphia: Drexel University, 1989.

Curley, Arthur, and Dorothy Broderick. *Building Library Collections*. 6th ed. Metuchen, N.J.: Scarecrow Press, 1985.

D'Elia, George. "The Development and Testing of a Conceptual of Public Library User Behavior." *Library Quarterly* 50, no. 4 (October 1980): 410-30.

"Denver P(ublic) L(ibrary) Reaches Out to Vietnamese Community." *Library Journal* 113, no. 20 (December 1988): 29.

Dorrell, Larry Dean. "Comic Books and Circulation in a Public Junior High School Library." Ph.D. diss., University of Missouri-Columbia, 1980.

Duncan, Patricia W., and William F. Goggin. "A Profile of the Lifetime Reader: Implications for Instruction and Resource Utilization." Paper presented at the 26th College Reading Association Annual Conference, Philadelphia, 28 October 1982. ERIC ED223994.

Edmonton Public Library User Survey. Edmonton, Alberta: Edmonton Public Library, 1976.

Evans, Dilys. "The YA Cover Story." *Publishers Weekly* 232, no. 29 (24 July 1987): 112-15.

Evans, G. Edward. *Developing Library and Information Center Collections*. 2d ed. Littleton, Colo.: Libraries Unlimited, 1987.

Frank, Jerome P., ed. "Book Design and Manufacturing: Competitive Market Spurs New Mass Market Cover Ideas." *Publishers Weekly* 236, no. 20 (17 November 1989): 30, 32.

———. "Book Design and Manufacturing: Mass Market Covers—Key Weapons in the Rack-Space War." *Publishers Weekly* 233, no. 3 (22 January 1988): 78-79.

———. "Book Design and Manufacturing: New Levels of Subtlety Mark Children's Book Jacket Art." *Publishers Weekly* 237, no. 3 (19 January 1990): 76-77.

Gallup Organization. *Book Reading and Library Use: A Study of Habits and Perceptions*. Princeton, N.J.: Gallup Organization, 1978.

———. *The Gallup 1985 Annual Report on Book Buying*. Princeton, N.J.: Gallup Organization, 1985.

_____. *The Gallup 1988 Annual Report on Book Buying*. Princeton, N.J.: Gallup Organization, 1988.

Genco, Barbara A. "Mass Market Books: Their Place in the Library." *School Library Journal* 35, no. 4 (December 1988): 40-41.

Gold, Joseph. *Read for Your Life: Literature as a Life Support System*. Markham, Ontario: Fitzhenry and Whiteside, 1990.

Goldhor, Herbert. "Are the Best Books Most Read?" *Library Quarterly* 29, no. 4 (October 1959): 251-55.

_____. "Evaluation of a Sample of Adult Books in the Kingston and St. Andrew Parish Library of Jamaica." Urbana: University of Illinois, Graduate School of Library Science, 1981a. ERIC ED201334.

_____. "A Report on an Application of the Inductive Method of Evaluation of Public Library Books." *Libri* 31, no. 2 (August 1981b): 121-29.

Gorman, G. E., and B. R. Howes. *Collection Development for Libraries*. New York: Bowker-Saur, 1989.

Griscom, Richard. "Periodical Use in a University Music Library: A Citation Study of Theses and Dissertations Submitted to the Indiana University School of Music from 1975-1980." *Public Librarian* 7, no. 3 (Spring 1983): 35-52.

Halldorsson, Egill A., and Marjorie E. Murfin. "The Performance of Professionals and Nonprofessionals in the Reference Interview." *College and Research Libraries* 38, no. 5 (September 1977): 385-95.

Hardesty, Larry. "Uses of Library Materials at a Small Liberal Arts College." *Library Research* 3, no. 3 (Fall 1981): 261-82.

Hole, Carol. "Click! The Feminization of the Public Library." *American Libraries* 21, no. 11 (December 1990): 1076-79.

Holland, Norman N. *5 Readers Reading*. New Haven, Conn.: Yale University Press, 1975.

Julien, Don. "Pioneering New Services: Videocassettes." *Wilson Library Bulletin* 59, no. 10 (June 1985): 664-67.

Kaehr, Robert E. "Bibliographic Instruction in the Public Library: To Have or Not to Have, That Is the Question." *Public Library Quarterly* 9, no. 4 (1989): 5-12.

Katz, Bill. "Perspective: The Allure of the New Books Section." *Collection Building* 10, nos. 3-4 (1990): 58-60.

Kiefer, Marjorie. "Cooperative Outreach Services for Seniors." *Illinois Libraries* 69, no. 10 (December 1987): 716-19.

Lange, Janet M. "Public Library Users, Nonusers, and Type of Library Use." *Public Library Quarterly* 8, nos. 1/2 (1987/1988): 49-67.

Little, Paul. "Collection Development for Bookmobiles." In *The Book Stops Here: New Directions in Bookmobile Services*, ed. Catherine Suyak Alloway, 59-70. Metuchen, N.J.: Scarecrow Press, 1990.

Madden, Michael. "Library User/Nonuser Lifestyles." *American Libraries* 10, no. 2 (February 1979a): 78-81.

_____. "Lifestyles of Library Users and Nonusers." *Occasional Papers* (of the University of Illinois Graduate School of Library Science), no. 137 (February 1979b): 1-44.

Manley, Will. "Facing the Public." *Wilson Library Bulletin* 64, no. 10 (June 1990): 89-90.

Mann, Peter H. *Books: Buyers and Borrowers*. London: Deutsch, 1971.

McBain, Ed. *Ghosts*. New York: Viking Press, 1980.

Mellon, Constance A. "Attitudes: The Forgotten Dimension in Library Instruction." *Library Journal* 113, no. 14 (1 September 1988): 137-39.

_____. "Library Anxiety: A Grounded Theory and Its Development." *College and Research Libraries* 47, no. 2 (March 1986): 160-65.

Mueller, Elizabeth. "Are New Books Read More Than Old Ones?" *Library Quarterly* 35, no. 3 (July 1965): 166-72.

"NEA Study Finds 56% of Americans Claim to Read Some Literature." *Publishers Weekly* 236, no. 8 (25 August 1989): 9-10.

Neill, Michael, and Jess Cagle. "When Elaine Duillo Paints It, A Romance Novel's Cover Is Worth a Thousand Steamy Words." *People Weekly* 31, no. 19 (15 May 1989): 141, 143.

Nell, Victor. *Lost in a Book: The Psychology of Reading for Pleasure*. New Haven, Conn.: Yale University Press, 1988.

"Paperback Has Nine Different Covers." *Unabashed Librarian*, no. 69 (1988): 17.

Parrish, Nancy B. "The Effect of a Booklist on the Circulation of Fiction Books Which Have Not Been Borrowed from a Public Library in Four Years or Longer." Master's project, University of North Carolina at Greensboro, 1986. ERIC ED282564.

Powell, Ronald R., Margaret A. T. Taylor, and David L. McMillen. "Childhood Socialization: Its Effects on Adult Library Use and Adult Reading." *Library Quarterly* 54, no. 3 (July 1984): 245-64.

Public Library Association. *Public Library Data Service Statistical Report '91*. Chicago: Public Library Association, 1991.

"Results of Pratt Market Study Show Nonusers Not Willing to Try." *Library Journal* 112, no. 13 (August 1987): 18.

Roberts, Thomas J. *An Aesthetics of Junk Fiction*. Athens: University of Georgia Press, 1990.

Robinson, Charles W. "Fees for Videocassettes — An Opportunity for Service and Growth." *Public Libraries* 26, no. 3 (Fall 1987): Fast Forward insert.

Ross, Catherine Sheldrick. "Readers' Advisory Services: New Directions." *RQ* 30, no. 4 (Summer 1991): 503-18.

Roy, Loriene. "Sources of Books for Adults in Eight Illinois Communities." *Illinois Library Statistical Report* 15 (November 1984): 1-24.

Sabine, Gordon, and Patricia Sabine. *Books That Made the Difference*. Hamden, Conn.: Library Professional Publications, 1983.

Saricks, Joyce G., and Nancy Brown. *Readers' Advisory Service in the Public Library*. Chicago: American Library Association, 1989.

Shaw, Ralph R. "The Influence of Sloping Shelves on Book Circulation." *Library Quarterly* 8, no. 4 (October 1938): 480-90.

Sherman, Steve. "Retailers Speak from Experience About Book Covers that Sell." *Publishers Weekly* 226, no. 17 (26 October 1984): 84-86.

Spiller, David. "The Provision of Fiction for Public Libraries." *Journal of Librarianship* 12, no. 4 (October 1980): 238-65.

Totterdell, Barry, and Jean Bird. *The Effective Library: Report of the Hillingdon Project on Public Library Effectiveness*. London: Library Association, 1976.

Van House, Nancy A. "A Time Allocation Theory of Public Library Use." *Library and Information Science Research* 5, no. 4 (Winter 1983): 365-84.

Van Styvendaele, B. J. H. "University Scientists as Seekers of Information: Sources of References to Books and Their First Use Versus Date of Publication." *Journal of Librarianship* 13, no. 2 (April 1981): 83-92.

Willits, Harold W., and Fern K. Willits. "Rural Reading Behavior and Library Usage: Findings from a Pennsylvania Survey." *Rural Libraries* 11, no. 1 (1991): 25-37.

Wittig, Glenn R. "Some Characteristics of Mississippi Adult Library Users." *Public Libraries* 30, no. 1 (January/February 1991): 25-32.

Wurman, Richard Saul. *Information Anxiety*. New York: Doubleday, 1989.

Youman, Nancy. "Marketing Solutions: Vintage's Novel Approach to Repackaging Classics." *Adweek's Marketing Week* 30, no. 39 (25 September 1989): 20-21.

Zill, Nicholas, and Marianee Winglee. "Literature Reading in the United States: Data from National Surveys and Their Policy Implications." *Book Research Quarterly* 5, no. 1 (Spring 1989): 24-58.

Zweizig, Douglas. "Predicting Amount of Library Use: An Empirical Study of the Role of the Public Library in the Life of the Adult Public." Ph.D. diss., Syracuse University, 1973.

Zwick, Louise Zarian. "Cuentos y Canciones Infantiles: Recordings in Spanish for Children." *School Library Journal* 35, no. 6 (February 1989): 23-26.

Price or Cost Decisions 5

During the past century, a large number of librarians have expressed informal laws recognizing that patrons consider various kinds of costs when making a decision to use the library. Ranganathan (1957) urged his colleagues to "save the time of the reader." Mooers (1960) warned librarians that "an information retrieval system will tend *not* to be used when it is more painful and troublesome for a customer to have information than for him not to have it." And Zipf (1949) objectively noted that "each individual [patron] will adopt a course of action that will involve the expenditure of the least effort."

But, as the years have passed, the laws have been refined to acknowledge that patrons actually weigh costs against benefits when choosing whether or not to use the library. Picture a large scale, with the costs of library use on one side and the benefits on the other. Patrons who perceive that the scale has tipped toward the benefits side will obtain the materials they need at the library. But patrons who feel that the costs outweigh the benefits will either obtain the materials they need from other sources (e.g., friends, bookstores, or other libraries) or decide that they can do without the information.[1]

There are several subtle points that librarians should consider with regard to the cost-benefit model described here. The first is that patrons are not "lazy" if they forgo using the library when they perceive the cost of doing so is too high. Rather, as Van House (1983a, 1983b) has noted, patrons are actually making choices based on rational assessments of their private costs and benefits. Therefore, librarians should refrain from implying that those who choose information sources other than the public library are "bad." Nor should librarians try to coerce patrons into using the library; informing patrons of benefits of library services is, of course, appropriate.

Second, each individual perceives the costs and benefits of library services differently. Perceptions of cost and benefit depend on a variety of factors, including the perceived likelihood of finding what patrons want[2], the amount of free time they have, and the discretionary income they possess. One person might feel that the costs of paying $2 to read a best-seller or of waiting 10 minutes in a checkout line are insignificant. Another might find the same costs so high that he or she will forgo using the library's services.

Another factor that influences a patron's perception of costs and benefits is the past experience with libraries in general or with one library in particular. For example, one marketing expert has pointed out that people who use the library infrequently may evaluate it negatively if they have even a few unsuccessful or frustrating experiences. In contrast,

> [f]requent users tend to evaluate the benefits offered by public libraries based on long-term usage experiences, which generate for them not only more user information but also better quality information. As a result, frequent users' expectations become more realistic, and the image which they develop of the library is reinforced by fulfilled expectations. The normal result is that users feel a strong commitment to the library and express their support through more physical as well as emotional involvement. Infrequent or non users, however, may exhibit a detached feeling of commitment and may even express disenchantment with the library and its services. (Ashton, 1985, 14)

Although this expert's point is technically correct, librarians should realize that they, too, can contribute to the frustrations of infrequent users by failing to design library systems that are easy to use.[3]

A third point to make is that the cost-benefit model of library use does not just apply to the patron's initial decision to use the public library, rather than some other information provider. It is also relevant to a later decision to use a particular collection or service within the public library. Consider the patron who decides to visit the library on two separate occasions. On the first, the patron looks for a novel in which he has a passing interest. When he discovers it is checked out to another patron, he considers filing a reserve request for it. But he does not bother, because he feels that such a request requires more effort than he is willing to exert for this book. On his second visit, the patron seeks a book that contains information he needs to make a decision about a permanent career change. Again, the book is already checked out. But this time the patron files the reserve request because he feels that the benefits of obtaining the information outweigh the costs of obtaining it.

What Costs Are Generally Associated with Using the Public Library's Collection?

Two kinds of costs are associated with borrowing materials from the public library. The first is the monetary cost, as in the case of a library that charges patrons fees for using items in the collection or fines for "misusing" them. Among the most common fees are those for borrowing certain types of materials, for filing reserve or interlibrary loan requests, and for obtaining a nonresident borrower's card. The most common fines are those charged for overdue materials and for lost or damaged materials.

The debate on whether or not public libraries should charge fees, and if so, for what services, has been ongoing for a number of years. Seven years ago, the National Commission on Libraries and Information Science (1985) summarized these arguments. These are repeated in figures 5.1 and 5.2.

Library services are a public good.

The U.S. tradition of free library services is damaged by charging fees.

Fees are illegal.

Fees are discriminatory.

Fees represent a form of double taxation.

Libraries will place emphasis on revenue-generating services.

Fees will have the long-term effect of reducing public support for libraries.

Fees might not be used to support library services.

The social benefits of library services are difficult to measure; therefore, a fee cannot be efficiently assigned.

It is difficult to define special services and basic services and to distinguish between them.

Private and public sector markets are separate and should remain separate.

The cost of administering and collecting fees outweighs the financial benefits of fees.

Most users have little need for fee-based on-line services.

If the service cannot be provided without a fee, the service should not be provided.

Improvements within library management and delivery of services would diminish the need for fees.

There is considerable staff resistance to fees.

Charging for a service subjects libraries to liability risks.

Reprinted, with permission, from the National Commission on Libraries and Information Science (1985, 4).

Fig. 5.1. Arguments against charging fees in public libraries.

Charging fees increases recognition of the value and importance of library services.

Fees encourage efficient use of public resources.

Fees promote service levels based on need and demand.

Fees encourage management improvements.

Fees limit waste and overconsumption.

Fees enhance investment in ongoing maintenance and repair of public facilities.

Fees encourage a better understanding of the financial limitations of the local government.

Premium service should be provided only to those willing to pay a premium.

The tradition of charging for services is part of American culture.

Fees control growth of and lower demand for services.

Escalating service costs make user fees a necessity.

Most library users can afford to pay a fee.

Without fees, public and academic libraries could not serve the larger community or nonresidents.

Fees cover only a small portion of the total cost of service provision.

Fees for most services are simple and inexpensive to collect.

Local policy may require libraries to charge for services.

Reprinted, with permission, from the National Commission on Libraries and Information Science (1985, 5).

Fig. 5.2. Arguments in favor of charging fees in public libraries.

In general, public librarians tend to value strongly the concept of a free public library and would, if fiscal conditions were ideal, refrain from charging fees of any type. Unfortunately, the financial capacity of the governmental bodies that fund public libraries is limited, to a large extent, by the amount of taxes the public is willing to pay; moreover, competition for funding among all governmental programs is great. In recent years, librarians have dealt with their financial constraints in two ways. They have worked to increase their internal efficiency by making existing services as cost effective as possible. And they have worked to increase the amount of money that they obtain from less traditional revenue sources.

Although libraries have spent time and effort in pursuing funding options like corporate donations, foundation grants, and endowment funds, they have also begun charging fees for some services.[4] For example, Phelan (1985) found, in a national survey of public libraries that served between 50,000 and 200,000 residents, that increasing overhead, materials, and new technology costs had caused most library directors to consider charging fees. Ninety-two percent of the libraries in this survey charged fees for at least one service.

Many libraries collect fees to help recover part of their costs for providing certain services. In some cases, substantial sums can be raised. For example, Robinson (1989) reported that the Baltimore County (Maryland) Public Library made over $800,000 in 1987 by charging $1 for each videotape borrowed. But in general, the percentage of total operating income resulting from fees is still quite small, an estimated 3 percent to 6 percent in most public libraries.

The decision to charge fees may be influenced by a number of different groups or individuals, including officials of the government body that funds the public library, state or federal policy makers who may place legal limits on the types of fees that may be charged, the library board, library administrators and staff, and patrons. However, Phelan's (1985) study showed that the decision about the need to charge fees was most often made by library staff themselves (see figure 5.3). Library staff or trustees generally determined the amount of the fee as well. These findings are not surprising. Although funding bodies may not always provide as much financial support as librarians would like them to, they do allow librarians a great deal of autonomy in deciding how to spend their budgets and in pursuing alternative fund-raising strategies.

Philosophy	Percentage of Libraries
Our local funding agent allows all decisions regarding fees for services to be made by library personnel.	53%
Our local funding agent would only permit fees to be assigned to those services not considered to be "basic" library services.	14%
Our local funding agent does not care whether fees are assigned to public library services or not.	10%
Our local funding agent would assign a fee to every public library service possible if no complaints about such fees were made.	7%
Our local funding agent is diametrically opposed to fees for public library services.	< 5%

Figures reported in Phelan (1985, 5).

Fig. 5.3. Philosophies of funding bodies regarding user fees in medium-sized public libraries.

But fees are not the only costs associated with borrowing materials from the public library. As economist Adam Smith noted more than 50 years ago, "The real price of everything, what everything really costs to the man who wants to acquire it, is the toil and trouble of acquiring it" (1937, 30). In fact, marketing studies conducted for many different profit and not-for-profit organizations have generally shown that user time and aggravation costs must be kept as low as possible in order for a product or service to show steady growth over the years.

As Van House has pointed out, the amount of time required to locate a desired item is influenced by both the user and the library. A patron can reduce the time it takes him to use the library by "increasing his or her own productivity: for example, by learning better how to use the library. Another way to reduce the time required would be to avoid unnecessary trips to the library; for example, by phoning ahead to see if materials are available.... The user can also reduce use time by shifting some of the effort of the information search to the library staff by asking for assistance" (Van House 1983a, 72). But librarians should also seek to reduce patron costs, whenever possible, by making libraries convenient to use. For example, public libraries can provide bibliographic instruction programs or dial-up access to the catalog for users who have computers.[5,6]

Consider for a moment the time, frustration, and monetary costs that a patron must bear to borrow an item from the public library. These include

1. the cost of reaching the library via walking, riding, or driving;

2. the cost of obtaining a borrower's card;

3. the cost of locating desired items;

4. the cost of standing in line to check out items;

5. the monetary cost (if any) of renting items;

6. the cost of returning borrowed items; and

7. the cost of paying fines when items are lost, damaged, or returned late.

Occasionally, the patron may be asked to pay other costs, either directly or indirectly. For example, the library might assume the patron is willing to travel to another branch to obtain an item. And in cases where the desired item is not owned by the library, is already checked out, or is misshelved, the patron may be asked to bear costs associated with

1. filing an interlibrary loan or reserve request;

2. waiting for the item to become available; and

3. returning to the library to pick up the item.

In other words, the patron's total costs in time and aggravation are potentially high.

Reviewing these cost factors can provide some insight into the relationship between cost and use. Practical examples and research findings are included when applicable.

The Cost of Reaching the Library Via Walking, Riding, or Driving

Generally, public libraries expect patrons to bear the costs of traveling to and from the library. Costs may include direct, out-of-pocket expenses for gasoline, parking, transit fares, or baby-sitting. Time is another cost, one whose importance is growing in a society in which adults of both sexes work outside the home.

Therefore, it is not surprising that public library use tends to be most prevalent among those who live close to the library and who feel that the library provides good hours of operation, convenient locations, and accessible parking. This implies that libraries can decrease the costs of patron use by locating branch outlets near where people live, work, and shop; by providing adequate free parking; and by tailoring library hours to meet the needs of patrons, rather than, for example, the needs of library staff.[7]

Although the cost of reaching the library is important, it is not explained in detail here. Rather, it is extensively covered in chapter 6, which discusses the effects of place (or distribution of materials) on library use.

The Cost of Obtaining a Borrower's Card

For residents of the public library's service area, the primary costs associated with obtaining a borrower's card are time and aggravation. One way that libraries can keep these costs low is by ensuring that patrons do not have to stand in line too long to get a card or (because there is inadequate signage) that they do not stand in the wrong line to get a card.

Another is by keeping the regulations that apply to who can get a borrower's card as simple as possible. One in-depth survey of circulation policies in public libraries showed that these regulations were excessively complex (Intner, 1987). Library staff will, of course, need to verify that those applying for cards are residents of the community served, since only residents pay the taxes that fund the library. Staff also need to verify the patron's address in case they later have to contact the patron about missing or overdue items. However, taking verification to an extreme (e.g., requiring patrons to show three pieces of identification that have both the patron's picture on them and a current mailing address) will discourage use and help perpetuate the tiresome stereotype of librarians as curmudgeonly types who want to keep library materials on the shelves rather than in the hands of borrowers.

One author has argued that the high number of regulations that apply to children seeking borrower's cards effectively makes children "second-class users" of the library (Vandergrift, 1989). For example, a statewide survey in New Jersey found that 36 percent of libraries would not issue borrower's cards unless children could print their names. Another 44 percent prevented children from obtaining a card until they had reached a certain age or grade level. And 27 percent would not issue cards unless parents cosigned the application forms (Razzano, 1986). This last restriction is more understandable, because in most states parents are liable for any debts, like fines for overdue or damaged materials, that their children incur.

There may be two types of fees associated with obtaining a borrower's card. The first is the small fee that some public libraries charge patrons who have lost their cards. Nuisance fees of this sort were instituted in hope that they would prevent patrons from repeating these errors. However, because nuisance fees do not actually prevent card loss, generate little revenue for the library, and represent a cost that can irritate patrons and hence discourage use, sound marketing strategies indicate they should be dropped.

A more valid fee is that charged for a nonresident borrower's card. Most libraries and the governmental bodies that fund them are understandably reluctant to provide services to those who are not paying for them, indirectly through tax monies or directly through a fee of this type.

There are few recently published studies that have reported the average nonresident fee currently charged by public libraries; the range appears to be from $10 to several hundred dollars per year. But library organizations and associations often recommend that libraries charge nonresidents an amount roughly equivalent to that the average taxpayer would have to pay. Some libraries have complicated formulas for determining this—like multiplying the assessed valuation of the nonresident's property by the millage rate charged for library services. An easier way to calculate this is to obtain, from the auditor at the beginning of the library's fiscal year, the number of households that actually pay taxes in the community. The library can divide the total library budget by this figure, then round the result to the nearest dollar to obtain a reasonable nonresident fee.

Not all potential users will wish to pay nonresident fees, particularly if they want to use the library on a short-term basis rather than regularly. A partial solution to this problem is for libraries to issue temporary borrower's cards for periods ranging from one week to a year, at a reduced rate. This lowers the cost to the nonresident without "cheating" the residents of the community the library serves.

The Cost of Locating Desired Items

The primary costs of locating desired items are those of time and aggravation. It takes time to check the catalog to see whether items are owned, to determine whether owned items are checked out, and to locate desired items on the shelf. Moreover, the user may experience various frustrations during the process.

The cost of using the catalog is one that appears to be high for many patrons. For example, 29 percent of patrons surveyed by the Edmonton (Alberta) Public Library reported finding the catalog so difficult to understand that they use it "only as a last resort" (Gajerski, 1989). This figure is, unfortunately, all too typical; the catalog of the average public library is used by only 20 percent to 50 percent of patrons seeking items in the collection.[8]

Some patrons legitimately bypass the catalog because they prefer to seek help directly from library staff, a practice that may save their time and give them greater satisfaction. Others bypass the catalog because they have simple requirements that lead them to believe they can manage without it. For example, they might be seeking a novel that is shelved alphabetically by author.

But many other patrons bypass the catalog because they find it inconvenient to use. One major reason for inconvenience relates to the number and location of catalog terminals (or microform readers). Librarians can reduce the cost of catalog use by installing enough catalog terminals, near the library's entrance and throughout the public service areas of the library, so that patrons can readily find unoccupied terminals.

Librarians can also reduce costs by designing catalogs that are easy to use. As figure 5.4 shows, a number of factors influence the success of catalog use. These will not be discussed in detail here, because one could write several books on the subject.[9] However, libraries can pay attention to these and can ensure that clear directions for catalog use are posted in each area where the catalog is located.

The number of terminals or microform readers available.

The accuracy of the information brought to the catalog by the patron and the form in which it is brought (for example, written or memorized).

The point of access chosen by the patron.

The amount of patron experience and training in using the particular form of catalog.

The number of entry points per item provided in the catalog.

The number of cross-references provided.

The order in which catalog entries are filed.

The extent of information included on a bibliographic record.

The size, complexity, and form of the catalog.

The quality of the labeling, guiding, and error messages given in the catalog.

The perseverance, diligence, and intelligence of the patron.

The availability and use of thesauri or other forms of controlled vocabulary used in the catalog.

These factors may vary depending on the form of catalog used: microform, card, book, or on-line.

Reprinted, with permission, from Baker and Lancaster (1991, 219).

Fig. 5.4. Factors that influence the success of catalog use.

Patrons must also bear the cost of determining whether the item is actually in the library. Most automated catalogs can tell patrons what items are available for circulation, which reduces this cost somewhat. This type of information is particularly helpful if a patron is using a systemwide catalog that indicates a desired item is at another branch, because a patron may be willing to travel to another location to get a title, if he is sure it will be on the shelf when he arrives. Librarians who do not provide access to on-line circulation information for other branches can reduce patron costs in a different fashion. They can inform patrons through signs posted near the catalog that reference librarians will be happy to call and check on the immediate availability of titles housed in other branches.

Even if the item is housed within the same building, the patron bears the cost associated with the time and aggravation of finding it. Eaton (1991) found that this cost was fairly small for people who were skilled in using libraries. However, the cost may be fairly large for the novice library user. For example, Mellon (1986) found that 80 percent of the freshmen who had to use a large academic library had some form of library anxiety. The response of one student was typical: "I ... was lost in the library for a very long time. It was like a big maze" (Mellon, 1986, 162). Librarians can reduce the cost of finding items in several ways. First, they can work to eliminate unnecessary complexity in the way the collection is laid out.[10] A few years ago, I visited a public library in the southeastern United States whose collection was laid out in a haphazard fashion. Patrons were confused by the fact that the general fiction collection (adult hardback titles) was located in several different areas and that the shelving of nonfiction, on three different floors, did not proceed logically from the 000s through the 999s of the Dewey Decimal System. Redesigning the floor plan and shifting items into a more logical order would have eliminated these problems.[11]

Another way to reduce patron costs of finding materials is to post maps of the collection. Maps may be posted near the main entrance, catalog terminals, elevator, and stairs. Maps are especially effective in large buildings or in buildings where the collection is housed on more than one floor.

Effective sign systems to guide patrons to the collections they are seeking will also reduce patron costs. The best signs use colors and lettering that can be readily read, have nonglare surfaces, and are large enough to be easily seen. They are also positioned effectively: at each point where the patron will have to make a decision about where to go, on a plane directly in front of the patron as he approaches a given area, and at eye level.[12]

Of course, reference staff can also reduce patron costs by showing them the location of desired items, but such cost reduction occurs only if patrons ask for help. A number of studies have shown that patrons are reluctant to do this for several reasons.[13] First, they do not want to "bother" a busy librarian. One possible solution is seeing that librarians refrain from performing other duties (e.g., selection) while they are scheduled on the desk, because such activity prevents them from making the kind of eye contact that will encourage patrons to ask questions. A second solution is scheduling enough staff on the reference desk to prevent long lines from forming, since such lines discourage many patrons from asking questions.

Other patrons hesitate to ask for help in locating items because they feel their questions are too simple or because they have not received satisfactory (for example, warm, caring, helpful) service from reference staff in the past. These problems can be resolved by training reference librarians to be sensitive to the needs of patrons and to refrain from implying that patrons should know. Another solution is to post signs by the catalog and reference desk that say: "No question is too simple. Please ask for help when you need it."[14]

Public librarians can also emulate those in the academic environment by offering short tours to show new borrowers where the various materials are kept. Most libraries will not, of course, have enough staff to give personalized tours to each person who is issued a borrower's card. However, they can arrange tours on a monthly basis, publicizing them on notices posted around the library and given to each person who requests a borrower's card.

Once the patron finds the general area where the item is housed, he will incur the cost of actually locating it on the shelf. This cost can be decreased in several ways. First, the library should ensure that materials are shelved in their correct locations. The library can do this by carefully training new shelvers, by working to reduce shelving errors when these occur, and by reading shelves periodically to correct misshelvings.[15] Second, the staff can reshelve materials that have been used within or outside the library quickly, ideally within one working day. Libraries that cannot reshelve every day should, at the very least, place carts of materials, already sorted and awaiting reshelving, on the floor near the relevant stack sections so that diligent patrons can browse for items there. Third, librarians need to realize that some patrons will not understand how to interpret various parts of the call number. For example, some patrons will have difficulty with technical notations like "quarto." Simple explanatory signs, posted at intervals around the stacks and at catalog terminals, can help alleviate this problem.

The Cost of Standing in Line to Check Out Items

The time spent waiting for service, or queue time, is dependent on the level of service that the library is willing to offer. Public libraries should schedule more circulation staff on the desk during the busiest periods. In most public libraries, this means during evening and weekend hours, although weekday lunch hours are also busy in many libraries. Unfortunately, in many libraries there tend to be fewer circulation staff on duty during these times; this trend should be reversed whenever possible. Libraries can also supplement circulation clerks with backup workers who can perform other duties (e.g., filing and shelving), helping at the desk whenever the line of borrowers grows long enough to cause patron inconvenience.

Another common problem is the patron who chooses a "short" checkout line that, due to lengthy or complicated transactions of another patron, turns out to be longer than anticipated. Libraries can equalize the number of minutes patrons have to wait by having patrons form one checkout line, roped off with velvet cords like those used by theaters and banks; the person at the head of the line is called to the next available clerk.

However, librarians should not assume that the cost of even this type of queue will be equal for all patrons. This is because the cost of a queue "is always discriminatory, because the same amount of time has different values to different people, depending on the opportunity cost of their time" (Van House, 1983a, 56).

The Monetary Cost (If Any) of Renting Items

The concept of "rental" collections is not new. As Giacoma (1989) noted, studies conducted in the 1920s, 1940s, and 1950s found that almost half the public libraries surveyed provided duplicate copies of best-selling titles for a small rental fee. One 1977 survey of 716 U.S. public libraries found that 10 percent charged for renting art prints, 13 percent for renting books, and 20 percent for renting films (Lynch, 1978). A survey of 170 California public libraries that same year found roughly similar percentages of public libraries that charged rental fees (Clark, 1977). So did a survey of Illinois public libraries in 1983. The latter study also reported that 5 percent to 6 percent of public libraries charged fees for renting records, 4 percent to 5 percent for renting audiocassettes, and 3 percent for renting 8mm films (Baker, 1983).

Unfortunately, only a few recent studies have examined the fees currently charged by a large sample of public libraries. Of these, none has extensively documented the levels and types of fees charged for renting materials. However, one American Library Association-funded survey of 619 U.S. public libraries of all sizes did ask how many were charging fees for three types of collections. This study found that 29 percent of the libraries surveyed charged fees for borrowing videocassettes, 23 percent for borrowing films, and 5 percent for borrowing art (Lynch, 1988).

Today, many large public libraries are designing and promoting fee-based services on a large scale. For example, in 1991 the County of Los Angeles Public Library received a large entrepreneurial loan to launch Audio Express, a fee-based cassette-by-mail service. Audio Express was designed to meet the needs of the many Los Angeles residents who face long commutes to work. Audio Express staff take patron requests for catalogs and tapes by mail, telephone, or telefacsimile, then mail cassettes to patrons for a fee. The rates were set to cover the costs of the cassettes and the promotion efforts, rather than to make a profit (Upfront, 1991).

The studies mentioned above indicate that libraries tend to charge rental fees for items that could be considered less central to the traditional library mission of providing quality books for the enlightenment of readers. Fees are most often charged for best-selling titles, videotapes, and audiocassettes. The reasons for this are currently unclear.

Optimistically, one would hope that this practice reflects the fact that many public librarians are adopting a societal-marketing orientation. That is, librarians may be limiting fees for "basic" collections of materials that will benefit society over the long run, realizing that such fees would discourage some community residents, generally those who can least afford it, from using the library. At the same time, librarians may be facing the realities of tight economic times by charging fees for "enhanced" or "value-added" services, those that will meet the short-term demands of patrons. For example, some librarians have decided they cannot afford to buy multiple copies in the quantities needed to meet immediate patron demand without hurting collection diversity. So they are purchasing a few copies of best-sellers for their regular collection (available to all patrons, albeit with a long wait) and providing multiple copies of these items in a rental collection.[16]

However, one could also argue that some librarians may be exhibiting elitist tendencies by charging fees for items that they personally value less: audiovisual and best-selling materials. The latter interpretation suggests that librarians would do well to examine their own motivations and biases when deciding whether they will charge fees for using various collections.[17]

The Cost of Returning Borrowed Items

There are several costs associated with returning borrowed items to the library. One is the cost of revisiting the library. Ideally, a library should absorb part of the cost of return travel by allowing patrons to return materials at any library outlet, not just the location where the item was originally borrowed.[18]

A second way libraries can reduce patron travel costs is to locate return drops for books and other items outside each library building. This will enable patrons to return items even when the library is closed. Most libraries do not allow items other than books to be placed in the book drop, because the weight of books on top of these may harm them. However, libraries should consider buying additional drops that could hold other types of materials as well. It is obviously not possible to have drops for all types of materials, because some (e.g., phonograph records) are damaged so easily that they must receive special handling. However, other popular media forms — like compact disks, videotapes, and audiocassettes — could be dropped into a container marked for them.

Libraries can also reduce patron costs by establishing, when the level of demand makes it possible, longer borrowing periods. Most library patrons prefer longer loan periods, because this allows them to use and return items more or less at their leisure and reduces the possibility of being charged an overdue fine. In fact, one study of 760 public libraries shows that libraries with longer loan periods (21 to 28 days) have annual circulation rates and per capita circulation rates that are significantly higher than those of libraries with loan periods of only 14 days (Nelson and Goldhor, 1987).[19]

Librarians need to remember that, if loan periods for high demand items are too long, patrons will be less likely to find these materials on the shelves. The Queens Borough (New York) Public Library discovered this when they lengthened the loan period for new fiction and popular nonfiction from 7 to 21 days. This policy change made these items so difficult to obtain that hundreds of patrons complained; the loan period was subsequently returned to its original level (Sivulich, 1989).

Allowing patrons to renew items can also reduce costs. However, some libraries have been reluctant to renew some or all types of items. For example, Goldhor (1990) found that 36 percent of a sample of Illinois public libraries did not permit renewals for any items. Many libraries prohibit renewals because they are time consuming and account for a rather small percentage of total circulation (1 percent to 9 percent in various studies).[20] But allowing renewals of materials with which the patron is not yet finished can increase patron satisfaction with the library and thus help balance the costs of using library services.

It is particularly important to consider allowing renewals when the library has a short, and therefore potentially inconvenient, loan period. In fact, Goldhor found that libraries with two-week loan periods had a renewal rate three times higher than that of libraries with four-week loan periods. This suggests that libraries with short loan periods should definitely consider allowing renewals. Many libraries already realize this; Goldhor's (1990) study shows that libraries with short loan periods were significantly more likely to allow renewals than those with longer loan periods.

Libraries should also allow telephone renewals, whenever the circulation system makes this possible, because this saves patrons the cost of travel time. Only one statewide study has addressed this issue. Baker (1985) found that 72 percent of a random sample of Illinois public libraries allowed such renewal. As figure 5.5 shows, this percentage declined as the size of the library increased. The lower rate of telephone renewals among larger libraries may have been due to the fact that more of these libraries had automated circulation systems, which can make it more difficult, although not always impossible, to do telephone renewals.

Population Served	Percentage
0-4,999 persons	88%
5,000-9,999 persons	80%
10,000-24,999 persons	73%
25,000 or more persons	39%

Figures reported in Baker (1985, 181).

Fig. 5.5. Percentage of Illinois public libraries allowing renewal of items over the telephone.

A final point is that both loan periods and renewal rates differ greatly by type of media. Generally, items in high demand (e.g., videotapes) tend to have the shortest loan period and the most restrictions on renewals.

The Cost of Paying Fines When Items Are Lost, Damaged, or Returned Late

Some patrons face an additional cost: paying fines when items are lost, damaged, or returned late. Most libraries charge patrons for damaged and lost works. Fines vary greatly for damaged items but are usually related to the amount of damage involved. Patrons are generally billed for the entire (original or replacement) cost of items that are lost; some libraries charge an additional fee to cover the cost of reprocessing the replacement works.

Most patrons are willing to pay a reasonable cost for works that they have damaged or lost. However, librarians will want to use their discretion in waiving some costs when the circumstances warrant. If, for example, a three-year-old child puts three videocassettes valued at $450 in the family aquarium, the library may want to compromise on the amount it charges the parent for replacing the works. Otherwise the library may permanently lose the family's patronage and goodwill.

A more common fee is that charged for overdue items. Overdue fines were originally established in hope that they would deter patrons from returning materials late. Although there is some evidence to suggest that fines do encourage patrons to return materials more quickly, the revenue raised by overdue fines may not always cover the cost of processing overdue notices.

This deficit has caused some libraries to eliminate fines entirely. For example, Adams (1991) reported on what happened when the Somerville (New Jersey) Free Public Library (SFPL) did this. SFPL hoped to cut patron costs and to increase use by eliminating all overdue fines. The year following this move, the library experienced an 11 percent increase in the number of residents who were registered borrowers, a 17.5 percent increase in the number of nonresidents who were registered borrowers, and a 19 percent increase in overall circulation. Findings like these suggest that the costs of charging overdues may outweigh their benefits.

Of course, libraries will need to take steps to see that eliminating overdues does not significantly reduce the total number of items returned to the library. For example, when the number of overdue works rose in response to its new no-fine policy, SFPL began mailing overdue notices and "blacklisting" patrons. Patrons could take out new items only when they had returned the old. This action caused the number of overdue works to decline to normal levels.

Other libraries have taken a more dramatic approach to ensure that overdue items are returned. They sponsor a forgiveness day or week, during which patrons can return materials, whether overdue for one day or many years, without paying fines. The Free Library of Philadelphia did this on a rather large scale in 1984. Stories in area newspapers alerted patrons to the event with intriguing leads like the following: "Somewhere in every house lurks an overdue library book; it's probably lying where no one will ever have to see it, alone and in the dark" (Milner, 1984, 629). The result of such publicity was that, during a single week, an estimated 35,000 patrons returned almost 160,000 overdue items valued at $1.5 million in what the library's public relations director called a "citywide absolution of guilt."

The Cost of Filing Reserve Requests

As was reported earlier, in the average public library, from 50 percent to 65 percent of the items that patrons are seeking at any one time are already checked out.[21] Today, most public libraries allow patrons to file cards to reserve such items as they are returned.

Patrons bear a number of different costs when they file reserve requests. The first is the time it takes to complete and turn in the reserve card. Libraries can reduce this cost by making cards readily available and ensuring that users do not have to stand in long lines to turn in the requests. For example, to avoid the latter problem, libraries may install boxes in which reserve cards can be dropped.

A second cost is the small fee that many libraries charge for reserving works. A few libraries charge this fee to deter patrons from making "frivolous" reserve requests. Such a practice is problematic, because most patrons will not take the time to file reserves for items that they do not really want. Many more libraries charge a small fee to help cover the costs of notifying the patron that a requested work is in.[22] Ideally, the latter fee should be charged only when it is necessary for economic reasons, because even such a small charge raises the cost of using the service.

There is also a cost associated with the delay in receiving the item needed. As one author has noted, "[d]elay time is a function of the library and the request to be filled.... Libraries cannot afford to have readily available all the information that anyone might need. Nor can they afford to have enough copies of heavily used materials to meet peak demands, so users must sometimes wait for them to be returned by others" (Van House, 1983a, 57).

Obviously, librarians will need to consider what is a reasonable period of delay, given the library's economic situation. Once this is determined, librarians can take steps to reduce delay time. Such steps may include purchasing multiple copies of books that are in high demand; reducing the length of the loan period for popular authors, titles, or subject areas; or leasing, from companies like Baker and Taylor Books, temporary supplemental collections of popular works. These techniques are discussed in more detail in chapter 9.

Occasionally, patrons will file so many reserve requests that a library cannot hope to fill them. Some libraries faced with this problem have decided to prohibit reserves for some types of materials. For example, many libraries take reserves for nonfiction videotapes but not for fiction videotapes. Libraries need to be aware, however, that decisions like these raise patron costs of using the collection. The following example illustrates this point.

In the mid-1980s, public libraries in the Montgomery County, Maryland, system stopped taking reserves on high demand (i.e., best-selling) titles. The library did this for two reasons. It wanted to conserve space on its overloaded computerized circulation system. It also wanted to "make the titles more available since sitting on reserve shelves waiting for people to pick them up took valuable reading time away from titles." However, in response to public complaints, the library conducted a survey that indicated that a majority of readers wanted the system reinstated. Patrons said they could not afford to buy all the books they wanted to read and could not afford the time to come into the library and check the shelves frequently for what they wanted. The library system paid attention to these patrons and lifted the moratorium on best-selling reserves (Best Seller, 1989).

A final cost of filing a reserve is that of returning to pick up the item. Many patrons do not pick up reserved items when they finally come. Such patrons are not "irresponsible"; they simply feel that the cost of waiting for reserved items has grown too large. Generally, patrons who do not pick up reserves have obtained desired items elsewhere (from friends, bookstores, or other libraries) or have decided they don't really need the items after all. These alternatives are especially likely to happen when delay time is excessive.

No one is currently studying, in an in-depth fashion, the length of time it takes public libraries to fill reserves. However, one recent survey indicates the length of time that medium-sized public libraries take to fill requests for materials that were checked out when the patron sought them, were located at another branch, or were at another library system. As figure 5.6 shows, fewer than half of the libraries surveyed were able to fill such requests within a week; a quarter had not been filled within one month (Public Library Association, 1991). These data indicate that public libraries could take further steps to lessen the cost of delay time.

Public Libraries Serving	Average 7-Day Document Delivery Rate	Average 30-Day Document Delivery Rate
100,000 to 249,999 people	47%	75%
50,000 to 99,999 people	39%	71%
25,000 to 49,999 people	39%	73%

So few large and small libraries reported these data that reliable national averages could be calculated only for medium-sized libraries.

Figures reported in Public Library Association (1991, 106-7).

Fig. 5.6. Average document delivery rates of medium-sized public libraries in the United States.

For many patrons, the cost of filing a reserve request, in terms of fees, initial filing time, delay time, and return travel time, is simply too high unless a patron is highly motivated to obtain a particular work. For example, 31 percent of patrons at the Edmonton (Alberta) Public Library preferred to "settle for something else instead" rather than to file reserve requests; 40 percent more (presumably regular users) said they would rather check the shelves on the next visit than file reserve requests (Gajerski, 1989).

Note that patrons will often file reserves for items that are "necessary" but not for items that are "nice, rather than necessary." For example, when Spiller (1980) surveyed 500 readers in five British public libraries, 63 percent said that they hardly ever filed fiction reserve requests because they did not find it worthwhile to do so; these same readers were much more likely to file reserve requests for specific nonfiction they were seeking.

The Cost of Obtaining Desired Materials from Another Branch Library

If a desired item is at a different branch from the one the user is patronizing, additional costs may arise. The first is travel. At least two factors influence whether a patron is willing to travel to a different branch to obtain a desired item. One is the "necessity" of obtaining the work. Although a patron may be willing to bear a higher cost to obtain a work that she considers essential to her information needs, she will be less likely to do so for a work she considers tangential. A second factor is the patron's perception of how convenient it will be for her to reach the branch. She might find it inconvenient, for example, to travel 15 miles to another branch until she realizes that branch is around the corner from her office. A patron who has to rely on the city's transit system may be less likely to travel to another branch than the patron who has a car.

But patrons should not have to assume all the costs associated with obtaining materials from a different branch. The library can absorb some costs by delivering requested materials to the branch where the requests were initiated within a reasonable time—ideally one week or less. In these instances, the patron will have to bear the cost of returning to the original branch to pick up the item; this may be more acceptable to the patron than traveling to a different branch, especially if she visits the library on a regular basis.

Libraries should also consider mailing requested items to patrons. Because of its expense, this option is generally reserved for patrons who cannot bear any costs of travel. For example, housebound patrons of the Akron-Summit County (Ohio) Library are generally serviced by a small collection of materials in the library's van. However, when a housebound patron has a special request, a librarian will locate the item and mail it the next day, rather than requiring that the patron wait two weeks for the van's next visit (Berry, 1990).

The Cost of Filing Interlibrary Loan Requests

A surprisingly small number of patrons take advantage of interlibrary loan services in medium-sized and large libraries. In fact, interlibrary loan accounts for less than 3 percent of the circulation of public libraries serving populations of more than 25,000 (National Center for Education Statistics, 1991).[23]

There are three major reasons for this low level of use. The first is that many patrons are not aware of interlibrary loan services, because few public libraries regularly and systematically promote these. Libraries that have made the effort have generally found it worthwhile, however. For example, one researcher asked 10 Illinois public libraries to conduct vigorous campaigns to advertise interlibrary loan services. These libraries used a variety of promotion techniques, including public service announcements on local radio and television stations; press releases and articles in local newspapers; bookmarks and flyers distributed to library users; signs posted within the library; buttons worn by staff; and staff suggestions to individual users. Interlibrary loan increased by an average of 38 percent in these libraries during the four-month period when these services were advertised (Goldhor, 1988).

A second factor that may inhibit interlibrary loan use in some libraries is the fees for these services. Although no recent studies have addressed this issue, several older studies show that approximately 10 percent of public libraries charge for interlibrary loan services.[24] The most common charge is for delivery of the requested item.

But patrons, who generally want to obtain desired materials immediately, tend to feel that the biggest cost of using interlibrary loan services is time. It takes time to complete a request form, to wait for the item to be found and sent to the requesting library, to wait to be notified by telephone or mail that the item is ready, and to return to the library to pick it up.

It is possible to increase the number of interlibrary loan requests by reducing these time costs. One academic library, the University of Illinois at Urbana-Champaign, has reduced these substantially. If a searcher fails to find an item in the library's on-line catalog, he receives an on-screen message that asks if he would like to search the holdings of other libraries in Illinois for the work. If he replies "yes," the computer searches the other catalogs and checks on the availability of the title. If the title is available, the work is sent to the user's campus mailing address. This interlibrary loan system is easy to use, has no fee, and delivers materials quickly, generally within a week. In two years the library increased the percentage of circulation that came from items requested via interlibrary loan from 3 percent to 8 percent (Potter, 1986).[25]

Although the system at the University of Illinois was originally developed in conjunction with other academic libraries in the state, public libraries within the state have ready access to it through 18 regional library systems. During October 1989, a total of 9,000 requests for interlibrary loans were handled by these regional systems (Sloan, 1990).

What Price Objectives Can a Library Adopt?

Marketing experts have identified four basic pricing objectives of profit and nonprofit organizations. These are maximizing use, recovering costs, maximizing profits, and discouraging use.

Maximizing Use

Because they feel that both the individual patron and society at large will profit from using the library, many public librarians try to maximize the use of their collections. Most try to do this by setting the price of using the collection, both in monetary and nonmonetary costs, as low as possible. Taking the various steps mentioned earlier in this chapter should reduce patron costs somewhat and ultimately lead to increased use. As noted in chapter 2, a number of libraries have claimed significant circulation increases after working to reduce patron costs while maximizing satisfaction levels.

Recovering Costs

Profit organizations would not survive if they did not both manage to recover the costs of their services and make a profit, however small. In the past, most public libraries have not had to depend on revenue generated from the sale of products or services. The library's offerings were subsidized through the use of tax money. But in today's tight fiscal climate, a library may not survive fiscally if it subsidizes the entire cost of each of the products and services it offers. So the library may compromise by setting prices that will help it recover part or all of its costs.

One library that has taken steps to recover costs is the Champaign (Illinois) Public Library and Information Center (CPLIC). A number of years ago, CPLIC was faced with tough financial times and a clientele that was demanding multiple copies of best-selling items. If CPLIC had purchased these works, it would have had to substantially reduce its purchase of other items in the collection, a choice it felt was incompatible with its mission. Instead, CPLIC purchased numerous copies of best-selling books and charged patrons $2 per week to "rent" them.[26] Once demand for the best-sellers had faded, CPLIC sold them for $5 a copy. Judith Drescher, former director of CPLIC, says the library kept track of how much money it made on each book through rental and sale. It was rare for a book to not recover the full cost of purchase. In many instances, the fees covered processing costs as well. All proceeds were funneled back into the rental collection to make it self-supporting (Drescher, 1991).

Maximizing Profits

Profit organizations occasionally set their prices fairly high in an effort to raise as much money as possible. Although few public libraries have this objective, their funding bodies might. For example, the Champaign Public Library and Information Center found there was one major drawback to its rental collection of best-sellers. When the city council realized the library was making money from the rental collection, money that could be used to ease CPLIC's financial woes without raising taxes, council members pestered the library board to either raise rental fees or charge fees for borrowing other types of materials, or both (Drescher, 1991).

DeCandido (1989) has described one study with interesting implications relating to the objective of maximizing profits in public libraries. In response to criticism by the business community and public officials, the Milwaukee Public Library conducted a study to see whether substantial nontax revenue could be realized through fees. The Public Policy Forum, a private, nonprofit, research organization that analyzes trends in taxation among local government units, found that cost-benefit analyses indicated only a limited number of library services could be self-supporting through a fee structure. One of these was rental of multiple copies of popular materials such as best-sellers and videos; another was researching and delivering items that would meet the information needs of area businesses.

Discouraging Use

Occasionally an organization will set prices to discourage people from using a particular product. This is sometimes done when the organization considers the product to be "bad" for some segment of the population. Consider, for example, the documented cases of librarians who have raised the costs of checking out sexually explicit materials by placing them in locked cases. This has usually been done to keep the materials out of the hands of children and teenagers.[27]

There are also instances of libraries raising costs to discourage certain classes of buyers. For example, the director of a public library on the East Coast resisted purchasing videotapes for years, because he felt the library should cater to book readers rather than "media junkies." The library board eventually persuaded the director to purchase the tapes to meet user demand. However, the director discouraged use of the tapes by charging high rental and overdue fees.

A more positive reason for discouraging use occurs when the library's budget does not keep pace with increases in collection use. The library can generally reduce its costs by shifting some nonmonetary costs to users. Consider the problems faced by the Iowa City (Iowa) Public Library (ICPL), which serves a highly educated university town and has a level of use far higher than that of the average public library. Between 1980 and 1991, circulation increased by 111 percent. But ICPL's budget (in 1980 dollars) increased by only 53 percent. This mean that ICPL could not hire enough staff to cope with the increased demand and had to stretch its collection to serve as many different users as possible.

One way ICPL coped was by discouraging use in an effort to avoid overtaxing personnel. High circulation of videotapes, which required staff-intensive screening between checkouts, was a particular problem. To solve it, ICPL lengthened the checkout period from two to seven days. This imposed a higher cost on patrons, because fewer tapes were available for checkout at any one time. However, the library succeeded in its purpose: videotape circulation declined by 35 percent to a level that could be handled by existing staff.[28]

ICPL also decided to stretch collections that were in short supply by setting limits to discourage heavy use by a small group of patrons. When compact disks were introduced, they were so popular that the shelves that housed them were always bare. So ICPL set a three-disk borrowing limit, instituted a seven-day loan period, and charged overdue fines of $1 per day. When collection funding improved and more disks were purchased, ICPL lengthened the loan period to three weeks and reduced the overdue charge to 20 cents per day.

Unfortunately, no recent studies have addressed the question of whether imposing fees to rent items will discourage use. Studies have shown that, when fees for on-line searching were instituted, use of previously free services dropped sharply.[29] This suggests that some patrons may cease using a collection if rental fees are charged. However, because the fees for on-line searching are much greater than those for renting materials, the drop in use of the latter may be much less significant.

Although many libraries do carefully consider issues relating to discouraging use,[30] others may discourage use without really thinking the matter through. For example, many libraries allow long queues to form for popular items in the collection, without assessing the cost to the library or the patron of doing so. Ideally, libraries should review their policies on a regular basis to ensure that poor service, overly stringent regulations, and unrealistic fees are not deterring use.

What Factors May Influence the Price Objectives That a Library Chooses?

The pricing objectives that a library sets depend on a number of different factors. Among the most important are the mission and roles that a library has adopted, the cost of providing certain types of materials, and the existence of one or more special situations that might require a library to consider encouraging or discouraging use.

Say that a public library has adopted two primary roles: *popular materials center* and *independent learning center*. In keeping with the former role, the library wants to buy multiple copies of the works of popular authors. But it also wants to build a diverse collection to meet the wide-ranging educational needs of its patrons. Because there is a potential for conflict here, library staff must thoughtfully consider possible pricing objectives.

In this case, library staff scrutinize the situation and decide they will try to maximize use of the collection by buying up to 10 copies of popular works when demand so indicates. But selectors feel that buying further copies to meet demand may limit the library's ability to maintain a diverse collection. They eventually decide to pass some of the costs of reading books by blockbuster authors to patrons, reducing the loan period for these works from three weeks to one.

There is evidence that librarians have sometimes set prices based on tradition (hence the refrain "but we've always charged 5 cents for overdues") or inattention (hence the long queues of reserves for blockbuster authors). Others may base prices on what other public libraries in the area are charging.[31] None of these practices is ideal, because the prices may have no relation to the cost the library is bearing to produce the product, local levels of demand for the product, or local prices set by the library's competition. A more thoughtful plan is for the library to use cost-oriented, demand-oriented, or competition-oriented pricing.

Under cost-oriented pricing, library staff fix the product's cost to correspond with the actual monetary cost incurred to provide that product. A national study of medium-sized public libraries shows that this method is the most common one used to determine fees (Phelan, 1985). Suppose that a library has a collection of popular books that it rents to patrons. The average book in the collection costs $30 to purchase and process and circulates 15 times. If staff charged patrons $2 for each circulation, the library would break even in terms of cost. Staff could funnel the fees earned back into the rental collection and have a self-supporting collection. Staff at another library with a similar collection may choose to subsidize part of the cost by charging patrons only $1 for each circulation.

Demand-oriented pricing examines the level of demand rather than the level of costs. Library staff members estimate how much value patrons see in a particular product and price that product accordingly, bearing in mind that patrons may continue to use popular items even if the cost rises slightly. The Princeton (New Jersey) Public Library bases its overdue fines on the availability of and demand for certain types of items. Fines range from 10 cents per day for an overdue book to $3 per day for an overdue video (Greiner, 1989).

There are two common forms of demand-oriented pricing in libraries. One is pricing that discriminates on a customer basis. Thus, a library may charge $1 for use of children's videotapes and $2 for use of adult videotapes. Many libraries set prices lower for those who could not otherwise afford to use library services. For example, the only overdue fines that senior citizen patrons of the Bay Village Branch of the Cuyahoga County (Ohio) Public Library System have to pay are those for videocassettes (Greiner, 1989).

The second form of demand-oriented pricing discriminates on a product basis. For example, the library may set a higher cost for new books than for old or for a popular product line (e.g., books-on-tape) than for a less popular one (e.g., 16mm films). Remember that costs here may not always be monetary. Libraries can set costs related to the patron's time and effort, such as shortened loan periods.

The third pricing strategy a library may adopt is competition-oriented pricing, that is, setting prices chiefly on the basis of what local competitors are charging. For example, a library that decides to charge fees for videotape rental may call all the video stores in town to determine the prices being charged for tape rentals, the length of time tapes can be rented, and the fee for returning late tapes, before it sets its own prices for videotape use.

What Factors Should a Library Consider When Changing the Price?

Librarians should review, on a regular basis, the price of using the collection to see if it should be reduced or increased. Generally, price increases are considered when the library's costs of doing business rise or when the level of demand for part of its collection expands significantly. For example, when a teacher requires 150 students to prepare reports on a particular state, the public library may place books about that state on reserve or limit the number of works that each student may check out.

In contrast, a library may consider reducing prices when its own costs are cut or when it wants to stimulate demand. It can also cut costs to gain part of the market share of its competitors. For example, one midwestern library noticed that circulation of the rental collection housed at its mall branch fell significantly when a bookstore moved in two doors away. When the branch quit charging fees for popular materials, use rose again, exceeding its previous level.

Libraries may, however, wish to estimate the effects of a price change on use before they permanently change the price of a particular product. Staff members can use three simple methods to estimate customer reactions to price changes. First, they can survey patron attitudes toward the proposed change. Two particularly valuable questions to ask patrons are

If the library increases the price of (a particular product) to X, would you still use it?

Would you be more likely to use (a particular product) if we reduced its cost from X to X?

Staff may also be able to predict customer reactions to a proposed price change by reviewing past-use data to determine the effect of earlier price reductions or increases on demand for a particular product. One city manager in the southeastern United States pressured his library to double fees for using certain materials. The library director provided statistics to the manager and the city council that showed that small fee increases in the past had little effect on usage but that larger increases caused circulation to fall. These data helped the director persuade city officials to raise user fees by only 30 percent.

Public libraries can also gauge customer reactions by actually changing the price of a product on a trial basis and examining the results. The Public Library of Des Moines (Iowa) did this several years ago. When city funding did not keep pace with the rate of inflation, the library materials budget suffered. The library wanted both to stretch its existing collection and to lessen the time that patrons had to wait to obtain reserves of new materials. So it temporarily reduced the length of its loan period from three to two weeks and eliminated the five-day grace period for overdue fines. When a large number of patrons complained, the library returned the loan period to its previous level, although it decided not to reinstate the grace period.

A final point is that existing library patrons may be fairly neutral about small increases in cost; after all, they have already decided that the benefits of using the library outweigh the costs. For example, a study by Phelan (1985) showed that medium-sized public libraries tended to charge very small user fees. Fifty percent of these libraries felt that initiating user fees for services had no effects on use; an additional 36 percent were unaware of changes in use. Only 10 percent said they had noticed a definite decrease in use since instituting fees. In these last cases, it seems likely that fees rose sharply enough that the costs of use outweighed the benefits patrons felt they received from the services.

Conclusion

There is a growing body of evidence that public library use is increasing. For example, Palmer (1991) found that circulation per capita has risen by 36 percent nationwide since 1980. Some of the increase may be due to the fact that the level of education of the general public has increased, and educational attainment is highly associated with both reading and library use.[32]

However, it is also reasonable to believe that part of the increase reflects advances that public librarians have made in reducing the costs of using the collection. The discussion above shows that some librarians are considering the effects of various types of costs on services and are making decisions to ensure that the costs of use do not outweigh the satisfaction patrons receive from such use. Ideally, this trend should both continue and spread.

Notes

[1]The Book Industry Study Group (1983) found that 80 percent of all books read are from sources other than the public library.

[2]Breadth of available selection has been identified as an important cost-benefit consideration in several studies. For example, Gallup (1985) found adult book buyers, when choosing which bookstore they would patronize, were often influenced more by the variety of selections offered. This was particularly true among those who visited bookstores frequently and bought books often.

[3]For example, even one-room libraries are more difficult for the average person to understand and use effectively than bookstores of the same size.

[4]Walker (1989) has even written a book that documents what libraries of all types are doing to make money by using fees.

[5]Diehl and Weech (1991a, 1991b) reviewed the literature on library use instruction and concluded that some users, presumably those most familiar with libraries, are satisfied with their library use skills; however, others desire use instruction.

[6]A recent nationwide poll indicated that 68 percent of those who use public libraries felt it would be valuable for them to have dial-up access to the catalog (Survey, 1991).

[7]Variables like these greatly influence the extent to which any media distribution outlet is used. For example, Gallup (1985) found that 38 percent of adult book buyers named location or hours as the factor that most influenced them to patronize a particular bookstore.

[8]See, for example, Krikelas (1972).

[9]For further information on studies that address these issues, see chapter 7 of Baker and Lancaster (1991).

[10]Little research has been conducted that relates specifically to library floor plans; however, various studies have indicated a strong correlation between the complexity of floor plans and user disorientation in general. See, for example, Weisman (1981).

[11]Myers (1979) is one of the few authors who has discussed the principles of designing open stack areas from a user's point of view.

[12]The most comprehensive guide to signs, by Pollet and Haskell (1979), discusses both theoretical principles of signage and practical considerations. Two other recommended works, which focus primarily on practical aspects, are by Mallery and DeVore (1982) and Reynolds and Barret (1981).

[13]Although most of these studies have been conducted in academic libraries, the results seem to hold true for public libraries as well. Among the more interesting are studies by Durrance (1986), Westbrook (1984), Murfin (1983), and Swope and Katzer (1972).

[14]For a more comprehensive picture of what libraries can do to make reference services more effective, see chapter 8 of Baker and Lancaster (1991).

[15]Various authors have described specific procedures for training and motivating shelvers, determining error rates, and reading shelves. Among the more useful are Kendrick (1991), Lowenberg (1989), and Schabo and Baculis (1989).

[16]Note that this distinction between basic and value-added services is being made increasingly, and, unfortunately, not just by librarians. For example, one management consultant firm, which specializes in advising municipalities on cost-allocation plans, told the New Mexico Municipal League that libraries should consider charging patrons for services that are "above and beyond what they normally provide." The firm recommended that fees be considered for such "extras" as adult education programs, story hours, and summer reading programs (Goldberg, 1990).

[17]An excellent overview of the ethical issues involved in charging fees for public library use is given in Giacoma (1989).

[18]The same principle applies to items checked out as part of a reciprocal borrowing agreement among a number of area library systems.

[19]The same study also found that 83 percent of the libraries that had shortened their loan periods allowed renewals, as opposed to only 33 percent of libraries with longer loan periods. This suggests that many libraries were trying to compensate for increasing patron costs in one area by decreasing them in another.

[20]See, for example, Goldhor (1990) and Baldwin (1979).

[21]See, for example, Gajerski (1989) and Kuraim (1983).

[22]For example, one study found that 71 out of 139 California libraries surveyed charged for a reserve notice postcard (Strong, 1984).

[23]This percentage is higher for smaller libraries, ranging from 4 percent for libraries serving populations of 10,000 to 25,000 persons to 18 percent for libraries serving fewer than 1,000 patrons (National Center for Education Statistics, 1991).

[24]See, for example, Strong (1984) and Lynch (1978).

[25]In the late 1980s, public libraries in Illinois gained access to this form of resource sharing by joining ILLINET Online. The database contains more than five million unique bibliographic records representing the OCLC cataloging activity of some 800 libraries of all types in the state. The system provides easy dial-up access to all libraries that can afford to purchase microcomputer terminals to tap into the system and to pay the costs of the telephone tolls. Titles are sent to participating libraries via a state-subsidized delivery system. For more information, see Sloan (1990, 1989) and Sloan and Stewart (1988).

[26]The Champaign Public Library and Information Center also purchased one or more copies of these titles for its regular collection, to ensure that patrons who could not afford to "rent" books had access to these items. Patrons could file reserves for items in the regular collection, but rental collection books were distributed on a first-come, first-serve basis only.

[27]This practice, of course, violates the American Library Association's "Library Bill of Rights." This one-page document is available from the American Library Association and has been reprinted in numerous texts devoted to collection development. See, for example, Evans (1987, 397).

[28]Note that when the Iowa City Public Library increased its videotape budget in response to patron requests for a bigger collection, videotape circulation rebounded quickly. It only took two years for use to surpass its previous level, even though the library left the seven-day loan period in place.

[29]See, for example, National Commission on Libraries and Information Science (1985).

[30]For example, Dubberly (1986) describes the thoughtful steps that the Seattle Public Library took to resolve similar cost-related issues.

[31]A study by Phelan (1985) showed that 19 percent of medium-sized public libraries did this to determine the fees they would charge.

[32]See, for example, Selsky (1989).

References

Adams, January. "A Year of Living Dangerously: Implementation of a No-Fine Policy at Somerville Free Public Library." *Public Libraries* 30, no. 6 (November/December 1991): 346-49.

Ashton, Dub. "Marketing and Communications: Activities that Support Library Growth." *Arkansas Libraries* 42, no. 4 (December 1985): 13-16.

Baker, Sharon L. "Fines, Fees, and Charges Levied." *Illinois Library Statistical Report* 7 (May 1983): 35-73.

_____. "Library Resources and Practices of Illinois Public Libraries: Analysis of the 1984 Supplemental Annual Report." *Illinois Library Statistical Report* 17 (May 1985): 142-96.

Baker, Sharon L., and F. Wilfrid Lancaster. *Measurement and Evaluation of Library Services.* 2d ed. Arlington, Va.: Information Resources Press, 1991.

Baldwin, Joe M. "Measuring the Efficiency of the Use of Books Borrowed from a Public Library." M.L.S. thesis, North Texas State University, 1979. ERIC ED178037.

Berry, Diana. "Creativity and Mobile Services." In *The Book Stops Here: New Directions in Bookmobile Services*, ed. Catherine Suyak Alloway, 253-61. Metuchen, N.J.: Scarecrow Press, 1990.

"Best Seller 'Reserves' Back by Popular Demand." *Unabashed Librarian* no. 71 (1989): 16.

Book Industry Study Group. *1983 Consumer Research Study on Reading and Book Purchasing.* New York: Book Industry Study Group, 1983.

Clark, Colin. "Charge for Service: The California Practice." *News Notes of California Libraries* 72, no. 2 (1977): 11-13.

DeCandido, Graceanne. "New Limited Fee Plan for Milwaukee Public Library." *Library Journal* 114, no. 2 (1 February 1989): 18.

Diehl, Susan J., and Terry L. Weech. "Library Use Instruction in the Public Library: A Survey of User Preferences." *Research Strategies* 9, no. 1 (Winter 1991a): 25-40.

_____. "Library Use Instruction Research and the Public Library." *Public Libraries* 30, no. 1 (January/February 1991b): 33-42.

Drescher, Judith. Telephone conversation on 11 December 1991.

Dubberly, Ronald A. "Managing Not to Charge Fees." *American Libraries* 17, no. 9 (October 1986): 670, 672-73, 675-76.

Durrance, Joan C. "The Influence of Reference Practices on the Client-Librarian Relationship." *College and Research Libraries* 47, no. 1 (January 1986): 57-67.

Eaton, Gale. "Wayfinding in the Library: Book Searches and Route Uncertainty." *RQ* 30, no. 4 (Summer 1991): 319-27.

Evans, G. Edward. *Developing Library and Information Center Collections*. 2d ed. Littleton, Colo.: Libraries Unlimited, 1987.

Gajerski, B. "Edmonton Public Library: 1989 User Survey." Edmonton Public Library, Edmonton, Alberta, 1989. ERIC ED327184.

Gallup Organization. *The Gallup 1985 Annual Report on Book Buying*. Princeton, N.J.: Gallup Organization, 1985.

Giacoma, Pete. *The Fee or Free Decision*. New York: Neal-Schuman, 1989.

Goldberg, B. "Make Libraries Pay Their Way, Advises Consultant (at New Mexico Municipal League Seminar)." *American Libraries* 21, no. 1 (January 1990): 13.

Goldhor, Herbert. "The Effect of Publicity on Interlibrary Loan Requests in Ten Illinois Public Libraries." *Public Libraries* 27, no. 4 (Winter 1988): 184-87.

_____. "Statistics of Renewals in Public Libraries." *Public Library Quarterly* 10, no. 2 (1990): 63-68.

Greiner, Joy, ed. "The Philosophy and Practice of Fines and Fees." *Public Libraries* 28, no. 5 (September/October 1989): 257-61.

Intner, Sheila S. *Circulation Policy in Academic, Public and School Libraries*. New York: Greenwood Press, 1987.

Kendrick, Curtis L. "Performance Measures of Shelving Accuracy." *Journal of Academic Librarianship* 17, no. 1 (March 1991): 16-18.

Krikelas, James. "Catalog Use Studies and Their Implications." In *Advances in Librarianship*, vol. 3, ed. Melvin J. Voigt, 195-200. New York: Seminar Press, 1972.

Kuraim, Faraj Mohamed. "The Principal Factors Causing Reader Frustration in a Public Library." Ph.D. diss., Case Western Reserve University, 1983.

Lowenberg, Susan. "A Comprehensive Shelf Reading Program." *Journal of Academic Librarianship* 15, no. 1 (March 1989): 24-27.

Lynch, Mary Jo. "Confusion Twice Compounded: Report of PLA Survey of Fees Currently Charged in Public Libraries." *Public Libraries* 17, no. 3 (Fall 1978): 11-13.

Lynch, Mary Jo, ed. *Non-Tax Sources of Revenue for Public Libraries*. Chicago: American Library Association, Office for Research, 1988.

Mallery, Mary S., and Ralph E. DeVore. *A Sign System for Libraries*. Chicago: American Library Association, 1982.

Mellon, Constance A. "Library Anxiety: A Grounded Theory and Its Development." *College and Research Libraries* 47, no. 2 (March 1986): 160-65.

Milner, Art. "Forgiveness Week." *Library Journal* 109, no. 6 (1 April 1984): 627-30.

Mooers, Calvin N. "Mooers' Law or, Why Some Retrieval Systems Are Used and Others Are Not." *American Documentation* 11, no. 3 (July 1960): ii.

Murfin, Marjorie E. "National Reference Measurement: What Can It Tell Us About Staffing?" *College and Research Libraries* 44, no. 5 (September 1983): 321-33.

Myers, Judy. "Designing Open Stack Areas for the User." In *Sign Systems for Libraries: Solving the Wayfinding Problem*, ed. Dorothy Pollet and Peter C. Haskell, 195-201. New York: R. R. Bowker, 1979.

National Center for Education Statistics. *Public Libraries in 50 States and the District of Columbia, 1989*. Washington, D.C.: U.S. Department of Education, Office of Educational Research and Improvement, 1991. Data Series: DR-LIB-89/90-1.1. NCES 91-343.

National Commission on Libraries and Information Science. "The Role of Fees in Supporting Library and Information Services in Public and Academic Libraries." Washington, D.C.: National Commission on Libraries and Information Science, 1985. ERIC ED258584.

Nelson, Susan, and Herbert Goldhor. "The Relationship Between the Length of Loan Period and Circulation in Public Libraries." *Illinois Library Statistical Report* 24 (August 1987): 3-20.

Palmer, Carole. "Public Library Circ Static, Spending Up 11.5%." *American Libraries* 22, no. 7 (July-August 1991): 659.

Phelan, Jody. "Fees for Services in Medium-Sized Public Libraries." *Iowa Library Quarterly* 23, no. 1 (Winter 1985): 2-11.

Pollet, Dorothy, and Peter C. Haskell, eds. *Sign Systems for Libraries: Solving the Wayfinding Problem*. New York: R. R. Bowker, 1979.

Potter, William Gray. "Creative Automation Boosts ILL Rates." *American Libraries* 17, no. 4 (April 1986): 244-46.

Public Library Association. *Public Library Data Service Statistical Report '91*. Chicago: Public Library Association, 1991.

Ranganathan, Shiyali R. *The Five Laws of Library Science*. 2d ed. Bombay, India: Asia Publishing House, 1957.

Razzano, Barbara Will. *Public Library Services to Children and Young Adults in New Jersey*. Trenton, N.J.: New Jersey State Library, Library Development Bureau, 1986.

Reynolds, Linda, and Stephen Barrett. *Signs and Guiding for Libraries*. London: Clive Bingley, 1981.

Robinson, Charles W. "Free or Fee Based Library in the Year 2000." *Journal of Library Administration* 11, no. 1/2 (1989): 111-18.

Schabo, Pat, and Diana Breuer Baculis. "Speed and Accuracy for Shelving." *Library Journal* 114, no. 16 (1 October 1989): 67-68.

Selsky, Deborah. "Library Market Outlook: American Reading Habits (and Education) on the Rise." *Library Journal* 114, no. 9 (15 May 1989): 22.

Sivulich, Kenneth. "How We Run the Queens Library Good (and Doubled Circulation in Seven Years)." *Library Journal* 114, no. 3 (15 February 1989): 123-27.

Sloan, Bernard G. "Future Directions for ILLINET Online." *Illinois Libraries* 72, no. 1 (January 1990): 40-44.

_____. "Resource Sharing at the Statewide Level: ILLINET Online." *Illinois Libraries* 71, nos. 3-4 (March-April 1989): 185-89.

Sloan, Bernard G., and J. David Stewart. "ILLINET Online: Enhancing and Expanding Access to Library Resources in Illinois." *Library Hi Tech* 6, no. 3 (1988): 95-101.

Smith, Adam. *An Inquiry into the Nature and Causes of the Wealth of Nations*. New York: The Modern Library, 1937.

Spiller, David. "The Provision of Fiction for Public Libraries." *Journal of Librarianship* 12, no. 4 (October 1980): 238-65.

Strong, Gary E. "Report on Fees and User Cost Sharing." *California State Library Newsletter*, no. 43 (July 1984): 5-6.

"Survey Reports Heavy Library Use: Anticipation of Home Computer Links." *Bulletin of the American Society for Information Science* 17, no. 4 (April/May 1991): 2-3.

Swope, Mary Jane, and Jeffrey Katzer. "The Silent Majority: Why Don't They Ask Questions?" *RQ* 12, no. 2 (Winter 1972): 161-66.

"Upfront News: Library Receives Entrepreneurial Loans." *Wilson Library Bulletin* 65, no. 7 (March 1991): 12.

Van House, Nancy A. *Public Library User Fees: The Use and Finance of Public Libraries*. Westport, Conn.: Greenwood Press, 1983a.

_____. "A Time Allocation Theory of Public Library Use." *Library and Information Science Research* 5, no. 4 (Winter 1983b): 365-84.

Vandergrift, Kay E. "Are Children and Teenagers Second-Class Users?" *Library Resources and Technical Services* 33, no. 4 (October 1989): 393-99.

Walker, Alice Sizer. *Making Money: Fees for Library Services*. New York: Neal-Schuman, 1989.

Weisman, Jerry. "Evaluating Architectural Legibility: Wayfinding in the Built Environment." *Environment and Behavior* 13, no. 2 (March 1981): 189-203.

Westbrook, Lynn. "Catalog Failure and Reference Service: A Preliminary Study." *RQ* 24, no. 1 (Fall 1984): 82-90.

Zipf, George K. *Human Behavior and the Principle of Least Effort*. Cambridge, Mass.: Addison-Wesley, 1949.

Place or Distribution Decisions

6

The third factor in the marketing mix that collection managers need to consider is place: how the library's products, in this case the items in the collection, are to be distributed to users. Distribution is a concern because the products the library offers are typically removed in space from the patron; they may also be removed in time, as in the case of a patron wanting something when the library is not open. To determine what forms of distribution will best resolve the various space and time issues that arise, librarians will need to ask themselves four major questions:

1. What types of distribution outlets can the public library use?

2. How should the library distribute items among its various outlets?

3. How should items be distributed among collections in a single library facility?

4. How can the library design its interior for maximum distribution effectiveness?

Each of these is discussed below.

What Types of Collection Distribution Outlets Can the Public Library Use?

When trying to determine the types and numbers of distribution outlets to be established, librarians should consider the costs of the various distribution options, the size of the geographic area served, and the nature of the library's clientele, including their ability or willingness to travel to use the collection. Because studies have consistently shown that overall library use is highest when patrons have convenient and ready access to the library building, librarians should try to find distribution solutions that strike a good compromise between the library's distribution costs and reasonable levels of customer convenience. That is, librarians should offer their services in as many places, with convenient locations and hours, as are affordable, then ask patrons to bear the rest of the cost of using these facilities, whenever the patrons are able to do so.

Seven distribution options exist: main libraries, full-service branches, minibranches, bookmobiles, deposit collections, home delivery services, and books-by-mail services. Each is discussed briefly below.

Main Libraries

The most economical decision is to have a single main library, because this reduces the need for duplicate collections.[1] Furthermore, because the library is concentrating its personnel and operating expenditures on one building only, it may be able to stay open a larger number of hours, making it more accessible to patrons, particularly those who work. Because the main library building tends to be quite large, it generally houses a sizeable and diverse collection that includes materials in all the formats that the library system collects. The main library collection tends to be particularly good at meeting the needs of patrons who read a great deal in one subject area, want items that are more esoteric or specialized, or want materials in a special format. Studies have shown that patrons with specialized needs, especially those associated with a formal educational program or career they are pursuing, may be willing to travel farther to use a main library rather than limit themselves to using materials at their local branch libraries (Gajerski, 1989; Gallup, 1976).

Some university libraries are choosing to operate a single facility, closing departmental libraries that are scattered around a campus and instead providing an extensive collection of materials in a main building. The single outlet option appears to work well at the university level as long as the campus is fairly small. Universities that have large campuses are not choosing to limit their distribution options to a single main library, because they have found that faculty and students would rather use more conveniently located departmental libraries.

But public libraries serve geographic areas that are much larger than a university campus. Although a single facility works well for many small towns, it is not as viable an option for larger communities. Various studies have shown that people want public library services close to where they work, shop, and live; most people are not willing to travel more than five miles out of their way to reach a library outlet (Childers and Van House, 1989; Hayes and Palmer, 1983; and Palmer, 1981). One recent study found that the closeness of the library is particularly crucial in neighborhoods where many residents have low socioeconomic and educational status: "People from these strata will not go to distant libraries partly because fewer of them own cars and partly because the perceived importance of library use is lower among them than among more-educated persons" (Shoham, Hershkovitz, and Metzer, 1990, 179). These patrons are less likely to use library services than the average patron because they perceive the costs of travel are higher and the benefits of library use lower.

Another potential problem with main library facilities is that they often lack free or easily accessible parking. This is most likely to be true when the library is in a downtown area, where the costs of real estate are high.

Full-Service Branch Libraries

Libraries in medium-size or larger communities can minimize patron travel time by supplementing a centrally located main library with full-service branch libraries near residential, shopping, and work areas.[2] As figure 6.1 shows, in 1989 the National Center for Education Statistics collected data on branch libraries from 8,715 public libraries in the United States. Eighty-four percent did not have branch libraries, presumably for economic reasons. The other 16 percent (1,409 libraries) had a total of 6,513 branch libraries. The average number of branches established among libraries that had branch libraries ranged from 51.3 in libraries that served a million or more residents to 1 for libraries that served a thousand or fewer residents.

Due to the smaller building size, the collections at branch libraries are generally substantially smaller than those at the main library. Some patrons prefer smaller collections because they find them less intimidating to use. However, small collections may not meet the needs of patrons who are seeking specialized works on a particular topic, who want a breadth of choices, or who want materials in a format that the branch does not carry.[3] For example, the videotape collection at the main facility of the Queens Borough (New York) Public Library (QBPL) contains foreign-language, how-to, juvenile-oriented, and feature films; permanent videotape collections at branch libraries are much smaller and do not generally contain how-to or foreign-language films (Sivulich, 1989). The Fairfax County (Virginia) Public Library is doubling the size of its audiotape collections (its goal is 100 files per branch) and still cannot meet patron demand (Annichiarico, 1991).

The small size of branch collections can be offset in a number of ways. One of the most common is tailoring selections to meet the specialized needs of the residents served. For example, QBPL designed a collection of popular and traditional Spanish-language materials for patrons at its Corona Branch, which serves a predominantly Hispanic clientele. Another way to stretch "fixed" branch collections is to supplement them with rotating collections of more specialized materials. QBPL has used this strategy to expand collections of videotapes at 17 branches; it rotates supplemental collections that contain 300 more specialized videotapes among the branches (Sivulich, 1989). One author has taken the notion of rotating collections to an extreme. Savage (1946) feels that branches should have a core collection of classics, standard reference works, and best-selling items (the last discarded when they have passed their usefulness); all other works should be rotated frequently among different branches so that each branch within a system has a continually renewed collection.

If they are sited properly and have good parking facilities and convenient hours (e.g., open many evening and weekend hours), branch libraries will be perceived as being readily accessible and will be heavily used. This use, combined with the smaller size and operating costs, often makes branch libraries more cost-effective than main library facilities.[4]

Size of Population Served	Number of Libraries Responding to Outlet Count	Number of Libraries with a Branch Library*	Percentage of Libraries with a Branch Library	Total Number of Branch Libraries	Average Number of Branch Libraries**
Total	8,715	1,409	16%	6,513	4.6
1,000,000 or more	18	16	89%	821	51.3
500,000 to 999,999	50	47	94%	927	19.7
250,000 to 499,999	84	75	89%	832	11.1
100,000 to 249,999	279	249	89%	1,385	5.6
50,000 to 99,999	479	321	67%	1,081	3.4
25,000 to 49,999	810	306	38%	766	2.5
10,000 to 24,999	1,591	238	15%	446	1.9
5,000 to 9,999	1,435	99	7%	170	1.7
2,500 to 4,999	1,354	37	3%	51	1.4
1,000 to 2,499	1,636	18	1%	28	1.6
Fewer than 1,000	961	2	0%	2	1.0
Not reported	18	1	0%	4	4.0

*No distinction was made in this survey between full-service branch libraries and minibranches.

**Among libraries that possess branch libraries.

Table compiled from figures reported in National Center for Education Statistics (1991, 21).

Fig. 6.1. Number of public libraries and their branches in the United States, cross-analyzed by size of population served.

In fact, branch libraries can reduce patron travel costs so much that people use the library who would not normally do so. For example, Behrman and Conable (1989) documented use by a number of nontraditional library users when the Fort Vancouver Regional Library opened a branch in a large shopping mall. The branch, which is open the same hours as the mall (71 per week plus extra hours during the Christmas season), is so busy that 60 percent of the children's collection is always checked out.

As Panz (1989) has noted, as metropolitan areas continue to expand in geographic size and as so-called "baby boomers" move into the suburbs, the need for branch libraries will increase. But if past trends are good indicators, library budgets will not increase as quickly as demand, which may cause difficulties in financing new buildings.[5] This has led various experts to predict that library systems will try to save money by building much smaller branches in the future.[6]

Minibranches

If a library cannot afford a full-service branch, it may consider establishing a minibranch instead. Unlike full-service branches, which provide story hours and other services, most minibranches limit themselves to providing materials for patron checkout. Because they are generally established to encourage impulse browsing, most minibranches are stocked with current and popular materials. To maximize use, these branches should be located in high-traffic areas with lots of parking and should be open during hours convenient for patrons. Because they can be staffed by nonprofessionals, minibranches are fairly cost-effective to operate.

One popular location for such minibranches is at rapid transit stations, where the library can provide service literally in the day-to-day path of potential users. One of the oldest rapid transit libraries was installed by the Montreal Public Library in the McGill metro station in 1981. During its first year of operation, this branch was used by almost 7,000 patrons. Of these, 68 percent had not previously possessed a library card (Lavigne, 1984). By 1988, this branch was circulating approximately 200,000 items per year. Other public libraries that operate minibranches in rapid transit centers include the Atlanta-Fulton Public Library, the Paris (France) Public Library, and the Miami-Dade (Florida) Public Library, which was the first to install a minibranch on the platform of an elevated transit system (World's, 1992; Mancini, 1989).

Many public libraries are also putting minibranches, rather than full-service branches, in shopping malls. The latter option can be an expensive one, since most malls charge a great deal to rent store space. However, a minibranch can be set up along a mall walkway at a much more reasonable cost. These walkway branches are frequently housed in portable kiosks. Public libraries in St. Paul, Cincinnati, and Fairfax County (Virginia) have used kiosk minibranches with good results (Wagner, 1987; Paine, 1985). The Wichita Public Library even installed a minibranch in a supermarket (Supermarket, 1986).

A few public libraries have set up minibranches as experimental facilities, to measure the potential demand for services among a particular group. The Multnomah County (Oregon) Library tried this strategy in 1988, when it established a minibranch for low-income and homeless residents of Portland. Initially funded by a Library Services and Construction Grant and donations, this branch was located in an area of low-income hotels and shelters and staffed by volunteers (Portland, 1989).

Bookmobiles

As figure 6.2 shows, 11 percent of the libraries in the United States use mobile facilities to provide a traveling collection of books and other materials. Many libraries arrange bookmobile stops at institutions that house potential users who might have difficulty traveling to the library. These may include senior citizen complexes, child care facilities, and schools. A few studies have shown that people who lack such service may quit using library services entirely. For example, 39 percent of the students served by an Ohio public library ceased using library services when the bookmobile stop at their school was discontinued (Bolt, 1984).[7] The cost of borrowing materials became too high when they did not have convenient access to the library's collection.

Other libraries use bookmobiles to serve groups that are intimidated by the library, since bookmobiles provide personalized services on a smaller scale that can help ease patron fears. For example, the Fresno County (California) Public Library schedules bookmobile stops at the camps of migrant workers. Librarians reasoned that the children of such workers would have few other opportunities to visit the library; many of their parents are or have been illegal aliens and are leery of large governmental institutions. Other barriers to use are the long hours the parents work and the fact that the parents themselves have no tradition of library use (Naismith, 1989). Other groups that may be intimidated less by the bookmobile than by main or branch library services include older persons who have not previously used the library, more conservative residents of highly rural areas (Philip, 1990), and Native Americans (Skrzeszewski, Huggins-Chan, and Clarke, 1990).

Libraries can also arrange for bookmobiles to frequent neighborhoods that do not have branch libraries, scheduling regular stops in the parking lots of apartment buildings, trailer courts, shopping malls, school buildings, housing projects, manufacturing plants, and the like.

Unfortunately, due to their limited size, bookmobiles cannot carry diverse or in-depth collections. Studies have shown that the average bookmobile contains between 2,000 and 3,000 books and has a tiny collection of periodicals and nonprint materials (Vavrek, 1990a; Abel, 1986).

Another disadvantage is that bookmobile stops are short, generally ranging from one-half to two-and-one-half hours and repeated an average of once every two weeks (Vavrek, 1990b). This intermittent service means that bookmobiles do not provide convenient access to the collection for many patrons. As a result, most libraries provide bookmobile services only when the library cannot afford to establish a branch library.

In some cases, the library may not have the capital to set up a branch in a growing neighborhood. A bookmobile parked in the neighborhood for an entire day once a week can meet the needs of an expanding service area and provide use statistics to help the library convince its funding body that a mini- or full-service branch is needed.

Size of Population Served	Number of Libraries Responding to Outlet Count	Number of Libraries with a Bookmobile	Percentage of Libraries with a Bookmobile	Total Number of Bookmobiles	Average Number of Bookmobiles*
Total	8,715	921	11%	1,140	1.2
1,000,000 or more	18	10	56%	51	5.1
500,000 to 999,999	50	35	70%	72	2.1
250,000 to 499,999	84	50	60%	77	1.5
100,000 to 249,999	279	156	56%	200	1.3
50,000 to 99,999	479	205	43%	252	1.3
25,000 to 49,999	810	215	27%	229	1.1
10,000 to 24,999	1,591	159	10%	166	1.0
5,000 to 9,999	1,435	49	3%	49	1.0
2,500 to 4,999	1,354	16	1%	16	1.0
1,000 to 2,499	1,636	17	1%	18	1.0
Fewer than 1,000	961	8	1%	9	1.1
Not reported	18	1	1%	1	1.1

*Among libraries that possess bookmobiles.

Table compiled from figures reported in National Center for Education Statistics (1991, 21).

Fig. 6.2. Number of public libraries with bookmobiles in the United States, cross-analyzed by size of population served.

In other cases, the geographic area to be served is too large and sparsely populated to make it cost-effective to set up a branch library. For example, the public library in Juneau, Alaska, received a state grant to serve rural readers in a region larger than Oregon, Washington, and California combined. The area is so huge, so sparsely populated, and has such poor roads that the library's "bookmobile" is an airplane, which flies material to more than 550 users. The users absorb a small part of the cost of the service: the price of mailing materials back to the library when they are finished with them (Ferrell, 1983).

Deposit Collections

Deposit collections can also be used to bring library materials to community residents who have difficulty traveling to libraries. Consider the case of a senior citizen complex that houses many elderly patrons who are no longer able to drive. Although some patrons might take the bus to the library, others would find the cost of doing so too high. So the library may establish, at the complex, a deposit collection—a small group of materials tailored to meet the needs of the residents that can be checked out at any time. As figure 6.3 shows, almost 1,100 public libraries in the United States are using deposit collections.

Other groups can benefit from deposit collections. For example, the Onondaga County (New York) Public Library provides rotating deposit collections of 25 read-aloud books to area preschools (Wyker, 1988). That library has also placed deposit collections of adult new reader titles in waiting rooms at health and welfare organizations (Outposts, 1988). The New York Public Library provides deposit collections for children and adults who live in homeless shelters (Behrmann, Bonitch, and Gottfried, 1988; Gonzalez and Gottfried, 1988). Other libraries provide them for prison inmates.

Because deposit collections are small, they need to be tailored to meet the needs of the client group. For example, a collection at a jail might include books and magazines for recreational reading as well as a variety of legal information. Although most deposit collections are composed primarily of hardback and paperback books, the library should add other formats when appropriate. For example, a deposit collection at a senior citizens' center may include large-print newspapers, magazines, and books, as well as books-on-tape. Libraries should rotate the materials in the deposit collections frequently to ensure that patrons have a variety of choices over time.

A few libraries have tried using a different kind of deposit collection, with good success. The Orange (New Jersey) Public Library (OPL) was the first to set up "read-and-return" collections of books that the library would otherwise discard (Scilken, 1971). It distributes the books in various outlets around the community (like banks, beauty parlors, and doctors' offices), marking them with a label that invites residents to take and read the book, returning it to the library when they are finished. For these collections, OPL chooses former best-sellers, mysteries, and "other books that will have instant appeal to the casual reader." Collections are placed in a simple book rack, with an accompanying sign, and are changed as frequently as demand indicates.

Size of Population Served	Number of Libraries	Number of Libraries Responding to Outlet Count	Number of Libraries with Deposit Collections	Total Number of Deposit Collections
Total	8,968	8,715	1,087	6,558
1,000,000 or more	19	18	11	27
500,000 to 999,999	50	50	35	612
250,000 to 499,999	84	84	45	770
100,000 to 249,999	279	279	109	1,478
50,000 to 99,999	479	479	139	1,159
25,000 to 49,999	810	810	160	854
10,000 to 24,999	1,592	1,591	236	797
5,000 to 9,999	1,435	1,435	152	391
2,500 to 4,999	1,354	1,354	94	268
1,000 to 2,499	1,637	1,636	78	114
Fewer than 1,000	961	961	27	39
Not reported	268	18	3	49

Tables compiled from figures reported in National Center for Education Statistics (1991, 21).

Fig. 6.3. Number of public libraries with deposit collections in the United States, cross-analyzed by size of population served.

Other libraries have also tried read-and-return collections. The Department of Public Libraries in Montgomery County, Maryland, has placed books in the county courthouse for use by citizens who have been called to jury duty (AL Aside, 1991). A slightly more ambitious program along these lines was established by the Cambridge (Massachusetts) Public Library, which placed thousands of donated paperbacks in a subway station and invited subway riders to borrow the books on the honor system (Watson, 1988).

Obviously, some of the materials in read-and-return collections are never returned. For example, the Orange (New Jersey) Public Library, which serves a low-income, lower-middle-class community, noted a return rate of 65 percent (Scilken, 1971). However, if librarians use donations or discards to stock these collections, they can raise community awareness about the library's collection at a relatively low cost.

Personal Delivery Services

Some public libraries also deliver items to the homes or offices of patrons. Those libraries that are interested in and can afford to provide the highest quality service send professional librarians to the offices or residences of patrons to interview them and determine their information needs. The librarians then choose materials from the collection to meet these needs. For example, the Broughton (Salford, England) Library purchased a van; added shelving, lights, and a small but choice collection of materials; and staffed it with professional librarians who visited patrons in their homes. The van, which was equipped with a hydraulic lift and nonslip flooring, could accommodate people in wheelchairs, who liked being able to supplement the librarian's recommendations with their own choices (Haydon, 1989).

In the United States, specially designed vans are being used by a number of libraries to serve the housebound. Other libraries, like the King County (Washington) Public Library, are using vans to serve institutions as well, because a new van can be purchased much more cheaply than a new bookmobile (Hawkins, 1980).

Because personalized, high-quality home delivery services are generally expensive (the Broughton Library reported serving 300 individuals a month with a staff of three professionals and one part-time clerk), most public libraries will need to consider ways to reduce costs. One method is to have librarians telephone patrons and select appropriate materials, then have nonprofessional staff members or volunteers deliver these items. This is an acceptable option as long as the professional obtains direct feedback from the patron about how well the selections worked.

Other libraries reduce costs by having volunteers perform the tasks performed by the delivery service. However, this option will be effective only if the following two conditions are met:

1. Volunteers can be recruited. This is a problem for two reasons. First, more women, who have traditionally filled volunteer ranks, are working for a living so have little time left to volunteer. Second, more nonprofit organizations than ever before are competing for the time of the remaining volunteers.

2. Volunteers are carefully trained. After all, the library will be asking them to perform professional work, like conducting readers' advisory and reference interviews and selecting materials to meet the patrons' needs.

Libraries also need to consider that volunteers have many other commitments and may not always be as "reliable" (that is, accountable for their actions) as paid library staff.

Libraries can reduce their out-of-pocket costs for delivery services in other ways. The most common is to limit the service to patrons who are physically unable to travel to the library, such as the housebound. A growing number of libraries also charge the patron for the delivery.

This option has been tried most frequently with the business community. Indeed, several studies show that many business people would rather pay for delivery service than take time to visit the library.[8] The Los Angeles County Public Library system used this knowledge to establish a service called FYI at its Norwalk Regional Library in 1989. FYI was designed to meet the collection-related needs of business people, government employees, and professionals who want accurate, up-to-date information to aid with their work but who lack the time to get it. The library provides FYI services on a full-cost recovery basis, billing the customer $65.47 per hour (its base cost) for finding the information, with an additional charge for other direct expenses incurred for searching databases, photocopying, and delivery. The library sends the information to the customer using fax, courier, or U.S. mail services, as the customer prefers (Los Angeles, 1989).

Books-by-Mail Services

This service is similar to delivery services except that materials are delivered to the patron's home and returned to the library via U.S. mail. A few public libraries, often those that serve highly rural areas with a widely dispersed population (like remote sections of Alaska), will deliver books by mail to patrons on a regular basis. Libraries that mail many items may even provide some type of printed bibliography, ideally an annotated one. Such a practice was followed by the Brazoria County (Texas) Library System when it distributed a catalog for large-print books to housebound patrons and residents of area nursing homes (Brazoria, 1989).

But until recently, because of the expense involved, most public libraries limited books-by-mail services to patrons unable to travel to a library facility. This practice is changing as libraries are realizing that patrons with limited time and some discretionary income may be willing to pay for such services. Consider Audio Express, a fee-based, audio-books-by-mail service developed by the Los Angeles County Public Library. Audio Express provides a shop-at-home catalog that offers a large selection of audio books: best-sellers, classics, mysteries, and general fiction as well as nonfiction titles, including business and language-instruction tapes. The library charges $10 per item for a 30-day rental; allows customer to place orders by mail, telephone, or telefacsimile; and accepts cash, checks, and major credit cards (County, 1992).

The Problem of Two-Way Distribution Channels

Distribution channels for most profit and nonprofit organizations are simplified by the fact that products tend to flow only one way: from the organization to the consumer. Consumers normally return products to the organization only when they are flawed (e.g., sour milk purchased at the grocery store) or do not fit (e.g., shoes that pinch one's feet). But products in libraries flow both ways. The library provides a collection of materials from which the patron borrows. The patron must then bear the cost of returning the item to the library.

This means that the library must make it easy for patrons to return products. The most common ways of doing this are

1. allowing materials borrowed at any library location to be returned to any other library location;

2. setting hours of operation that are convenient for the patron;

3. installing book returns and returns for other materials, whenever possible, so the patron can easily return items when the library is closed; and

4. reducing or eliminating fines for overdue materials.

Because these strategies were discussed in chapter 5, they will not be repeated here.

Are Librarians Making Effective Choices About Their Collection Distribution Options?

The question of whether librarians are making wise distribution decisions, and thus becoming as responsive as possible to both the long-term needs of society and the short-term needs of patrons, is one that has no definitive answer at this time. Certainly most librarians are working very hard to benefit society in the long term. For example, they are establishing collection distribution outlets for many diverse and specialized groups of patrons. Among the most common of these are children, young adults, senior citizens, the housebound, African-Americans, Native Americans, the foreign born, the homeless, the incarcerated, and migrant workers.

However, there are indications that some librarians may be ignoring important issues when making distribution choices. This problem could cause libraries to provide services that are less effective and less cost-effective in meeting patron needs than they might be—a serious problem during this time of limited funding. Research data on the bookmobile, the distribution outlet that has been the most studied in recent years, will be used to illustrate the points made.

If librarians are to make wise distribution decisions, they should perform a number of tasks. First, they should keep separate budget statistics for each distribution outlet so that comparisons among outlets can be made. Most librarians are not keeping such statistics. For example, of those public libraries with bookmobiles that answered a series of nationwide surveys, only 22 percent had separate bookmobile budgets (Vavrek, 1990a).

Second, librarians should calculate cost-effectiveness figures (cost per circulation or use) for each distribution outlet. Although it is impossible to tell how many libraries calculate these figures, a review of the literature shows that few are publicly reporting them. This situation should be changed, because the few studies that have been conducted show substantial differences in the costs of borrowing an item from various distribution outlets. For example, Tutton (1990) and Vavrek (1990a) have found that bookmobile items can be circulated for as much as $1.30 less per item than items housed at the main library or branch libraries.

Third, librarians should weigh these cost-effectiveness figures against indicators of the benefits that individuals or society might be receiving from each distribution outlet. Again, the literature shows little evidence that this is being done.

Ideally, librarians should also survey patrons who use each distribution outlet to determine the extent to which the outlet is meeting their collection needs. In fact, several nationwide studies conducted by the Center for Rural Librarianship found that 7 out of 10 libraries with bookmobiles have not surveyed bookmobile users (Vavrek, 1990a).

Fifth, librarians should carefully consider everyday matters pertaining to each distribution outlet. Consider, for example, the matter of bookmobile stops. One statewide study of bookmobile services found that more than 90 percent of the libraries surveyed did not use a formal survey to choose potential stops; only 27 percent used population and census tract maps. Although most bookmobile librarians looked at what stops had been used in the past and at patron requests for service, they did not always evaluate these thoughtfully before deciding on stops that would be continued or added. Another problem noted was that, although patrons wanted evening and weekend hours for bookmobile stops in suburban neighborhoods and rural communities, fewer than 5 percent of the libraries scheduled such stops (Abel, 1986).

Finally, librarians should use any data that they have collected to draw up long-range plans for improving service at each distribution outlet. In fact, two-thirds of public libraries with bookmobiles have no long-range plans directing or guiding bookmobile service (Vavrek, 1990a).

Some libraries are considering decisions like these thoughtfully. For example, Tutton (1990) has described in some depth the procedures that the Warren-Newport (Illinois) Public Library uses to determine cost-effectiveness figures for its bookmobile. And the Middletown (Ohio) Public Library routinely considers 20 different criteria when scheduling bookmobile stops (Mort, 1990). However, these libraries appear to be the exception rather than the rule.

One should not generalize too much from the data presented here, because recent published studies on distribution outlets are generally scarce. Nevertheless, the evidence suggests that

1. librarians may not be weighing decisions about the types of distribution outlets they offer as carefully as they might; and

2. research is needed to determine the relative costs and levels of effectiveness of various distribution outlets.

How Should the Library Distribute Items Among Its Various Outlets?

Another major decision librarians must make concerns how particular items will be distributed among various outlets—the main library, full-service branches, minibranches, bookmobiles, and deposit collections.[9] As the previous discussion of price decisions indicates, patrons will be happiest when they can get everything they want or need at the library outlet that is most convenient for them. Obviously, neither the budgets nor the buildings of most public libraries are large enough to allow this. So librarians are forced to make tough choices about how many copies of a work should be purchased and in what distribution outlets these will be placed.

Librarians who have adopted a societal-marketing orientation, one that emphasizes both the short-term demands of patrons and the long-term interests of the community, need to consider two major factors when determining how they will distribute items among various collection outlets. The first is the levels of use that similar products or product lines have received at different distribution outlets. Betts (1986) has compiled a list of specialized subjects that generally receive less use and thus may benefit from being housed only at the main library or at large branch libraries. These include "art history, literary criticism, original works of literature by minor authors, science and technology beyond the general interest and practical level, academic social science, philosophy and religion (other than 'personal' religion), law and economics" (Betts, 1986, 45). Libraries will need, of course, to examine their own use data to determine whether these or other subjects would benefit from such treatment. Once this has been done, decisions about where to place items should be fairly straightforward. For example, the head selector may send several copies of the latest recreational videotape to a suburban branch library that has had consistently heavy circulation for this type of item in the past, and no copies of the videotape to a minibranch in the midst of the city's financial district that has had little demand for similar items.

A second factor that should influence the number of copies that should be purchased and the outlets to which these are sent is the long-term needs of special target markets. For example, prisoners served by a deposit collection may need information about drug rehabilitation programs, legal matters, and career options. A large group of Korean immigrants served by a branch library may need information on learning English as a foreign language and on obtaining citizenship.

The particulars of determining the levels of use and needs of special target markets will not be discussed here, because chapter 8 covers them in more detail. However, the following example illustrates how librarians can use this information to make distribution decisions.

The ABCD library serves 50,000 residents in the Midwest. It has its main building in the county seat, three branch libraries in neighboring towns, a bookmobile, and deposit collections at the jail and the senior citizens' center. The head selector chooses to handle each of the following purchases differently, keeping in mind past levels of use and the needs of different client groups:

1. A new edition of a cookbook that has circulated steadily in the past. The selector decides to buy eight copies. She places three of these in the main library, one in the bookmobile, and one at each branch.

2. A new book about living well during one's retirement years. The selector purchases four copies. She places one in the main library, one in a branch library that serves a large elderly population, one in the deposit collection at the senior citizens' center, and one on the bookmobile, which stops at three housing complexes for the elderly.

3. A recent book on careers in psychology. Because demand for very specialized career development books has been relatively low, the selector purchases only one copy and places it in the main library.

These placement decisions seem to be reasonably effective ones, given the library's budget limitations and the nature and composition of its clientele. Nevertheless, some potential use will be lost by not having a work at a particular outlet the day a patron looks for it, because not every patron will be willing to bear the cost of obtaining a work from a different library outlet.

Public libraries can increase the likelihood that patrons will be able to obtain desired items when they need them by adopting a three-tiered distribution strategy. First, the library can set up a centralized selection program to do formula buying of materials that are likely to be in demand and to distribute them to relevant outlets in as timely a fashion as possible. Second, the library can ask its professional selectors, who are responsible for making purchases for various collections at the main library or other distribution outlets, to develop local collections to meet the special needs of their clientele. Both of these strategies are explained in more detail in chapter 9. And third, as mentioned earlier, the library can design a quick and efficient delivery system to link distribution outlets. This three-fold strategy has been used by the King County (Washington) Library System (Julien, 1985). It appears to be successful because it emphasizes short-term and long-term needs of the library's clientele, while reducing the costs that patrons must bear when using the library.

How Should Items Be Distributed Among Collections in a Single Library Facility?

Selectors also need to determine how items are to be distributed within a library building—that is, in which collections they are to be placed. A fully integrated collection would contain materials of all types (for all ages, of all formats, on all subjects and genres, etc.) housed in a single shelving range; the other extreme is to have each different type of collection shelved separately.

Decisions about whether integration or separation is the most feasible option are generally made after considering two factors: patron needs and practical considerations. Librarians can ask themselves four questions when considering patron needs:

1. Do patrons have special needs that an integrated collection might not serve?

2. Will patrons be helped or hindered by the size of an integrated collection?

3. Will patrons need special help in using a collection due to the complexity of accessing information in it?

4. Do patrons prefer to have other collections housed separately for ease of use?

Two other questions will help librarians weigh practical considerations related to integration:

1. Do librarians need ready access to a subset of the collection so they can help patrons?

2. Do the physical characteristics of certain materials make it unrealistic for them to be interfiled?

Once these questions have been answered, librarians should find it relatively easy to make decisions about how to distribute items among the various collections.

Do Patrons Have Special Needs That an Integrated Collection Might Not Serve?

Patrons sometimes have specialized needs that may be better met by a separate collection than an integrated one. For example, most libraries divide children's book collections to meet the needs of children in various developmental stages.[10] Picture books teach very young children basic concepts, like shapes, colors, and the letters of the alphabet. Easy readers use simple vocabularies to encourage children who are just learning to read, while juvenile fiction and juvenile nonfiction categories are reserved for more advanced readers. A 1987 nationwide survey of a sample of public libraries also showed that 84 percent had separate collections of materials for young adults (Fry, 1989).

Obviously, works will sometimes be suitable for more than one age group. Consider Ursula K. Le Guin's series *The Earthsea Trilogy*, which can be enjoyed by both teenagers and adults. Librarians should consider placing copies of works like this in each relevant collection. This will increase the likelihood that the titles will be found and enjoyed by patrons, particularly those who select their works by browsing rather than via the catalog.

Librarians will also wish to consider housing, in separate collections, materials for adult new readers and foreign-language works. Interfiling these works with the regular collection can greatly limit their use, because people who are just learning to read or to speak English may be unable to search the catalog for these works and may be nervous about asking for help. Each of these separate sections should be marked with an appropriate sign to enable those who have difficulty reading English to find it easily. The sign marking foreign-language materials should be bilingual; that marking the adult new reader collection should contain an appropriate symbol, like a picture of an adult reading.

Large-print books are another collection that most patrons prefer to be kept separate. This is because patrons tend to request large-print works only when failing eyesight makes it difficult for them to read normal-sized print; integrating these works among the regular collection makes them much more difficult to find.

Will Patrons Be Helped or Hindered by the Size of an Integrated Collection?

Occasionally, a library's size may influence the number and types of collections that are housed together. For example, a number of branch libraries with very small collections have placed their collections of juvenile, young adult, and adult nonfiction in one integrated section.[11] This practice increases the likelihood that patrons will find at least one work on each subject being sought. Moreover, it allows older patrons to choose works of a simpler style without embarrassment and encourages younger people to select works that are in line with their reading skills, even if these works are officially "adult" works. Interfiling juvenile, young adult, and adult nonfiction is particularly helpful when the library is trying to meet the needs of students writing reports, because students can find in a single location works that address a topic in a simple or a more complex fashion. Libraries will, however, need to shelve such collections at a height appropriate for both children and adults.[12]

Large libraries may wish to subdivide collections instead of integrating them to alleviate the information overload that patrons face when using large collections. Such overload occurs when patrons are faced with too many choices. Because libraries routinely expect patrons to make selections from among thousands of items, the potential for information overload is high. It is even greater when patrons are not looking for specific items or subject areas but rather are browsing among all the items on the regular shelves for one or two works that will somehow satisfy their information needs (Baker, 1986b).

Various studies have shown that a majority of patrons want libraries to subdivide their fiction collections by genre.[13] Such categorization performs a useful readers' advisory function by making it easier for people to select the type of novel they want. Moreover, it alerts browsers to less popular works within a particular genre, reducing their reliance on a small number of popular authors and titles (Baker, 1988; Baker and Shepherd, 1987). These factors help explain why fiction that is categorized circulates significantly more than fiction that is not (Baker, 1988).

Fiction categorization is especially useful in libraries that do not (and most do not) provide subject headings for fiction in their card catalog.[14] It is also particularly useful for paperback collections, because it helps counteract the fact that these are not generally organized in any order whatsoever, a nonarrangement that increases the patron's cost of using the collection.

One major question is: When does a collection grow large enough that narrowing devices like genre fiction classification are needed to help patrons choose material? Two studies shed some light on this issue. The first found that information overload was experienced in a library with about 4,700 books in its fiction collection but not in a library with 1,300 (Baker, 1986b). The second found that patrons in a library with 6,000 works of fiction experienced information overload but patrons in a library with 2,500 books did not (Baker, 1988). These findings suggest that libraries with collections smaller than 2,500 books may not need to categorize fiction by genre, and those with collections larger than 4,700 items should consider doing so. Libraries with collections that fall in the middle of this range may wish to survey patrons further to determine their preferences.

Many patrons also prefer to have nonfiction grouped by reader interest categories (that is, those that correspond to user needs and interests) rather than by Dewey Decimal number. Common categories include cooking, marriage/sex, psychology, music, religion, computers, travel, and sports. This type of categorization was first used on a widespread basis by the Detroit Public Library in the early 1940s (Rutzen, 1952).

Many British libraries use some form of reader interest categorization; however, in the United States, this strategy is more widely used by bookstores than public libraries. This is unfortunate, because such categorization can increase patron use of and satisfaction with the collection. For example, one researcher studied the effects of reorganizing fiction for children, using reader interest categories marked with symbols instead of words. The arrangement reduced the cost of using the collection among children who could not yet readily understand an author arrangement of fiction and helped foster a sense of independence and self-worth among these small users (Williams, 1973).

Few libraries have researched the effects of using reader interest categorization in the scientific manner Williams used. However, those libraries that have tried this practice report positive results. For example, the Metropolitan Library System in Oklahoma City, Oklahoma, discovered that the more books are arranged by popular subdivisions, the more use patrons make of them (Little, 1979). And a library system in South Africa reported that the circulation of nonfiction displayed in reader interest categories increased by an average of 70 percent in six of its libraries (Venter, 1984).

Proponents suggest that a collection of up to 30,000 nonfiction volumes can be completely handled using a reader interest categorization system. Obviously, this type of grouping will be useful for smaller collections, like collections of paperbacks and collections housed on bookmobiles, in minibranches, and in small branch libraries.[15] Libraries with larger collections of nonfiction may wish to catalog all new works received within the Dewey Decimal System, then add a reader interest label above the regular call number on current and popular works only. Labeled titles can then be shelved by reader interest category in an area designed for browsers and ideally located near the library's entrance. When use of these items declines over time, the library can remove the reader interest labels and shelve the works in the regular stacks.

Obviously, the types of subdivisions mentioned here are useful for any large collection, not just the book collection. For example, libraries can establish readily understandable interest categories for their sound recordings (categories like folk, rock, jazz, and classical), then arrange works within them by the name of the person(s) recording the work or the composer. This type of grouping will be much easier for the average patron to understand than the Alpha-Numeric System for Classification of Recordings (ANSCR) that many public libraries use today. Libraries can also subdivide large collections of sound recordings and of videotapes.

There are a number of practical decisions librarians will need to make if they wish to subdivide their collection into genre fiction or reader interest categories. For example, they will need to consider how many and what type of categories they will use for the subdivision. These matters are discussed more in chapter 10, which gives specific, practical advice on methods that libraries can utilize to promote use of their collections.

Will Patrons Need Special Help in Using a Collection Due to the Complexity of Accessing Information in It?

There is also evidence that collections should be kept separate if the methods used to access them are particularly difficult for the average patron to understand. For example, those libraries that serve as official depositories for U.S. government publications generally cannot afford to list all the publications they receive in the library's catalog; instead, they provide access to these works through a complicated system of precompiled indexes. Because many patrons and not a few librarians have difficulty using these indexes, libraries often encourage use of government publications by housing these works in a separate area and providing specially trained staff to help people access them. In fact, one academic library found that use of government publications decreased by 60 percent when that collection was merged with another (Van de Voorde, 1989).

Many public libraries collect other works that may be difficult for the average person to access. The most common are those containing local history or genealogical information, which may not be indexed anywhere. Libraries may wish to house these materials separately and to provide a knowledgeable staff member to assist patrons in using them, especially if this collection is large.

Do Patrons Prefer to Have Other Collections Housed Separately for Ease of Use?

Most library patrons want new works of all types housed separately, so they can browse among all the recent titles. This preference has been documented by studies that show the following:

1. Circulation of new titles is significantly higher when they are placed in a separate section than when they are interfiled in the regular stacks.

2. Circulation of works displayed in the new titles section drops off immediately and significantly when they are moved to the regular stacks.[16]

These findings imply that patrons find the cost of searching for new titles in the regular stacks to be too high.

Another collection of new and popular materials that most patrons prefer to have separated from the regular collection are works that the library obtains on a lease-purchase plan from vendors like Baker and Taylor Books. A small percentage of libraries lease best-selling works instead of purchasing multiple copies. This is because unwanted materials can be sent back to the vendor when demand fades, and works with continuing demand can be purchased at a reduced cost for the permanent collection. Again, the library should consider keeping these new and popular works separate to reduce patron costs of finding them.

Patrons, particularly browsers, may also have difficulty locating fiction and biographies if these are classified within the Dewey Decimal System. Most public libraries house fiction separately and arrange it alphabetically by author and title, and they arrange separate collections of biographies alphabetically by subject of the biography and then author.[17]

Two other kinds of items that many patrons prefer to be housed separately are recreational videotapes and recreational books-on-tape. This is because many patrons come into the library specifically seeking a "fun videotape" to watch or a "good tape" to listen to when they are driving or exercising.

The situation is more complicated when it comes to nonfiction videotapes and nonfiction books-on-tape. Some patrons are looking for tapes on a particular subject, rather than of a particular format. This has caused some libraries to interfile these works with the regular nonfiction collection; others file them separately by format.

A few libraries have experimented with both. For example, the Dover (New Hampshire) Public Library tried interfiling nonfiction videocassettes with nonfiction books. But they stopped the practice after a six-month trial period because of extremely negative patron response. The library discovered that most patrons who checked out videotapes were not looking for topical information; they wanted to borrow something on videotape and wanted all videotapes, fiction and nonfiction, housed in one area for easy browsing (Action, 1989).

A number of librarians have suggested that patrons would find it easier to locate items in particular formats if they were integrated with the book collection. For example, Libretto (1983) recommends this treatment for magazines on popular subjects like cooking and interior design. However, the findings of the Dover study suggest that libraries should survey patrons to determine which methods of access will keep their costs of using the collection low.

Do Librarians Need Ready Access to a Subset
of the Collection So They Can Help Patrons?

Occasionally, a collection may need to be kept separate so that library staff will have better access. For example, reference works should be located near the reference desk so librarians can answer patron questions. However, librarians need to be aware that there are several problems with placing too many works in a reference collection. First, separating reference materials from nonfiction materials on the same subject may make it more difficult for patrons, particularly the large number who bypass the catalog, to find the information they need. Second, although reference librarians prefer a collection that is large enough to answer many questions, they have difficulty keeping track of all the materials in collections that are too large; this can decrease the efficiency of their searches.[18] Finally, because large reference collections are more time consuming to maintain, they often contain a higher percentage of dated materials. Although any work in a library can theoretically be used for reference purposes, these problems imply that librarians should carefully consider which items are in great demand as reference sources and need to be shelved accordingly and which should be placed in the regular stacks.

Nolan (1991) recently noted that librarians can regularize this decision-making process by assigning someone to oversee the entire reference selection and deselection process. This will help ensure that all necessary items are ordered and that consistent decisions about the placement of items are made. The library should also set criteria for what items belong in the reference collection. In general, says Nolan, works should be placed in the reference collection only if they

a. have a reference-like format, which makes them convenient to use for looking up information quickly;

b. are used frequently by reference librarians;

c. are authoritative;

d. are current; and

e. have unique coverage.

Careful scrutiny of the reference shelves using such criteria should help librarians ensure that the size of the reference collection stays at a manageable level.

Do the Physical Characteristics of Certain Materials Make It Unrealistic for Them to Be Interfiled?

Two format considerations also need to be examined when librarians are determining whether they will interfile materials or keep them separate. The first is the issue of "oversize" works. Public libraries handle these items in various ways. A few libraries turn oversize books spine up and interfile them with the regular books so that the patron will not face the additional cost of tracking down an oversize item. This practice is acceptable if the work is an ephemeral one that will be discarded in a few years anyway. However, because spine-up shelving will eventually damage most works, it is not suitable for items that the library expects to retain for a long time (e.g., local history items).

Other oversize shelving practices are better for the books but have a higher cost to patrons. For example, some libraries shelve oversize works on a separate section at the end of each range or on a separate range at the end of the entire collection. Still others, reasoning that patrons will not browse the lowest shelf anyway, shelve oversize books flat on that shelf. These practices are confusing to many patrons, who tend not to realize that oversize works are shelved elsewhere; they assume, when they can't find the works in their proper call number order on the regular shelves, that the items are checked out. Libraries can counteract this problem by posting signs at the end of each stack range to inform patrons where books marked "Oversize" are shelved.

Another issue librarians will need to consider is where to house works of different formats. Since the mid-1970s, various authors have suggested that libraries should consider interfiling materials of all formats in a single shelving system.[19] Weihs, for example, argues that interfiling by format "saves time for both patrons and staff because it eliminates the need to search in several places, reduces the number of directional questions a patron may have to ask, and generally eliminates the necessity of retrieving items from a storage area. Intershelving presents the entire range of materials on a given subject in a single location. If nonbook materials are shelved separately, patrons may fail to find useful items" (Weihs, 1984, xii). Weihs's last point is particularly true when patrons are browsing or when they do not realize that nonbook materials are listed in separate catalogs.

Other authors suggest that interfiling materials according to user needs will increase the circulation of all library materials.[20] Unfortunately, no rigorous studies have been conducted to verify that circulation increases were caused by the interfiling rather than other factors.

There are some logistical problems that need to be overcome if a public library chooses to interfile. First, the library must purchase special containers for each type of medium it chooses to interfile, as figure 6.4 illustrates. These containers help reduce the likelihood that the items they contain (e.g., magazines or phonograph records) will be damaged when they are interfiled with books and other media on the regular shelves. The containers also prevent small items (e.g., pamphlets and filmstrips) from being lost among other works. Unfortunately, purchasing these containers adds significantly to the cost of processing each item. Although this cost is not too great for libraries that purchase a relatively small number of nonprint items, it may be prohibitive for those with larger media collections.[21]

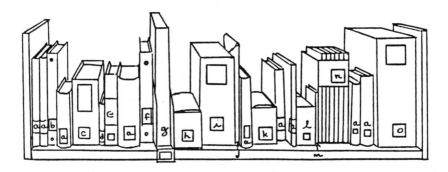

a. book; b. binder containing microfiches; c. box containing filmstrips; d. book-like album containing a single sound cassette; e. videotape cassette in container; f. binder containing slides; g. clip-on holder containing a motion picture in a box; h. motion picture loop cartridge in container; i. box containing slide carousel; j. envelope containing a single Viewmaster slide; k. microfilm reel in container; l. box containing microopaque cards; m. pamphlet binder containing a single picture; n. Princeton file holding issues of a current periodical; o. kit housed in a box

Reprinted, with permission, from Weihs (1984, 14).

Fig. 6.4. Intershelving materials in various formats.

A second potential problem is that interfiling may decrease retrieval efficiency in some instances. For example, it may take a patron more time to retrieve microfiche copies of newspapers and magazines that are interfiled by subject among the rest of the collection, then search through the library to find a microfiche reader. The library could lower this cost by housing microfiche items in numerical order in a storage cabinet located next to a bank of microfiche readers.[22]

Interfiling may be physically impossible in other cases due to the size or bulkiness of the materials involved. For example, a small percentage of public libraries have collections of art—prints, sculpture, and the like—that they lend to patrons; others have long-playing 16mm films that are too large to fit on normal-sized library shelves.

Another potential problem with interfiling is theft. A few older studies indicate that theft rates for interfiled nonprint media are no higher than those for books.[23] However, many libraries may be unwilling to store recreational videotapes, which are often quite expensive, on the regular shelves. One alternative is, of course, to shelve empty videotape containers in the stacks, keeping the tapes themselves behind the circulation desk to deter theft.

The costs involved in purchasing containers for shelving, the bulkiness of some formats, the desire to maintain retrieval efficiency, and the potential for theft explain why few public libraries have tried interfiling their entire collections. Nevertheless, a growing number of libraries are interfiling some formats (e.g., filmstrips and nonfiction sound cassettes), because such interfiling can improve access to nonprint materials that patrons are seeking by content, rather than by form.

Final Comments on Integration

A number of libraries currently label the spines of works in a special collection and then interfile them among the regular stacks, rather than housing them separately. This tactic is less effective than it might be because it requires patrons to search through the stacks looking for works with a particular kind of label. A double-process search like this raises the cost of using the collection. This greater cost explains why genre fiction titles that were marked with spine labels and interfiled in the stacks of the Davidson County (North Carolina) Public Library circulated significantly less than genre fiction works housed in separate collections (Baker, 1988).

Note that although separate collections do seem desirable in many cases, it is preferable to integrate all types of materials in a single catalog whenever possible. This is because many patrons erroneously believe that the main catalog lists everything the library owns.[24] A nationwide study conducted eight years ago documented that only 38 percent of public libraries actually had an integrated, multimedia catalog (Intner, 1984). This percentage may be slightly higher today because some libraries with on-line catalogs put most forms of media within these.

Libraries that do not have integrated catalogs should consider establishing them.[25] Obviously, reducing patron costs is reason enough for doing this. However, a multimedia catalog may also help reduce claims that libraries are guilty of a subtle form of censorship when they fail to make patrons aware of all the separate collections they own.[26] Libraries that choose, for some reason, not to establish an integrated catalog should at least place large signs at the main catalog that inform patrons of the presence of other catalogs or of uncataloged materials (e.g., government publications and vertical file materials) in separate shelving or storage areas.

Librarians should also consider ways to link patrons who bypass the catalog to separate collections that they might find interesting. One of the simplest ways to do this is to use shelf dummies. For example, a shelf dummy placed next to Thomas J. Peters's book *In Search of Excellence* might refer patrons to the book-on-tape of the same title, which is housed elsewhere. A dummy can refer those browsing among books on baroque music to phonograph records and compact disks on this topic. A dummy can also inform patrons that a library has removed works in a particular subject area to a special display on that topic. Small signs, posted in strategic areas within the stacks, can also link patrons to related collections.

How Can the Library Design Its Interior for Maximum Distribution Effectiveness?[27]

One comprehensive article on the topic of people's orientation needs in libraries notes that "[u]nfamiliar environments make special demands upon us. Even the simplest of settings can involve a jumble of information that has to be sorted and processed before it becomes meaningful" (Pollet and Haskell, 1979, 3). Even the smallest public libraries can be confusing and frustrating to the patron, because they contain a wide variety of different things: many kinds of collections, organized in different fashions; storage units of all sizes and shapes to house these; furniture for lounging and studying; service desks of all kinds; and dozens of miscellaneous items like signs, photocopying machines, busts of

Shakespeare, plants, vending machines, and coat racks. These items all serve important functions, but their accumulated mass can cause the patron to feel disoriented.

As a library and its collections grow, there is a higher potential cost with finding desired items. Although the cost will lessen as the patron becomes familiar with the layout of the collections, it is particularly high for the person who is not a regular library user. However, librarians can reduce patron frustrations by planning interiors that make it easy for everyone to find items.

Profit-making companies have a great incentive for providing ideal distribution facilities, because their survival depends on selling large quantities of their products. Public libraries do not have this incentive, because they do not go out of business when their distribution mechanisms are ineffective. Nevertheless, librarians who are service-oriented will want to reduce patron costs by improving the layouts of their collections, as well as the sign systems that mark these collections.

What Effects Will the Placement of Various Collections Have on the Use of Items Within Them?

One of the most important distribution decisions a public library will need to make is which collections it will place near the entrance, which at the far end of the building, and which in between. The problem is compounded if a library spreads its collections over several floors.

This decision needs to be considered in light of evidence showing that collections near the entrance will tend to be used significantly more than collections housed farther away. In one of the earliest studies on the subject, Carnovsky (1935) describes how the physical location of books in a small browsing library influenced their use:

> There is one section of shelving which directly confronts the student when he enters the room. During the first month of the library's operation, I placed the fiction in this section. During the second month I moved all the fiction to another section and substituted non-fiction on the more accessible shelves. In spite of the fact that fiction was still quite accessible, there was apparent a noticeable drop in the proportion of fiction circulated as compared with the period when fiction was on the section more easily accessible. At the end of the second month, I again restored the books to their original sections and once again the fiction resumed a circulation very similar to that of the first month. (Carnovsky, 1935, 474)

It is not surprising that the circulation of works nearest the library's door was higher, because it costs patrons more, in terms of time, to use collections that are less accessible.

Other researchers have found that use of reference works increased dramatically when they were moved closer to the entrance (Harris, 1966) and that circulation of a large variety of fiction and nonfiction works increased significantly when they were moved from the regular stacks and displayed more prominently (Baker, 1986a, 1986b; Taylor, 1982; Goldhor, 1981, 1972; Mueller, 1965).

If a library's primary goal is to maximize use of its collection, the staff will want to scrutinize circulation records, determine which kinds of items are most heavily used, and place these by the door. This will help ensure that patrons can obtain these materials with as little cost as possible. This strategy has been used with some success by the Phoenix Public Library (PPL), which has a "Popular Library" within its central library. The popular library collection consists of new books, best-selling titles, paperbacks, popular magazines, and a rental collection. The collection is housed immediately inside the main entrance, adjacent to the circulation desk. As such, it is the first stop in the library's traffic pattern and accommodates the needs of browsers, who comprise a large part of the clientele of PPL. As Webb notes, "A person who requires specific information — a researcher or an independent learner — passes through the Popular Library to the subject departments where the bulk of the library's collection will be located, including the reference tools, the scholarly journals, the older, more technical books, books on specialized topics, and educational books such as test tutors and licensing exams" (1985, 64).

Note that placing popular works near the entrance may cause their use to rise even further. This could have positive effects, such as higher patron satisfaction and an overall circulation increase. However, there may be negative effects as well. The first is that more patrons will be selecting works from these areas, thus increasing competition for already popular titles. This competition could decrease the patron's chances of finding items on the shelves when they are needed. The result may be lower user satisfaction unless the library adopts corrective strategies, like purchasing more copies of these types of works or establishing shorter loan periods for them. These strategies may be most appropriate when a library has adopted the role of *popular materials center*.

A second problem is that locating the most-used items near the door may reduce the likelihood that patrons will venture farther into the building to seek less popular, but not necessarily less worthy types of materials. Libraries that want to avoid this problem should consider a different placement strategy: enticing patrons farther into the building by placing popular items at the back of the facility, rather than near the entrance. This strategy has been used with some success by the Woodlawn Branch of the Baltimore County (Maryland) Public Library (BCPL). Library staff felt that patrons would be willing to take extra time and effort to retrieve highly popular items. So they placed two of their most-used collections, new books and videocassettes, at the rear of the library. Staff determined the path that patrons would need to follow to get these items and marked it with brightly colored footsteps. Finally, they chose worthy but less popular items and arranged them along this path in special subject displays that were angled for maximum visibility. BCPL felt that this placement technique increased the use of less popular subject areas without significantly decreasing the use of the new fiction or videocassettes.

Libraries do need to be aware, however, that not all materials will be popular enough to entice users farther into the building. The collections that would seem to have the best enticement potential are videocassettes and new materials, particularly fiction. Individual libraries can identify other local collections that have this type of drawing power by scrutinizing their overall circulation patterns.

How Should the Library's Shelving Be Arranged to Reduce Patron Costs in Locating Items?

To date, research on designing user-friendly shelving arrangements in public libraries is fairly scarce.[28] Nevertheless, there are some fairly simple principles for arranging shelving of all types that librarians should follow whenever practical considerations, such as the building's architecture and the need to maintain visual control over certain types of materials, make this possible.

The first principle is *group like collections together*. This will make it easier for patrons to browse among them. For example, the library should place the general fiction collection and any genre fiction collections in the same area, rather than scattering them throughout the building; this will reduce the costs of patrons who read more than one kind of fiction. Librarians should group most closely together those types of works that studies have documented are likely to be used by the same groups of patrons. As figure 6.5 shows, the Gallup Organization (1985) asked buyers of various categories of fiction materials to check other categories that they were most and least likely to read or buy. Librarians can note common affinities and place related collections together. Information on nonfiction purchases, shown in figure 6.6, can be used to lay out nonfiction into reader interest categories.

The second shelving principle is *group all items in a single collection within a single range of shelves*. This will eliminate the confusion that can be caused when a range of similar materials is broken by furniture, equipment, or service areas. Occasionally, a library will need to violate this rule for some reason. For example, one midwestern public library has split its range of juvenile nonfiction into two sections; this allows the librarian working the service desk to maintain visual control over the entire children's room. If building considerations make it necessary to split stacks, it should post signs, at the point where the stacks split, to inform patrons where the shelving continues. This is particularly important in cases where stacks are split between floors.

A third principle librarians should follow when arranging shelving is *avoid placing shelving around the perimeter of the stacks, perpendicular to the regular ranges of shelves*, because this placement may confuse patrons. Again, if building considerations make this necessary, the library should post signs that explain this arrangement.

Note that shelving principles 2 and 3 do not imply that the library must arrange all materials on long, parallel rows of shelving. Indeed, wide U-shaped bays of books, like those shown in figure 6.7 on page 135, invite patrons into their depths and so encourage browsing.[29] Rather, principles 2 and 3 suggest that libraries should use a self-orienting arrangement of materials that establishes clear traffic patterns that patrons can readily understand.

(Text continues on page 136.)

Fiction Categories Almost Always Checked	Most Likely Category to Check Also	Second Most Likely to Check Also	Least Likely to Check Also
Action/Adventure	Mystery/Suspense/Spy	Popular Fiction	Occult/ Supernatural
Historical Fiction	Autobiography/ Biography	Historical Nonfiction	Occult/ Supernatural
Humor	Autobiography/ Biography	Popular Fiction	Western; Investment/ Economics/ Income Tax
Mystery/Suspense/ Spy	Popular Fiction	Action/Adventure	Investment/ Economics/ Income Tax
Occult/Supernatural	Mystery/Suspense/Spy	Popular Fiction	Western
Popular Fiction	Autobiography/ Biography	Mystery/ Suspense/Spy	Western
Romance	Mystery/Suspense/Spy	Cookbooks	War/Military
Science Fiction	Action/Adventure	Popular Fiction	Investment/ Economics/ Income Tax
War/Military	Historical Fiction	Historical Nonfiction	Romance; Cookbook
Western	Action/Adventure	Historical Fiction	Occult/ Supernatural

Reprinted, with permission, from the Gallup Organization (1985, 127).

Fig. 6.5. Fiction categories book buyers were most and least likely to buy.

Nonfiction Categories Almost Always Checked	Most Likely Category to Check Also	Second Most Likely to Check Also	Least Likely to Check Also
Autobiography/ Biography	Historical	Popular Fiction	Western
Cookbook	Home and Garden/ How-To-Do-It	Autobiography/ Biography	War; Western
Health/Diet/Exercise	Home and Garden/ How-To-Do-It	Cookbook	Western
Historical Nonfiction	Historical Fiction	Autobiography/ Biography	Occult/ Supernatural
Home and Garden/ How-To-Do-It	Cookbook	Health/Diet/ Exercise	Western
Investment/ Economics/ Income Tax	Home and Garden/ How-To-Do-It	Autobiography/ Biography	Western
Leisure	Popular Fiction	Humor	Occult/ Supernatural
Reference/ Instruction	Home and Garden/ How-To-Do-It	Autobiography/ Biography	Occult/ Supernatural
Religious	Home and Garden/ How-To-Do-It	Autobiography/ Biography	Occult/ Supernatural

Reprinted, with permission, from the Gallup Organization (1985, 129).

Fig. 6.6. Nonfiction categories book buyers were most and least likely to buy.

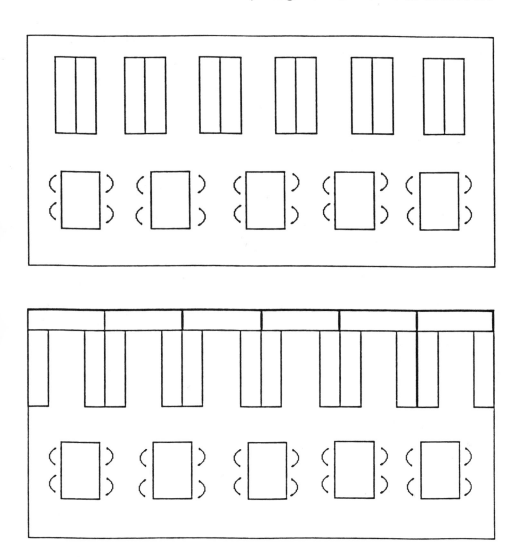

Fig. 6.7. Shelves arranged in a standard layout and in U-shaped bays.

Two other principles relate more to the need to make users aware of the shelving arrangement used than to the arrangement itself. The first of these is *use color cues to alert patrons to the location of separate collections*. For example, a library may choose to paint the shelves that hold easy readers bright yellow, those that hold juvenile nonfiction red, and those that hold juvenile fiction blue. Another library may choose to use floor tiles of different colors to mark the paths to various collections.

The last principle is *use effective sign systems to mark the location of various collections*. In general, signs for each major collection should be large enough to read from the library's door. (When collections are housed on different floors, signs should inform patrons of this as well.) Signs should be positioned appropriately: neither so high that the patron will fail to see them, nor so low that they are hidden behind bookcases or other furniture. Some libraries make the mistake of placing signs parallel to the traffic flow where few people will notice them; a better practice is to place signs perpendicular to the patron's line of vision so they can be seen when approached. The library should use multisided signs if the area to be marked is one that patrons can approach from more than one direction.

Libraries should also label each stack section with signs to indicate their contents. In years past, most libraries have labeled stack sections with a call number range (e.g., 658-747). Although such numbers serve as a location device, they do not encourage browsing, because most patrons do not know what the numbers mean. For this reason, some libraries have added subject headings to indicate the most popular areas housed within these stack sections. Such subject headings have the highest potential for increasing browsing when they

1. are large enough to be read easily;

2. use popular, easily understood terms (not necessarily Library of Congress subject headings, which often utilize more formal, traditional terms); and

3. are of medium specificity (like South American history) rather than too broad (e.g., history) or too narrow (e.g., Brazilian history, 1901-date).

Rather than using hand-lettered or homemade signs that look unprofessional and are hard to read, libraries should order professional signs. These should use a single, basic, easily readable typeface and be printed in high-contrast colors (e.g., black and white).

As mentioned in chapter 6, a number of guides can help libraries design effective sign systems, including Mallery and DeVore (1982), Reynolds and Barrett (1981), and Pollet and Haskell (1979). Lubans and Kushner (1979) also spell out principles that can be used to evaluate the effectiveness of existing sign systems.

Conclusion

This chapter suggests that librarians need to consider issues of place, or distribution, if they wish to make their collections truly responsive to the needs of individual users and the community as a whole. Although some libraries are examining these issues, others need to weigh these matters more thoughtfully, after considering the levels of use their products are receiving at different distribution outlets and the long-term needs of special client groups. Further research is obviously needed, particularly on the cost-effectiveness of various distribution outlets, the effects that separation and integration have on use of the collection, and the effectiveness of various collection layout arrangements.

Notes

[1] In 1991, there were 1,282 main library facilities in the United States (*The Bowker Annual*, 1991).

[2] It is beyond the scope of this book to consider the particulars of choosing the best site for a branch. Readers interested in this topic may refer to Koontz (1990), who reviews the general literature on site location, then gives a market-based model for predicting the use of new or relocated public library facilities.

[3] Indeed, Detweiler (1986) found that the circulation per volume falls off sharply when the size of a library's collection drops below 50,000 volumes.

[4] Rawlinson (1990) quotes statistics that show that branch libraries account for 82 percent of the circulation of library systems, even though they receive only about 54 percent of book funds and 57 percent of total operating expenditures.

[5] Hall (1987) provides a good overview of the current sources that public libraries are using to finance building projects.

[6] See, for example, Mason (1985).

[7] Lack of transportation is a particular barrier among children and teenagers. For example, 48 percent of librarians questioned in a nationwide survey felt that lack of transportation was a major or moderate barrier to use of the public library by teenagers (Fry, 1989).

[8] See, for example, Baker (1991).

[9] Most public libraries do not have separate collections to meet the needs of patrons who use books-by-mail services (or even, in some cases, deposit collections). Rather, librarians fill patron requests by "borrowing" materials from collections housed at the main and branch libraries.

[10]Birckmayer (1988) provides a brief introduction to the development stages of children and gives suggestions for how librarians can respond to these stages.

[11]Kralick (1977) found that although patrons accept the practice of interfiling nonfiction works for all ages, they are not as comfortable with the idea of interfiling fictional works for all ages. They felt that many adult novels were, because of subject matter and language, unsuitable for nonadults.

[12]Readers who wish more information on the practice of interfiling nonfiction for all ages should refer to Kralick (1977).

[13]See, for example, Baker (1988), Spiller (1980), Briggs (1973), and Borden (1909).

[14]Many patrons seeking fiction bypass the card catalog, but such subject headings would be useful for those who do not. In recent years, various groups have taken a more active role in recommending that public libraries should routinely add fiction subject headings in the catalog. For example, the American Library Association (1990) has issued guidelines for establishing subject access to individual works of fiction. And the Library of Congress and the Online Computer Library Center are sponsoring a pilot project designed to add subject headings to computerized bibliographic records for works of fiction (Libraries, 1992).

[15]For example, and as Little (1979) notes, the Metropolitan Library System in Oklahoma City, Oklahoma, uses more than 20 reader interest categories to organize collections of 4,000 to 6,000 uncataloged paperbacks on its bookmobiles.

[16]See, for example, Mueller (1965).

[17]Of course, some librarians still favor classifying these works within the Dewey Decimal or Library of Congress classification systems. Sapp (1986) gives a broad overview of the ways in which these and other classification systems provide access to fiction.

[18]This problem is discussed in some detail in chapter 8 of Baker and Lancaster (1991).

[19]See, for example, Tiffany (1978) and Hart (1976b).

[20]See, for example, Wilson (1976).

[21]Many school libraries, which have substantially smaller collections than the average public library, interfile materials with some success (Weihs, 1984).

[22]Sinkule (1986) discusses, in a comprehensive fashion, ideal storage and viewing facilities for microforms.

[23]See, for example, Stoness (1976) and Hart (1976a).

[24]See, for example, Markey (1983) and Matthews and others (1983).

[25]This issue is discussed in more detail in Intner and Smiraglia (1987).

[26]See, for example, Smith (1977).

[27]This section limits itself to discussing how the interiors of main, full-service-branch, and minibranch libraries might be designed to improve distribution effectiveness. Readers who are interested in designing the interiors of bookmobiles should refer to Hole and Topping (1990).

[28]Academic libraries have explored the matter in a bit more detail. See, for example, Myers (1979).

[29]On a consulting visit some years ago, this author saw the successful use of such nooks at the Cockeysville and Pikesville branches of the Baltimore County (Maryland) Public Library.

References

Abel, Joanne. "A Survey of Bookmobile Service in North Carolina." *North Carolina Libraries* 44, no. 4 (Winter 1986): 225-29.

"Action Exchange: Self-Service AV Collections; Software to Track Attendance." *American Libraries* 20, no. 1 (January 1989): 30.

"AL Aside—Ideas." *American Libraries* 22, no. 2 (February 1991): 123.

American Library Association. *Guidelines on Subject Access to Individual Works of Fiction, Drama, Etc*. Chicago: American Library Association, 1990.

Annichiarico, Mark. "Spoken Word Audio: The Fastest-Growing Library Collection." *Library Journal* 116, no. 9 (15 May 1991): 36-38.

Baker, Sharon L. "The Display Phenomenon: An Exploration into Factors Causing the Increased Circulation of Displayed Books." *Library Quarterly* 56, no. 3 (July 1986a): 237-57.

_____. "Improving Business Services Through the Use of Focus Groups." *RQ* 30, no. 3 (Spring 1991): 377-85.

_____. "Overload, Browsers and Selections." *Library and Information Science Research* 8, no. 4 (October-December 1986b): 315-29.

_____. "Will Fiction Classification Schemes Increase Use? Results of an Experimental Study." *RQ* 27, no. 3 (Spring 1988): 366-76.

Baker, Sharon L., and F. Wilfrid Lancaster. *The Measurement and Evaluation of Library Services.* 2d ed. Washington, D.C.: Information Resources Press, 1991.

Baker, Sharon L., and Gay W. Shepherd. "Fiction Classification Schemes: The Principles Behind Them, and Their Success." *RQ* 27, no. 2 (Winter 1987): 245-51.

Behrman, Sara, and Gordon Conable. "There's a Library at the Mall." *Wilson Library Bulletin* 64, no. 4 (December 1989): 31-33.

Behrmann, Christine, Yolanda Bonitch, and Harriet Gottfried. "The Library Serves Homeless Children." *The Bookmark* 46, no. 3 (Spring 1988): 198-99.

Betts, Doug. "Public Library Bookstock Management." *Library Review* 35 (Spring 1986): 39-51.

Birckmayer, Jennifer. "Developmental Needs of Youth in These Changing Times." *The Bookmark* 46, no. 3 (Spring 1988): 161-65.

Bolt, Nancy M. *Brown County, Ohio, Need for Library Service and Cooperation Among Libraries.* Columbus: State Library of Ohio, 1984.

Borden, William A. "On Classifying Fiction." *Library Journal* 34, no. 6 (June 1909): 264-65.

The Bowker Annual: Library and Book Trade Almanac. 36th ed., ed. Filomena Simora. New Providence, N.J.: R. R. Bowker, 1991.

"Brazoria County Library System Distributes Catalog for Large-Print Books." *Texas Libraries* 50 (Fall 1989): 102.

Briggs, Betty S. "A Case for Classified Fiction." *Library Journal* 98, no. 22 (15 December 1973): 3694.

Carnovsky, Leon. Personal correspondence. Cited by Harriet R. Forbes. "The Geography of Reading." *ALA Bulletin* 29, no. 8 (August 1935): 470-76.

Childers, Thomas, and Nancy A. Van House. *The Public Library Effectiveness Study: Final Report*. Philadelphia: Drexel University, College of Information Studies, 1989.

"County of Los Angeles Public Library Offers New Service to Los Angeles County Commuters." *Public Libraries* 31, no. 1 (January/February 1992): 9.

Detweiler, Mary Jo. "The 'Best Size' Public Library." *Library Journal* 111, no. 9 (15 May 1986): 34-35.

Ferrell, Nancy. "Alaska's Flying Library." *Library Journal* 108, no. 6 (15 March 1983): 554-55.

Fry, Ray M. "Services and Resources for Young Adults in Public Libraries: Report of the NCES Survey." In *Bowker Annual: Library and Book Trade Almanac, 1989-1990*, 34th ed., ed. Filomena Simora, 414-23. New York: R. R. Bowker, 1989.

Gajerski, B. "Edmonton Public Library: 1989 User Survey." Edmonton Public Library, Edmonton, Alberta, 1989. ERIC ED327184.

Gallup Organization, Inc. *The Gallup 1985 Annual Report on Book Buying*. Princeton, N.J.: Gallup Organization, 1985.

_____. *The Role of Libraries in America: A Report of the Survey Conducted by the Gallup Organization, Inc. for the Chief Officers of State Library Agencies of Arizona, Florida, Idaho, Illinois, Iowa, Kentucky, Maryland, Massachusetts, Mississippi, Nevada, New York, North Carolina, Pennsylvania, South Dakota, Wisconsin, Wyoming, and the American Library Association*. Frankfort: Kentucky Department of Library and Archives, 1976.

Goldhor, Herbert. "The Effect of Prime Display Location on Public Library Circulation of Selected Adult Titles." *Library Quarterly* 42, no. 4 (October 1972): 371-89.

_____. "Experimental Effects on the Choice of Books Borrowed by Public Library Adult Patrons." *Library Quarterly* 51, no. 3 (July 1981): 253-68.

Gonzalez, Mario, and Harriet Gottfried. "Library Service to the City's Homeless." *The Bookmark* 46, no. 4 (Summer 1988): 223-31.

Hall, Richard B. "Trends in Financing Public Library Buildings." *Library Trends* 36, no. 2 (Fall 1987): 423-53.

Harris, Ira. "The Influence of Accessibility on Academic Library Use." Ph.D. diss., Rutgers University, 1966.

Hart, Thomas L. "Dare to Integrate." *Audiovisual Librarian* 21, no. 8 (October 1976a): 18-19.

Hart, Thomas L., ed. "Integrated Shelving of Multimedia Collections." *School Media Quarterly* 5, no. 1 (Fall 1976b): 19-30.

Hawkins, Marilyn. "Seattle's Bookmobile Metamorphosis." *Wilson Library Bulletin* 54, no. 7 (March 1980): 442-46.

Haydon, John. "Salford's Mobile Service for the Housebound." *Library Association Record* 91, no. 1 (27 January 1989): 42.

Hayes, Robert M., and E. Susan Palmer. "The Effects of Distance Upon Use of Libraries: Case Studies Based on a Survey of Users of the Los Angeles Public Library." *Library and Information Science Research* 5, no. 1 (Spring 1983): 67-100.

Hole, Carol, and Russ Topping. "Designing Bookmobile Interiors." In *The Book Stops Here: New Directions in Bookmobile Service*, ed. Catherine Suyak Alloway, 135-56. Metuchen, N.J.: Scarecrow Press, 1990.

Intner, Sheila S. "Access to Media: Attitudes of Public Librarians." *RQ* 23, no. 4 (Summer 1984): 424-30.

Intner, Sheila, and Richard Smiraglia. *Policy and Practice in Bibliographic Control of Nonbook Media*. Chicago: American Library Association, 1987.

Julien, Don. "Pioneering New Services: Videocassettes." *Wilson Library Bulletin* 59, no. 10 (June 1985): 664-67.

Koontz, Christine M. "Market-Based Modelling for Public Library Facility Location and Use-Forecasting." Ph.D. diss., Florida State University, 1990.

Kralick, John E. "The Integration of Non-Fiction Collections." Master's thesis, University of California at Los Angeles, 1977.

Lavigne, Nicole. "International Developments: A Library in the Metro Station." *Public Library Quarterly* 5, no. 2 (Summer 1984): 47-57.

"Libraries." *Chronicle of Higher Education* 28, no. 19 (15 January 1992): A22.

Libretto, Ellen V. "Merchandising Collections and Services." In *New Directions for Young Adult Services*, ed. Ellen V. Libretto, 49-60. New York: R. R. Bowker, 1983.

Little, Paul. "The Effectiveness of Paperbacks." *Library Journal* 104, no. 20 (15 November 1979): 2411-16.

"Los Angeles County Public Opens Fee-Based Service." *Wilson Library Bulletin* 64, no. 1 (September 1989): 18-19.

Lubans, John, Jr., and Gary Kushner. "Evaluating Signage Systems in Libraries." In *Sign Systems for Libraries*, ed. Dorothy Pollet and Peter C. Haskell, 115-23. New York: R. R. Bowker, 1979.

Mallery, Mary S., and Ralph E. DeVore. *A Sign System for Libraries: Solving the Wayfinding Problem*. Chicago: American Library Association, 1982.

Mancini, Donna. "On the Move: Rapid Transit Commuter Libraries." *RQ* 29, no. 1 (Fall 1989): 15-18.

Markey, Karen. "Thus Spake the OPAC User." *Information Technology and Libraries* 2, no. 4 (December 1983): 381-87.

Mason, Marilyn Gell. "The Future of the Public Library." *Library Journal* 110, no. 14 (1 September 1985): 136-39.

Matthews, Joseph R., Gary S. Lawrence, and Douglas K. Ferguson, eds. *Using Online Catalogs: A Nationwide Survey; A Report of a Study Sponsored by the Council on Library Resources*. New York: Neal-Schuman, 1983.

Mort, Ann. "Scheduling: Where and When." In *The Book Stops Here: New Directions in Bookmobile Service*, ed. Catherine Suyak Alloway, 74-79. Metuchen, N.J.: Scarecrow Press, 1990.

Mueller, Elizabeth. "Are New Books Read More than Old Ones?" *Library Quarterly* 35, no. 3 (July 1965): 166-72.

Myers, Judy. "Designing Open-Stack Areas for the User." In *Sign Systems for Libraries: Solving the Wayfinding Problem*, ed. Mary S. Mallery and Ralph E. DeVore, 195-201. New York: R. R. Bowker, 1979.

Naismith, Rachael. "Library Service to Migrant Farm Workers." *Library Journal* 114, no. 4 (1 March 1989): 52-55.

National Center for Education Statistics. *Public Libraries in 50 States and the District of Columbia: 1989*. Washington, D.C.: U.S. Department of Education, Office of Educational Research and Improvement, 1991.

Nolan, Christopher W. "The Lean Reference Collection: Improving Functionality through Selection and Weeding." *RQ* 52, no. 1 (January 1991): 80-91.

"Outposts for New Reader Books." *Unabashed Librarian*, no. 66 (1988): 11.

Paine, Anne W. "Consideration of Portable Structures in Meeting Library Needs." *Illinois Libraries* 67, no. 9 (November 1985): 813-15.

Palmer, E. Susan. "The Effect of Distance on Public Library Use: A Literature Survey." *Library Research* 3, no. 4 (Winter 1981): 315-54.

Panz, Richard. "Library Services to Special Population Groups in the 21st Century." *Journal of Library Administration* 11, nos. 1/2 (1989): 151-71.

Philip, John J. "Bookmobile Service: Justification to the Nonbeliever (Or to the Weak of Heart)." In *The Book Stops Here: New Directions in Bookmobile Service*, ed. Catherine Suyak Alloway, 1-7. Metuchen, N.J.: Scarecrow Press, 1990.

Pollet, Dorothy, and Peter C. Haskell, eds. *Sign Systems for Libraries: Solving the Wayfinding Problem*. New York: R. R. Bowker, 1979.

"Portland Reading Room Receives Funding." *Wilson Library Bulletin* 63, no. 5 (January 1989): 15.

Rawlinson, Nora. "The Central Library: A Final Attraction." *Library Journal* 115, no. 10 (1 June 1990): 6.

Reynolds, Linda, and Stephen Barrett. *Signs and Guiding for Libraries*. London: Clive Bingley, 1981.

Rutzen, Ruth. "Shelving for Readers." *Library Journal* 77, no. 6 (15 March 1952): 478-82.

Sapp, Gregg. "The Levels of Access: Subject Approaches to Fiction." *RQ* 25, no. 4 (Summer 1986): 488-97.

Savage, Ernest A. *Manual of Book Classification and Display for Public Libraries*. London: Allen & Unwin, 1946.

Scilken, Marvin H. "The Read and Return Collection: A Scheme for Overcoming Librarians' Reluctance to Buy Multiple Copies of Popular Books." *Wilson Library Bulletin* 46, no. 1 (September 1971): 104-5.

Shoham, Snunith, Sara Hershkovitz, and Dalya Metzer. "Distribution of Libraries in an Urban Space and Its Effects on Their Use: The Case of Tel Aviv." *Library and Information Science Research* 12, no. 2 (April/June 1990): 167-81.

Sinkule, Karen L. "Problems with Promoting Use of Microform Documents." *RQ* 26, no. 1 (Fall 1986): 21-29.

Sivulich, Kenneth G. "How We Run the Queens Library Good (and Doubled Circulation in Seven Years)." *Library Journal* 114, no. 3 (15 February 1989): 123-27.

Skrzeszewski, Stan, June Huggins-Chan, and Frank Clarke. "Bookmobile Services to Native Peoples: An Experiment in Saskatchewan." In *The Book Stops Here: New Directions in Bookmobile Service*, ed. Catherine Suyak Alloway, 312-21. Metuchen, N.J.: Scarecrow Press, 1990.

Smith, Susan Jane. "Arrangement and Access Paths: A Study of Their Effect on Intellectual Freedom." Master's thesis, University of Chicago, 1977.

Spiller, David. "The Provision of Fiction for Public Libraries." *Journal of Librarianship* 12, no. 4 (October 1980): 238-66.

Stoness, B. Jeanne. "Integration of Print and Non-Print Resources." *Expression* 1, no. 1 (Spring 1976): 34-37; and in *NYLA Bulletin* 24, no. 8 (October 1976): 1-2, 10-11.

"Supermarket Libraries Appeal to Customers." *Library Journal* 111, no. 20 (December 1986): 30.

Taylor, Margaret Ann Thomas. "The Effect of Bibliographic Accessibility upon Physical Accessibility of Materials in a Public Library Setting." Ph.D. diss., University of Michigan, 1982.

Tiffany, Constance J. "The War Between the Stacks." *American Libraries* 9, no. 8 (August 1978): 499.

Tutton, Mary. "A New Perspective on Bookmobile Costs." In *The Book Stops Here: New Directions in Bookmobile Service*, ed. Catherine Suyak Alloway, 32-38. Metuchen, N.J.: Scarecrow Press, 1990.

Van de Voorde, Philip E. "Should Reference Service for U.S. Government Publications and General Reference Be Merged? A Case Study." *Government Publications Review* 16, no. 3 (May/June 1989): 247-57.

Vavrek, Bernard. "Mapping the Bookmobile: Recent Surveys." In *The Book Stops Here: New Directions in Bookmobile Service*, ed. Catherine Suyak Alloway, 9-15. Metuchen, N.J.: Scarecrow Press, 1990a.

_____. "Rural Road Warriors." *Library Journal* 115, no. 5 (15 May 1990b): 56-57.

Venter, Trude. " 'n Rangskikkingsmetode om die gebruik van nie-fiksie in openbare biblioteke te bevorder." *South African Journal for Librarianship and Information Science* 52, no. 4 (December 1984): 109-12.

Wagner, Elaine. "A Library in a Skyway." *Minnesota Libraries* 28, no. 10 (Summer 1987): 324-28.

Watson, Tom. "Read and Return." *Wilson Library Bulletin* 62, no. 9 (May 1988): 53-54.

Webb, T. D. *Reorganization in the Public Library*. Phoenix, Ariz.: Oryx Press, 1985.

Weihs, Jean. "Accessible Storage of Nonbook Materials." Phoenix, Ariz.: Oryx Press, 1984.

Williams, Dianne T. McAfee. "A Study to Determine the Effectiveness of an Interest Grouping Classification for Primary Grade Children." Master's thesis, Western Michigan University, 1973.

Wilson, De Etta. "On the Way to Intershelving: Elements in the Decision." *Hawaii Library Association Journal* 33 (1976): 43-51.

"World's First Library in an Elevated Transit System Opens in Miami." *Public Libraries* 31, no. 1 (January/February 1992): 8-9.

Wyker, Shirley. "Welcome to the Public Library: Serving Children in Day-Care." *The Bookmark* 46, no. 3 (Spring 1988): 193-94.

Promotion Decisions

7

Obviously, redesigning collections to meet community needs, setting prices for using collections as low as is economically feasible, and making effective placement decisions are vital keys to attracting and retaining public library patrons. But as Sherman has noted, some librarians make the mistake of "feeling that library services and materials are important in themselves and therefore it is unnecessary to publicize them. Inherent value, like virtue, will win out. The good will triumph. Truth will reign" (1980, 6). The reality, of course, is that it may not. A library needs to consciously and actively inform potential users about the existence of its collection in an effort to persuade them of the value of using these materials. The goal of promotion efforts is to make the target market aware of the library's resources and to inform them of the benefits of using these resources. Patrons can then weigh these benefits against the costs they will face in using the collection. An individual will use the collection only if he is convinced that the benefits of such use outweigh the costs.

In developing any promotional campaign, library staff should consider a number of broad questions:

1. What target market is the library trying to reach with a particular promotion campaign?

2. What type of response is being sought from the target market?

3. What type of message will the library try to convey to the target market?

4. What techniques can the library use to promote its products?

5. How often should promotion occur?

6. How will the library evaluate the results of its promotion efforts?

Each is discussed on the following pages.

What Target Market Is the Library Trying
to Reach with a Particular Promotion Effort?

Libraries can direct their promotion efforts toward a variety of target markets. These include

1. *community residents in general.* For example, a library might promote its collection via advertisements in a local newspaper or magazine or through public service announcements on a local radio or television station.

2. *one or more groups of community residents who have a common bond.* For example, a librarian might present a booktalk to the science fiction club, give area genealogists a tour that emphasizes the local history collection, or speak to senior citizens about resources that can aid them in stretching their retirement incomes.

3. *library users in general.* For example, a library might promote a special collection via a brochure mailed to all registered borrowers. It could also set up, within a particular library building, different "point-of-purchase" displays emphasizing amateur detective stories, classical music, travel guides, or other subsets of the collection.

4. *individual patrons.* For example, the library might provide a readers' adviser, who will promote the collection, one work at a time, to patrons who are having trouble finding items that they would like to read, watch, or listen to.

Promotion efforts will be most effective if the library lets information about the community dictate which target markets should be pursued. A library that has followed the procedures spelled out in *Planning and Role Setting for Public Libraries* (McClure and others, 1987) will have an advantage over libraries that have not followed this or a similar systematic planning process, because the former will have

1. collected information about the community, the residents, and the extent to which they are aware of and use the library;

2. chosen primary and secondary roles from among those listed in *Planning and Role Setting for Public Libraries*; and

3. written a mission statement, ideally a tightly focused one like those discussed in chapter 3.

Libraries can then examine the chosen roles and determine which target markets to pursue. As noted in chapter 3, libraries generally will want to pursue first those target markets that need their products and that can be reached in a cost-effective fashion. For instance, a library that has chosen a role of *preschoolers' door to learning* may wish to direct a substantial part of its promotion resources to making young children and their parents who are library users more aware of the different collections that will meet their needs. A library that has selected the role of *formal education support center* may choose, as a major target market, students who attend the junior high and high schools that are only two blocks from the main library.

The library then will want to develop goals and objectives related to these roles and the library's mission, that the staff will try to meet. As Bunge (1984) has noted, a goal is a clear but general statement of what the library intends to accomplish over the planning period. Thus, one promotion-related goal for the library that has chosen the role of *formal education support center* might be to make high school students more aware of the ways that the public library's collection can meet their curriculum-related needs.

An objective is a specific target for action, related to a particular goal, that must be attained within a specific time frame. One promotion-related objective that falls under the goal listed above might be the following: By December of this calendar year, make 60 percent of those taking classes in general science, biology, chemistry, and physics aware that the public library has resources in its collection that can help them with their science-fair projects. The more time a library takes to make its promotional goals and objectives clear, the easier it will find it to plan promotion activities to meet these, to budget for relevant promotion activities, and to evaluate the success of these efforts.[1] Budgeting is an especially important issue, because a library will need to determine, at an early date, how it will allocate its promotion budget among different target markets.

Librarians should keep two different concepts in mind when making budgeting decisions. First, promotional budget allocations should reflect the roles the library has chosen for itself in its strategic planning process. *Planning and Role Setting for Public Libraries*, for example, suggests that a library should allocate 40 percent to 50 percent of its overall budget to support the primary roles it has chosen to emphasize, 30 percent to 40 percent more to support its secondary roles, and the final 20 percent to support all other aspects of library services. Libraries can use these percentages as a rough guide to allocating their promotion budgets. If, for example, the library has chosen two primary roles of *preschoolers' door to learning* and *reference library*, it could spent 50 percent of its total promotion budget to publicize children's materials and reference works to relevant target markets, like preschoolers and their parents, day-care workers, business people, people searching for career and consumer information, and genealogists.

A second concept to keep in mind is that of market potential—that is, the degree to which a particular target market is likely to use the library. Marketers who work for profit-making organizations generally allocate their full promotion budgets on the basis of market potential. If public libraries adhered strictly to this practice, they would spend a great deal of money promoting resources to groups that are already using the library heavily and none promoting resources to groups that are not using the library at all.

Libraries that are following a societal approach may want to modify this practice somewhat. They may spend the bulk of their promotion budgets trying to reach those two groups of community residents who have the greatest market potential—library users and people who use the kinds of materials that libraries offer but who do not currently use libraries. However, because libraries are trying to benefit society as a whole, they may want to devote a small portion of the budget to efforts to reach out to people who "need" library services but are less likely to use them—that is, traditional nonuser groups like the culturally disadvantaged and the nonreading public.

What Type of Response Is Being Sought from the Target Market?

In their promotion efforts, librarians are obviously seeking to increase use of the collection. A number of profit-making organizations try to increase use by training their salespersons to adopt hard-sell promotion techniques, like overstating the benefits of using a product, using slick, memorized sales presentations, and making negative comments about products offered by competitors. Most businesses that use these kinds of pressure-selling tactics are trying to maximize their immediate sales.

But public libraries are less interested in maximizing current sales and more interested in maximizing the number of repeat customers—customers who will use libraries again and again because they have been satisfied in the past. This means that librarians will want to take a different approach to promotion, one that involves studying the customers' requirements, then making suggestions about works that will meet these requirements. This approach assumes that patrons will be more likely to use public library collections if staff show they have the long-term interests of patrons in mind.

Although use of the collection is the desired outcome of a library's promotion efforts, it may not be the immediate result. This is because, as Kotler (1982) points out, customers of any organization must move through six different "buyer readiness stages" before use will occur. These are awareness, knowledge, liking, preference, conviction, and action. Staff members will be able to promote the library most effectively if they determine which stage a majority of potential users are in and focus their promotion efforts accordingly.

In some instances, the target market will not be aware of the library's existence. For example, high school students who attend rural schools may not be aware that the public library in the county seat serves the entire region. If awareness is low, staff will wish to devote their initial promotion efforts to building name recognition of the library.

In other cases, the target market may be aware of the library but may not know much about the collections and services it offers. Promotion efforts should be geared toward transmitting key information about the library and its resources. For example, the public library in Coppell, Texas, uses a Welcome-Wagon-type service to inform new residents about the library's collections and services (Action, 1992).

If the target audience members know about the library but do not like it (e.g., because they find it too costly or frustrating to use), library staff will need "to find out why and then develop a communications program to build up favorable feeling. If the unfavorable view is rooted in real inadequacies..., a communications campaign would not do the job. The task would require first improving the [library] and then communicating its quality" (Kotler, 1982, 359).

Sometimes a target audience will like the library but still prefer to obtain reading, listening, and viewing materials from other information outlets. In such instances, staff will want to stress the benefits of using the library's collection. For example, a library could discuss, in its promotion campaign, the wide range of materials that it offers and the currency of its collection. The Los Angeles County Public Library did this when it launched a major publicity drive that emphasized various benefits of using the collection under one unifying slogan that proclaimed "The best things in life are still free" (Los Angeles, 1991).

A target audience may prefer the library to other information outlets but may not have developed the conviction to use it. Therefore, librarians will want to stress that using the library will help patrons meet their needs. As chapter 4 indicates, this task is easiest when members of the target market already use the types of materials that libraries offer. It is much more difficult to convince hard-core nonusers that they will benefit from using materials in the library's collection.

Finally, some members of a target market may be convinced that they should use the library's collection but may still have failed to act on this conviction for a variety of reasons. The marketing task thus becomes motivating the potential patron to take action. For example, the library may get patrons to check out a best-selling work from its rental collection by reducing the rental price from $2 to $1.

Libraries can determine the buyer awareness stage of a target market in a variety of ways. Most libraries today do this by maintaining regular contacts with members of the target market. For example, the children's librarian may obtain a very rough idea of the buyer readiness stage of children by talking with children who already visit the library or with librarians and teachers from area elementary schools. This type of informal information gathering is very inexpensive. However, librarians should realize it may not produce fully accurate data. After all, children who visit the library have already decided to use the library; this means that they are not truly representative of all children in the community. Information obtained from other librarians and teachers may also be somewhat biased, because they are not members of the target group.

For this reason some libraries are beginning to undertake more formal marketing research. Often this is done by organizing one or more focus groups, consisting of 6 to 10 members of each target market, then probing member knowledge and feelings about the library and its resources. This technique will be most effective if the library

1. uses multiple focus groups to obtain a more in-depth look at a broad spectrum of the target market;

2. includes both users and nonusers in these discussions; and

3. uses moderators who have a broad knowledge of both public libraries and marketing practices to guide the discussions.

The Iowa City (Iowa) Public Library (ICPL) followed these principles when it sponsored six focus groups to determine how it could better serve the needs of area business people. Sixty-eight business people attended, representing six different kinds of businesses (e.g., nonprofit agencies and service businesses).

ICPL found that business people were using few library resources, primarily because group members, as a whole, were aware of the library but lacked knowledge about how its collections could meet their needs. These business people felt that the library should publicize its business services in a more concentrated and more targeted fashion by working closely with the Chamber of Commerce, heads of local government agencies, and trade associations like the area Board of Realtors. Participants felt the two most effective means of promotion would be press releases in the Chamber of Commerce newsletter and small group tours targeted to specific types of businesses (Baker, 1991).

Although focus group discussions are fairly cost-effective (ICPL spent a total of $830, not including staff costs, on the six discussions it sponsored), a library may occasionally find it worthwhile to formally survey its target market. This is because such surveys can, if well designed, measure the exact buyer awareness stage of a large number of persons in the target market. They can also determine why certain attitudes exist, so that causal factors can be addressed during promotion efforts. Currently, few public libraries use such marketing surveys, probably because of their high cost. They also require a rather sophisticated knowledge of research design in order to obtain accurate results—knowledge that library staff may not have.[2] However, a library may be able to solve this problem if it can persuade local market researchers or students in a marketing program at a local university to donate their time to design the survey, implement it, and interpret the results.[3]

What Type of Message Will the Library Try to Convey to the Target Market?

Promotion can convey three different types of messages to target markets: information messages, persuasion messages, and reminder messages. The type of message chosen will depend on the buyer awareness stage that the bulk of the target market is in.

At times a library will want to use information messages to gain the attention of potential customers. Such messages inform target markets about the services the library offers and the collection of materials it contains. Information messages may also be used to clarify the library's image, to correct false impressions, or to reduce consumer fears.

At other times, the library may wish to use persuasion messages. Such messages state how library resources can be of benefit to the patron, in an effort to convince customers to engage in library use now. For example, the Lincoln Library in Springfield, Illinois, used the following text on a poster advertising a research workshop for students: "Get a Running Start on Your Term Paper! This year be prepared when term paper time rolls around. The library is offering a free workshop (on Saturday, October 3, from 9:30-11:00 a.m.) to show you short-cuts in library research. The skills you'll acquire will help you find more information in less time for term papers and other school projects" (Tuggle and Heller, 1987, 92).

The library may also wish to use reminder messages. These are designed to jog patrons' memories about the kinds of works that are available and the benefits of using these. For example, residents of the area served by the Fairbanks (Alaska) Public Library were reminded of the variety of works in the library's collection each week when a local radio station separately aired five book reviews, representing the fields of best-selling fiction, nonfiction, children's books, homemaking books, and technical books for the layperson (Sherman, 1980).

The library will want to develop, for each promotion effort, creative messages that will attract a potential user's attention, hold his interest, arouse his desires, and cause him to act, that is, to use library materials. However, giving instructions on how to write such messages is beyond the scope of this book. Librarians who wish to learn more about generating memorable and attention-getting messages, selecting messages most likely to appeal to the target market, and implementing these can refer to standard public relations texts. Recent books that discuss these matters in some detail include Brody and Lattimore (1990), Klein (1990), and Tucker and Derelian (1989). Works by Leerburger (1989) and Tuggle and Heller (1987) address the subject from a library perspective, as do two marketing newsletters: *Marketing Library Services* and *Marketing Treasures*.

What Techniques Can the Library Use to Promote Its Products?

The techniques that can be used to "sell" library collections are limited only by the imaginations of staff members. Although some librarians have stuck to tried-and-true methods of promoting their collections, like writing public service announcements and listing the types of items that can be obtained at the library on the side of book bags, others have advertised their wares on matchbook covers, parade floats, rapid-transit vehicles, and hot-air balloons.

The most commonly used promotional methods fall into four categories. *Personal selling* is a technique used most often by the professional staff—the readers' advisory and reference librarians who promote the collection, one item at a time, to patrons who want a particular kind of work and the outreach librarians who present booktalks, speeches, and slide-tape presentations that emphasize the collection's contents to interested groups. But nonprofessional staff members, whether they are working behind the circulation desk or in the stacks shelving items, may also be asked to recommend items or to explain the different types of works that are available. *Promotional activities*, like summer reading programs, talks by local authors, and point-of-purchase displays located at strategic points within the library, can also inform patrons of the variety of works in the collection. *Mass-media promotion* generally involves advertising the library's products in local newspapers and magazines and on television or radio stations. *Targeted information pieces*, like brochures, book lists, posters, signs, and newsletters can also be used, both within and outside the library, to feature interesting product items (e.g., a recently published atlas of local historical maps) or product lines (e.g., large-print books and books-on-tape).[4]

As Wood has so cogently noted, the library's goal is to choose "the medium or combination of different media (often called 'media mix') that will best satisfy budgetary constraints and achieve the [promotion] campaign's objectives.... [But] there are no givens in media selection, no rules whose faithful, mechanical application assures success" (1988, 11). There are three broad factors, however, that should influence the choice of promotion medium:

1. the target market

2. the message content

3. the cost

The relationship between each of these factors and promotional media commonly used in public libraries is shown in figure 7.1.

Libraries will need to consider two issues related to the target market. The first is its size and diversity. For example, advertisements in the local newspaper about the broad spectrum of materials in the collection will reach a bigger and more heterogeneous audience than a public service announcement that is aired on a local classical music station.

But various characteristics of the target market should also be considered before choosing a promotion technique—characteristics like psychographic factors (e.g., extent of library use, life-style, and leisure interests) and demographic factors (e.g., age, educational level, and occupation). A library that is trying to reach existing patrons may use a different promotional technique than one trying to promote the collection to some subset of community residents who may not be current users. For example, a library can place brightly colored signs and displays around its building to promote, to current users, various sections of the collection, like works that can help with school assignments or that feature people who appear regularly in the news. But it may buy ads on a rock-and-roll radio station to try to convince teenagers to use its collection of phonograph records and compact disks and use direct mail to tell first-time parents about its collection of materials on child raising.

The content of the message will also influence the choice of promotion media. One important factor in message content is the aspect of the collection that is being promoted. If the library is publicizing something of on-going interest to the public (e.g., investment guides), it can choose a medium with a long shelf life—like posters, which may hang for months. However, if the library is publicizing something of seasonal interest (e.g., holiday materials) or a collection-related event (e.g., a forthcoming talk by a local author), it will need to use a medium that can reach the public in a timely fashion: a newspaper feature story, a radio or television announcement, or a newsletter announcement.

The complexity of message content is another factor that should be considered. Short messages can be featured on posters and signs. Detailed technical information, like the types of collection sources that area businesses will find useful, is best conveyed in a news article or an information brochure.

(Text continues on page 159.)

Technique	Target Market	Message Content	Types of Costs Incurred
NEWSPAPER feature stories, photographs, or advertisements	Newspapers provide good overall market coverage for community residents in general.	Messages in news stories can range from simple to complex; they can inform, persuade, or remind. Messages in advertisements should be simple and capture attention immediately; they can inform, persuade, or remind. The message is very timely and therefore especially useful for promoting current collection-related events or for informing the public about recent changes in the cost of using the collection. Because the medium is fairly transient, messages about on-going features of the collection will need to be repeated periodically. Effective graphic design may be used to help gain attention.	Staff time: to write stories, design advertising copy, take photographs, develop graphic materials, and work with media representatives to ensure good coverage and placement of material Advertising: purchased by the column inch Supplies
MAGAZINE/NEWSLETTER feature stories, photographs, or advertisements	General interest magazines can provide average to good market coverage for community residents in general. Special-interest magazines, like the Chamber of Commerce newsletter, are good for reaching highly specialized target markets.	Messages in news stories can range from simple to complex; they can inform, persuade, or remind. Messages in advertisements should be simple and capture attention immediately; they can inform, persuade, or remind. The medium can be used to convey messages about current collection-related events if the marketer allows for the lead time required for publication. Because the medium is fairly transient, messages about on-going features of the collection will need to be repeated periodically. Effective graphic design may be used to help gain attention.	Staff time: to write stories, design advertising copy, take photographs, develop graphic materials, and work with media representatives to ensure good coverage and placement of material Advertising: purchased by the column inch (may be free in some special-interest publications) Supplies

(Fig. 7.1 continues on page 156.)

Fig. 7.1. Promotional techniques commonly used by libraries.

Technique	Target Market	Message Content	Types of Costs Incurred
TELEVISION OR CABLE TELEVISION feature stories, advertisements, or public service announcements	Television can provide average to good market coverage for community residents in general.	Messages in news stories can be simple or of medium complexity; they can inform, persuade, or remind. Messages in advertisements and public service announcements should be simple and capture attention immediately; they can inform, persuade, or remind. The message is very timely and therefore especially useful for promoting current collection-related events or for informing the public about recent changes in the cost of using the collection. Because the medium is fairly transient, messages about ongoing features of the collection will need to be repeated periodically.	Staff time: to plan stories, develop advertising copy or script, design graphic materials, and work with media representatives to ensure good coverage and placement of material Advertising: may be purchased by the minute Supplies
RADIO feature stories, advertisements, or public service announcements	Radio can provide average to good market coverage for community residents in general. Radio stations that follow a specific format (e.g., rock, classical music, information) can reach highly selective target audiences.	Messages in news stories can be simple or of medium complexity; they can inform, persuade, or remind. Messages in advertisements and public service announcements should be simple and capture attention immediately; they can inform, persuade, or remind. The message is very timely and therefore especially useful for promoting current collection-related events or for informing the public about recent changes in the cost of using the collection. Because the medium is fairly transient, messages about on-going features of the collection will need to be repeated periodically.	Staff time: to plan stories, develop advertising copy or script, and work with media representatives to ensure good coverage and placement of material Advertising: may be purchased by the minute Supplies

(Fig. 7.1 continues on page 157.)

Technique	Target Market	Message Content	Types of Costs Incurred
DIRECT MAILINGS— newsletters, information brochures, book lists, or posters	Direct mail can provide average to good market coverage for community residents in general, library patrons in particular, or a small, specially targeted group. Target markets may vary greatly in size, from a few dozen to thousands.	Messages in newsletters, brochures, and book lists can range from simple to complex; they can inform, persuade, or remind.	Staff time: to write copy, take photographs, develop graphic materials, compile mailing list, and mail materials
		Messages on posters should be simple and capture attention immediately; they can inform, persuade, or remind. The medium can be used to convey messages about current collection-related events if the marketer allows for the lead time required for publication and mailing.	Printing costs
			Supplies
		Because the medium is fairly transient, messages about on-going features of the collection will need to be repeated periodically.	Postage
		Effective graphic design should be used to help gain attention.	
POSTERS AND SIGNS placed within the building	Posters/signs, if appropriately designed and positioned, can reach library users effectively.	Messages on signs and posters should be simple and capture attention immediately; they can inform, persuade, or remind.	Staff time: to write message and develop graphic materials
		The message can be timely and therefore especially useful for promoting current collection-related events.	Printing costs
		The message can also be enduring and therefore especially useful for promoting on-going features of the collection or the costs of using various materials.	Supplies
		Effective graphic design should be used to help gain attention.	

(Fig. 7.1 continues on page 158.)

Technique	Target Market	Message Content	Types of Costs Incurred
POINT-OF-PURCHASE DISPLAYS within the building	POP displays, if appropriately designed and positioned, can reach library users effectively.	Messages on accompanying signs should be simple and capture attention immediately; they can inform, persuade, or remind. Effective graphic design may be used to help gain attention.	Staff time: to pull materials for the display, refill the display as it empties, and develop graphic materials Furniture to house the display Supplies
SPEECHES OR BOOKTALKS presented to the target market, inside the library or outside its doors	Speeches and talks can reach specially targeted groups of community residents and library patrons.	If carefully designed and delivered, message can effectively promote collection-related events, the collection as a whole, or individual product lines or items. Slides and graphics can accompany talk to help gain attention.	Staff time: to prepare and deliver talk, develop graphic materials, and travel to group meeting places Supplies
INDIVIDUAL RECOMMENDA-TIONS given by readers' advisers and reference librarians	Recommendations are designed to reach individual library patrons rather than targeted groups of users.	Messages can promote individual product items or lines in the collection.	Staff time: to help patrons on an individual basis

A final factor that will influence the choice of promotion media is the actual out-of-pocket cost to the library. One distinction that librarians may find useful is the difference between advertising and publicity:

Advertising: Any paid form of personal presentation and promotion of ideas, goods, or services by an identified sponsor.

Publicity: Nonpersonal stimulation of demand for a product, service, or business unit by planting commercially significant news about it in a published medium or obtaining favorable presentation of it upon radio, television, or stage that is not paid for by the sponsor. (Kotler, 1975, 201)

That is, a library must set aside part of its budget to pay for advertising that it develops. However, when a library uses publicity, it actually finds or creates eye-catching, timely, well-written news stories related to the products in the collection, then tries to persuade the news media to use these. This allows it to promote its wares without direct cost, other than staff time.

As Kotler has noted, "Publicity has three qualities that make it a worthwhile investment. First, it may have higher veracity than advertising because it appears as normal news and not sponsored information. Second, it tends to catch people off guard who might otherwise actively avoid sponsored messages. Third, it has high potential for dramatization in that it arouses attention coming in the guise of a noteworthy event" (1975, 212).

Unfortunately, publicity efforts have a large hidden cost: the library's marketing person will have to spend a great deal of time trying to gain the goodwill of people in the various news media, particularly area newspapers, television stations, and radio stations. Otherwise, the library may not be able to get media representatives to air public service announcements, take publicity photographs, cover newsworthy events, or print press releases from the library.

Large urban libraries are at a disadvantage here, because the larger the city, the more nonprofit groups are competing for free publicity. This has caused some larger libraries to begin budgeting money for paid advertising. In 1991, the Los Angeles County Library set aside $600,000 for a two-year campaign designed to increase library use and the number of card holders. The library did this so it would not have to depend on the news media to air or print its promotional materials. It also wanted to reach community residents during prime time, when public service announcements usually are not aired (Los Angeles, 1991). The New York Public Library has conducted several large paid advertising campaigns over the years, including one describing the role the library played in making Dr. Seuss a household name, in developing the Polaroid camera, in creating Ripley's Believe It or Not, and in other behind-the-scenes contributions (New York, 1986).

Other libraries should consider using paid advertising, at least occasionally, because this will give them more control over the frequency and size of their promotion efforts. For example, they will be able to designate how large their ads are and where these are placed. However, although librarians acknowledge the value of paid advertising, they don't use it as often as they might. This trend is typical of nonprofit organizations in general, which fear that any donated advertising they receive (e.g., public service announcements) will be withdrawn if they show that they are willing to purchase advertising space (Kotler, 1982).

How Often Should Promotion Occur?

Several factors should influence the frequency of a library's promotion efforts. One is the buyer awareness state of the target audience. This is because it will take stronger and more frequent promotion efforts to convince people who have little awareness of, knowledge of, and liking for the library's collection to use it. An astute group of public, school, university, and special librarians from Fairbanks, Alaska, recognized this principle more than 20 years ago when they organized a joint effort to increase community awareness of the cramped, underused, and understaffed public library. During a one-year period, the librarians produced photographic spreads of library facilities for area newspapers; got local movie theaters, television stations, and radio stations to play film and sound clips advertising library services and collections; featured weekly reviews of works in the collection in area newspapers and on the radio; set up exhibits of best-selling works of the twentieth century in the library and at the Fairbanks International Airport; and distributed lists of works about Alaska and its history. Promotion efforts increased the community's knowledge of and use of the library and its collection and helped convince the city of Fairbanks to fund a new library building (Sherman, 1980).

Another factor that can affect the frequency of promotion efforts is the extent to which a product's use will vary seasonally. For example, works on gardening, white water rafting, winter vacations, and holidays show cyclical patterns of use. That is, use is very high during one part of the year and very low during others. It will be most cost-effective for libraries to time promotion of seasonal works when natural interest is beginning to ripen in the product and during the height of interest. For example, a public library could promote its collection of college catalogs from September through December, a time when many high school seniors must begin narrowing the list of schools that they are considering attending.

There are several other patterns that a library may follow when it is promoting a particular collection. It could use burst advertising—promoting the collection heavily all at one time—to obtain maximum attention. For example, shortly before Black History Week, a library can arrange for information on resources related to this to appear in a feature story in the local newspaper and in public service announcements on the local radio and television stations. It can also mail flyers to area social studies teachers and display biographies of famous black Americans near the circulation desk.

Because the effects of burst advertising are temporary, it is best used when a short-term promotion effort is desired, like the seasonal effort mentioned above. One noncollection-related example in a public library in North Carolina illustrates this point. Owens (1987) arranged for a burst of advertising on the library's information and referral service in a variety of places: the local newspaper, radio and cable television channels, and posters and brochures distributed throughout the community. As expected, the advertising blitz had an immediate effect: calls to the information and referral service increased by tenfold. However, six weeks after the promotion campaign had ended, calls had fallen to their pre-publicity levels.

Continuous promotion is more appropriate for materials that will be used on a regular basis, like the parenting collection. Such promotion is designed to recur at regular intervals (e.g., once a month) to remind potential patrons that a particular collection is available. However, one problem with continuous promotion is that, if used too frequently, it may be ignored by both the news media and the public.

To overcome this difficulty, libraries can use intermittent advertising— promoting a particular collection in small bursts. Promotion of this type can generate more attention in the news media than continuous advertising, while reminding potential patrons of a collection on an irregular basis. This is particularly true if library promotion efforts take advantage of existing demand for subject areas. For example, the library can tie promotion efforts into local, national, or world events or trends. It might, for instance, promote its collection of materials on the breakup of the former Soviet Union or on the anti-Japanese sentiment that is arising in various parts of the United States.

How Will the Library Evaluate the Results of Its Promotional Efforts?

One step in promotion that is often forgotten (but should not be!) is evaluating the results of promotion efforts. This step is important because not all types of promotion will be able to increase the target market's awareness or use of the collection. For example, one author found that promoting works on cable television did not significantly increase their use (Auld, 1978). Obviously, a library will want to modify or drop promotion efforts that have had little effect on user behavior. It will also want to determine which promotion efforts are most cost-effective.

One technique that organizations sometimes use to measure promotion effectiveness is the exposure count. That is, a library can note the quantitative relationship between the news media coverage it received and the estimated audience it reached. The ABCD Public Library might find that news media coverage included 200 column inches of news and photographs in the local newspaper, which has a circulation of 8,500 persons; 40 minutes of air time on the local radio station, which has an estimated audience of 5,300; and 10 minutes of air time on the local television station, which reaches an estimated 12,800 persons. If this time and space had been purchased at standard advertising rates, it would have cost the library $10,500. Unfortunately, exposure counts of this sort only estimate the number of people reached and give no indication of whether community residents changed their behavior toward using the library because of the promotion efforts. Thus, they do not really measure effectiveness.

If the library has the financial resources to do so, it may find it more useful to determine instead the extent of the target market's attitude change toward the library. That is, the library should try to find out whether the target market's awareness, knowledge, liking, etcetera, have increased. If a library has already developed a formal market survey to measure these states, it can simply resurvey the target market to determine the extent to which an attitude change has occurred.

An even better way to measure the effectiveness of promotion efforts is to measure their effects on use of the library. Good librarians often conduct experiments to see whether promotion efforts work. That is, they promote a particular collection and then step back and watch to see whether use increases. However, because they have not had the necessary research training, many librarians fail to establish appropriate experimental controls—to make sure that the promotion effort caused use to increase rather than some other factor.

Researchers have sometimes faulted librarians for not taking time to set up rigorous experiments with scientific controls. But it is not always practical for a library to do this. Indeed, as Baker (1989) has indicated, public libraries should set up formal experiments to measure the effects of their promotion efforts only if

1. the change has the potential to greatly improve use or to save a large sum of money over time;

2. staff members or consultants are available who are willing to conduct the research and who have an in-depth knowledge of the principles of hypothesis testing, causality, study design, and statistics;

3. the library is willing to endure the inconvenience of changing its procedures for a short time and of collecting statistics associated with the study;

4. the library is willing to bear the expense of the study; and

5. the library is prepared to use results of the study to make changes.

Many public libraries lack the staff, resources, or commitment to do all these things.

This does not mean that libraries should forgo evaluation efforts entirely. Rather, libraries that do not have time to comprehensively evaluate the success of their promotion efforts can

1. rely on promotion methods that trained researchers have shown will increase patron knowledge of and use of materials; and

2. use quick-and-dirty but effective techniques to evaluate the success of their promotion efforts.

Although individual public libraries do not always have the incentive to engage in research, library researchers do, because the classes they take and the jobs they hold often require this. Over the years, a number of researchers have worked with libraries to determine formally whether and why a particular promotion effort works. For example, a review of various research studies shows that book lists significantly increase patron awareness and use of listed titles, but only when they receive wide distribution within the library, that is, when they are consistently placed in works that patrons are checking out, are consistently promoted by library staff, or are prominently displayed is high-traffic areas.

Book lists that are not prominently displayed in the library or are distributed outside library doors may not significantly increase use of the listed titles.[5] Research results like these can increase the understanding of all librarians about whether and why a particular promotion method will work.

Libraries also can use quick-and-dirty evaluation techniques. Because such techniques lack scientific controls, the results cannot be generalized to the field as a whole. However, they can give a library a rough estimate of how well a particular promotion technique worked in that institution.

Consider, for example, the method that Smith used to evaluate the effectiveness of individual staff promotion of works they felt patrons would find interesting. At the beginning of each month, Smith placed two quart mason jars in the circulation area. He filled the first with 300 pennies and left the second empty. Each time a staff member convinced a patron to check out an additional work or file a reserve on a work he had not yet read, the employee moved a penny from the first to the second jar. At the end of the month, Smith counted the pennies in the second jar and informed circulation staff how much of the monthly circulation total was due to these individual promotion efforts. If staff had increased use significantly, Smith rewarded them by taking them out to lunch (Smith, 1992). This evaluation system worked because it provided a simple yet quick measure of the results of promotion efforts.

Conclusion

The best promotion efforts are thoughtful ones that are related to a public library's overall mission, goals, and objectives. Libraries that carefully determine the target markets they will try to reach, the specific products or collection-related events they will promote, the best techniques for reaching these audiences, and the optimum frequency of their promotion efforts should have the greatest potential for increasing target market awareness and use of the collection.

Notes

[1]For a short overview of the various types of costs (for signage, exhibits, photography, etc.) that most libraries will incur when promoting their wares, see Chartrand (1983).

[2]A number of texts in the field give general principles for conducting effective surveys. See, for example, Powell (1991).

[3]Mueller-Alexander (1991) lists the advantages and disadvantages of using these and other alternative sources for marketing research.

[4]It is beyond the scope of this theoretical text to discuss the practical details of writing press releases and public service announcements, designing effective and colorful posters, constructing units to house displays of materials, and the like. Librarians who wish to learn more about these matters may refer to the many

practical guides on these subjects, including Schaeffer (1991), Everhart (1989), Tuggle and Heller (1987), Franklin (1985), Rummel and Perica (1983), Bronson (1982), and Sherman (1980).

[5]See, for example, Baker (1986), Parrish (1986), Wood (1985), Taylor (1982), Powell (1982), Goldhor (1981), and Auld (1978).

References

"Action Exchange: Promoting the Library to New Residents." *American Libraries* 23, no. 5 (May 1992): 371-72.

Auld, Lawrence W. S. "The Effect on Public Library Circulation of Advertising via Cable Television." Ph.D. diss., University of Illinois at Urbana-Champaign, 1978.

Baker, Sharon L. "Improving Business Services Through the Use of Focus Groups." *RQ* 30, no. 3 (Spring 1991): 377-85.

_____. "Overload, Browsers, and Selections." *Library and Information Science Research* 8, no. 4 (October-December 1986): 315-29.

_____. "Problem Solving Through Experimental Research: The Need for Better Controls." *Library Trends* 38, no. 2 (Fall 1989): 204-14.

Brody, E. W., and Dan L. Lattimore. *Public Relations Writing*. Westport, Conn.: Quorum Books, 1990.

Bronson, Que. *Books on Display*. Washington, D.C.: Metropolitan Washington Library Council, 1982.

Bunge, Charles A. "Planning, Goals, and Objectives for the Reference Department." *RQ* 23, no. 3 (Spring 1984): 306-15.

Chartrand, Margaret. "Budgeting for a Public Relations Program." In *Persuasive Public Relations for Libraries*, ed. Kathleen Kelly Rummel and Esther Perica, 32-39. Chicago: American Library Association, 1983.

Everhart, Nancy. *Library Displays*. Metuchen, N.J.: Scarecrow Press, 1989.

Franklin, Linda Campbell. *Display and Publicity Ideas for Libraries*. Jefferson, N.C.: McFarland, 1985.

Goldhor, Herbert. "Experimental Effects on the Choice of Books Borrowed by Public Library Adult Patrons." *Library Quarterly* 51, no. 3 (July 1981): 253-68.

Klein, Erica Leery. *Write Great Ads: A Step-by-Step Approach*. New York: John Wiley, 1990.

Kotler, Philip. *Marketing for Nonprofit Organizations*. Englewood Cliffs, N.J.: Prentice-Hall, 1975.

_____. *Marketing for Nonprofit Organizations*. 2d ed. Englewood Cliffs, N.J.: Prentice-Hall, 1982.

Leerburger, Benedict A. *Promoting and Marketing the Library*. Rev. ed. Boston: G. K. Hall, 1989.

"Los Angeles County PL Conducts $600,000 PR Drive." *Library Journal* 116, no. 6 (1 April 1991): 19.

Marketing Library Services. Newsletter issued 8 times per year. For subscription information, write P.O. Box 2286, Abington, Mass. 02351.

Marketing Treasures. Bimonthly newsletter. For subscription information, write Chris Olson and Associates, 857 Twin Harbor Drive, Arnold, Md. 21012.

McClure, Charles R., Amy Owen, Douglas L. Zweizig, Mary Jo Lynch, and Nancy A. Van House. *Planning and Role Setting for Public Libraries: A Manual of Options and Procedures*. Chicago: American Library Association, 1987.

Mueller-Alexander, Jeanette M. "Alternate Sources for Marketing Research for Libraries." *Special Libraries* 82, no. 3 (Summer 1991): 159-64.

"New York Public Library Undertakes Public Service Advertising Campaign." *Wilson Library Bulletin* 60, no. 8 (April 1986): 11.

Owens, Jo Ann B. "A Study of Methods Used to Publicize I & R Services in Public Libraries." Master's project. Greensboro, N.C.: University of North Carolina, Department of Library Science and Instructional Technology, 1987.

Parrish, Nancy. "The Effect of a Booklist on the Circulation of Fiction Books Which Have Not Been Borrowed from a Public Library in Four Years or Longer." Master's project, University of North Carolina at Greensboro, 1986. ERIC ED282564.

Powell, Ronald. *Basic Research Methods for Librarians*. 2d ed. Norwood, N.J.: Ablex, 1991.

_____. "The Effect of a Booklist on Library Circulation." Unpublished manuscript, University of Illinois at Urbana-Champaign, 1982.

Rummel, Kathleen Kelly, and Esther Perica, eds. *Persuasive Public Relations for Libraries*. Chicago: American Library Association, 1983.

Schaeffer, Mark. *Library Displays Handbook*. New York: H. W. Wilson, 1991.

Sherman, Steve. *ABC's of Library Promotion*. 2d ed. Metuchen, N.J.: Scarecrow Press, 1980.

Smith, Duncan. Telephone interview. 12 February 1992.

Taylor, Margaret Ann Thomas. "The Effect of Bibliographic Accessibility upon Physical Accessibility of Materials in a Public Setting." Ph.D. diss., University of Michigan, 1982.

Tucker, Kerry, and Doris Derelian. *Public Relations Writing: A Planned Approach for Creative Results*. Englewood Cliffs, N.J.: Prentice-Hall, 1989.

Tuggle, Ann Montgomery, and Dawn Hansen Heller. *Grand Schemes and Nitty-Gritty Details: Library PR That Works*. Littleton, Colo.: Libraries Unlimited, 1987.

Wood, Elizabeth J. *Strategic Marketing for Libraries: A Handbook*. Westport, Conn.: Greenwood Press, 1988.

Wood, Richard J. "The Experimental Effects of Fiction Book Lists on Circulation in an Academic Library." *RQ* 24, no. 4 (Summer 1985): 427-32.

A Product-Analysis Approach to Collection Evaluation[1]

8

Although some authors have stated that product analysis is one of the most neglected aspects of marketing in libraries,[2] McGinn (1988) has more accurately noted that librarians have been trying to ascertain customer needs in various ways for many years, although they have not always used marketing terms to describe what they are doing.

Collection evaluation is, in fact, a form of product analysis—one that has been occurring in some fashion since public libraries first opened their doors. But librarians have to a large extent relied on informal, sporadic, subjective, and unsystematic methods to evaluate both the quality of a collection and the nature of its use. This pattern is understandable because libraries have tended to have too few staff and other resources. However, it contributes to the building of collections that are less effective in meeting patron needs than they might be.

Today, there are numerous signs that librarians are recognizing that excellent collections, designed to meet the long- and short-term needs of the community, are vital to fulfilling a library's goals. An emphasis on continuous and comprehensive product analysis, or collection evaluation, can help accomplish these goals. Product analysis is particularly important in a time when leaner budgets have forced librarians to shift their efforts from buying everything they need to buying only the "best" items for their clients.

A number of authors have described various collection evaluation techniques that libraries of various sizes and types can use.[3] Generally, such techniques fall into two broad classes:

1. *materials-centered evaluation techniques*, which focus on the materials themselves and generally address such issues as collection size, quality, and diversity; and

2. *client-centered evaluation techniques*, which focus on the quality and quantity of collection use.

Most libraries will want to use both materials-centered and client-centered approaches to develop balanced, comprehensive collections that they feel their patrons will like. For example, librarians at the Skokie (Illinois) Public Library measure collection quality, size, and diversity by checking collection holdings against a number of lists of recommended works. They examine various measures of use and availability such as turnover rate, title fill rate, and document delivery rate. And they seek patron suggestions about how the collection might be improved (Jacob, 1990a).

This chapter recommends that public libraries consider putting into place a product-analysis approach to collection evaluation that involves four separate tasks:

1. identifying currently owned items that are heavily used

2. identifying currently owned items that are lightly used or not used

3. identifying items that are not in the collection but are desired by patrons and potential patrons

4. identifying other barriers that inhibit use of the collection

This chapter explains why libraries should consider performing these four tasks. At the request of practitioners, it also describes specific evaluation techniques and procedures to accomplish these tasks. These are spelled out in some detail in the figures that accompany the text.

Because of limited resources, some libraries may not be able to adopt all of the evaluation approaches recommended here. In the short term it is better for a library to adopt fewer approaches and carry them out on a regular and consistent basis than to perform many different tasks sporadically, when time permits. However, if a library wants to obtain a strong base of information to aid with collection management decisions, it should consider phasing in, over time, as many of these approaches as possible.

This four-tiered approach to product analysis assumes that it is appropriate to emphasize past, current, and potential use of the collection. After all, all the roles a public library selects for itself, from *popular materials center* to *formal education support center*, are theoretically based on the use of the library by community residents. Note, however, that the product-analysis recommendations given here include several measures of collection quality, size, and diversity. They are not, therefore, totally oriented toward use.

A second assumption is that no measure of use is perfect. Circulation statistics, for example, can tell us that the patron was interested enough in a book's subject, author, or title to check it out but not whether he actually read or enjoyed the item.[4] Librarians need to take this limitation into account when interpreting the results.

A third assumption made is that past use of specific authors, titles, genres, or subject areas is a good predictor of present or future use. This assumption has been shown to be valid in numerous studies. For example, Eggers (1976) found that 93 percent of the books returned to the Iowa City (Iowa) Public Library had circulated in the previous year. And Brooks (1984a, 1984b) showed that past circulation records could be used to forecast overall circulation trends for a public library. Past use accurately predicts future use because the general interests of library patrons change very slowly. Changes likely to significantly affect the use of a collection as a whole will occur over very long periods of time.

One limitation of the product-analysis approach described in this chapter is that it requires that a public library have some means of identifying the use of specific titles. Libraries with automated circulation systems may have a slight advantage here, because most of these systems can be programmed to generate circulation information for each copy of a work.

Many libraries that lack automated circulation systems already maintain the circulation history of each item by recording, on cards or date labels affixed somewhere in or on the books, the date on which the borrowed item is due back in the library. If the library does not discard old date-due cards or paste new date-due labels over old ones that are already filled, the librarian can examine the entire circulation history of the work — a practice that is particularly helpful when making weeding decisions.

Those libraries that do not record circulation information in each work (for example, those using a transaction-card circulation system where the date-due cards placed in circulating titles are removed when the item is returned) will want to begin recording it. The simplest way to do this is to attach a blank date-due label to each circulating item and stamp that label every time the item is checked out. Because the use of some works is seasonal, most libraries will want to consider collecting a full year's worth of circulation data to provide a reliable base of information on which to make weeding decisions.

Identifying Currently Owned Items That Are Heavily Used

As part of product analysis, a library should frequently and systematically identify items in its collection that are so heavily used that patrons have difficulty obtaining them. The library can then work to make these items more readily available.

In the past, some librarians assumed that only best-selling items were in such high demand that patrons couldn't readily obtain them. One study, conducted over 20 years ago in 11 branches of a public library system in Maryland, illustrates the fallacy of this assumption. Moreland (1968) systematically and regularly checked the availability of 122 modern classic titles like *Gone with the Wind, Black Like Me*, and *Fahrenheit 451*. Whenever all copies of a title were checked out at any branch, new ones were immediately purchased, processed, and put on the shelves at that branch. Although the library bought an average of 16 copies of each title for each branch library over the 11 months of the study, it still had not reached the point where at least one copy of every title was always available when a patron wanted it.

During this stage of product analysis, the evaluator will be trying to determine the types of work that are consistently used so that purchase of these can be consistently emphasized in the future. Certain genres (e.g., mysteries and romances), certain formats (e.g., videotapes and compact disks), and certain subject areas (e.g., popular psychology books, cookbooks, and books on career planning) are consistently used very heavily in many public libraries.

The person evaluating the collection will also want to identify those authors whose works are heavily used. This is particularly relevant for fiction collections. In fact, Spiller (1980) has shown that most public library patrons have, in their heads, lists of 10 or 20 fiction writers whose works they want to read. Once a patron has found one of these authors, he tends to want to read all the books that author has written within a particular series that has captured the patron's attention. For example, a patron might want to read all of John MacDonald's series about a modern-day knight-errant named Travis McGee or all of Elizabeth Peters's mysteries featuring archaeologist Amelia Peabody.

The evaluator should also identify specific titles that are in such high demand that patrons have difficulty obtaining them, so that the immediate problem can be corrected. Each library will need to determine the percentage of patron requests it will try to meet immediately. As has been noted throughout this book, the average public library can immediately fill only 50 percent to 65 percent of patron requests. But most public libraries will want to improve their performance and to set higher goals for title availability.

There are a number of different methods librarians can use to identify titles, authors, and types of works that are being heavily used. The three major ones recommended here are practical approaches to accomplishing these tasks:

1. scrutinizing reserve lists

2. examining circulation records of individual works

3. examining circulation totals

Scrutinizing Reserve Lists to Identify Heavily Used Works

Most public libraries have some means of reserving for one patron a title that is checked out to someone else. Therefore, the evaluator can examine the reserve list and identify a portion of the works that patrons are requesting. This process will underestimate patron desire for heavily used titles, because not every person who wants to borrow an item will make the effort to reserve it. However, the practice of scrutinizing reserve lists is still recommended for libraries of all sizes and levels of resources. This is because the scrutiny process requires a minimal amount of staff time to identify quickly many works that patrons are having difficulty finding. Directions for identifying heavily used works using reserve lists are given in figure 8.1.

Examining Circulation Records to Identify Heavily Used Titles

Another way to identify heavily used works is to regularly and routinely scrutinize their circulation records. When the library's circulation system is both automated and flexible, this will be relatively easy to do. The library can simply request printouts of all items that have circulated heavily (that is, more than X times in X months). The evaluator then checks the shelves and notes circulation patterns of these titles and of other works by these authors.

(Text continues on page 172.)

Using Reserve Lists to Identify Heavily Used Works

1.   Publicize the fact that patrons can file reserves. The promotion should be continuous, so that new patrons as well as old can discover the service, but it may be simple. For example, the library can post notices at the catalog, on the ends of the stack sections, and elsewhere that read:

> "If the library owns a title that you want but it is not on the shelf, please stop at the reference desk. We will reserve the item for you and notify you when it has been returned."

Also, ask staff at public service desks to routinely remind patrons that they can file reserve requests.

2.   Whenever possible, do not charge patrons a fee to file reserve requests. Librarians have often argued that charging a minimal fee for reserves deters the "frivolous abuse" of reserve services. However, there is little evidence that such abuse occurs. What's more, if the library wants an effective collection, it needs to actively encourage patron feedback about what titles are and are not immediately available for use. Charging even a nominal amount to file a reserve notice may actually discourage this feedback, because use of library services may decline when fees are imposed (Giacoma, 1989; Huston, 1979).

3.   Review reserve requests frequently. The demand for the average title tends to be very strong during a short, intense period when the publisher or the news media are promoting it. During this period of initial popularity, demand for a title may grow rapidly. There may be only two reserve requests for an item when it is first published but 20 by the end of a four-week period. To keep on top of demand for works at the peak of their popularity, reserve lists should be reviewed every week.

4.   Examine reserve lists for specific titles. Try to fill these within a short period—ideally no longer than one to two months. Remember that even a two-month waiting period is less than ideal. By the time a reserve request is placed, processed, and filled, the patron may have forgotten that he wanted the item, borrowed a friend's copy, obtained the item at another library, or purchased it himself.

As chapter 9 notes, a library can fill reserve requests in a variety of ways: purchasing popular items in multiple copies, obtaining these works on a lend-lease plan like those offered by Baker and Taylor Books, or shortening the length of the loan period for copies already owned.

5.   Remember that providing only enough copies to meet the demand for patrons who are interested enough in a particular title to place a reserve on it won't guarantee that the library has enough copies to meet the current browsing demand for the item. Consider ordering one or more extra copies to help meet this demand as well.

6.   Note specific authors, genres, and subject areas for which reserves are consistently filed. Such trends may be most apparent if past reserve data is analyzed quarterly. Modify future selection practices to guarantee higher availability rates for these works.

Fig. 8.1. Directions for using reserve lists to identify heavily used works.

Identifying heavily used titles is more difficult if the library has a manual circulation system or an automated system that is not flexible enough to generate printouts of heavily used works. In the past, some libraries have tried to identify heavily used titles by taking a sample of the circulation titles. Unfortunately, any sample will fail to identify all titles that are heavily used and that might benefit from duplication or from some other treatment to improve their availability.

A better practice is to train staff who check in returned materials to quickly and routinely scan the date due stamps in each item and list heavily used items on a form created for this purpose. The evaluator then checks the shelves and notes the circulation patterns of other copies of that title.

Note that the manual method of screening circulation records to identify heavily used titles can be time consuming and, therefore, difficult for many libraries to phase in completely. Libraries with limited staff resources can, however, consider performing this type of screening for limited sections of the collection—those that contain works for which demand is particularly heavy, like videotapes. Directions for, and forms associated with, screening returned works are provided in figures 8.2, 8.3, and 8.4.

Examining Circulation Totals to Determine Heavily Used (and Lightly Used) Classes of Materials

Most public libraries keep statistics on the number of items that have circulated in various

1. user groupings (e.g., children, young adult, and adults);

2. formats (e.g., recordings and 16mm films);

3. genres (like classic fiction and mysteries); and

4. subjects (from reader interest categories like car repair, to broad or narrow groupings within the Dewey Decimal Classification System, like the 100s or the 590s).

Such totals can provide information on which classes of materials are heavily used or, for that matter, poorly used. Librarians can modify their selections accordingly. For example, the Metropolitan Library System in Oklahoma City, Oklahoma, used its knowledge of the fact that 84 percent of nonfiction circulation fell into only 33 Dewey Decimal categories to guide selections for its bookmobile collections (Little, 1990). And the Skokie (Illinois) Public Library (SPL) has even developed a spreadsheet that lists circulation statistics with other collection-related data, like the number of shelves occupied, the volume count, and the budget allocation for each area. The spreadsheet breaks down information for each Dewey 10 area (i.e., 000, 010, 020, 030) and each subject or format (e.g., fiction and art prints). SPL staff feel that consolidating these data in one comprehensive document allows them to tell quickly which areas of the collection need immediate attention (Jacob, 1990b).

(Text continues on page 176.)

Screening Returned Works

1.   Determine the availability rate that the library wants to achieve. Although studies have found that the average public library meets 50 percent to 65 percent of patron requests for specific items, libraries that want to provide excellent service should try to better this percentage.

2.   Determine, from figure 8.3, the peak circulation rate for achieving the desired availability rate. The peak circulation rate refers to the point at which the availability rate will drop below a certain level. Suppose a library has a 21-day loan period for books and wants to achieve a 70 percent availability rate. It will want to identify all books that circulated six or more times per year, since these items will be off the shelf for an estimated 30 percent of the time or more.

The peak circulation rate will change when the loan period does. Suppose the same library wants to achieve a 70 percent availability rate for compact disks, which have a two-week loan period. The peak circulation rate for these items would be nine circulations.

3.   Record, on the appropriate line of the *Form for Identifying Heavily Used Items* (see figure 8.4), the peak circulation rates for works of various kinds.

4.   Have circulation staff routinely scan the date-due stamps in each item as they check in returned materials. Have staff record, on the *Form for Identifying Heavily Used Items*, works that fall at or above the peak circulation rate.

Note that it will be quicker for staff to quickly identify recent date-due stamps if the library changes, in January of each year, the color of the ink that it uses to stamp due dates. For example, it could use blue ink one year, red the next, and black the third.

5.   As each form is completed, check the shelves, noting circulation patterns of other copies of these titles and of other works by these authors. Modify future selection practices to increase the availability of heavily used items.

Fig. 8.2. Directions for screening returned works.

Peak Circulation Rates for Achieving Selected Availability Rates

DESIRED AVAILABILITY RATE*	LOAN PERIOD, IN DAYS	PEAK CIRCULATION RATE	LOAN PERIOD, IN DAYS	PEAK CIRCULATION RATE	LOAN PERIOD, IN DAYS	PEAK CIRCULATION RATE	LOAN PERIOD, IN DAYS	PEAK CIRCULATION RATE
91-95%	7	4	14	2	21	1	28	1
86-90%	7	7	14	3	21	2	28	2
81-85%	7	10	14	5	21	3	28	2
76-80%	7	12	14	6	21	4	28	3
71-75%	7	15	14	7	21	5	28	4
66-70%	7	17	14	9	21	6	28	4
61-65%	7	20	14	10	21	6	28	5
56-60%	7	23	14	11	21	7	28	6
51-55%	7	25	14	12	21	8	28	6
46-50%	7	28	14	14	21	9	28	7
41-45%	7	31	14	15	21	10	28	8
36-40%	7	33	14	16	21	11	28	8

*These availability rates were calculated by

1. multiplying the annual circulation of each item by the length of the loan period to obtain a rough estimate of the number of days that an item will be absent from the shelves;

2. subtracting this figure from 365 to estimate the number of days the item will be on the shelf and ready for patron use; then

3. dividing the resulting figure by 365 to estimate the percentage of time that the item is on the shelf and available for patron checkout.

Fig. 8.3. Peak circulation rates for achieving selected availability rates.

Identifying Heavily Used Items

Class: _____ Peak circulation rate: _____ Class: _____ Peak circulation rate: _____

Class: _____ Peak circulation rate: _____ Class: _____ Peak circulation rate: _____

Class: _____ Peak circulation rate: _____ Class: _____ Peak circulation rate: _____

Class: _____ Peak circulation rate: _____ Class: _____ Peak circulation rate: _____

Circulation Staff: Please print below the author, title, and call number of each item that has circulated at or above the peak circulation rate.

Author's Name	Title	Call Number

When this page is full, please forward it promptly to the person in charge of collection evaluation.

Fig. 8.4. Form for identifying heavily used items.

Although there are many different methods of analyzing circulation records, the three recommended here are fairly simple. Evaluators can

1. examine circulation totals to see if the use of a class of items is rising or falling;

2. calculate the stock turnover rate for each class of items; and/or

3. calculate the relative use of each class.

Examining Circulation Totals to See If the Use of a Class of Items Is Rising or Falling

Determining whether the use of a class of items is rising or falling is a simple task that can be easily performed by libraries of all sizes and with all resource levels. The library simply examines the percentage of circulation accounted for by that class over several years. Suppose that the library breaks circulation down by format. It might find that, although circulation for the entire collection increased by only 5 percent during the entire three-year period, the circulation of compact disks was 10 percent higher in 1990 and 23 percent higher in 1991 than in 1989. This reveals an ever-increasing demand for these items—one to which the selector should be alerted. Directions for, and the form associated with, determining whether the use of a particular class of items is increasing or waning are shown in figures 8.5 and 8.6.

Calculating the Stock Turnover Rate for Each Class of Items

Calculating stock turnover rate is more time consuming than merely examining trends in use, because it requires that a library know both the number of volumes held in a particular class and the total annual circulation of that class. It then divides total circulation by total holdings to obtain the turnover rate—the average annual circulation per item. Various authors have recommended that libraries of all sizes consider calculating turnover rate for as many classes of items as staff resources allow, because this measure enables a library to compare demand levels for related classes of items.[5] A librarian who knows that the average fiction turnover rate is 1.5 can quickly see that mystery fiction, which has a turnover rate of 6.0, is in more demand than westerns, which have a rate of 0.4. Libraries that do not keep information on the number of volumes held or the annual circulation of different classes of items should begin to record it, whenever this is feasible. Directions for, and the form associated with, calculating the stock turnover rate for each class of items are shown in figures 8.7 and 8.8.

(Text continues on page 182.)

Determining Whether the Circulation of Each Class Is Rising or Falling: Directions

1. Determine for which classes of materials the library has separately recorded annual circulation figures. Record these in column 1 of figure 8.6. Some common classes that the library may keep separate circulation figures for are

Subject Area
>   Broad classification (e.g., 700-799 of the Dewey Decimal Classification System — the arts)
>   Narrower classification (e.g., 740-749 of the Dewey Decimal Classification System — drawing and the decorative arts)
>   Topic-specific classification (e.g., 747 of the Dewey Decimal Classification System — interior decoration)

Genre

General Fiction	Fantasy Fiction	Adventure Fiction
Mystery Fiction	Classic Fiction	Historical Fiction
Romance Fiction	Horror Fiction	Short Stories
Science Fiction	Western Fiction	

Reading Level

Adult	Children's	Easy Reader
Young Adult	Picture Book	

Format

Hardback book	Compact disk	8mm film
Paperback book	Phonograph record	Art print
Large-print book	Videotape	Magazine
Book-on-tape	16mm film	Government publication
Audiocassette		

Location

Main library	Branch library	Bookmobile

2. Record the total annual circulation of items in these classes for the last three years in columns 2, 3, and 4 of the form.

3. Examine these circulation figures to determine whether the use of each class is rising or falling over time.

4. Circle with a black pen those classes whose use has risen significantly during the last three years. Consider allocating more of the materials budget to purchasing works in these classes.

5. Circle with a red pen those classes whose use has fallen significantly during the last three years. Examine these to determine if there is anything wrong (e.g., circulation may be decreasing because no new books in this area have been purchased) or if lack of use seems to reflect a simple decline in popularity of this type of work (e.g., 16mm films). Once the reasons for declining use have been identified, consider changing selection patterns for these classes of works.

Fig. 8.5. Directions for determining whether the circulation of each class is rising or falling.

Determining Whether the Circulation of Each Class Is Rising or Falling

Column 1 Class	Column 2 Total 199__ Circulation	Column 3 Total 199__ Circulation	Column 4 Total 199__ Circulation

Fig. 8.6. Form to determine whether the circulation of each class is rising or falling.

Calculating the Stock Turnover Rate of Various Classes: Directions

1. Determine for which classes of items the library has information on both the total number of volumes held and the total annual circulation. Record these in column 1 of figure 8.8. Group related classes (e.g., all types of adult fiction) together on the form for ease of interpreting the findings.

Some common classes that the library may keep separate records for are

Subject Area
> Broad classification (e.g., 700-799 of the Dewey Decimal Classification System represents the arts)
> Narrower classification (e.g., 740-749 of the Dewey Decimal Classification System represents drawing and the decorative arts)
> Topic-specific classification (e.g., 747 of the Dewey Decimal Classification System represents interior decoration)

Genre

General Fiction	Horror Fiction
Mystery Fiction	Western Fiction
Romance Fiction	Adventure Fiction
Science Fiction	Historical Fiction
Fantasy Fiction	Short Stories
Classic Fiction	

Reading Level

Adult	Picture Book
Young Adult	Easy Reader
Children's	

Format

Hardback book	Videotape
Paperback book	16mm film
Large-print book	8mm film
Book-on-tape	Art print
Audiocassette	Magazine
Compact disk	Government publication
Phonograph record	

Location

Main library	Branch library	Bookmobile

2. Record in column 2 the total annual circulation of each class.

3. Record in column 3 the total number of volumes held in each class.

4. Divide the figure in column 2 by that in column 3 to get the stock turnover rate. Record this figure in column 4.

5. Add the annual circulation figures from column 2 and record here. _____

6. Add the total volume figures from column 3 and record here. _____

7. Divide the figure in line 5 by the figure in line 6 and record the average stock turnover rate for the collection as a whole here. _____

(Fig. 8.7 continues on page 180.)

Fig. 8.7. Directions for calculating the stock turnover rate of various classes.

Calculating the Stock Turnover Rate of Various Classes: Directions — *Continued*

8. Compare the average stock turnover rate for one class with those of the collection as a whole and of related classes. This will help identify areas in which there is particularly heavy demand.

9. Circle with a black pen those classes with turnover rates significantly higher than average. These are classes for which there is currently heavy demand. Ask the selector to strengthen these classes to better meet demand.

10. Circle with a red pen those classes with turnover rates significantly lower than average. Examine these underused classes to determine if anything is wrong. For example, a low use of western might be caused by a lack of interest in this genre among library patrons, but it could also be the result of a dingy, outdated, unappealing collection. Ask the selector to change purchasing patterns to resolve the problems identified.

Calculating the Stock Turnover Rate of Various Classes

Column 1 Class	Column 2 Total Yearly Circulation	Column 3 Total Number of Volumes Held	Column 4 Stock Turnover Rate

Fig. 8.8. Form for calculating the stock turnover rate of various classes in the collection.

Calculating the Relative Use of
Each Class of Items

Circulation totals are even more revealing when they are expressed in terms of relative use. Relative use is a measure that compares the amount of use that a portion of the collection actually receives with the amount of use expected. Suppose that works on economics comprise 3 percent of the total adult nonfiction collection and chemistry 4 percent. Logically, economics should receive 3 percent of the total circulation and chemistry 4 percent. But economics actually accounts for 15 percent of the nonfiction circulation and chemistry for only 1 percent. Economics is an overused class and chemistry an underused class.

Whenever possible and appropriate, relative use calculations should be made by fine rather than broad classes. For example, a breakdown of the 640s, an overused class that contains items relating to home economics and family living, might show that all the overuse comes from 641.5, cookbooks, although the other subclasses are either underused or used at the level expected.

Relative-use figures can be calculated by subject area, genre, reading level, or format. For example, when the Metropolitan Library System in Oklahoma City, Oklahoma, did a relative-use analysis, it found that uncataloged paperbacks represented 16 percent of the collection but accounted for 26 percent of its use. This figure, and analyses that showed that the cost per circulation for paperbacks was less than one-third the cost for hardbacks, led that library to greatly expand its collection of paperback materials (Little, 1979).

One obvious question is "How much does use of a class have to vary from what would logically be expected before it is considered overused or underused?" Mills (1982) correctly notes that it is misleading to examine the raw differences between the percentage of holdings and the percentage of circulation of each class. A subject that occupies 0.6 percent of the collection and receives 0.8 percent of the use would be equivalent, using these calculations, to one that occupied 3.5 percent of the collection and received 3.7 percent of the use. But the discrepancy between holdings and use is 33 percent for the smaller class and only 6 percent for the larger.

Mills suggests that librarians should instead multiply the relative use factor (the percentage of use divided by the percentage of holdings) by 100 to create the percentage of expected use (PEU). This PEU concept is easy for many librarians to understand because it suggests that the expected use of a subject will be 100 percent. The librarian then ranks the PEUs of various classes in a continuum from high to low then designates cutoff points to represent overused and underused classes. For example, classes with PEUs below 80 percent may be labeled underused and those with PEUs above 120 percent overused.[6]

Librarians should be cautious when interpreting relative-use data because the data indicate a deviation from expected behavior but do not explain why this deviation exists. For example, a class could be underused because it contains dated materials, because it contains materials too specialized or technical to meet the needs of patrons, or because the subject matter itself is simply not popular with the library's patrons. The evaluator needs to identify the reasons for underuse or overuse before discussing possible solutions to the problem with the selector.

Because relative-use figures can help libraries identify major collection strengths and weaknesses, they are recommended for libraries of all sizes. Indeed, libraries like the Baltimore County (Maryland) Public Library (BCPL) use them frequently. BCPL has even experimented with allocating shelf space based on the relative use of each Dewey area, weeding sections of low interest to allow for more buying in those of high interest (Rawlinson, 1981). Relative-use figures will be easier to calculate if a library has an automated circulation system that can be programmed to generate information on the number of titles and holdings in a particular class.[7] Libraries lacking such a system will have to spend more time manually calculating relative-use figures. These libraries may wish to phase in relative-use calculations, as staff resources allow. For example, a library could begin calculating relative-use figures for fiction and audiovisual materials one year, add nonfiction from the 000s to the 490s the next, and the remainder of the nonfiction the third. Directions for, and the form associated with, calculating the relative use of each class are shown in figures 8.9 and 8.10.

(Text continues on page 187.)

Calculating the Relative Use of Various Classes: Directions

1. Record, at the top of figure 8.10, the total number of volumes in the circulating collection and the total annual circulation for the collection as a whole.

2. Determine for which classes of items the library knows the total number of volumes held and the total annual circulation. Record these in column 1. Group related classes (e.g., all types of adult fiction) together on the form for ease of interpreting the findings.

Some common classes that the library may keep separate records for are

Subject Area
    Broad classification (e.g., 700-799 of the Dewey Decimal Classification System represents the arts)
    Narrower classification (e.g., 740-749 of the Dewey Decimal Classification System represents drawing and the decorative arts)
    Topic-specific classification (e.g., 747 of the Dewey Decimal Classification System represents interior decoration)

Genre
    General Fiction   Horror Fiction
    Mystery Fiction   Western Fiction
    Romance Fiction   Adventure Fiction
    Science Fiction   Historical Fiction
    Fantasy Fiction   Short Stories
    Classic Fiction

Reading Level
    Adult   Picture Book
    Young Adult   Easy Reader
    Children's

Format
    Hardback book   Videotape
    Paperback book   16mm film
    Large-print book   8mm film
    Book-on-tape   Art print
    Audiocassette   Magazine
    Compact disk   Government publication
    Phonograph record

Location
    Main library   Bookmobile
    Branch library

3. Record in column 2 the total number of volumes held in each class.

(Fig. 8.9 continues on page 185.)

Fig. 8.9. Directions for calculating the relative use of various classes.

Calculating the Relative Use of Various Classes: Directions— *Continued*

4.   Divide each figure in column 2 by the total number of volumes in the circulating collection to obtain the percentage of the total collection occupied by that class. Record these percentages in column 3.

5.   Record in column 4 the number of items that circulated in each class during the past year.

6.   Divide each figure in column 4 by the total annual circulation for the collection as a whole to obtain the percentage of circulation accounted for by that class. Record these figures in column 5.

7.   Divide the figures in column 5 (percentage of circulation) by those in column 3 (percentage of holdings) and multiply by 100 to obtain the percentage of expected use (PEU). Record these figures in column 6.

8.   On a separate sheet of paper, list the PEUs of all classes in rank order. Place the class with the highest PEU at the top, and the lowest at the bottom.

9.   Define the thresholds that represent overused and underused classes. For example, a library may declare classes with PEUs of 120 or above as overused and ones with a PEU of 80 or below as underused.

10.   Purchase more materials, following market-based selection practices, to strengthen overused classes.

11.   Examine underused classes to determine what is wrong. For example, low use of works on South American history might be caused by a lack of interest in the collection, but it could also be the result of the library having an outdated collection of overly technical works on the subject. Change selection practices to resolve the problems identified.

Calculating the Relative Use of Various Classes

Total number of volumes
in the circulating collection: _____

Total annual circulation for
the collection as a whole: _____

Column 1 Class	Column 2 Total Volumes in Each Class	Column 3 Percentage of Collection Occupied by Each Class	Column 4 Annual Circulation of Each Class	Column 5 Percentage of Circulation Accounted for by Each Class	Column 6 Percentage of Expected Use (PEU)

Fig. 8.10. Form for calculating the relative use of various classes.

Identifying Currently Owned Items That Are Not Used

Librarians generally identify poorly used items as part of the weeding process. And most librarians agree that there are many valid reasons to weed, even on an irregular basis. A major one is to stretch shelf space. As public libraries continue to collect newly published items and to diversify by purchasing materials in the new formats that patrons are requesting, their space needs will continue to grow. Yet the governmental bodies that fund libraries cannot always afford to replace crowded facilities; the average public library building is used for 40 or more years (Holt, 1989; Lushington and Mills, 1980). And voters can fail to approve building projects even when the library's funding agency supports this. A recent study found that voters turned down one-quarter of the bond issues proposed in the United States to fund new library buildings or to renovate or expand existing ones (Hall, 1990).

Identifying poorly used items also allows librarians to improve the reliability of the collection by eliminating outdated, erroneous information. Leaving obsolete materials on the shelves can decrease rather than increase patron satisfaction—something that should be avoided whenever possible. Removing obsolete titles and materials in poor physical condition makes it easier for patrons to choose from the titles that remain, thus reducing the costs of using the collection. And weeding outdated works should encourage librarians to search aggressively for replacement items.

But evaluators should also examine poorly used items to determine patterns of nonuse. These patterns indicate a lack of fit between the library's target market and its products—that is, the items in its collection. Recording information about nonuse provides objective data that can help selectors make better decisions about future purchases. It also alerts the library to "good" but little used works already in the collection that might be promoted.

Screening Items in the Circulating Collection to Determine Poorly Used Titles

Libraries will need to consider three questions when screening the collection to identify poorly used titles. The first is "How often should the collection be screened?" Generally, if the collection is small and staff resources permit, an evaluator should try to identify unused works each year (Slote, 1989). Larger libraries and libraries with limited staff resources should try to identify unused titles in each section of the collection at least every other year.

The second question the library must ask is "When should screening take place?" It will be easier for an evaluator to clearly identify trends in use if he examines an entire section of similar works in a fairly short period of time. An evaluator might screen all westerns during the third week of March, all nonfiction videos during the second week of May, and all car-repair books during the fourth week of August.

A final question the library should address is "What is a poorly used title?" This answer will vary greatly depending on the section being examined. A library may consider a book-on-tape that circulates only three times per year poorly used and a philosophical work that circulates the same amount very popular. Nevertheless, the question "What constitutes little or no use?" will be relatively easy to answer if the library knows the stock turnover rate (i.e., the annual circulation per volumes held) for each section of the collection. If the library has followed the procedures spelled out earlier in this chapter, it will have calculated the stock turnover rates for works of different formats, genres, and subject areas and for works designed for use by patrons of different age levels (i.e., children, young adults, and adults).

The library can then multiply the turnover rate by the percentage of the collection that the library is interested in weeding. Titles that fall below the resulting figure will represent the least-used section of the collection and can be considered for weeding. Libraries with severely overcrowded shelves may want to weed as much as 20 percent of the collection. Libraries that want to increase the size of their collection over time may want to weed less stringently, although weeding at least 5 percent to 10 percent of the collection per year is recommended to maintain collection vitality.

The directions for, and forms associated with, screening items in the circulating collection to determine poorly used titles are given in figures 8.11 through 8.14.

Screening Items in the Noncirculating Collection to Determine Poorly Used Titles

Although many libraries identify poorly used works in their circulating collections, generally as part of the weeding process, they often fail to review works in their noncirculating collections: reference works, journals, microfiche, and the like.[8] Yet having collection management information on these works is just as important, especially in light of studies that show that in-house use of materials is generally as high or higher than circulation.[9]

Libraries have often failed to record in-house use because they feel it will take too much time to do so. In part, this is because of an erroneous assumption that the library must record the in-house use of all materials that are consulted but not borrowed. In fact, this is not recommended; much evidence supports the fact that both the general subjects and the individual titles used within a library are largely the same as those borrowed to be used outside the library (Baker and Lancaster, 1991). Therefore, public libraries can save themselves a great deal of effort and expense by recording in-house use information only for those items that do not circulate: microfiche, periodicals, reference works, and the like.

(Text continues on page 194.)

Screening Unused Items in the Circulating Collection

1. Determine which sections of the collection will be screened and how often.

2. Determine when each section will be screened.

3. Answer, for each section, the question "What constitutes little or no use?" An easy way to determine this is to do the following:

a. Divide the total annual circulation of works in this section by the number of holdings in this section to obtain the stock turnover rate (average circulation per title).

b. Determine the percentage of the collection that will be weeded. This figure should be in the 5% to 20% range.

c. Multiply this percentage by the stock turnover rate of a particular section of works. Works whose average yearly circulation falls below this represent that percentage of the collection that is least used. For example, if a library wants to weed 10% of its mystery collection (which has a stock turnover rate of 11.0), it would consider weeding any title whose average yearly circulation fell below 10% x 11.0 — that is, below 1.1.

4. Identify all works whose annual circulation falls at or below this cutoff point. If the library has an automated circulation system, request a printout of all works that meet this criterion, then have a clerical staff member turn these items spine up on the shelves. If the library is not automated, ask a clerical staff member to physically examine the date due slip in each work and turn spine up all low-use items.

Studies have shown that libraries can predict, with less than a 10% error rate, future use of individual items from a single year's worth of circulation data. This error rate will be an acceptable one for most libraries; however, a library can reduce it even further by calculating the average annual circulation rate for each item using circulation records from the past two or three years.

5. Examine spine-up works at the shelves (rather than having the clerk place works on a cart that is moved to the evaluator's desk for screening). This will allow use of each item to be placed in context with other items for that age group, by that author, or of that format, genre, or subject area.

6. Examine each item, noting the title, author, genre, and format. Determine, based on standard weeding criteria, whether the item should be removed from the collection. The most common criteria, other than use, are physical condition, currency, and quality or value of contents (Slote, 1989). Therefore, useful screening questions include the following:

a. Is the work in good physical condition?

b. Does the work contain dated, obsolete, or inaccurate information?

(Fig. 8.11 continues on page 190.)

Fig. 8.11. Directions for screening unused items in the circulating collection.

Screening Unused Items in the Circulating Collection — *Continued*

c.   Is the work valuable enough, for some other reason, to keep in spite of low use? For example, is the work:

listed in *Fiction Catalog, Public Library Catalog*, or on one of ALA's "Notable Books" lists?

written by an author who lives in this city, state, or region?

recipient of a prize or award for its high quality?

part of a series that is not being discarded in its entirety?

one of only a few works of its type, genre, or subject area?

one that has a larger social or historical significance?

7.   Place, on a book cart, titles that are to be weeded: those that are not well used, that contain inaccurate or obsolete information, that are in poor condition, and that are not valuable to the library for some other reason.

8.   List works that would normally be discarded because of low use, but that are deemed valuable enough to be kept, on the *Form for Identifying "Good" but Unused Titles in the Circulating Collection That May Benefit from Promotion* (see figure 8.12). Give completed forms to the person responsible for promoting this section of the collection.

9.   Record the names of authors whose works have received little or no use on the *Form for Identifying Authors with Unused Works in the Circulating Collection* (see figure 8.13). These authors are likely to remain unused over time, although the reasons for this nonuse may vary. For example, the author may not be well known among the local clientele or may write in a dated or technical style. And an author's popularity may wane after his death, because he is no longer creating a demand for his product by writing new works. De-emphasize future purchases of these authors, when relevant.

10.   Note other consistent trends of nonuse on the *Form for Identifying Types of Items in the Circulating Collection That Are Poorly Used* (see figure 8.14). Some of these trends are consistent across many public libraries, like low levels of use of older works in the hard sciences or of subject areas that many people would consider technical or esoteric—like the finer points of differential calculus. Other trends, peculiar to a specific library and clientele, are noticed only with careful scrutiny. For example, a public library in a retirement community may discover that "lust-full" novels (westerns like the Longarm series and "bodice-ripper" romances) are not generally popular with its patrons but that "old-fashioned" stories, like Zane Grey's westerns or Faith Baldwin's romances, are.

Be careful not to make erroneous assumptions when identifying possible reasons for low or falling use. For example, do not mistakenly assume that interest in "high technology" science fiction is dying out if, in fact, the collection is too old to interest the science fiction fans who use the library.

De-emphasize future purchases in these areas, when relevant.

11.   Take the cart of items to be weeded to the technical processing area. Follow the library's standard procedures for removing these works from the collection.

**Identifying Unused Titles in the Circulating Collection
That May Benefit from Promotion**

Directions

1.   List, in the spaces provided, the section of the collection screened, the date the screening occurred, and the call number, author, and title of "good" works that have been lightly used or unused.

2.   Share this information with those responsible for promoting the use of this section of the collection—through book lists, book displays, booktalks, newspaper column listings, or other means.

Section Screened: _____ Date Screened: _____

Call Number	Author's Full Name	Title of Work

Fig. 8.12. Form for identifying "good" but unused titles in the circulating collection that may benefit from promotion.

Identifying Authors with Unused Works in the Circulating Collection

Directions

1.   List, in the space provided, the section of the collection screened, the date this screening occurred, and the full name of each author whose works have been lightly used or unused.

2.   De-emphasize these works in future purchases, when appropriate.

Section Screened: _____ Date Screened: _____

Last Name	First Name	Middle Initial

Fig. 8.13. Form for identifying authors with unused works in the circulating collection.

Identifying Items in the Circulating Collection That Are Poorly Used

Directions

1. List, in the space provided, each type of work whose use is low and give possible explanations for each.

2. De-emphasize these kinds of works in future purchases, when relevant.

Type of Work   Possible Reasons for Low Use

_____

_____

_____

_____

_____

_____

_____

_____

_____

_____

_____

_____

_____

_____

_____

_____

_____

_____

_____

Fig. 8.14. Form for identifying types of items in the circulating collection that are poorly used.

Although various methods of measuring in-house use exist, the one recommended here is a practical method of recording use on a day-to-day basis.[10] The library simply places signs near items that do not circulate that ask patrons to put items they have used on tables or in specially marked areas, rather than reshelving them. Staff members collect these items at least once a day, stamp (on a label fixed to the inside front or back cover of the item) the date on which the items were used, then reshelve the items. These stamped labels serve the same purpose as the date-due labels in circulating titles: they provide a permanent record of use in each work. When evaluators are ready to screen certain sections of the collection, they can rather quickly scan the labels to identify heavily used items — or, for that matter, poorly used ones.

This method of recording in-house use will underestimate use to some extent, because some patrons will ignore the signs and reshelve items anyway (Rubin, 1986a, 1986b). However, because an underestimate is better than no estimate, this method is recommended as a practical and viable way of recording data that can be used to make collection management decisions for noncirculating items. Directions for, and the form associated with, screening the noncirculating collection to identify poorly used items are given in figures 8.15 and 8.16.

(Text continues on page 198.)

Screening the Noncirculating Collection to Identify Poorly Used Items

1. Determine which sections will be screened and how often.

2. Determine when each section will be screened.

3. Answer, for each section, the question "What constitutes little or no use?"

The library will need to determine this rate separately for each section of the collection. To do this,

a. draw a random sample of items from the section under investigation;

b. add the total number of uses recorded during the last year on the date-used label affixed to each work (that is, add together the total annual use figures for each of the works in the sample);

c. divide this figure by 100 to give the average annual use per item;

d. determine the percentage of the collection to be weeded (from 5% to 20%); and

e. multiply this percentage by the average annual use per item to obtain a cutoff point for weeding.

4. Identify all works whose annual use falls at or below this cutoff point. Have a clerical staff member physically examine the date-used label affixed to each work and turn spine up all low-use items.

Studies have shown that libraries can predict, with less than a 10% error rate, future use of individual items from a single year's worth of use data. This error rate will be an acceptable one for most libraries; however, a library can reduce it further by calculating the average annual use rate for each item from date-used records that cover two to three years.

5. Examine spine-up works at the shelves (rather than having the clerk place works on a cart that is moved to the evaluator's desk for screening). This will allow use of each item to be placed in context with other items for that age group, by that author, or of that format, genre, or subject area.

6. Examine each item, noting the title, author, genre, and format. Determine, based on standard weeding criteria, whether the item should be removed from the collection. The most common criteria, other than use, are physical condition, currency, and quality or value of contents (Slote, 1989). Therefore, useful screening questions include the following:

a. Is the work in good physical condition?

b. Does the work contain dated, obsolete, or inaccurate information?

(Fig. 8.15 continues on page 196.)

Fig. 8.15. Directions for screening the noncirculating collection to identify poorly used items.

Screening the Noncirculating Collection to Identify Poorly Used Items — *Continued*

c.   Is the work valuable enough, for some other reason, to keep in the collection in spite of low use? For example, is the work

listed in *Fiction Catalog, Public Library Catalog,* or on one of ALA's "Notable Books" lists?

written by an author who lives in this city, state, or region?

recipient of a prize or award for its high quality?

part of a series that is not being discarded in its entirety?

one of only a few works of its type, genre, or subject area?

one that has a larger social or historical significance?

7.   Place, on a book cart, titles that are to be weeded: those that are not well used, that contain inaccurate or obsolete information, that are in poor condition, and that are not valuable to the library for some other reason.

8.   List, on figure 8.16, specific titles (e.g., series of reference works) and types of works that the library should consider discontinuing or de-emphasizing in future purchases due to low use.

9.   Take the cart of items to be weeded to the technical processing area. Follow the library's standard procedures for removing these works from the collection.

Identifying Noncirculating Items with Low Use

Directions

1. List, in the space provided, specific titles or types of works whose use is low and give possible explanations for each.

2. De-emphasize these kinds of works in future purchases, when relevant.

Title/Type of Work   Possible Reasons for Low Use
_____

_____

_____

_____

_____

_____

_____

_____

_____

_____

_____

_____

_____

_____

_____

_____

_____

_____

_____

Fig. 8.16. Form for identifying noncirculating items with low use.

Identifying Items That Are Not in the Collection but Are Desired by Patrons and Potential Patrons

The third task in a comprehensive marketing-based evaluation program differs considerably from the first and second tasks. Rather than identifying currently owned items that are unused or heavily used, evaluators work to identify items that are not in the collection but that might be purchased to meet the needs of community residents.

In the past, librarians have often done this informally, as the opportunity arose. For example, a librarian might examine a collection after hearing a patron complain that she was unable to find a current price guide for antique furniture. But the type of program recommended here is a more active one in which evaluators regularly and systematically seek information about specific authors, titles, and types of works that might be added to the collection.

This chapter does not advocate spending a great deal of time soliciting the recommendations of people who are hard-core nonusers. As earlier chapters have noted, people who fall into this category do not tend to read or to use the types of media that public libraries stock. Therefore, they are unlikely to be interested in making purchase suggestions.

However, libraries are encouraged to solicit ideas on how the collection might be improved from a second group of nonusers: those defined as "potential patrons" because, although they do not use the public library, they do use the types of resources that the library offers. As noted in previous chapters, some potential patrons may be unaware of what the library has to offer; they never developed the library habit as children and simply don't think of it as a source for the types of materials they need. Others may be aware of the library's services but find that the collection does not meet their needs. One library director in Illinois said she learned a lot when she got married. Her new husband told her that he quit using the library because he had found it was unlikely to have on the shelves at the time he sought them two types of materials: recent materials about new computer software programs and current best-selling books. The librarian actively solicited his suggestions and those of other potential patrons before working with staff to change the library's purchasing patterns.

One problem, of course, is identifying groups of potential patrons so their suggestions can be obtained. An easy and cost-effective way of doing this is to identify clubs or organizations that these people might belong to, then work with these groups and their representatives. Historical societies and science fiction clubs are good examples of organizations that may contain potential patrons, but there are many less obvious ones as well. For example, a computer club could provide recommendations about software that might be purchased, a mothers' club about child development materials, and a gourmet club about cookbooks.

Librarians can seek, from each group that agrees to help, concrete information about the types of items and the specific authors and titles that group members would find useful. The librarian can check these suggestions against the library's current holdings, upgrade the collection as necessary, and promote the improved collection to the group that helped make it better as well as other potential users.

Because of the time commitment involved in performing each of these tasks, libraries will be unable to contact all clubs and organizations that could be of help. Therefore, they will need to decide how many market segments they can feasibly serve and which of those groups identified should be targets in their marketing efforts. As chapter 3 notes in some detail, this decision will be influenced by the roles the library has chosen to pursue, the size and diversity of the target markets, the viability of reaching each market segment, and possible humanitarian or public relations advantages associated with serving particular target markets.

There are several different approaches evaluators can use to collect information about the kinds of materials that might be added to a particular collection. These are examining interlibrary loan records, analyzing unanswered reference and readers' advisory questions, soliciting patron suggestions for new purchases, and surveying patrons and potential patrons using questionnaires or focus group interviews.

Identifying Wanted Items by Examining Interlibrary Loan Records

Many public libraries automatically consider ordering for their own collections the materials that are requested on interlibrary loan. Ideally, this is done in light of the library's mission and the roles it has chosen for itself. For example, a library fulfilling the role of *popular materials center* might purchase, rather than borrow, materials written by authors with continuing popularity (such as Carl Sagan or Dorothy Gilman), current materials on popular subjects, and duplicate copies of popular titles. The same library would consider borrowing requested titles that are not likely to have a broad-based appeal—like a book detailing how sod houses were built in northwest Iowa in the nineteenth century, a first novel written in German, or a biography of a lesser-known astronomer.

The practice of reviewing interlibrary loan requests at the time they are made is a valuable one, because it enables the library to quickly obtain titles desired by patrons. Moreover, studies have shown that most interlibrary loan requests are for current, in-print titles and that works purchased as a result of interlibrary loan requests tend to have circulation rates comparable to those of titles selected by library staff.[11]

Nevertheless, librarians should, on a regular basis, examine past interlibrary loan requests to determine whether there are specific types of materials for which recurring requests are made, so that purchasing patterns can be changed. For example, a public library that has installed a CD-ROM version of InfoTrac may note a number of loan requests for magazines that are indexed in that database but not owned by the library; it can subsequently purchase the most requested of these titles. Analyzing interlibrary loan requests by author, format, genre, and subject area is an especially useful exercise. Such analysis can even be done via computer if the library has a circulation system or interlibrary loan subsystem that can be programmed in this fashion.[12]

Libraries of all sizes and resource levels can perform the type of interlibrary loan screening recommended here because it is simple and requires only a small amount of staff time. However, because interlibrary loans account for less than 3 percent of the circulation of most public libraries,[13] librarians should, whenever possible, supplement this kind of screening with other forms of feedback about the types of works patrons and potential patrons want added to the collection. Figure 8.17 lists directions for screening interlibrary loan records.

1. Review, on a monthly basis, each title that has been requested on interlibrary loan.

2. Check to see whether works by this author are being heavily used. If so, consider changing selection practices so future demand can be met.

3. Check to see whether other works in this subject area, genre, or format are being heavily used.

4. If so, consider changing selection practices so future demand can be met.

Fig. 8.17. Directions for screening interlibrary loan requests.

Identifying Wanted Items by Analyzing Unanswered Reference and Readers' Advisory Questions

Many libraries record the subject matter of all reference questions that they cannot answer, so they can determine whether specific sections of the nonfiction collection need to be augmented. Libraries can record similar information about unanswered readers' advisory questions to meet the needs of patrons who request aid with finding fiction and other popular materials. Both of these practices are excellent ones that can be adopted by libraries of all sizes and resource levels, because they are fairly simple and require little staff time to accomplish. Directions for, and the form associated with, screening unanswered reference and readers' advisory questions are shown in figures 8.18 and 8.19.

Identifying Wanted Items by Soliciting Patron Suggestions for New Purchases

Today, most libraries collect and record suggestions for purchase in a sporadic rather than systematic fashion. This manner of record-keeping results in fewer suggestions being collected and in some not being attended to. However, libraries of all sizes and resource levels can cheaply and easily make capturing

(Text continues on page 203.)

Screening Unanswered Reference and Readers' Advisory Questions

1. Have reference staff record the nature of each reference or readers' advisory question that was unanswered. Note this information on a simple form of the type shown in figure 8.18.

2. Have reference staff review, at least once a month, each question that was recorded on this form to see whether it is related to the roles that the library has chosen to serve. A library should be able to answer questions that are related to both the primary and secondary roles it has chosen. For example, a library that has adopted a role of *preschoolers' door to learning* should own one or more sources that would answer a question about the general developmental stages of children. However, one could not fault the library for lacking a source that would answer a question about the technical specifications of the type of laser beams that are used in eye surgery, if the library had ruled out the role of *research center*.

3. Forward role-related questions to the person responsible for selection in each area. They should consider making purchases that will help the library answer these types of reference and readers' advisory questions.

Fig. 8.18. Directions for screening unanswered reference and readers' advisory questions.

Listing Unanswered Readers' Advisory and Reference Questions

Directions

1.   Record below each reference or readers' advisory question that could not be answered. List additional questions on separate sheets.

_____

_____

_____

_____

_____

_____

_____

_____

_____

_____

_____

_____

_____

_____

_____

_____

_____

_____

_____

_____

Fig. 8.19. Form for listing unanswered readers' advisory and reference questions.

these suggestions a normal and systematic part of the routine if they train each staff member who works at a public service desk to ask each patron whether he found what he was looking for. This practice takes only a small amount of time but can readily identify specific titles that are being sought. Moreover, having their comments solicited makes patrons feel that the library is paying attention to their needs. Directions for, and the form associated with, soliciting patron suggestions are shown in figures 8.20 and 8.21.

Identifying Wanted Items by Surveying Patrons and Potential Patrons Using Questionnaires or Focus Group Interviews

Over the years, literally hundreds of surveys have asked patrons and potential patrons what they like to read, watch, and listen to. Results of many of these studies have been interesting but rather general. For example, Lucas (1980) found that patrons tended to read in the areas of their life interests (e.g., career and family patterns, hobbies). She also discovered that libraries that served residents with higher levels of education need a wider range of materials, because these residents tend to have a broader range of reading interests. More recently, Gajerski (1989) documented that patrons of the Edmonton (Alberta) Public Library wanted additional copies of the most popular books and magazines, more audiovisual materials, and a larger range of current magazines and newspapers.

Although general studies like these can help libraries determine what broad patterns of collection development they might strive for over time, most libraries will want to obtain more specific suggestions about the types of materials that patrons and potential patrons desire for their collections. This will be easier to do if the library does one of two things:

1. Asks for in-depth comments about one section of the collection at a time. Ideally, this will be a section that is given priority in the library's strategic plan or that has been identified as greatly in need of improvement. For example, the library could focus on improving its collection of travel books, easy readers, science fiction works, or recreational videotapes.

2. Focuses on a particular target market. For example, the Chicago Public Library used a survey to determine the collection-related needs of one group of public housing residents before developing plans for library service to public housing communities in general (Spiller, 1989). Chang and Har-Nicolescu (1983) determined that Asian-Americans had strong needs for materials on obtaining citizenship, English-language instruction, other continuing education programs, career counseling, health services, community cultural groups, and events celebrating their culture. In some instances, the choice of target market will be dictated by the roles the library has chosen to play. In others, it will be influenced by the section of the collection under examination. For example, a library that is interested in updating its career development materials could solicit suggestions for improvement from high school students, guidance counselors, and area career development specialists.

(Text continues on page 206.)

Soliciting Patron Suggestions:
Directions

Ideally, staff members who work at each public service desk (circulation, reference, audiovisual, etc.) should

1.   ask each patron who visits the desk: "Were you looking for a specific item or type of work today? (If so,) did you find what you wanted?"

Asking these questions alerts staff to patrons whose needs are not fully satisfied. Staff can then ask follow-up questions about whether patrons checked the catalog or asked the reference librarian for help. If not, patrons can be given further assistance.

2.   ask patrons who are still unable to find what they wanted if they would complete a purchase suggestion form of the type shown in figure 8.21.

Note that some libraries will want to save time by requesting that the patron complete one of the order cards that staff routinely uses, rather than figure 8.21. This is acceptable as long as the order card

a.   is short and easy to complete;

b.   requests information about desired authors, titles, subject areas, genres, and formats; and

c.   asks the patron if he wishes to discuss his collection needs further with a librarian.

3.   give each completed form to the person responsible for selecting materials in that section of the collection.

Fig. 8.20. Directions for soliciting patron suggestions.

Purchase Suggestion Form

The library welcomes your suggestions for purchase. Please list below works that you would like to see added to the collection. We will consider every purchase suggestion seriously, although, due to budget considerations, we may not be able to order everything you want. Thank you.

Subject area, genre area, or format of work desired:

Title desired:

Full name of author, composer, or producer of this work:

Publisher and publication date (if known):

If you would like someone on our staff to call you to discuss your request, please list your name and telephone number below.

Fig. 8.21. Purchase suggestion form.

Two popular methods of obtaining in-depth comments about a collection are the patron questionnaire and the focus group interview. Questionnaires are often used when a library wants to survey a target market that is comprised of some subset of library users—like people with children in tow or people browsing through the compact disks. Staff can simply ask these users to complete and return questionnaires during a regular library visit.

Questionnaires can also be effective if the library wants to reach a target market outside the library that has an easily identifiable set of members. For example, the Atwood-Hammond (Illinois) Public Library had students in local junior high and high school classes complete questionnaires to determine their general levels of interest in reading, the places where they obtained reading material, and the types of books they most liked to read (Obert, 1988). It will, of course, cost more to survey target markets outside the library, because the librarian must travel to the group to distribute the surveys or mail them to members of the target market. Directions for using materials preference questionnaires and a sample questionnaire are shown in figures 8.22 and 8.23.

Directions for Conducting Focus Group Studies

Unfortunately, there are many target markets, like women who work outside the home, that have many members but no identifiable membership list. These target markets will be difficult for libraries to survey cheaply—a major consideration given existing resource levels. Therefore, libraries that wish to learn what types of items people in these target groups desire should consider conducting focus group interviews instead.[14]

Focus groups are comprised of 10 to 15 users or potential users who have an interest in the section of the collection being evaluated and who are willing to donate one to two hours of their time to sharing their knowledge. A moderator interviews the group by guiding a joint discussion about specific steps the library can take to meet the collection-related needs of group members. Ideally, the interviews are taped to give the library a record of all suggestions made.

The main purpose of focus groups is to solicit patron suggestions about what an ideal collection might contain, but they provide several other benefits. First, the interactions that occur during focus group discussions often reveal why patrons feel the way they do—revelations that are crucial if a library desires to increase levels of use or satisfaction with the collection. When the Iowa City (Iowa) Public Library (ICPL) wanted to improve its business collection, staff members questioned seven groups of people from various types of businesses (e.g., service, manufacturing, and retail businesses) about the ideal collection that would meet their needs. The focus groups revealed that few business people actually used library resources to help them in their work. The main reason for these low levels of use was lack of knowledge about what the library had to offer, because few people read the library's newsletter or saw (because they did not visit the library) the signs, brochures, and other materials promoting business resources that were displayed in the library building (Baker, 1991a).

(Text continues on page 209.)

Using Materials Preference Questionnaires

1. Determine whether the library will pass out questionnaires to all persons in the target market or a sample of the same. The former can be done if the number of persons in the target market is relatively small. If the target market is large, the library can obtain reliable information about how the collection may be improved if it draws a representative sample. Read Hernon and McClure (1990) and other standard research guides in the field for information on choosing a representative sample.

2. (If the library is surveying a group of people other than its own users,) ask for cooperation from group leaders and/or members of the target market.

3. Design a survey form that asks members of the target market about

a. their knowledge of the collection under study;

b. their use of this collection;

c. their general suggestions for improving this collection; and

d. their specific suggestions for authors, titles, and types of works that the library might buy.

An example of this type of survey, designed for distribution to all those who browsed among or who checked out a work from the videotape collection during a two-week period, is shown in figure 8.23.

The questionnaire should be short, easy to complete, and worded in a clear and unbiased fashion. Read Powell (1991) or other standard research guides in the field for information on designing effective questionnaires.

4. Pretest the questionnaire by asking five to six members of the target group to complete it. Review each question asked with each person surveyed to ensure that its meaning is clear and unambiguous.

5. Revise the questionnaire in light of pretest comments.

6. Photocopy as many copies of the revised questionnaire as needed.

7. Distribute the questionnaire.

8. Tally and summarize the results.

9. Consider changing selection practices, when relevant, as a result of these findings.

Fig. 8.22. Directions for using materials preference questionnaires.

Videotape Preference Questionnaire

Thank you for agreeing to take five minutes to give us your suggestions for improving our collection of videotapes.

The library has a number of different collections of videotapes. For each kind listed, please check whether you were aware of this collection, whether you have used it during the last year, and (if so) how often this use occurred.

Videotape Collection	Were you aware of this collection?		Have you used this collection during the last year?		If so, state approximately how many times
	Yes	No	Yes	No	
Horror films					
Science fiction films					
Comedy films					
Action/adventure films					
Drama					
PBS television shows (e.g., "Nova")					
Music videos					
Exercise videos					
How-to-do-it videos					
Walt Disney movies					
Other children's films					

Are there any specific films that you would like the library to purchase for its collection?

Do you have any other suggestions on how the collection might be improved?

If you would like to talk further about this matter with the librarian who is responsible for this collection, indicate your name, address, and telephone number below.

Please return completed forms to the circulation desk. Thank you for your time and your suggestions.

Fig. 8.23. Videotape preference questionnaire.

A second side benefit is that focus group participants are often able to provide useful suggestions about how a library can promote its collection to the types of people whom the participants represent. For example, participants in the focus group study mentioned above suggested that ICPL should publicize its business collection and services in the Chamber of Commerce newsletter, which most of the businesses in town received, and through small tours designed to meet the needs of specific target markets—like real estate agents and governmental employees.

A third benefit is that focus group participants may learn more about resources in the collection simply by listening to their colleagues talk. The library can also distribute, at the end of each session, information on the resources in the collection and can give short tours. Those who attended the business focus groups at ICPL said that these discussions had made them more aware of and more likely to use the collections (Baker, 1991a).

If the library can afford to, it should schedule more than one focus group for each collection under discussion. This will increase the number of suggestions for improvement. It will also help the library determine which issues are most important to participants, because these will be mentioned repeatedly in different groups. The Orange (New Jersey) Public Library followed this practice in 1990 when it scheduled a series of 10 focus groups: five each focused on determining the collection-related needs of (a) parents who wanted to expose their children to reading and other library services and (b) adults who came to the library to check out popular materials for their own use (Baker, 1991c).

Directions for surveying community residents via focus group discussions are given in figure 8.24. These assume that the library has already determined the collection and the target markets on which they will focus.

(Text continues on page 212.)

Conducting a Focus Group Interview

As part of the initial planning for the interview, the librarian should

1.   Develop a list of questions that focus specifically on this collection. The questions should be open-ended to encourage discussion and should be placed in a logical order. They should concentrate on the participants' current impressions of this collection, their levels of use or nonuse of this collection, and their suggestions for how this collection might be improved. Typical questions might include:

What do you know about the library's collection of materials on _____?
Do you or does anyone you know use the collection now?
If so, how?
If not, why not?
What do you currently like about this collection?
How might the library improve this collection?
Could the library do anything to promote use of this collection more effectively?

2.   Have the list of questions typed up for later distribution to focus group participants.

3.   Decide how many focus groups will be planned. Scheduling more than one will allow the library to obtain a broader base of suggestions and to identify themes common to all groups.

4.   Choose the dates and times of the focus group interviews. Many patrons will find it convenient to attend on weekday evenings or weekend afternoons. Allow one and one-half hours for each session. This time period is long enough to allow in-depth discussion to develop but short enough to recruit willing participants.

5.   Choose the location(s) where the focus group interviews will be held. Ideally, interviews should take place within the library to permit participants to review, if they choose, the library's collection. Choose meeting rooms capable of seating 10 to 20 people around a conference table.

6.   Determine whether interviews will be limited to current patrons or will include potential patrons as well. Although it may be harder to persuade potential patrons to participate, they may have better insight than current patrons about why an existing collection is not used.

7.   Solicit from library staff, friends, trustees, and patrons, the names, addresses, and telephone numbers of people who might be willing to donate one to two hours to answer the library's questions. The librarian should ask about three times as many people to come as will be needed, because there is a large dropout rate between the number of persons invited and the number who actually participate.

(Fig. 8.24 continues on page 211.)

Fig. 8.24. Directions for conducting a focus group interview.

Conducting a Focus Group Interview — *Continued*

8. Write to possible participants, explaining what the library is trying to accomplish and giving the dates and times of the interviews. Include the list of questions that will be asked, so they can think about the issues in advance. Include self-addressed stamped postcards so those invited can inform the library which, if any, focus group session they will be attending.

9. Choose someone to serve as moderator. The moderator should be empathetic and possess good social and communication skills so group members will feel comfortable talking freely in a group of strangers. He should also have some training in soliciting comments in a way that will not bias results. Note that, whenever possible, the moderator should not be a library staff member, since this may inhibit critical comments from group participants.

10. Call and remind focus group participants about the interviews two to three days before they are scheduled to come.

On the day of each focus group study, the librarian should

1. Have a volunteer make coffee for participants, run the tape recorder during the actual session, and record the names of all persons who attend.

2. Make sure that the moderator understands what needs to be done. This person must greet participants, explain the library's purpose in conducting this sort of study, ask the questions that have been decided on, encourage discussion among participants, obtain clarification when necessary, and tactfully move the discussion forward if anyone tries to dominate the discussion.

After the focus group interview is finished, the librarian should

1. Write thank-you notes to all who attended.

2. Have the tape recording transcribed.

3. Class the suggestions into broad categories for easy review.

4. Determine which of the suggestions are both appropriate and affordable.

5. Change selection practices, when appropriate.

Identifying Other Barriers That Inhibit Use of the Collection

The fourth task in the product-analysis approach to collection development is identifying other barriers that inhibit use of the collection. As Kantor (1976) notes, these may be related to factors associated with

1. acquisitions (e.g., the library may not own the needed item);

2. circulation (e.g., another patron may be using the title);

3. library errors (e.g., misshelving may prevent the item from being located); or

4. patron errors (e.g., a patron may look for Ellis Peters's latest novel in the general fiction collection rather than in the mystery section).

The easiest way to identify these barriers is to conduct a materials availability study. Such a study can determine the percentage of materials that are immediately available when patrons seek them. It can also determine the extent to which each of the above barriers is hindering availability.

Availability (or fill-rate) studies fall into two broad categories. In a citation-based availability study, the library examines the roles it has chosen to emphasize, then compiles lists of citations that represent the needs of patrons that are related to each of these. Suppose, for example, that a library has identified primary roles of *popular materials center* and *children's door to learning* and secondary roles of *independent learning center* and *formal education support center* for area high schools and community colleges. Such a library may wish to have, in its citation pool, a sample of items that

1. have appeared on various best-selling lists during the last six months;

2. are listed in four standard bibliographies appropriate for a broad audience of children and adults: *Children's Catalog, Elementary School Library Collection, Fiction Catalog*, and *Public Library Catalog*; or

3. are contained in the bibliographies and reading lists used by teachers at the high schools and community colleges that the library serves.

The evaluator checks each citation in the pool against the library's catalog to see if it is owned, determines whether owned items are available for circulation, and, if not, determines why. Because the time necessary to compile a good citation pool can be extensive, and because citation-based availability studies provide no information about patron skills in using the catalog or in locating desired items, this book recommends that libraries should conduct patron-based availability studies instead.

The popularity of patron-based availability studies has risen during the last few years, in part because this type of measurement is promoted in *Output Measures for Public Libraries* (Van House and others, 1987). In such a study, staff distribute questionnaires that ask patrons entering the library on selected days to record the specific items or types of items they are seeking and whether these are found.

Planning Materials Availability Studies

There are several guidelines public libraries should follow when planning this type of materials availability study. The first is that the library should consider conducting separate availability studies at each of its major outlets. This is because availability rates from one location may not be representative of all libraries within the system. For example, central libraries tend, because they have larger collections, to have higher fill rates than branch libraries.[15] Fill rates may also vary from branch to branch, depending on the size of the collection, the composition of the clientele, the success of branch librarians in targeting their collections to meet patron needs, and other factors.

The second guideline is that the library should conduct separate availability studies for print materials and nonprint materials. This practice is recommended because availability rates differ significantly by format. Higher levels of demand, as for popular videotapes and books-on-tape, account for some of this difference. Another large portion may result from using different methods and procedures for acquiring, processing, and storing audiovisual materials than for print materials.

The third guideline is that to ensure that the data collected are representative of all library users, the library should collect information on a fairly large number of items that patrons are requesting. Collecting a sample of 500 requests will ensure that the library obtains reliable data on the total percentage of patron needs that it is filling (Kantor, 1984). It will also allow the library to break down information by class (that is, by format, genre, or broad subject area) during the analysis stage. Such breakdowns are desirable because availability rates can differ by class. Ideally a library would work first on correcting those rates that are lowest, such as those for highly popular formats, genre areas, or subjects. If this type of fine analysis is contemplated, the evaluator needs to avoid the temptation of breaking down the sample into too many small subdivisions, each containing only a handful of items. This is because availability rates calculated on a handful of items may not be representative of the total group of items. To yield data on which accurate availability figures may be calculated, each of these smaller classes should contain no fewer than 75 items.

The library should also take steps to encourage as many patrons as possible to participate in the study. This will increase the likelihood that the data collected will be representative. Participation can be increased if the evaluator posts signs throughout the library that inform patrons that a study is in progress and that librarians will request their cooperation. It will also be helpful for the library to assign someone to distribute blank questionnaires as patrons enter the library and collect completed ones as they leave.

Finally, the library should use a fairly sophisticated questionnaire to measure availability rates, rather than the questionnaire recommended in *Output Measures for Public Libraries*. That latter form, shown in figure 8.25, will collect accurate information on title fill rate. After all, success in that case is an objective measure: either the title is found or it is not.

However, it is almost impossible to determine a real, rather than an inflated, browsing fill rate using this survey form, because most library patrons, when asked whether they found "something" to meet their needs, will say yes. In fact, almost all of the libraries using this form report filling more than 90 percent of their patrons' browsing needs.[16]

Using this form will also produce subject and author fill rates that are artificially high, because the questionnaire does not discriminate between patrons who are fully satisfied with the item they checked out and those who are partially successful. For example, a bicyclist may have wanted a book describing, in some detail, bicycle tours through the Cotswolds in England but settled for a book that lists the names of organizations that offer English biking tours. A fiction reader may have settled for one of Robert Ludlum's earlier novels when he really wanted to read that author's latest work. To effectively determine subject and author fill rate, an evaluator needs to determine, at minimum, whether the patrons' needs were fully satisfied, partly satisfied, or not satisfied.

Finally, the form shown in figure 8.25 does not allow calculation of a genre fill rate, although public libraries typically check out as much fiction as nonfiction. A revised questionnaire, the Print Materials Availability Survey (figure 8.26), corrects each of these problems. Directions for completing the Print Materials Availability Survey are in figure 8.27.

Analyzing Materials Availability Data

Regardless of the type of availability study performed, the evaluator's main purposes are to

1. note how often items were located; and

2. if they were not located, to determine why.

A library will want to note the percentage of title, author, subject, and genre searches that were fully or partly successful for two reasons. First, these figures can document the difficulties that patrons have in finding what they want and convince library staff that improvements need to be made.[17] Second, these figures can serve as baseline availability rates. Once a library has determined why patrons were unsuccessful in their searches and has established programs to help correct these problems, it can remeasure availability rates and compare them to these baseline figures to see how much improvement has resulted.

(Text continues on page 219.)

LIBRARY SURVEY

Form number _____

Library _____   Date _____

PLEASE FILL OUT THIS SURVEY AND RETURN IT AS YOU LEAVE.

We want to know if you find what you look for in our libraries. Please list below what you looked for today. Mark "YES" if you found it, and "NO" if you did not find it.

TITLE	
If you are looking for a specific book, record, cassette, newspaper, or issue of a magazine, please write the title below. Include any reserve material picked up.	

NAME OF WORK	FOUND?
(Example)	
• Gone with the Wind	YES NO
1.	
2.	
3.	
4.	
5.	

SUBJECT OR AUTHOR	
If you are looking for materials or information on a particular subject or a special author today, please note each subject or person below.	

SUBJECT OR AUTHOR	DID YOU FIND SOMETHING?
(Examples)	
• how to repair a toaster	
• any book by John D. MacDonald	YES NO
1.	
2.	
3.	
4.	
5.	

BROWSING   If you were browsing and not looking for anything specific, did you find something of interest?

YES _____   NO _____

OTHER   _____ Check here if your visit today did *not* include any of the above activities. (Example) using the photocopy machine.

COMMENTS   We would appreciate any comments on our service and collections on the back of this sheet.   THANK YOU!

Fig. 8.25. Library survey (materials availability form) from *Output Measures for Public Libraries*.

Print Materials Availability Survey

Our library is interested in improving the quality of our collection. If you are seeking a book, magazine, newspaper, pamphlet, or other printed item today, could you please take time to complete this survey? You may return it to any staff member as you leave. Thank you.

Date _____

If you are looking for a printed work with a specific TITLE, please complete SECTION 1. Otherwise, skip to SECTION 2.

SECTION 1.

Please list below each title that you sought today, then tell whether you found it.

TITLE OF WORK	Did you find this work in our collection?	
	Yes	No
Example: Gone with the Wind		
1.		
2.		
3.		
4.		
5.		
6.		

If you are looking for a printed work by a specific AUTHOR, please complete SECTION 2. Otherwise, skip to SECTION 3.

SECTION 2.

Please list below the name(s) of each AUTHOR you sought today, then tell whether you found a work by this author that met your needs.

AUTHOR (list last name, then first name)	Did you find a work by this author that met your needs?		
	Yes	No	Partially
Example: Shakespeare, William			
1.			
2.			
3.			
4.			
5.			
6.			

(Fig. 8.26 continues on page 217.)

Fig. 8.26. Print materials availability survey.

Print Materials Availability Survey — *Continued*

If you were seeking a fictional (that is, imaginary work) of a particular GENRE or TYPE, please complete SECTION 3. Otherwise, skip to SECTION 4.

SECTION 3.

Some people like to read books of a specific type or genre. Some common types are:

Mystery fiction	Fantasy fiction	Historical fiction
Romance fiction	Classic fiction	General fiction
Science fiction	Horror fiction	Large-print fiction
Western fiction	Adventure fiction	Short stories

Please indicate below the type or genre of fiction that you sought and tell whether you found something in our collection that met your needs.

Type of fiction sought	Did you find something in our collection that met your needs?	
	Yes	No
Example: Science fiction	X	
1.		
2.		
3.		
4.		
5.		

If you were seeking a factual work on a particular SUBJECT, please complete SECTION 4.

SECTION 4.

Many people like to read works about a particular subject—like materials that discuss World War I, spelunking, a famous person, or how to sew. Please indicate below the subject of each factual work that you sought and tell whether you found something in our collection that met your needs.

SUBJECT	Did you find a work on this subject that met your needs?		
	Yes	No	Partially
1.			
2.			
3.			
4.			
5.			

Thank you for taking time to help us with this survey!

Completing the Print Materials Availability Survey:
Directions

This survey was designed for patrons who are looking for print materials. The library should conduct a separate availability study if it wishes information from patrons looking for audiovisual materials. Also, each branch library should conduct its own availability study, because fill rates may differ significantly from one library location to another.

The library should choose two weeks of the year in which to conduct the study. One of these should be in March or October, because public library circulation is typically highest then. The other week should be chosen from the winter or summer months.

In preparation for each week of the survey, the evaluator should

1.   Photocopy a week's supply of the survey form shown in figure 8.26. In many libraries, 60% to 70% of the patrons who enter will be seeking print materials. Some librarians may know the average number of patrons who visit the library each week (i.e., the door count). If so, the librarian can multiply this figure by .70 to determine the number of forms needed. The librarian must, to obtain reliable data, collect information on 500 patron requests. If the total number of desired requests has not been collected by the end of the specified week, the librarian should extend the survey until the requests have all been gathered.

2.   Sharpen a supply of pencils that patrons can use to complete survey forms.

3.   Arrange for a volunteer to distribute forms to every patron who is seeking printed materials during that week and to gather completed forms before the patron leaves the library.

4.   Arrange for a staff member to check the catalog, shelves, and circulation records at the end of each day of the survey to see why certain titles were not found.

5.   Tell all staff members when the survey will be distributed.

6.   Prepare a box in which completed surveys may be dropped and place it near the door of the library.

During each survey week, the volunteer should

1.   Realize that it is important to get as many patrons as possible to complete the form, because the reliability of the results will be higher when this is done.

2.   Ask each patron entering the library if he is (a) seeking print materials and (b) willing to complete the form.

3.   Give a blank questionnaire to patrons who say "yes." People who visit the library more than once during the week should be given a separate form to complete each time they are seeking materials.

At the end of each survey day, the librarian should check the catalog and circulation records for each title in section 1 that was not found, to see why the books were unavailable. Determine the reason for nonavailability, using the codes shown in instruction 1 of the section entitled *Directions for Determining How to Increase the Library's Title Fill Rate* (see figure 8.29). Mark this code in the right margin of the *Print Materials Availability Survey*, next to the corresponding title.

At the end of the survey week, the librarian should complete the forms shown in figures 8.28 through 8.32 to determine the title, author, genre, and subject fill rate and to identify ways that these might be increased.

Fig. 8.27. Directions for completing the print materials availability survey.

Determining the exact reasons why patrons were unsuccessful is not terribly difficult. On the same day patrons complete their searches, library staff should check the catalog, the shelves, and the circulation area to determine why each desired item was not found. The evaluator examines the results in some detail, determines which of four barriers to availability is causing the problems, then recommends corrective action to prevent, or at least decrease, the chances of these problems recurring. Logically, most libraries proceed by trying to improve first those factors that show the lowest probability for success or that are expected to give the most improvement for the least cost. If the problem is not a collection development issue, the evaluator passes on the information to the appropriate person to correct.

Forms for analyzing the Print Materials Availability Survey are in figures 8.28 through 8.32.

(Text continues on page 226.)

Determining the Library's Title Fill Rate

1.   Count the total number of titles sought
by all patrons (from section 1 of the *Print
Materials Availability Survey*) and list this
figure here.   _____

2.   Count the total number of titles found by
all patrons (from section 1 of the *Print
Materials Availability Survey*) and list this
figure here.   _____

3.   Divide line 2 by line 1 to obtain the
library's TITLE FILL RATE.   _____

4.   Review the results. The average public library fills 50% to 65% of
patron requests for specific titles. A library will want to obtain as high
a title fill rate as it possibly can, given its financial resources.

Fig. 8.28. Directions for determining the library's title fill rate.

Determining How to Increase the Library's Title Fill Rate

1.   Count the total number of titles from the *Print Materials Availability Survey* that were marked with each of the two-character codes listed below. List these figures in the spaces provided. Add the figures within each section to obtain the total number of titles that were unavailable because of a particular group of factors.

ACQUISITIONS BARRIERS AFFECTING AVAILABILITY

Code   *Reason for Nonavailability*

A1.   The library does not own the title.   _____

A2.   The library has ordered the title, but it has not yet
          been received.   _____

A3.   The library has received the title, but it has not yet
          been cataloged and processed.   _____

   TOTAL NUMBER OF TITLES THAT WERE UNAVAILABLE
   BECAUSE OF BARRIERS RELATED TO ACQUISITIONS   _____

CIRCULATION BARRIERS AFFECTING AVAILABILITY

Code   *Reason for Nonavailability*

C1.   The item is checked out to another borrower.   _____

C2.   The item is long overdue from another patron. No
          replacement decision has been made.   _____

   TOTAL NUMBER OF TITLES THAT WERE UNAVAILABLE
   BECAUSE OF BARRIERS RELATED TO CIRCULATION   _____

LIBRARY ERRORS AFFECTING AVAILABILITY

Code   *Reason for Nonavailability*

L1.   The item is unavailable because it is being rebound,
          repaired, recataloged, or relabeled.   _____

L2.   The item is "Missing."   _____

L3.   The item is checked in but is not reshelved.   _____

L4.   The item is misshelved.   _____

L5.   The call numbers on the item and in the catalog do
          not agree (e.g., book is marked FIC GREEN; catalog
          is marked MYST FIC GREEN; patron cannot find
          the title).   _____

L6.   A staff member is using the item but has failed to
          check it out.   _____

   TOTAL NUMBER OF TITLES THAT WERE UNAVAILABLE
   BECAUSE OF LIBRARY ERRORS   _____

(Fig. 8.29 continues on page 222.)

Fig. 8.29. Directions for determining how to increase the library's title fill rate.

Determining How to Increase the Library's Title Fill Rate — *Continued*

PATRON ERRORS AFFECTING AVAILABILITY

Code   Reason for Nonavailability

U1.   Even though the title is in the correct place on the
shelf, the patron does not locate it.   _____

TOTAL NUMBER OF TITLES THAT WERE UNAVAILABLE
BECAUSE OF PATRON ERRORS   _____

2.   Read the information given below to determine causes of low availability rates and possible solutions for increasing them. The best way to proceed is to improve first the factor or factors that are causing the most problems or that are expected to give the greatest improvement for the least cost.

Acquisitions Factors That Affect Availability Rates

If many titles sought by users have not been ordered, the library's collection development policies may be at fault. Sometimes the reason for an acquisitions problem is easy to identify. For example, the fill rate for books may have decreased when a portion of the book fund was reallocated to purchase magazines.

At other times, it may be necessary to get a better idea of where the acquisitions problem lies by breaking down the availability figures by the type of work requested. For example, a librarian may determine, through scanning, that most of the titles not available are mysteries and could allocate a higher percentage of the collection budget to that genre.

In yet other cases, the availability problem may be related to difficulties with receiving or processing items. This is particularly likely in larger libraries with a big cataloging backlog. This problem is related less to the library's selection practices than to the priority placed on the quick processing of new materials and can be corrected by eliminating the backlog.

Circulation Factors That Affect Availability Rates

Often a print item that a patron is seeking will be checked out to another user. Although occasional circulation "interference" is normal, most libraries own a number of titles that are so popular that all copies are regularly checked out. That is, the number of copies of a single work present on the shelves also influences availability. As discussed in an earlier section of this chapter, the most common methods for increasing the likelihood that popular works will be available when patrons want to use them are to purchase more copies of popular titles or shorten the length of their loan periods. These strategies for increasing availability are discussed in some detail in chapter 9.

Library Errors That Affect Availability Rates

A library error occurs when the catalog indicates ownership but the title is not in circulation or on its allotted shelf. The book may be missing or it may be in some area not identified in the catalog.

The library can correct the problems of misshelving and slow reshelving by maintaining full strength in the reshelving unit. It can reduce the missing titles problem by installing an electronic security system, inventorying the collection and eliminating the catalog cards for those items not found, or dealing, on a case-by-case basis, with titles thought to be missing. If a book is found to be missing, the selector for that area should determine, as quickly

(Fig. 8.29 continues on page 223.)

Determining How to Increase the Library's Title Fill Rate—*Continued*

as possible, whether or not the item is to be replaced. If so, the order should be placed immediately, and the replacement copy processed as soon as it arrives. If not, the catalog should be corrected.

A more difficult problem is created by books that are temporarily located somewhere other than their regular places on the shelves. These may be sitting on a staff member's desk or awaiting rebinding or repair. This problem can be solved, at least partially, in those libraries with automated catalogs that list such temporary locations. Nonautomated libraries can reduce this type of error by installing signs that direct patrons to check with library staff members when they cannot find specific items. Such signs should be located at the catalog and at various entrances to and strategic locations within the stacks.

Occasionally, a different problem arises: the actual location of an item is changed but the catalog is not. This may happen, for example, if the library marks a book with a genre label and shifts its location but fails to mark the catalog entry. Again, the solution is simple but not inexpensive. The catalog record for any item that has permanently changed its location should be updated to reflect the change.

Patron Errors That Affect Availability Rates

The term "patron error" is somewhat misleading, because it implies that the error is entirely the patron's fault. This is not always true. For example, patrons may be unable to locate the picture book section simply because it was not marked with an appropriate sign. In fact, one set of researchers confirmed that "patron errors" decrease as patron familiarity with the idiosyncracies of a particular library increases (Rinkel and McCandless, 1983). Librarians should, therefore, try to anticipate simple and frequently occurring patron errors and plan ways to avoid them.

Many patrons err when searching the catalog for specific titles because they lack basic catalog-use skills. Providing bibliographic instruction, reference librarian help, or clear directions on how to use the catalog may reduce this kind of error.

A related error occurs when the patron correctly locates a title in the catalog but then (1) incorrectly records the call number or (2) relies on short-term memory of the number when trying to retrieve the book. Providing pencils and paper slips on which patrons can record the number or installing printers at on-line catalog terminals may reduce these types of errors.

Some patrons, even when they have the correct call number, may look in the wrong location for an item. Librarians can help correct this problem by designing better guiding and orientation systems. They can also post signs, at the catalog and in the stacks, encouraging patrons to ask for help, because fill rates tend to increase when the librarian helps the patron search for materials.

Determining the Author Fill Rate

1. Examine section 2 of the *Print Materials Availability Survey*. Count the total number of authors sought and record this information here. (Note: If an author is listed here by more than one patron, count each listing separately.)

                     _____

2. Count the total number of authors that were found and record this information here. (If an author is listed here by more than one patron, count each listing separately.)

                     _____

3. Divide the figure listed on line 2 by the figure on line 1. List the AUTHOR FILL RATE here.

                     _____

4. Determine whether this is an acceptable fill rate. Remember that the average public library can provide only 50% of the items that its patrons have requested. When the fill rate is unacceptable, it is generally due to acquisitions or circulation factors. The librarian can review the discussion of acquisitions and circulation barriers that appear in figure 8.29 to see what steps may be taken to improve the fill rate.

Fig. 8.30. Directions for determining the author fill rate.

Determining the Genre Fill Rate for Fiction

1. Examine section 3 of the *Print Materials Availability Survey*. Count the total number of times a patron indicated that a genre was sought and record this information here.   _____

2. Count the total number of times a patron indicated that a genre was found and record this information here.   _____

3. Divide the figure listed on line 2 by the figure on line 1. List the GENRE FILL RATE here.   _____

4. Determine whether this is an acceptable fill rate.

5. If the fill rate is not acceptable, count the number of times each genre (e.g., classic fiction) was sought and the number of times each was found. Determine if a particular genre (e.g., mystery fiction) accounted for most of the problems. If so, the library should consider purchasing more fiction of this type, shortening the length of the loan period, or taking some other action (e.g., using rotating deposit collections, soliciting donations of works) that would increase availability.

Fig. 8.31. Directions for determining the genre fill rate for fiction.

Determining the Subject Fill Rate

1. Examine section 4 of the *Print Materials Availability Survey*. Count the total number of times a patron indicated that a subject was sought and record this information here. _____

2. Count the total number of times a patron indicated that a subject was found and record this information here. _____

3. Divide the figure listed on line 1 by the figure on line 2. List the SUBJECT FILL RATE here. _____

4. Determine whether this is an acceptable fill rate.

5. If the fill rate is not acceptable, scan the data to see whether specific subject areas contributed heavily to the problem. If so, the library should consider purchasing more works in these subject areas, shortening the length of the loan periods, or taking some other action to increase availability.

Fig. 8.32. Directions for determining the subject fill rate.

Conclusion

The type of product analysis recommended here is very different from collection evaluation done on an irregular or infrequent basis for puposes of weeding or inventory control. It requires that a library make a conscious choice to devote resources to systematically and comprehensively collecting data about how the collection is used or not used, as well as what it does not contain. Although a program of this sort is not inexpensive, the data it provides can be used to make consistent collection management decisions that can increase availability of desired titles and types of materials. The growing use of automated circulation systems in many libraries will make much of this data collection easier, although libraries with manual systems can use any or all of the techniques recommended here.

Finding competent staff to coordinate collection evaluation efforts would also make data collection easier. Currently, many public libraries do not assign evaluation duties to one person; rather they expect each of their selectors to become familiar with evaluation methods and then to evaluate that subset of the collection for which he purchases material. Because this often involves duplication of effort, it is quite wasteful of resources. Moreover, some of the tasks mentioned here (e.g., the materials availability study) are best conducted as part of an integrated evaluation plan. Ideally, the coordinator assigned to head such a plan should have both an in-depth understanding of collection development principles and practices and a solid knowledge of research methods to ensure that the data gathered are reliable and valid.

One further point needs to be made. Although the major purpose of undertaking these product-analysis tasks is to aid in the selection and promotion of library materials, evaluation data may also be examined to confirm that the library has chosen an appropriate set of roles for itself. That is, if the library has chosen the role of *independent learning center*, data collected during this analysis process should show that patrons are in fact using the materials that support such a role. In a few cases, however, a comprehensive and objective analysis may reveal that the roles a library has selected are inappropriate. For example, one public library in the Midwest that has begun to do more collection evaluation is realizing that it should have chosen *popular materials center* as one of its primary roles, because more than half its circulation comes from providing resources for its patrons' recreational reading and use. That is, the product analysis has caused the library to rethink whether the roles it has selected are in line with the needs of its patrons.

Notes

[1]The ideas expressed in this chapter are an expansion of those first developed in Baker (1991b).

[2]See, for example, Condous (1983).

[3]See, for example, Baker and Lancaster (1991), Powell (1990), American Library Association (1989), Wortman (1989), Robbins and Zweizig (1988), and Magrill (1985).

[4]Only a few studies have examined this issue. These have generally found that patrons both use and enjoy the materials they check out from the library (see, for example, Baker, 1983). This is not surprising because most patrons examine the works at least superficially at the library and leave on the shelves those that they are not interested in using.

[5]See, for example, Van House and others (1987).

[6]An alternative option is to calculate the mean PEU, determine the standard deviation, then label classes with PEUs that are one or more standard deviations above or below the mean as overused or underused. This practice, which has been described in some detail by Dowlin and Magrath (1983), will classify about a third of the classes of materials as underused or overused and therefore in need of some attention.

[7]Some automated systems are so flexible that they allow relative use to be calculated by subject and location simultaneously (see, for example, Nimmer, 1980). This is quite useful because branch libraries within the same system might receive different amounts of use in the same subject area because of different interests of the clients they serve.

[8]A few libraries do regularly analyze the in-house use of back issues of newspapers and periodicals in storage, because patrons must request access to these (see, for example, Lenahan, 1989).

[9]In a review of in-house use studies in all types of libraries, Baker and Lancaster (1991) found that ratios of in-house use to circulation ranged from 0.1:1 to 11.2:1.

[10]Rubin (1986a, 1986b) provides an excellent review of these.

[11]See, for example, Roberts and Cameron (1984), Pritchard (1980), and Trevvett (1979).

[12]See, for example, O'Connell and Miller (1977).

[13]See, for example, National Center for Education Statistics (1991).

[14]Two works that give a more comprehensive description of the focus group process are Drabenstott (1992) and American Library Association (1988). Other works that describe how individual public libraries have used the focus group process to identify problems and make changes are Baker (1991a) and Hutton and Walters (1988).

[15]See, for example, Detweiler (1980).

[16]See, for example, Public Library Association (1989).

[17]See, for example, Mansbridge (1986) and Kuraim (1983).

References

American Library Association. *Guide to the Evaluation of Library Collections*. Chicago: American Library Association, 1989.

_____. "To the Sharper Image: Using Focus Groups to Find Out What the Public Really Wants." Audiotape of a panel discussion presented at the American Library Association Conference, New Orleans, 9 July 1988.

Baker, Sharon L. "An Adult User Survey." *Illinois State Library Statistical Report* 7 (May 1983): 1-33.

_____. "Improving Business Services Through the Use of Focus Groups." *RQ* 30, no. 3 (Spring 1991a): 377-85.

_____. "Public Libraries." In *Collection Management: A New Treatise*, ed. Charles B. Osburn and Ross Atkinson, 395-416. Greenwich, Conn.: JAI Press, 1991b.

_____. "Results of Focus Group Interviews, December 1990, for the Orange Public Library." Unpublished consultant's report, University of Iowa, School of Library and Information Science, 1991c.

Baker, Sharon L., and F. W. Lancaster. *Measurement and Evaluation of Library Services*. 2d ed. Arlington, Va.: Information Resources Press, 1991.

Brooks, Terrence A. "Naive Vs. Sophisticated Methods of Forecasting Public Library Circulations." *Library and Information Science Research* 6, no. 2 (April 1984a): 205-14.

_____. "Using Time-Series Regression to Predict Academic Library Circulations." *College and Research Libraries* 45, no. 5 (November 1984b): 501-5.

Chang, Henry, and Suzine Har-Nicolescu. "Needs Assessment of Library and Information Service for Asian American Community Members in the United States." In *Task Force on Library and Information Services to Cultural Minorities*, 79-99. Washington, D.C.: National Commission on Libraries and Information Science, 1983. ERIC ED241015.

Condous, Crystal. "Non-Profit Marketing—Libraries' Future?" *Aslib Proceedings* 35, no. 10 (October 1983): 407-17.

Detweiler, Mary Jo. "Availability of Materials in Public Libraries." In *Libraries' Effectiveness: A State of the Art*, ed. Neal K. Kaske and William G. Jones, 76-83. New York: American Library Association, 1980.

Dowlin, Ken, and Lynn Magrath. "Beyond the Numbers: A Decision Support System." In *Proceedings of the 1982 Clinic on Library Applications of Data Processing*, ed. F. W. Lancaster, 27-58. Urbana: University of Illinois, Graduate School of Library and Information Science, 1983.

Drabenstott, Karen Markey. "Focused Group Interviews." In *Qualitative Research in Information Management*, ed. Jack D. Glazier and Ronald R. Powell, 85-104. Englewood, Colo.: Libraries Unlimited, 1992.

Eggers, Lolly. "More Effective Management of the Public Library's Book Collection." *Minnesota Libraries* 25, no. 2 (Summer 1976): 56-58.

Gajerski, B. "Edmonton Public Library: 1989 User Survey." Edmonton Public Library, Edmonton, Alberta, 1989. ERIC ED327184.

Giacoma, Pete. *The Fee or Free Decision*. New York: Neal-Schuman, 1989.

Hall, Richard B. "The Votes Are In." *Library Journal* 115, no. 11 (15 June 1990): 42-46.

Hernon, Peter, and Charles R. McClure. *Evaluation and Decision Making*. Norwood, N.J.: Ablex, 1990.

Holt, Raymond. *Planning Library Buildings: From Concept to Completion*. Metuchen, N.J.: Scarecrow Press, 1989.

Huston, Mary M. "Fee or Free: The Effect of Charging on Information Demand." *Library Journal* 104, no. 16 (15 September 1979): 1811-14.

Hutton, Bruce, and Suzanne Walters. "Focus Groups: Linkages to the Community." *Public Libraries* 27, no. 3 (Fall 1988): 149-52.

Jacob, Merle. *Collection Development Plan for the Skokie Public Library.* Skokie, Ill.: Skokie Public Library, 1990a.

_____. "Get It In Writing: A Collection Development Plan for the Skokie Public Library." *Library Journal* 115, no. 14 (1 September 1990b): 166-69.

Kantor, Paul B. "Availability Analysis." *Journal of the American Society for Information Science* 27, nos. 5-6 (September 1976): 311-19.

_____. *Objective Performance Measures for Academic and Research Libraries.* Washington, D.C.: Association of Research Libraries, 1984.

Kuraim, Faraj Mohamed. "The Principal Factors Causing Reader Frustration in a Public Library." Ph.D. diss., Case Western Reserve University, 1983.

Lenahan, Nancy M. "Use of Periodicals and Newspapers in a Mid-Sized Public Library." *Serials Librarian* 16, nos. 3-4 (1989): 1-7.

Little, Paul. "Collection Development for Bookmobiles." In *The Book Stops Here: New Directions in Bookmobile Service*, ed. Catherine Suyak Alloway, 59-73. Metuchen, N.J.: Scarecrow Press, 1990.

_____. "The Effectiveness of Paperbacks." *Library Journal* 104, no. 2 (15 November 1979): 2411-16.

Lucas, Linda Sue. "The Range of Life Interests and Reading Interests Among Adult Users of Public Libraries in Communities of Various Sizes." Ph.D. diss., University of Illinois, 1980.

Lushington, Nolan, and Willis N. Mills, Jr. *Library Designed for Users: A Planning Handbook.* Hamden, Conn.: Library Professional Publications, 1980.

Magrill, Rose Mary. "Evaluation by Type of Library." *Library Trends* 33, no. 3 (Winter 1985): 267-95.

Mansbridge, John. "Availability Studies in Libraries." *Library and Information Science Research* 8, no. 4 (October-December 1986): 299-314.

McGinn, Howard F. "Libraries and Marketing: New Worlds—Old Worlds." *North Carolina Libraries* 46, no. 3 (Fall 1988): 126-31.

Mills, Terry R. "The University of Illinois Film Center Collection Use Study." Unpublished report. University of Illinois, Graduate School of Library and Information Science at Urbana, 1982. ERIC ED227821.

Moreland, George B. "Operation Saturation: Using Paperbacks, Branch Libraries in Maryland Conduct an Experiment to Equate Book Supply with Patron Demand." *Library Journal* 93, no. 10 (15 May 1968): 1975-79.

National Center for Education Statistics. *Public Libraries in 50 States and the District of Columbia: 1989.* Washington, D.C.: U.S. Department of Education, Office of Educational Research and Improvement, 1991.

Nimmer, Ronald J. "Circulation and Collection Patterns at the Ohio State University Libraries, 1973-1977." *Library Acquisitions: Practice and Theory* 4, no. 1 (1980): 61-70.

Obert, Beverly. "Collection Development Through Student Surveys and Collection Analysis." *Illinois Libraries* 70, no. 1 (January 1988): 46-53.

O'Connell, Michelle D., and A. Patricia Miller. "COCTAILS: Automated Interlibrary Loan Statistics at Health Sciences Library, SUNYAB." *Bulletin of the Medical Library Association* 65, no. 2 (April 1977): 250-54.

Powell, Nancy, ed. *Pacific Northwest Collection Assessment Manual.* 3d edition. Salem: Oregon State Library Foundation, Pacific Northwest Conspectus Database, 1990.

Powell, Ronald R. *Basic Research Methods for Librarians.* 2d ed. Norwood, N.J.: Ablex, 1991.

Pritchard, S. J. "Purchase and Use of Monographs Originally Requested on Interlibrary Loan in a Medical School Library." *Library Acquisitions: Practice and Theory* 4, no. 2 (1980): 135-39.

Public Library Association. *Public Library Data Service Statistical Report '89.* Chicago: Public Library Association, 1989.

Rawlinson, Nora. "Give 'Em What They Want." *Library Journal* 106, no. 20 (15 November 1981): 2188-90.

Rinkel, Gene K., and Patricia McCandless. "Application of a Methodology Analyzing User Frustration." *College and Research Libraries* 44, no. 1 (January 1983): 29-37.

Robbins, Jane, and Douglas L. Zweizig. *Are We There Yet? Evaluating Library Collections, Reference Services, Programs, and Personnel.* Madison: University of Wisconsin-Madison, School of Library and Information Studies, 1988.

Roberts, Michael, and Kenneth J. Cameron. "A Barometer of 'Unmet Demand.' " *Library Acquisitions: Practice and Theory* 8, no. 1 (1984): 31-42.

Rubin, Richard. *In-House Use of Materials in Public Libraries*. Urbana: University of Illinois, Graduate School of Library and Information Science, 1986a.

_____. "Measuring the In-House Use of Materials in Public Libraries." *Public Libraries* 25, no. 4 (Winter 1986b): 137-38.

Slote, Stanley J. *Weeding Library Collections*. 3d ed. Littleton, Colo.: Libraries Unlimited, 1989.

Spiller, David. "The Provision of Fiction for Public Libraries." *Journal of Librarianship* 12, no. 4 (October 1980): 238-65.

Spiller, Deborah J. "Library Service to Residents of Public Housing Developments: A Study and Commentary." *Public Libraries* 28, no. 6 (November-December 1989): 358-61.

Trevvett, Melissa D. "Characteristics of Interlibrary Loan Requests at the Library of Congress." *College and Research Libraries* 40, no. 1 (January 1979): 36-43.

Van House, Nancy A., Mary Jo Lynch, Charles R. McClure, Douglas L. Zweizig, and Eleanor Jo Rodger. *Output Measures for Public Libraries*. 2d ed. Chicago: American Library Association, 1987.

Wortman, William A. *Collection Management: Background and Principles*. Chicago: American Library Association, 1989.

Marketing-Based Selection Practices

9

If collection evaluation is the first step in the marketer's program of collection management, selection is the second. But today's libraries face two major stumbling blocks in selecting materials for integrated collections that will meet the varying needs and desires of a wide spectrum of patrons. The first, as Bryant (1987) notes, is the tendency in most libraries to subdivide selection responsibilities in a variety of ways (e.g., by subject, reading level, and format) and then assign them to a number of different people, each of whom brings his own selection philosophy to the process. Although this can add richness to the library's collection development program, it can also "inhibit the collection's systematic development if pursued without leadership. At some point, inconsistencies in approach to collection development are discovered; some segments of the collection are growing disproportionately to others in terms of the literature from which they are derived, the use they receive, and the relationship of patron need to the avowed mission of the library" (Bryant, 1987, 114).

The second barrier to systematic collection development is a tendency for librarians to begin their selection with subjective impressions of which purchases have worked in the past and which have not. Although there is no doubt that subjective impressions can help librarians make valid selection choices, studies have shown that the more objective data the librarian has available, the more likely that collection development decisions will be made wisely.[1]

This chapter discusses how a library can work to resolve both of these problems and build collections that are consistent with a societal-marketing orientation. Such collections are developed with the needs of individual patrons and the community as a whole in mind. A library can achieve this by taking four steps to establish marketing-based selection practices throughout the entire library system. These steps are

1. writing a collection development policy that indicates how the roles it has chosen will influence collection development;

2. reviewing materials budget allocations to ensure that these are consistent with what the library is trying to accomplish;

3. establishing a centralized selection unit to do formula-based purchasing; and

4. asking professional selectors to review the objective data that have been collected about past and present use of the collection, then follow the three marketing principles when making selections (see page 247).

Each of these steps is discussed below.

Writing a Collection Development Policy That Indicates How the Roles Chosen Will Influence Collection Development

As noted in chapter 3, many public libraries today are analyzing the information-related needs of their communities, then choosing two to four primary and secondary roles on which they will focus. Although role setting, in general, can help libraries stretch limited resources wisely, it can also provide blueprints that can aid in collection development efforts. For this reason, libraries should indicate, in their collection development policies, the roles chosen and the effects of these choices on collection development efforts.[2] One library system that has followed this tactic is the Minneapolis Public Library and Information Center. A primary role for its Washburn Community Library is "to provide support to adults and children in their endeavors to learn. Library staff members make frequent contacts with local schools and the library provides a wide range of materials to support classroom assignments of elementary and secondary students. The library provides materials and services to children and those working with or intending to work with children, for the ultimate purpose of encouraging reading. It provides a collection which meets the needs of many adult students who are enrolled in formal education or independently learning about a topic of interest" (Minneapolis, 1990, 86).

This particular collection development policy illustrates the fact that branch libraries may choose to emphasize different roles from either the central library or other branches. For example, the central library in Minneapolis has chosen *reference library* as a primary role and *popular materials center* and *research center* as secondary roles, while the Roosevelt Community Library has chosen *popular materials center* and *children's door to learning* as its primary roles. Role selection oriented to specific branch libraries, rather than to the system as a whole, is appropriate whenever the clients of different branches have different needs and should be spelled out in the collection development policy.

Reviewing Materials Budget Allocations to Ensure That These Are Consistent with What the Library Is Trying to Accomplish

Most public libraries today spend between 15 percent and 25 percent of their total operating budget on materials (National Center for Education Statistics, 1991). Public libraries that adopt a societal-marketing orientation will want to ensure that most of these funds are used to foster the roles the library has chosen and to strengthen collections that do not meet patron demand, without detracting from the library's ability to meet the long-term interests of its community. Therefore, a library will want to examine its budget allocations for materials, determine how much money it is spending on materials for different user groups and on various formats, genres, or subject areas, and make any necessary corrections.

Each library will need to address three major questions in its review. The first two require fairly concrete answers about how allocations will be made among different classes of materials: Are budget allocations for materials in line with the roles the library has chosen? Should budget allocations be changed because of information collected during the product analysis stage? The answer to the third question — How will the library's duplication policy influence how much money will be spent within a particular budget category? — is more complex because it requires that the library make a major philosophical decision. Each of these issues is discussed below.

Are Budget Allocations in Line with the Roles the Library Has Chosen?

One of the strengths of *Planning and Role Setting for Public Libraries* (McClure and others, 1987) is its recommendation that a library funnel the bulk of its personnel and monetary resources toward improving the quality of collections and services that support from one to four roles carefully selected to meet community needs. The question that arises, therefore, is: how much money should be directed toward each primary and secondary role? As figure 9.1 shows, McClure and others (1987) recommend that public libraries should consider directing 40 percent to 50 percent of their resources toward pursuing their primary roles and 30 percent to 40 percent toward their secondary ones. Maintenance roles, which by definition are those on which the library is not focusing, should receive only 20 percent.

Although these budget breakdowns were originally recommended for overall library activities, a public library can use these percentages as a rough guideline when determining whether it needs to reallocate its materials budget. For example, a library that has chosen a primary role of *popular materials center* and a secondary role of *children's door to learning* will not want to spend 70 percent of its materials budget on purchasing a large and diverse collection of adult nonfiction. Rather, it should devote about 40 percent to 50 percent of its budget to purchasing popular materials (both fiction and nonfiction) in all formats and another 30 percent to 40 percent to purchasing materials for children. The remaining 20 percent can be spent on other areas — like the local history and reference collections.

One library that has followed this practice is the Crawford Memorial Library (CML) in Monticello, New York. CML serves a resort community whose population ranges from 20,000 in the winter to almost 100,000 in the summer. But its annual circulation was only about 46,000 items — much lower than might be expected. The new director felt this was due to the library's failure to match collection resources to community needs. He followed the procedures specified in *Planning and Role Setting for Public Libraries* and determined that CML should concentrate on only two roles: *children's door to learning* and *popular materials center*. He then raised the percentage of the materials budget that was devoted to each role. For example, the percentage allocated to purchasing children's materials was temporarily increased from 10 percent to a full 50 percent to help correct glaring deficiencies in that area (Barrish and Carrigan, 1991).

Level of Priority	Large Libraries or Libraries with Extensive Resources	Branch/Small Libraries or Libraries with Moderate Resources	Effort/Commitment Level
Primary	1-2 Roles	1 Role	40%-50%
Secondary	1-2 Roles	1-2 Roles	30%-40%
Maintenance Level	Remainder of Library Roles and Activities	Remainder of Library Roles and Activities	20%

Reprinted with permission from McClure and others (1987, 43).

Fig. 9.1. Recommended number of role priorities.

Should Budget Allocations Be Changed
Because of Information Collected During
the Product Analysis Stage?

At this time a library will also wish to examine three types of information gathered during the product analysis stage to determine whether it should shift money from one budget category to another. Information collected on the *Form to Determine Whether the Circulation of Each Class Is Rising or Falling* will indicate whether allocations should be increased or decreased because of strong and continuing changes in use patterns. Information recorded on the *Form for Calculating the Stock Turnover Rate of Various Classes in the Collection* and the *Form for Calculating the Relative Use of Various Classes* will indicate which classes of materials (subject areas, genres, and formats) are overused and underused. The library will want to reduce allocations for collections that are underused because they are not being demanded by patrons (e.g., 16mm films). It can then use these monies to "fix" classes that are underused because they contain materials that are inappropriate for clients (e.g., materials that are out-of-date or overly technical) and to strengthen overused classes so they will better meet patron demand.

How Will the Library's Duplication Policy Influence
How Much Money Will Be Spent Within a
Particular Budget Category?

As has been noted throughout this book, most public libraries have title availability rates of 50 percent to 65 percent. This means that 35 percent to 50 percent of a library's patrons cannot find, on the shelves and ready for checkout, specific titles they are seeking on any one day. The most common reason for these low availability rates is that the titles sought are checked out to other users (Kuraim, 1983). This fact is not too surprising because about 80 percent of the circulation in the average library comes from about 20 percent of its works.[3] In other words, the bulk of patrons are competing for a small percentage of titles.

The question then becomes: what can libraries do to improve their availability rates? The germ of the answer is noted in an observation made more than 15 years ago by Buckland (1975) that three major factors influence the availability rate of a specific title:

1. the level of patron demand for it

2. the number of copies the library provides for users

3. the length of its loan period

Changes in any of these will directly affect the likelihood of a book being checked out to another user.

The level of patron demand for a title is generally influenced by factors outside the librarian's control, except in specific cases where the library is promoting the work. For example, demand may rise suddenly when a local teacher assigns 100 students to read Nathaniel Hawthorne's *The Scarlet Letter* or when a particular book is mentioned on the television show "Nova." Because the library has no influence over promotion efforts that it does not institute itself, it is generally forced to rely on two methods of increasing the availability of titles. It can

1. duplicate titles that are, or are predicted to be, heavily used; or

2. shorten the length of the loan period for popular works.

Duplicating Titles That Are, Or Are Predicted to Be, Heavily Used

Today, librarians are increasingly making the decision to systematically duplicate popular items. This action represents a shift in buying patterns, because until about 15 years ago, most libraries were hesitant to purchase more than one or two copies of most works for each branch within their systems. As Robinson noted in 1976, "Although recent studies have shown that a considerable number of duplicate copies are necessary to satisfy patron demands for popular titles, libraries ordinarily minimize duplication. There is little attempt to utilize the dicta that 'nothing sells merchandise like merchandise' by having adequate quantities at the point of sale. The effect of this lack of availability on customer reaction to library service is largely unknown, but it would appear to inhibit repeat business" (1976, 2). Why, then, have librarians been so reluctant to purchase multiple copies of popular works? The answer is rather complex.

First, broad-scale evaluation efforts used to be the exception rather than the rule. As a result, few librarians realized how often popular works were off the shelf and, therefore, unavailable for patron use. Moreland (1968) describes one of the earliest studies to explore this issue. An in-house survey at the Montgomery County (Maryland) Library revealed that 25 percent of its patrons were dissatisfied with library service. Of these, 65 percent noted that the books they wanted were not on the shelves when they wanted them. To combat this problem, librarians at 11 branches identified 122 titles that they felt were in continuous demand. Most of these were modern-day classics—like *Fahrenheit 451, To Sir with Love*, and *Black Like Me*. Each librarian chose 60 titles from this list, ordered at least 10 (uncataloged) paperback copies of each, then placed the books in their collections. The librarians checked the shelves at regular intervals to ensure that patrons could always find a copy of each work, reordering books in multiples of five whenever the supply of a title on hand was reduced to three copies. During the 11-month study period, these 11 branches bought a total of 21,821 copies of the 122 titles. But they still had not yet reached the satisfaction point—the point where one copy was always available—for all titles selected by each branch.

This experiment in duplicate buying was originally designed to raise user satisfaction. But its real value lay in making staff at the Montgomery County Library realize that their former purchasing patterns, which emphasized buying only one or two copies of each work for each branch, were inadequate. This and other published studies since that time have reinforced this concept for the larger library world.

A second reason that public librarians have been reluctant to duplicate works was because they feared they would end up spending the bulk of their materials budgets on best-selling titles. But, in actuality, many kinds of items are in short supply on the shelves of most libraries: modern-day classics like those in the Montgomery County study as well as older classics like *The Adventures of Huckleberry Finn* and *Vanity Fair*; recent materials in popular subject areas, like cooking, child care, income tax preparation, and home maintenance; items that have received various kinds of awards for their quality, like a Grammy, Oscar or Pulitzer prize; materials by authors with long-standing reputations, such as Dorothy Sayers and Robert Heinlein; materials in highly used genre areas, like mysteries and romances; and materials in popular formats, such as compact disks, books-on-tape, and videotapes.

A third reason that libraries have been hesitant to purchase multiple copies is that they feel it is somehow "wasteful" to discard duplicates once demand for these titles has faded. But it is actually no more wasteful to discard a duplicate copy that circulated 20 times during a two-year period than a title that circulated 20 times over 10 years. Moreover, libraries have two "less wasteful" options for disposing of duplicate copies. They can sell these works in periodic book sales or in prominently placed displays housed in each branch, then use the receipts to buy more popular works. Or they can place them in the type of read-and-return collections that are described more fully in chapter 6. Collections like this invite the public to peruse displays of works in public places (from transit stations to courthouses to banks), take home titles that interest them, then return the works to the library when they are finished. Read-and-return collections are an excellent means of increasing the library's visibility in the community, especially among people who would not normally visit a library.[4]

Other libraries have resolved the "wastefulness" issue by using lend-lease plans for popular items.[5] For example, libraries that subscribe to the Adult Book Leasing System offered by Baker and Taylor Books receive, on a monthly basis, an annotated listing of items in high demand — both prepublication books and current best-sellers. The lists include popular nonfiction, general fiction, and "category" books — large-print items, biographies, historical novels, westerns, science fiction, and adventure and suspense fiction. A library can lease 100 or more books per month, which are fully processed and ready to be shelved, and can return the items to Baker and Taylor for credit when they are no longer needed.

But the major reason that librarians have been hesitant to systematically duplicate popular works is that they have realized that their materials budgets are not infinitely expandable. A library that buys multiple copies of some titles will be forced to purchase fewer different titles overall, an action that can significantly affect collection diversity.

For this reason, some libraries are currently duplicating only a small number of works. For example, a few libraries check, on a regular basis, the availability of a "core" collection of titles — those considered to be classic within a genre or subject — and order one or more extra copies of those titles that are not present on the shelves.[6] Other libraries duplicate titles that have many reserves on them, that are consistently used for school assignments, or that have been identified, using procedures like those described in chapter 8, as circulating at a very high rate. In general, duplicating a small percentage of materials in the collection has little effect on overall collection diversity.

But some public libraries have chosen to duplicate much more heavily. For example, the Baltimore County (Maryland) Public Library (BCPL) buys far fewer titles than other public libraries of its size (Wisotzki, 1989). In fiscal year 1988-1989, BCPL planned to use its adult fiction budget of $870,000 to buy about 1,100 new fiction titles that it feels will be popular with patrons. BCPL determines the number of copies to be purchased for the system by examining various factors related to demand, including the use of past titles by the same author; the use of other works in the same genre, subject area, or format; the amount of money the publisher or distributor is spending to advertise a particular work; and whether the work will be featured on major radio and television talk shows.

BCPL purchases best-selling fiction titles in the largest quantities — generally from 190 to 450 copies for the system's 23 branch libraries. Fewer than 20 titles are bought at a rate of more than 450 copies for the system, although BCPL duplicates works by two blockbuster authors much more heavily. The largest branch receives 125 copies of each new title by Danielle Steel and Sidney Sheldon; the smallest full-service branch gets 30 copies. In contrast, BCPL may purchase as few as eight copies of "literary" fiction, sending two copies to the largest branch, one to a few of the others, and none to the smaller branches.

The range of different nonfiction titles that BCPL purchases is also substantially less than that purchased in most public libraries of its size. In fiscal year 1988-1989, BCPL planned to buy about 5,100 new titles with its budget of $770,000. The number of copies of each title varies from 1 to 20 per branch. The average is 30 for the system as a whole, which gives the highest circulating branch four copies.

As various studies have shown, duplication of popular works increases the probability of their being available when desired and causes user satisfaction to rise.[7] Unfortunately, duplication on a very large scale uses up funds that could be spent in other ways, including the addition of new titles. For this reason, some libraries have opted to increase availability rates in a different way: by shortening the length of the loan periods for popular works.

Varying the Length of the Loan Period

Shortening the loan period seems, at first, to be a simple solution to the problem of increasing the availability rates of popular titles. But in reality the issues are as complex as those that surround purchasing multiple copies of popular works.

For example, Buckland (1975) concisely describes the dilemma regarding the length of time a borrower is allowed to keep a particular book. Borrowers want to be able to find the works that they desire on the library's shelves; this is most likely to occur when the library assigns short loan periods. But borrowers also want long loan periods, so they can use materials at their leisure. This conflict of interest suggests that the library should weigh, in its decision-making process, the costs that individual patrons must bear as a result of having shortened loan periods against the benefits other patrons will receive as a result of increased availability rates.

A library could, of course, increase title availability by shortening the loan periods for its entire collection. For example, some years ago the Beverly Hills (California) Public Library determined that patrons could find approximately 55 percent of the works they wanted on the shelves if the library had a four-week loan period; if the loan period was reduced to three weeks, the availability rate would rise to 60 percent; a two-week loan period would yield a rate of 66 percent (Newhouse and Alexander, 1972).

But cutting loan periods for the total collection does not always make the best sense. As noted earlier in this chapter, about 20 percent of the works in most public libraries account for about 80 percent of the use. Shortening the overall loan period would increase the availability for those titles that are heavily used. But there appears to be little reason to shorten the length of the loan period for the 80 percent that are already sitting on the shelves when patrons want them.

A few libraries have taken the opposite tack and instituted demand-dependent loan policies that apply to each item in the collection. For example, when a university library in England learned that its users could find what they wanted only 60 percent of the time, it reprogrammed its own privately designed, automated circulation system to match the demand-level of a particular item with a loan period that it deemed suitable. If a title was highly popular, indicated by a very recent circulation, the computer automatically gave it a loan period that could be as short as three days. If the title had circulated less recently, the loan period was longer — from two weeks to two years, depending on how long it had been since the work was borrowed.

The results were dramatic: title availability rose to 90 percent. Overall demand for library materials rose too, by 200 percent in a two-year period, as patrons found that they could consistently locate needed items on the shelves. Although such an increase in use under a standard system would have caused title availability rates to take a rapid plunge, the adaptive properties of loan periods that were fully dependent on demand helped keep title availability levels high (Buckland, 1983, 1975).

Unfortunately, most automated circulation systems of the turnkey type (those used in most of the automated public libraries in the United States) are not flexible enough to compute different loan periods for each title based on its past demand. Nor do circulation staff have time to manually compute loan periods for each title being checked out. So libraries generally use preset loan periods of different lengths for various classes of materials.

Under this system, the library should establish shorter loan periods for those types of materials that are overused and which, if the library follows the product-analysis procedures spelled out in chapter 8, have already been identified. These include

1. works in popular formats. For example, a library could set a loan period of three days for videotapes, one week for compact disks, two weeks for books-on-tape, and four weeks for books.

2. works in classes that are overused. For example, a library could set a two-week rather than four-week loan period for the four sections of its print collection that are most heavily overused: new books, mysteries, diet books, and child-care manuals.

3. works that circulate highly during some seasonal period. For example, a library could set one-week loan periods for holiday books during the month before that holiday and for state and federal income tax guides between January 15 and April 15 each year. It could set even shorter loan periods for (or place on reserve within the building) works that relate to a class assignment that has been given to a large number of students in the area.

4. works by a particular author. For example, a library could set a four-week loan period for most authors, a two-week loan period for those authors who have a strong following, and a one-week loan period for "blockbuster" authors.

5. particular titles. For example, a library could set a one-week loan period for works that appear on various best-seller lists, like the lists of fiction and nonfiction titles that appear in the Sunday *New York Times* and of the top 10 sound recordings in *Rolling Stone* magazine.

A library that is instituting a number of shortened loan periods can help offset the cost of these for patrons in three ways. First, it can allow renewals for as many types of materials as possible, from books to videotapes, to keep overdue charges caused by the shortened loan periods low. Second, it can permit renewals of materials over the telephone as well as in person, whenever the circulation system makes this feasible. Finally, the library can set its daily overdue fines at the lowest possible level.

Finding the Correct Balance Between Duplication and Loan Periods

All public libraries should take action to raise their availability rates as high as they possibly can. But individual libraries will need to decide for themselves how this will be accomplished. Neither solution discussed here is perfect. Shorter loan periods are inconvenient for patrons; reducing them too far may raise the cost of using the library so high that patrons become irritated and, in the worst-case scenario, decide the cost is not worth the effort. But purchasing or leasing duplicate copies of items is expensive; it uses money that could be spent on buying a greater variety of titles, thus reducing collection diversity. The decision about which techniques to emphasize will be made easier if a library remembers three important principles.

The first is that actions taken to reduce availability rates should be in keeping with the primary and secondary roles the library has selected for itself. For example, a library that has chosen a role of *independent learning center* will be committed to building a widely varied collection of self-help materials in all formats and relevant to the needs of all ages. Therefore, it may want, to a large extent, to rely on reducing loan periods to increase title availability, because mass duplication of a large number of different items would inhibit collection diversity. In contrast, the library that has chosen a role of *popular materials center* is more likely to feel that mass duplication of current and popular works in a variety of formats is an appropriate strategy to follow.

The second principle that should govern the decision-making process is that librarians should not think in absolute terms. That is, they do not have to concentrate solely on duplication or solely on reducing loan periods. Rather, as Buckland (1975, 1983) notes, they should consider these strategies as interrelated means of increasing availability. Librarians can do this by asking two simple questions:

1. Are loan periods already so short that the borrower's convenience is being hurt?

2. Is duplication already so high that the inevitable loss of different titles is hurting?

When the answer to the first question is "yes," the library should consider duplication. When the answer to the second question is "yes," the library should consider shortening the loan period. In other words, the library should set one threshold for reducing the loan period and another for acquiring more duplicate copies.

The third principle is that any decision should be made in the best interests of the library system—not just an individual branch library. The Baltimore County Public Library adhered to this principle when it designed a plan to solve a selection problem that was occurring in two of its branches. Because these branches had many patrons who were heavy readers of adult fiction, they often had reserve lists of 50 to 100 patrons for many of the new but not best-selling fiction titles. The branches did not want to purchase too many copies of these works, because doing so would greatly limit the number of different fiction titles that could be provided. But it would have taken many months for them to meet this kind of reserve demand if they had simply reduced the length of the loan period for these titles. So BCPL developed a computer program to match reserves with the number of copies ordered at a particular branch. When either branch had one and one-half times more holds than copies ordered, the program subtracted 25 percent of the available copies due to each of the other branches in the BCPL system. These copies were then earmarked, for one circulation only, to the branch with the outstanding reserves (Wisotzki, 1989).

A Final Note on Materials Allocation Decisions

In actuality, the decisions a library makes regarding its materials allocation budget are fairly complex. This is particularly true for large library systems, because such decisions often need to be made separately for each branch library. Therefore, it is important to formally record these decisions in the library's collection development policy so that selectors throughout the system can be made aware of them.

Establishing a Centralized Selection Unit
to Do Formula-Based Purchasing

In the past 10 years, a number of public libraries have tried to make the time-consuming and costly task of selection more efficient by establishing a centralized selection unit—that is, by having a small group of people make some selection decisions for the entire library system. The composition of centralized selection units has varied from library to library. Some employ only professional librarians; others only paraprofessionals; some a mixture of the two. Some units select all materials for the system as a whole; others perform specific selection tasks.

This chapter recommends that public libraries establish a centralized selection unit to do formula-based purchasing. The unit would be staffed by paraprofessionals but supervised by a professional librarian. Its main responsibility would be to buy the types of materials that appear on various lists and for which clear-cut purchasing rules can be devised: best-sellers, award-winning titles, and reserved items. It would also compile a series of lists that would alert professional selectors throughout the system to items receiving regional or national promotion in the news media.

A central selection unit of this type is cost-effective because it greatly reduces the number of different people who are engaged in the never-ending chore of list checking. It thus frees professional librarians from what is essentially a routine activity, allowing them to spend more time on selection tasks that require professional judgment and action: from reviewing results of collection evaluation efforts to reading reviews and identifying titles that will fill collection gaps and meet patron needs. The centralized unit also encourages the quick purchase and processing of new materials in high demand—a practice that helps ensure they are available for patron use at the peak of popularity.

Staff in the central selection unit should perform four major tasks. First, they should purchase materials in all formats, genres, and subject areas that appear on various best-selling lists that the unit supervisor has identified as being appropriate bases for library purchases. Lists that represent both print and nonprint formats and that cover all genre and subject areas are printed in various trade and nontrade magazines and newspapers, like *The New York Times, Publishers Weekly*, and *Rolling Stone* magazine, and in information updates from jobbers like the Ingram Book Company and Baker and Taylor Books.

Purchases should be based on formulas devised by the unit supervisor that specify how many copies of materials of various types should be bought for the system and what their initial loan periods should be. Any given formula may take into account a number of different factors. These include

1. the library's role

2. the library's policies regarding duplication and loan periods

3. the popularity of the author (remember the duplication rates that the Baltimore County Public Library used for Sidney Sheldon and Danielle Steel!)

4. the popularity of the genre or subject area

5. the cost of the item (materials that cost more than a given dollar amount may be ordered in smaller quantities than other items)

6. the format (materials in some formats may be ordered in smaller quantities than others)[8]

Staff will then determine how many copies will be distributed to each branch. Again, this is done on a formula basis. For example, a branch whose circulation represents 21 percent of the total systemwide circulation may get 21 percent of the copies of an ordered title.

A second task of the central selection unit should be to focus on lists of "best items" and award-winning titles that the unit supervisor has identified as relevant to the library's needs. These may include "notable" lists, like those issued by the American Library Association and various professional or educational groups like the National Science Teachers Association; annual compilations of editor's choices of best books, like those listed in *School Library Journal*; and lists of materials that have won various private awards, like those receiving the Hugo or Nebula awards for science fiction and fantasy.

Most of these high-quality titles should already be owned by the library; the professional selectors throughout the system will have ordered them previously when they saw favorable initial reviews in the library press. This means that the task of the central selection unit will be verifying that these items are owned, duplicating them in appropriate quantities, and deciding how the copies will be distributed to branch libraries. Formulas for purchasing multiple copies of these items may be based on the same factors that were used to develop formulas for purchasing best-selling items.

Purchasing extra copies of reserve titles is the third task that a central selection unit should undertake. In fact, the unit can follow the procedures given in figure 8.1 of chapter 8 to identify reserved titles that are in heavy demand. Libraries should try to fill reserve requests as quickly as possible. For example, the Queens Borough (New York) Public Library orders one copy of best-selling titles for every three reserves (Sivulich, 1989). The library's policies should help dictate how many copies of high-demand titles should be ordered and what type of loan periods should be assigned to these.

Some centralized selection units have set up programs designed to process their reserve orders quickly and efficiently. For example, the Cuyahoga County (Ohio) Public Library allows patrons to file reserves several months before an anticipated best-seller is received. Reserve requests note both the date that the request was made and the patron's "home" branch. When multiple copies of these titles are received, the central selection unit assigns each copy to an "owning" branch but sends the item directly to the home branch of the patron who was first to file the reserve. Whenever a reserved title is checked in at a branch, the automated circulation system informs the clerk that a reader is waiting for this item at a different branch. The item is then sent, via the intra-library delivery system, to the next patron on the reserve list. When no more reserves are left on a particular title, the item is sent to the owning branch and placed on the browsing shelves (Berlin, 1989).

The fourth task of the central selection unit is to compile, for use by professional selectors in each area, lists of works that are not yet best-sellers but are receiving or will receive lots of news media attention and so will have reasonably heavy demand. Paraprofessional staff will generally rely on two major sources for this information. The first are trade magazines. For example, the publisher's advertisements, the "Forecasts" and "Rights" columns, and the seasonal announcements that appear in *Publishers Weekly* often include information about how much money will be devoted to advertising a particular title, how large the first print run will be, and whether the item will be featured by the Book-of-the-Month or other special interest book club, promoted in a national magazine or on an author's tour, or made into a television or feature film.

Paraprofessional staff can also peruse information releases from library jobbers that indicate the amount and type of publicity that items in some formats are receiving. For example, both the Ingram Book Company and Baker and Taylor Books issue a weekly microfiche that lists books that will be talked about on national television shows like "Donahue" and "Good Morning America," featured in popular magazines like *Time, Working Woman*, and *People* or on author tours in major U.S. cities, and made into feature films or television movies. The *Get Ready Sheet*, a low-cost announcement service for librarians, includes similar information.

The centralized selection unit should sort the lists that result from this perusal of promotion information by class (that is, subject, genre, age level, or format), then distribute relevant lists to the persons responsible for selection of these classes of materials. Because titles on this list are those for which there is likely to be a high initial demand, the lists should be updated frequently, preferably every week, and forwarded to the selector for quick action.

Note that some libraries have established centralized selection units to handle all materials to be purchased throughout the system. This was done, for example, in 1987 by the Metropolitan Library System (MLS) in Oklahoma City, Oklahoma. MLS felt that centralized selection would reduce the overall time spent on selection, allow orders to be placed more quickly, and foster a systemwide selection philosophy—a goal that the library had found difficult to meet when a large number of professional staff were choosing materials. But other libraries, like the Cuyahoga County (Ohio) Public Library, have limited the tasks of their central selection unit to formula-based purchasing. CCPL took this action after examining its service area closely. Because its more than two dozen branches serve a surburban area with a population of over 600,000 people of diverse socioeconomic, cultural, and ethnic backgrounds, the library decided to give each branch a materials budget and the autonomy to select materials to meet the special needs of its patrons.

No research has explored whether there is a difference in effectiveness between centralized selection units that do formula-based purchasing only and units that purchase all materials for the library system. However, staff reactions to the latter have often been mixed, especially during the initial days of the change to centralized selection. In part, this has been due to the reluctance of professional librarians to turn the "fun" task of selection over to someone else. But it has also been caused by a feeling on the part of some staff members that centralized selection staff, who generally have no direct contact with patrons, will not be able to purchase materials that will fully meet user needs.

In fact, a few older studies suggest that librarians who have patron contact on a day-to-day basis are more familiar with what patrons are requesting and, as a result, better able to choose works that reflect what their patrons want. For example, Turow (1978) asked selectors of children's books in a public library to tell whether "a general impression of what children want" was an important factor in their choice. Ninety-one percent of branch librarians, all of whom had daily contact with their patrons, thought this criterion was "very important." None of the system coordinators, who had no public service duties but were responsible for purchasing books for branches without children's librarians, rated this criterion as more than "somewhat important." In an academic library, Evans (1969) found that public service librarians routinely selected a higher percentage of titles in demand among patrons than their nonpublic service counterparts.

But other studies have verified that materials selected by librarians who have gathered extensive data on past patterns of use in their libraries and on their clients' current needs also receive higher levels of use — levels that are indicative of a good match between patrons and the collection.[9] These data seem to suggest that a centralized selection staff that has access to the types of product analysis data recommended in this book will also be able to make effective selection decisions. Further research is obviously needed on these issues.

Asking Professional Selectors to Review Objective Data on Collection Use, Then Follow Three Marketing Principles When Making Selections

Although the percentage of formula-based selections is rising, the bulk of materials for most public libraries will be ordered by professional selectors who have developed expertise in purchasing materials of a certain subject, genre, or format.[10] This portion of the chapter recommends that libraries follow three broad marketing principles when making selections. These principles should not supersede the library's consideration of role choice issues when making selections (although libraries that have chosen different roles may apply these principles somewhat differently). Nor should they replace the standard selection criteria that libraries have used for a number of years, like currency; literary or artistic merit; accuracy of the information presented; and appropriateness to the audience of the item's reading level, writing style, and depth of coverage of a topic.[11] Rather, librarians should use their understanding of these three marketing principles to enrich and supplement the other two factors, so that the most effective decisions can be made. Each of the marketing principles is discussed below.

Marketing-Based Selection Principle #1

If an item or type of item hasn't been used, don't buy it again.

Profit-making organizations regularly review the vitality of their products, withdrawing them when there is no demand. As chapter 8 noted, libraries should do the same thing. But because past use of materials predicts future use, libraries should also avoid purchasing products that are highly similar to those that have been withdrawn.

There are four kinds of materials to which the no-use, no-purchase principle applies. The first is individual items that the library is considering replacing due to their poor physical condition. If such items have not been consistently used in the past, it will not generally be cost-effective for a library to replace them or even to rebind them.

The second kind of work that selectors will want to de-emphasize are titles by authors for whom there is little demand. If a library has followed the product-analysis recommendations in chapter 8, these authors will already have been listed on the *Form for Identifying Authors with Unused Works in the Circulating Collection*. The no-use, no-purchase principle does not imply that librarians should curtail purchasing all but the most popular authors. Most librarians will want to foster diversity by buying many titles by authors whose works are not best-sellers but who have developed a readership among patrons. And, depending on the roles it has chosen, a library may also want to purchase the works of first-time authors or foreign authors. But in general, selectors should avoid continuing to purchase works of authors who have generated little interest among patrons over time.

Selectors will also want to avoid buying the kinds of materials listed on the *Form of Identifying Types of Items in the Circulating Collection That Are Poorly Used* and the *Form for Identifying Noncirculating Items with Low Use*. For example, if full-length biographies of obscure Greek philosophers have not been used in an *independent learning center*, the selector could bypass similar works in the future and instead purchase full-length biographies of philosophers who are better known or collective biographies containing information on a number of different philosophers. The selector for the *popular materials center* in the retirement community that didn't like "lustful" novels could de-emphasize purchases of the "sweet-and-savage" romances that his patrons avoid and buy "gentle" romances instead.

Finally, selectors will want to de-emphasize purchases in classes of materials that receive little use by patrons. For example, there may be no demand for materials in technologically dated formats like Beta videotapes and 8mm films. The selector can easily identify such classes by reviewing information contained on the *Form to Determine Whether the Circulation of Each Class Is Rising or Falling*, the *Form for Calculating the Stock Turnover Rate of Various Classes in the Collection*, and the *Form for Calculating the Relative Use of Various Classes*.

Occasionally, a selector will want to violate the no-use, no-purchase principle for a valid reason. For example, the selector in a library that has chosen the role of *independent learning center* may be interested in purchasing some works of fiction of exceptionally high quality even though the natural audience for these is small. When this is the case, the selector should proceed under the following corollary: If works with anticipated low use are purchased, they should be consciously and consistently promoted to encourage use. That is, the library must make a long-term commitment to systematically promoting these works, both when they are initially received and throughout their lives, using the types of promotion methods that are discussed in chapter 10. Otherwise, they are likely to sit unused on the shelves.

Marketing-Based Selection Principle #2

If an item or type of item has been or is likely to be used heavily, duplicate it or assign a shortened loan period so that a patron's chance of finding it on the shelf is increased.

Selectors will need to pay particular attention to the purchase of materials that are likely to be used heavily if they want to meet the short- and long-term demands of patrons. This is true regardless of the roles that the library has chosen.

Although the central selection unit can easily use standardized formulas to order best-selling titles and titles that are being heavily reserved, professional selectors will want to handle the ordering of other types of materials that are currently, or are expected to be, heavily used. In the past, most selectors in public libraries limited their decision making to the number of copies to be purchased. However, this book recommends that selectors also should be responsible for determining the length of the loan period, because both factors affect patron success in obtaining titles. Selectors will need, of course, to refer to the library's policies on duplication and length of the loan period to make these decisions.

Two documents can help the selector identify titles that will benefit from duplication or loan-period reductions. These are the *Form for Identifying Heavily Used Items* and the list of titles, compiled and forwarded by the centralized selection unit, that are being heavily promoted in the regional or national news media. In each case, the selector's job is to try to predict the level of demand for these titles then decide what multiple-copy-loan-period combination will best meet demand. Obviously, the library does not want to end up with a large number of unused copies on the shelves; but neither does it want to provide so few copies of a work that it falls far short of meeting patron demand. Whenever possible, selectors should aim for a multiple-copy-loan-period combination that allows the library to meet the needs of those who have filed reserves as well as those who are browsing for a good work to read, watch, or listen to. Checking use records of other titles by these authors, in these subject or genre areas, or in these formats can help the selector more accurately predict the extent of demand. So can reviewing the factors that affect use of a particular item, which are extensively detailed in chapter 4.

The selector will also want to consider initial duplication or shorter loan periods for new works that are being added in classes that are being heavily demanded by patrons. Such classes can readily be identified from the *Form to Determine Whether the Circulation of Each Class Is Rising or Falling*, the *Form for Calculating Stock Turnover Rate*, and the *Form for Calculating Relative Use*. If the highly educated patrons who frequent a public library in a university town prefer mysteries and classic fiction to romance novels and westerns, the selector makes his choices accordingly. If works in particular subject areas (e.g., child care books, car repair manuals, financial planning guides) have been highly popular in the past, they are likely to be so in the future. The same is true of works in particular formats (e.g., books-on-tape).

Marketing-Based Selection Principle #3

If an item or type of item is not in the collection but may be useful to patrons, buy the work if levels of potential use justify the expense of its purchase. Place greatest emphasis on purchasing works that support the library's primary and secondary roles.

If a library has followed the product-analysis procedures spelled out in chapter 8, it will have identified in several ways the items that are not owned but are desired: through the review of interlibrary loan requests and of unanswered reference and readers' advisory questions, through patron completion of purchase suggestion forms and materials preference questionnaires, and through comments made during focus group interviews. Individual selectors will identify other nonowned titles, both new and retrospective ones, through their perusal of standard selection sources like *Booklist, Public Library Catalog*, and *Fiction Catalog* and through advertisements and catalogs from publishers and media distributors. The resulting list of possible purchases will include individual titles, works by specific authors, and materials in certain subject areas, genres, or formats.

Selectors will generally wish to order items on this list that are inexpensive, that fall within the roles the library has selected, and that are likely to be used by patrons. Suppose, for example, that a committee of English teachers gives the public library a list of the novels that are being read in the literature classes of area high schools and colleges. A library that has selected a role of *formal education support center* may try to buy all these items. A library serving the role of *popular materials center* might buy those novels on the list that are likely to be popular with other patrons, like Mark Twain's *The Adventures of Huckleberry Finn*. But it might bypass items it feels will have a narrower readership, like George Eliot's *Mill on the Floss*.

Items that are more costly, that clearly fall outside the scope of the collection, or that appear to represent the interests of a single patron (like a book on how to compose film scores) rather than an interest that other patrons might have (like a general book on folk music) are treated more cautiously to prevent the selector from overspending in areas that are unrelated to the library's primary and secondary roles. This will reduce the likelihood that the library will be unable to buy needed works because it has already spent all monies allocated for a particular class of materials, a problem that Kovacs (1990) found was common in all types of libraries. In most cases, librarians should order specialized, technical, or expensive items on interlibrary loan, rather than purchase them.

It will not always be easy to determine which titles are likely to be used by patrons. However, a selector increases the chance of making a good purchase by checking the circulation records of works by the same author, in the same subject or genre area, or in the same format. For example, a selector who is thinking about ordering Nancy Thayer's new novel may determine how extensively her past novels have circulated, especially in comparison with other novels owned by the library, before making a purchase decision. This type of review, and a review of factors that affect use of library materials (see chapter 4), can help selectors predict, with some degree of accuracy, not only whether a particular item should be purchased but also in what quantities.

Conclusion

The four-part plan spelled out in this chapter requires that the library's administration assumes responsibility for encouraging a systemwide approach to incorporating marketing principles throughout the selection process. The first two steps, incorporating role choice decisions into the collection development policies and reviewing budget allocations to ensure that these are in keeping with marketing principles, will encourage librarians to focus their choices in common directions that were established after full consideration of long-term community needs. The third step, establishing a centralized selection program to do formula-based purchasing, will increase the speed with which certain kinds of selections will be made and processed, providing better patron service while freeing professional selection staff from the nonprofessional task of list checking. And advocating adoption of the three marketing-based selection principles will encourage staff to consistently add considerations of patron demand to factors that they normally consider when making selections: factors related to role choice and to the quality and suitability of the title for a particular collection. The result should be a collection that fully embodies the concept of a societal-marketing orientation—one that meets both the short-term demands of patrons and the long-term needs of the community.

Notes

[1]See, for example, Krueger (1983).

[2]A variety of sources give information on a number of different elements that should be included in collection development policies. See, for example, Cassell and Futas (1991), American Library Association (1989, 1987), Evans (1987), and McClurg (1985).

[3]See, for example, Britten (1990) and Trueswell (1969).

[4]See, for example, Hart (1990) and Scilken (1971).

[5]Unfortunately, several studies have shown that lend-lease plans may not be particularly cost-effective. See, for example, Tod (1983).

[6]See, for example, Eggers (1976).

[7]See, for example, Almony's (1978) review of the literature on this subject.

[8]For example, the Minneapolis Public Library and Information Center (1990) purchases fewer duplicate copies of videotapes than of books.

[9]See, for example, Diodato and Diodato (1983) and Evans and Argyres (1974).

[10]For example, the Queens Borough Public Library allocated $312,500 for centralized ordering in fiscal year 1990-1991, out of a total materials budget of $4.25 million (Oldick, 1992).

[11]Two recent works that review these selection criteria in more detail are Cassell and Greene (1991) and Kovacs (1990).

References

Almony, Robert A., Jr. "The Concept of Systematic Duplication: A Survey of the Literature." *Collection Management* 2, no. 2 (Summer 1978): 153-65.

American Library Association. *Guide for Writing a Bibliographer's Manual.* Chicago: American Library Association, 1987.

_____. *Guide for Written Collection Policy Statements.* 2d ed. Chicago: American Library Association, 1989.

Barrish, Alan, and Dennis Carrigan. "Strategic Planning and the Small Public Library: A Case Study." *Public Libraries* 30, no. 5 (September/October 1991): 283-87.

Berlin, Susan. "Best Sellers and Public Service: Can Public Libraries Provide Both?" *Reference Librarian*, nos. 27-28 (1989): 451-57.

Britten, William A. "A Use Statistic for Collection Management: The 80/20 Rule Revisited." *Library Acquisitions: Practice and Theory* 14, no. 2 (1990): 183-89.

Bryant, Bonita. "The Organizational Structure of Collection Development." *Library Resources & Technical Services* 31, no. 2 (April 1987): 111-22.

Buckland, Michael K. *Book Availability and the Library User.* New York, Pergamon Press, 1975.

_____. *Library Services in Theory and Context.* New York: Pergamon Press, 1983.

Cassell, Kay Ann, and Elizabeth Futas. *Developing Public Library Collections, Policies, and Procedures: A How-to-Do-It Manual for Small and Medium Sized Public Libraries.* New York: Neal-Schuman, 1991.

Cassell, Marianne K., and Grace W. Greene. *Collection Development in the Small Library*. Chicago: American Library Association, 1991.

Diodato, Louise W., and Virgil P. Diodato. "The Use of Gifts in a Medium-Sized Academic Library." *Collection Management* 5, nos. 1-2 (Spring-Summer 1983): 53-71.

Eggers, Lolly. "More Effective Management of the Public Library's Book Collection." *Minnesota Libraries* 25, no. 2 (Summer 1976): 56-58.

Evans, G. Edward. *Developing Library and Information Center Collections*. 2d ed. Englewood, Colo.: Libraries Unlimited, 1987.

_____. "The Influence of Book Selection Agents upon Book Collection Usage in Academic Libraries." Ph.D. diss., University of Illinois, 1969.

Evans, G. Edward, and Claudia White Argyres. "Approval Plans and Collection Development in Academic Libraries." *Library Resources and Technical Services* 18, no. 1 (Winter 1974): 35-50.

The Get Ready Sheet. Utica, N.Y.: Mid-York Library System, annual.

Hart, Katherine H., and Ann W. Grice, eds. "Field Notes." *Public Libraries* 29, no. 5 (September-October 1990): 263.

Kovacs, Beatrice. *The Decision-Making Process for Library Collections: Case Studies in Four Types of Libraries*. Westport, Conn.: Greenwood Press, 1990.

Krueger, Karen. *Coordinated Cooperative Collection Development for Illinois Libraries*. Springfield: Illinois State Library, 1983.

Kuraim, Faraj Mohamed. "The Principal Factors Causing Reader Frustration in a Public Library." Ph.D. diss., Case Western Reserve University, 1983.

McClure, Charles R., Amy Owen, Douglas L. Zweizig, Mary Jo Lynch, and Nancy Van House. *Planning and Role Setting for Public Libraries: A Manual of Options and Procedures*. Chicago: American Library Association, 1987.

McClurg, Patricia. *Selection of Library Materials in the Humanities, Social Sciences, and Sciences*. Chicago: American Library Association, 1985.

Minneapolis Public Library and Information Center. *Collection Development Policy*. Minneapolis, Minn.: Minneapolis Public Library and Information Center, 1990.

Moreland, George B. "Operation Saturation." *Library Journal* 93, no. 10 (15 May 1968): 1975-79.

National Center for Education Statistics. *Public Libraries in 50 States and the District of Columbia: 1989*. Washington, D.C.: U.S. Department of Education, Office of Educational Research and Improvement, 1991.

Newhouse, Joseph P., and Arthur J. Alexander. *An Economic Analysis of Public Library Services*. Lexington, Mass.: Lexington Books, 1972.

Oldick, John. Conversation with Sharon L. Baker on 15 May 1992.

Robinson, William C. "The Utility of Retail Site Selection for the Public Library." *Occasional Papers* of the University of Illinois, Graduate School of Library Science, no. 122 (March 1976): 1-52.

Scilken, Marvin H. "Information Exchange: The Read and Return Collection — A Scheme for Overcoming Librarians' Reluctance to Buy Multiple Copies of Popular Books." *Wilson Library Bulletin* 46, no. 1 (September 1971): 104-5.

Sivulich, Kenneth G. "How We Run the Queens Library Good (and Doubled Circulation in Seven Years)." *Library Journal* 114, no. 3 (15 February 1989): 123-27.

Tod, Mary. "The Law of Slow Learning: Marketing at the Dallas Public Library." *Public Library Quarterly* 4, no. 2 (Summer 1983): 29-38.

Trueswell, Richard W. "Some Behavioral Patterns of Library Users: The 80/20 Rule." *Wilson Library Bulletin* 43, no. 5 (January 1969): 458-61.

Turow, Joseph. "The Impact of Differing Orientations of Librarians on the Process of Children's Book Selection: A Case Study of Library Tensions." *Library Quarterly* 48, no. 3 (July 1978): 276-92.

Wisotzki, Lila. "Duplicate, Circulate: Demand Buying." Paper presented at the Collection Development Conference, Public Library Association, 19 March 1989, Chicago, Illinois.

Marketing-Based Promotion Practices

10

If evaluation, or product analysis, and selection are the first and second steps in a comprehensive program to market the public library's collection, promotion is the third. Note that some marketers tend to think of promotion in a fairly narrow fashion—that is, advertising and publicizing a library's collection. Although this definition was used in chapter 7 to introduce librarians to basic promotion concepts, this chapter discusses promotion from a wider perspective—defining promotion activities as a broad spectrum of techniques that libraries have adopted to increase patron awareness or use of the resources in the collection.

The major premise of this chapter is that promotion efforts will be most effective when they are carefully thought out. Indeed, they should occur as part of a well-planned program that considers several major questions:

1. What aspects of the collection can be promoted?

2. What factors should guide librarians making promotion decisions?

3. What internal promotion techniques have been shown to be effective in increasing use or user awareness of the collection?

4. What external promotion techniques have been shown to be effective in increasing use or user awareness of the collection?

Each is discussed below.

What Aspects of the Collection Can Be Promoted?

Over the years, mounting evidence has shown that public libraries can increase patron awareness and use of many different kinds of materials by using tried-and-true promotion techniques. For example, Baker's (1986b) review documented that book lists and displays, when properly designed, have increased the circulation of old books, new books, biographies, randomly selected works of fiction and nonfiction, works on general topics like inflation as well as specialized ones like poetry by contemporary women, popular titles, and titles that have not circulated in years. These findings suggest that libraries can pretty much choose which aspects of their collections they want to promote: the collection as a whole, specific product lines and items within it, collection-related events, or changes in the cost of using library resources.

Promoting the Collection as a Whole

Many libraries have chosen to promote a broad spectrum of materials in the collection to a specific target market or an entire community of prospective users. For example, the St. Paul (Minnesota) Public Library once used a publicity campaign called "Raising Readers" to encourage children and their parents to become more aware of the collection, while the Mobile (Alabama) Public Library put together a slide-cassette show that highlighted, in verse, works of different formats, on different subjects, and by different authors (Tuggle and Heller, 1987).

Promoting a Specific Product Line

A library can also promote product lines, or groups of works that have a common

1. subject or theme. For example, the Houston (Texas) Public Library received $135,000 from the National Endowment for the Humanities to provide a learning and reading program for adults called CITY! The library publicized works related to this theme through press releases, television public service announcements, flyers, calendars, and posters, including one that read "Loving, Warring, Lying, Scheming, Building, Coping, Dreaming—The City in Fiction and Film (Tuggle and Heller, 1987).

2. genre or subgenre. For example, the library might distribute book lists of "bodice-ripper" romances, cleric detective stories, adult westerns, or hard science fiction.

3. format. The library might feature, in an article in the local Chamber of Commerce newsletter and in a booktalk at a chamber meeting, books-on-tape that businesses could use for training purposes, like Thomas J. Peters and Robert H. Waterman, Jr.'s *In Search of Excellence: Lessons from America's Best Run Companies*.

4. author. For example, the library might have its readers' adviser talk, in a 15-minute radio interview once a month, about the life and writings of a prolific author whose works are entertaining, informative, or insightful.

5. title. The library might pull together, in a small display near the circulation desk, all versions of an especially worthy title, regardless of format. For example, it could feature Jane Austen's *Pride and Prejudice* in hardback, paperback, large-print, books-on-tape, "classic comic," and videocassette forms.

Promoting a Specific Product Item

Libraries can also promote specific items in the collection in a variety of fashions. For example, one public radio station played, on a weekly basis, reviews taped by librarians from the Fairbanks (Alaska) Public Library in five fields: best-selling fiction, nonfiction, children's books, homemaking books, and technical books for the layperson (Sherman, 1980). Libraries also commonly promote individual items in booktalks, on book lists distributed within and outside the library, in displays, via individual reference or readers' advisory interviews, and through other means.

Promoting a Collection-Related Event

Collection-related events, like talks by local authors, also lend themselves to promotion. In fact, many libraries create various eye-catching events that will allow a series of stories to be generated in the local news media, as well as provide interesting or entertaining experiences for participants. For example, librarians from the Springfield (Massachusetts) City Library worked with community leaders and city schools to celebrate the 350th birthday of the city. Because Springfield is the hometown of Theodor (Dr. Seuss) Geisel, the library decided to emphasize its collection by sponsoring a four-month "Seussamania" festival. Librarians dressed up as the Cat in the Hat or Sneetches and visited each classroom in nine elementary schools to introduce the less familiar Seuss books. The library displayed hundreds of pieces of sculpture and other children's artwork portraying Seuss characters, sponsored a performance of *The Lorax* by a children's theater group, and held a Seuss-fest of singing. News media coverage was extensive and circulation of children's books increased 50 percent systemwide during the festival (Youthreach, 1986).

Another example of a collection-related event was the auction sponsored by the Salt Lake City (Utah) Public Library. The library wrote notable individuals (movie stars, sports heroes, writers, politicians, and the like) and asked each to explain in writing what book had made a difference in his or her life. The staff purchased copies of relevant works then auctioned them, along with the letter from the celebrity, at a gala reception. News media coverage of the auction was excellent and helped to increase awareness of the library's collection as a potential agent for change in people's lives (Tuggle and Heller, 1987).

Promoting a Change in the Cost of Using the Collection

Libraries should also inform patrons whenever they change the price of using the collection. This may be done in cases where the cost goes down, as when the library offers a two-for-one special on its rental collection of popular materials. But it should also be done when the cost rises, as when the library reduces the loan period in order to stretch a limited collection to better meet patron demand.

Publicizing cost changes allows patrons to decide for themselves whether the benefits of using the collection will continue to outweigh the costs. Moreover, if the library takes time to explain why costs are rising or falling, patrons may gain a better understanding of library services in general.

What Factors Should Guide Librarians Making Promotion Decisions?

A number of factors should influence librarians who are making decisions on what to promote and how to promote. The most important appear to be the roles the library has chosen to play; a library's ability to meet the demand it will generate by its promotion efforts; the buyer-awareness state of prospective patrons; and an understanding of how consumers process promotional information.

The Roles the Library Has Chosen to Play

The most effective promotion decisions take into consideration the roles the library has selected for itself. In part, this is because role choice provides a basis from which the library can determine what target markets it will direct promotion efforts toward. A library that has chosen the role of *independent learning center* may devise a series of rotating displays that feature, for learners browsing in the library, the various kinds of self-education resources in the collection. A *formal education support center* may determine what types of library-related school assignments will be given during a particular month, then distribute to relevant classes lists of materials on the subjects.

Generally the library proceeds by gathering information about each market segment's knowledge of and use of the collection via the kind of focus group interviews and patron questionnaires mentioned in chapters 7 and 8. This information should enable the library to determine which promotional techniques will be most successful in reaching the target market. For example, the Iowa City Public Library discovered, via focus group interviews, that the best promotional medium to reach area business people was the local Chamber of Commerce newsletter (Baker, 1991).

A Library's Ability to Meet the Demand It Will Generate by Promotion Efforts

Another factor that should influence librarians who are making promotion decisions is the level of demand they are likely to generate by their efforts. In general, librarians should avoid promoting items if the resulting demand will be so high that they cannot meet it. For example, it is a bad idea to list, in a newspaper that has a potential readership of 5,000 patrons, the name of a new résumé book of which the library owns only one copy. Better alternatives would be promoting, via the newspaper, résumé books that are owned in multiple copies or publicizing the library's entire line of résumé books.

Librarians can also avoid creating too much demand by paying attention to a particular product's life cycle. As noted in some detail in chapter 4, although a few products have life cycles that are faddish (very rapid) or cyclical (seasonal) in nature, most have a four-stage life cycle:

1. the introductory stage, in which demand for an item is slow

2. the growth stage, in which demand for the product increases rapidly

3. the maturity stage, in which demand levels off then wanes

4. the decline stage, in which demand falls sharply

Librarians should consider promoting products in the introductory stage of their life cycles as these are acquired. Profit-oriented businesses regularly follow this tactic by informing clients of new products as soon as they become available. Indeed, because new products may die on the shelf if they are not brought to the attention of potential customers, businesses devote more money and attention to promoting new items than those in any other stage of the product life cycle. Libraries have generally followed the lead of businesses by displaying new materials prominently within the building—a tactic that significantly increases their use.[1] But they can also promote works outside the library's doors. Works in new formats, works by first-time authors, and works with local interest, like a newly published book featuring historical maps of the area, are particularly good products to emphasize in promotion efforts.

Bookstores and other media distributors that are interested in making a profit also concentrate on promoting products that are in heavy demand. These are products in the growth stage of the life cycle—like many titles being featured on radio and television talk shows—or that have a faddish life cycle—like exposé books. But most public libraries do not have enough money to purchase unlimited quantities of the works for which patrons are clamoring. Generally, a library will want to promote titles that are already in high demand only if

1. such promotion is in keeping with the roles it has chosen (e.g., *popular materials center*); and

2. it is prepared to allocate additional resources to meeting the demand that results.

Many libraries (e.g., those who have chosen the roles of *reference library* or *independent learning center*) may not wish to spend additional money to buy or lease extra copies of popular items because this would curtail their ability to purchase a more diverse collection.

Librarians also need to deal with the problem of temporarily heavy demand for products that receive cyclical use—like holiday materials. Promoting these works during their off-season will most likely be futile. However, librarians need to handle promotion efforts during the "in" season carefully to ensure that they are not creating levels of demand they cannot meet. One good way of doing this is reducing the length of the loan period on in-season titles before promoting them.

Many libraries will also find it valuable to promote each product that is in the mature stage of its life cycle—that is, a product whose use has waned. This decline often results from the fact that new titles tend to receive more publicity than old ones. As the publicity surrounding these new items fades, so does patron awareness of these titles; they become "lost" on the shelves and their circulation declines. Thus, inventories of these mature works, which comprise the bulk of the collections in many public libraries, build up unless libraries take steps to increase patron knowledge of these items.

Although librarians will not want to promote mature items that are out of date, they can effectively publicize those that are of good quality (e.g., classic videotapes), that contain information that has not become obsolete, and that are neither so esoteric nor so technical that they will fail to interest a number of patrons. However, librarians will want to observe results of their promotion efforts closely, because some mature products may have outlived their usefulness. As Dragon (1983) notes, librarians should resist the temptation to let optimism get in the way of experience when they are promoting mature products.

Finally, librarians will want to weed, rather than promote, most items that are in the decline stage, unless there is some overriding reason for keeping them (e.g., they are unique local history materials).

The Buyer Awareness State of Prospective Patrons

As chapter 7 has explained in some detail, customers may fall into any of six different "buyer readiness" stages. They can be aware of the public library's existence, have knowledge about its collection and services, develop a preference for using it as opposed to another media outlet, develop the conviction to use its collection and services, and act on that conviction. These buyer readiness stages can affect both what will be promoted and how that promotion will occur.

If general public awareness and knowledge of library resources are low, the library may wish to promote a broad spectrum of materials in the collection to its entire community of potential users. Tuggle and Heller (1987) cite a number of instances where public libraries have used this technique. For example, the King County (Washington) Public Library developed a television public service announcement that featured a member of the Seattle Supersonics walking through the stacks, listing the subjects covered by the collection.

A library can also choose to promote the entire collection or a subset of the same to one or more target markets that have a low awareness and knowledge of library services. For example, a public library that serves as a *formal education support center* for a college community may decide to promote its collection at the beginning of each semester at orientation sessions for new students and faculty members.

But people will not move beyond the awareness and knowledge stages to those of liking, preference, conviction, and action, unless they perceive that the benefits of using the library outweigh the costs. People tend to determine for themselves the costs that they will face in using the library. But they may need to have the benefits of using a particular collection pointed out.

Generally, libraries should point out benefits in a straightforward fashion if patron awareness and knowledge of the collection are low. The State Library of Pennsylvania developed a series of promotional pieces that did just this and could be used by any public library in the state. A typical example was "Do it yourself! Find out how at the library. And put the money you save in the bank. Your public library. We have the answers" (Tuggle and Heller, 1987, 93). Indirect approaches may be used for those who have already indicated a preference for using the library's collection as opposed to other media distribution outlets. For example, materials that are displayed attractively may sell themselves to people who are already in the library building.

An Understanding of How Consumers Process Promotional Information

As Engel and others (1973) have noted, consumer information processing occurs in four steps:

1. Consumer senses are activated when they are exposed to different stimuli—in this case, the variety of techniques that libraries use to promote their collections.

2. In order for the exposure-promotion to be effective, it must in some way capture the consumer's attention. If, for example, the local newspaper has run a feature story on the library's collection of travel books, the consumer must both glance through the paper and notice this particular story.

3. The consumer must then comprehend what the stimulus is. That is, he must take in and make some attempt at understanding the promotion message. For example, he can read the travel-book article and notice the types of resources that he would find of benefit.

4. Finally, the consumer must retain the promotion information in his memory where it can be used to aid his decision about using library resources. This decision will involve weighing information about the benefits of using the library against information about the costs of using it.

Three major findings are apparent when one reviews the research surrounding these steps. The first is that capturing the patron's attention may be difficult. Prospective patrons receive far more promotion information than they retain, because they selectively filter out information they do not want, need, or understand.[2] For example, a person with no children may ignore displays, book lists, news stories, and the like that feature the library's collection of picture books and easy readers.

Second, consumer motivation to acquire and process promotional information is relatively low in many situations.[3] Motivation is highest for items that are high in cost and, therefore, risk, like a new car. However, it is low for items that are low in monetary cost, like most of the products in the library's collection. But libraries can increase this motivation by showing how their services and resources will benefit individual patrons or groups of patrons.

Finally, consumer information processing is affected negatively by time constraints.[4] That is, consumers whose time is severely limited cannot process promotional information as effectively as those who have more time. This means that the library should, whenever possible, use promotion techniques that are not time intensive. These will generally be those techniques that patrons find easy to understand and to use.

Taken together, these research findings suggest that librarians can increase user awareness or use of library materials if and only if they promote products that are perceived as being of benefit to potential patrons, using promotion techniques that capture the attention of and require little effort from that user. The findings also imply that techniques that capture the attention of large numbers of library users will increase awareness and use levels significantly more than techniques that catch the attention of a smaller user audience.

A major question is which promotional techniques capture the attention of and require little effort from the user. The next two sections of this chapter provide a quick overview of the research that has been done on techniques that promote library materials both inside and outside the building.

What Internal Promotion Techniques Have Been Shown to Be Effective in Increasing Use or User Awareness of the Collection?

The answer to this question is not a simple one and requires a basic understanding of several points relating to the needs of patrons who are browsing for something good to read, watch, or listen to.

First, as Webb (1985) notes, browsers are one of four major categories of library users:

1. group participants, who attend programs in the library

2. independent learners, who visit the library frequently when seeking information about specific topics, especially those related to educational or career needs, but whose use may lag once these needs are satisfied

3. researchers, who make extensive and in-depth use of the library to answer particular inquiries

4. browsers, who visit the library at frequent intervals to obtain materials in some broad class like compact disks, serious contemporary fiction, or craft books that will meet their needs, which are generally recreational.

Group participants generally use the library's meeting facilities, then leave; as a result, they use few resources in the collection and have minimal contact with staff. Because independent learners and researchers tend to realize that they need help in locating specific pieces of information, they often ask questions of staff and use catalogs, indexes, and other bibliographic control devices to find materials. But browsers, for a variety of reasons, often serve themselves, even if this means that their search for "something good" is not as effective or efficient as possible.

Second, various studies have shown that the number of browsers in public libraries outweighs the number of users who are searching for specific items or for works on a narrow subject. For example, one of the most comprehensive studies of public library use found that 68 percent of patrons were browsing for something of interest to them, 31 percent sought specific subjects, and 8 percent were looking for a specific author or title (Totterdell and Bird, 1976).

Third, the larger the library's collection, the more likely that browsers will experience some information overload. As Baker (1986b) has noted, information overload occurs when people are faced with too many choices. Feelings of confusion and inadequacy can result, making it difficult for some individuals to make decisions. As one patron who visited a large library commented, "Using the library is a scary prospect.... I know that nothing in here will hurt me but it all seems so vast and overpowering" (Mellon, 1986, 160). Because patrons are expected to make selections from among hundreds or thousands of items, their potential for experiencing information overload is very real. Indeed, overload may be more prevalent among patrons than librarians realize, especially in medium-sized and large libraries. This is particularly true when patrons are not looking for specific documents but rather are browsing among all the materials on the regular shelves for one or two items that will somehow satisfy their information needs. For example, Baker (1986a, 1988) found that many patrons experience some degree of overload when browsing among adult fiction collections that were as small as 3,000 to 4,000 volumes.

Fourth, because browsers enter the library with only a nebulous idea of what resources they might like to use, they are open to influence from a variety of factors when selecting materials. Point-of-sale methods of promotion, like book displays and other in-library advertising of works, can help reduce overload by focusing a browser's attention on a smaller set of items. Many people like this type of promotion method, which can

1.   expose patrons to items they have never heard of but would like to use;

2.   remind patrons of authors or titles they have heard about and would like to borrow; or

3.   trigger patron recognition of latent needs that they have not previously acted upon.

Fifth, the most cost-effective internal promotion strategies will be those that are easy for browsers to use and understand and that expose a large number of browsers to a small set of materials (e.g., point-of-purchase displays). Internal promotion strategies that focus on smaller numbers of browsers at a time, like the kind of individual "selling" done by a readers' adviser, can also increase use or user awareness but may not be as cost-effective.

Display Shelving

Unlike bookstores and other media distribution outlets, many libraries have persisted in using old-fashioned shelving methods that do not effectively highlight the products in their collections. For example, although bookstores display their wares face front to entice patrons to use them, a majority of public libraries still pack standard shelving units with hundreds of books housed spine out. Yet when Long (1986) divided a group of 300 titles into equal parts, shelving one face front and the other spine out in a branch of the Durham (North Carolina) Public Library, she discovered that the former circulated significantly more than the latter. Although few libraries are rigorously testing the effects of using display shelving, a number note that both use of and user satisfaction with their collections increased when they installed display shelving.[5]

Other librarians have not yet realized that books placed on eye-level shelves will circulate more than books placed on the top shelf. But as Spiller notes, many browsers are influenced by shelf height when making their selections: "When respondents sought a specific book, its position on the shelf was rarely of importance. When browsing at random, however, 29 percent of respondents felt they were influenced to some extent by the height of the shelf, in the way that supermarket shoppers are more prone to impulse buying of goods at eye level. There were 27 specific complaints against top shelves, 17 of these because of the difficulties caused by wearing bifocals. Forty-eight respondents singled out bottom shelves for criticism, a gamut of medical complaints (blood pressure, bad back, arthritis, dizziness, etc.) being held responsible for their inaccessibility" (Spiller, 1980, 249). Problems with shelf height are not limited to display units for books. For example, some libraries display phonograph albums on two-tiered record racks, although many patrons will not stoop to browse those items housed on the lower tier.

Libraries that are refurbishing older buildings or furnishing new ones should consider buying special display shelving to counteract these problems. Shelving manufacturers offer many units that display works both spine out and face out. Some of these are designed to fit in small spaces in crowded libraries — like the narrow, 20-inch-wide, end-of-range display shelving used by the Queens Borough Public Library (Sivulich, 1989). Other manufacturers solve the shelf-height problem by designing lower shelves that kick out and tilt upward slightly, so that patrons can read titles without stooping. Still others offer shelving units topped with lighted headers that inform patrons what types of works are housed there. And almost all offer display shelving for a variety of works, including record albums, magazines, books-on-tape, and videocassettes as well as books. Shelving of this sort is featured in news articles and in the advertisements of various library shelving manufacturers, in the general library literature.[6] *Publishers Weekly* also features, on a regular basis, articles that discuss new kinds of shelving and list the names of firms that can design shelving systems for maximum effect.[7]

Libraries that cannot afford to purchase new furniture can maximize the effectiveness of their existing shelving in several ways. First, they can avoid placing works on the top and bottom shelves of standard eight-shelf units, because few patrons will browse these anyway. This assumes, of course, that the library either has adequate shelf space or can obtain it by adding extra shelving units or weeding its collection.

A library can also tilt bottom shelves by lowering, one or two notches, the rear shelf supports only. Shaw (1938) was one of the first to try this. He tilted the four bottom shelves of one section of fiction at the Gary (Indiana) Public Library. He then placed an equal number of books on each of seven shelves in this section and in an adjacent section in which the bottom shelves were left straight. Shaw found that books housed at eye level (on shelves two, three, and four) of the "straight" section, circulated significantly more than books housed on shelves five, six, and seven of that section. But in the tilted section there were no significant differences between the circulation of books housed at eye level and those on the lower shelves. Although tilting the shelves did not cause the overall circulation of the stack section to increase, it did distribute use more evenly among all the shelves. Patrons could see titles on the bottom shelves without stooping; this reduced their cost of choosing these works.

A third way to help counteract the shelf height problem is to shift the shelves at regular intervals so that no work stays too long on the bottom shelves. For example, a library could keep a three-shelf buffer at the beginning and end of its fiction stacks, then shift shelves, on a yearly basis, so that works formerly on shelves two to four move to shelves five to seven and vice versa. Many nonfiction and audiovisual works would also benefit from this kind of shifting.

Libraries that cannot afford to buy special display shelving can also train pages to shelve books face out whenever this is feasible. For example, and as Libretto (1983) notes, shelvers can display titles face out at the end and on top of shelves and can place titles with multiple copies alternately spine out and face out.

Point-of-Purchase Displays

Many libraries entice their patrons to try something different by designing attractive point-of-purchase displays of library materials. These generally focus on a particular product line like spy stories, government publications, materials on child care, or the works of Mark Twain. Libraries have also mixed fictional and nonfictional works together when they are linked by some theme. For example, a library might display nonfiction works about ancient human beings with Jean Auel's *Clan of the Cave Bear* and other novels focusing on that time period.[8]

Librarians who want their point-of-purchase displays to be effective should note the following findings from the literature. First, point-of-purchase displays will increase both use and user awareness of the materials they contain only when they are placed in highly visible and accessible locations of the library; point-of-purchase displays in less accessible locations will not (Baker, 1986a).

Second, as Libretto (1983) notes, librarians should assess the library's normal traffic flow and position displays in those areas that are most traveled by and readily accessible to patrons. Particularly effective locations for displays are

1. near the entrance, which is the most heavily trafficked area of the building;

2. at the end of cross aisles in heavily traveled areas; and

3. at or near the circulation desk or any other public service desk where patrons have to wait in line.

Whenever possible, display units should be located at an angle so that the approaching patron can easily see them (that is, head on or at no more than a 45-degree angle to the patron's line of vision).

Third, librarians should avoid setting up point-of-purchase displays that contain materials patrons cannot immediately check out. For example, libraries should not display single-copy titles in the windows of the building or in locked display cases. Such displays actually frustrate patrons by drawing their attention to materials that they cannot obtain readily and easily.

Although some researchers who have studied the display phenomenon used standard library book carts to house displays because of their convenience and portability, this practice is not the most effective one. Ideally, libraries should locate materials on shelves or flat surfaces that are at eye level (between 36 and 60 inches from the floor) for easy visibility. The tops of many card catalogs may be an appropriate height, although libraries can also buy special display shelving or can construct pyramid-like structures that can house materials at this height.[9] Many libraries also display works in "dumps" (cardboard display units) that they have obtained from their jobbers or local bookstores.[10]

A fifth finding is that "fixed" displays should be changed frequently. Fixed displays are those with a specific nonchanging group of titles on them. The circulation increases experienced with a fixed display fall off within about four weeks because repeat patrons quickly borrow from the display everything that they want (Baker, 1986a). Libraries that cannot afford to change a fixed display once a month should instead set up "rotating" displays—those with more generic titles on them. For example, as items in a "fantasy" display are checked out, shelvers can refill the display from the larger fantasy collection.

Displays should have simple and colorful headers or signs whenever possible to attract patrons to the display. Some libraries have used subject-related signs to make it easy for patrons to quickly determine whether the displays contain anything of interest to them. For example, the Queens Borough (New York) Public Library keeps signs in stock for more than two dozen subject areas that lend themselves to merchandised display (Sivulich, 1989). But librarians can also top displays with "generic" signs that can be reused later. These might include such headings as "Staff Favorites," "Recommended Titles," "Items Other Patrons Have Enjoyed," or even "Books with Yellow Covers."

Seventh, because point-of-purchase displays are a visual promotion device, librarians should ensure that they contain materials that are visually appealing. Regardless of their content, works with plain, dull, or rebound covers will seem less interesting to most patrons than works with bright and colorful covers.

Libraries do need to be aware of two potential problems with using displays. The first relates to the need to train shelvers to straighten and restock displays on a regular basis, so that they do not look messy or bare. The second and more serious issue is that it may be difficult for patrons and staff to find items that have been taken from their regular location on the shelves and placed in a temporary display. This suggests that library staff, particularly shelvers and those who work at public service desks, need to be alerted whenever the subject of a point-of-purchase display is changed, so that desired items can be readily found.

Book Lists and Lists of Other Materials

The value of book lists is not that they make particular works more visible and physically accessible, but that they help alleviate overload by focusing patron attention on a smaller group of titles in which they might be interested. However, special attention needs to be paid to the techniques used to distribute book lists if they are to work effectively. Book lists will significantly increase patron selection of the materials they contain only when they are distributed widely and in a manner that requires little patron effort to obtain them (Baker, 1986b).

Consider, for example, the fact that one researcher failed to increase use of book list titles when, following the test library's usual practice, she left them out for voluntary patron pickup on top of the card catalog and in other locations throughout the building (Taylor, 1982). Many patrons did not visit those sections of the library where the book lists were placed. Even those who did still had to have their attention captured by the book list, among all the other stimuli competing for their attention, had to comprehend what the list was, and had to consciously pick up the list before they could consider using it as a selection aid. Any breakdown in this process resulted in the book list not being used.

The research on this subject has identified three effective distribution techniques:

1. Force-feeding the book lists to patrons to ensure that they come into visual contact with the list without having to expend effort to locate and pick it up. For example, when Golden (1983) put a copy of a book list into each set of items an adult patron borrowed, use of the titles on the list increased significantly. The Prince George's County (Maryland) Memorial Library System used this strategy recently to increase use of its nonfiction collection (Service, 1989).

2. Placing the lists, with a large accompanying sign, just inside the door of the library for patron pickup. When Parrish (1986) used this technique to promote 35 fiction titles that had not been checked out in four years or more, the titles were checked out 33 times during the following eight-week period.

3. Asking staff to distribute these lists to patrons who ask relevant reference or readers' advisory questions. One academic library did this to help interested patrons identify genre fiction materials classed within the Library of Congress schedule (Wood, 1985). Again, use of these titles was significantly higher than that of similar titles that were not so promoted.

It is important for libraries using book lists to note that these are somewhat less effective than point-of-purchase displays for increasing use. For example, Goldhor (1981) found that titles placed on a book list increased their circulation by four times; titles placed on display increased their circulation by seven times. The lower effectiveness of book lists as a promotion medium is not surprising. Displays require only that the patron notice an item of interest, pick it up, and check it out. Book lists require that the patron notice the list, comprehend the information on it, search through the stacks for items of interest, some of which may not be present on the shelves, then check these out. The extra effort required to use a book list thus reduces to some extent its ability to increase use of the titles it contains.

Note that annotated and unannotated book lists that contain works focusing on a single subject or genre area have been shown to be equally effective in increasing use of the titles they are promoting.[11] However, when more than one genre or subject area is featured on a single book list, annotations can help patrons focus their selection more quickly.

Although librarians may take time to compile their own book lists, they will often find it more cost-effective to use lists that someone else has put together. Such lists on a wide variety of subjects are featured in journals like *The Unabashed Librarian*, are indexed in *Library Literature*, and are distributed during "swap-and-shop" sessions at library conferences. A library will, however, need to delete titles that are not owned from these already prepared lists.

Librarians will also want to avoid sending patrons to the shelves for works that are already checked out. For this reason, librarians should consider featuring on their book lists

1. titles for which they have multiple copies;

2. authors who have written several works of fiction rather than just one or two titles; and

3. subject headings and call numbers of popular nonfiction areas rather than specific nonfiction titles.

Fiction Categorization

Although librarians generally do not think of fiction categorization as a promotion device, studies show that this technique can significantly increase awareness and use of materials that are so classed. For example, Baker (1988) found that fiction titles marked with "mystery" or "romance" designations circulated more than similar works that received no genre markings.

This increase in the use of classified titles is not surprising, because such categorization performs two useful readers' advisory functions. First, it makes it easier for people to select the type of novel they want. This is important because studies have shown that a majority of persons seeking fiction look for works "of a particular type or kind."[12] Yet many patrons become frustrated and confused, that is, they experience some degree of overload, when looking for a "good" title among all those that a library offers. Subdividing the collection by category helps patrons narrow their choices and alleviate this overload (Baker, 1988).

Fiction categorization also helps patrons identify authors previously unknown to them who write the type of book they like. This is important because most fiction readers try to expand their list of favorite authors — a short list that is generally already exhausted — by browsing for the genre of book that they like (Spiller, 1980). Indeed, one study found that fiction categorization alerted browsers in various sizes of libraries to desirable works in a particular genre that were less well known, thus reducing their reliance on a small number of popular authors and titles (Baker, 1988).

Because fiction categorization makes it easier for patrons to choose the kinds of works they think they will like, thus reducing their cost of using library materials, it is not surprising that a majority of patrons want libraries to subdivide their fiction collections by genre. For example, when Reader (1982) surveyed patrons at a public library in Hertfordshire, England, he found that 70 percent were very satisfied with the library's practice of categorizing fiction into seven different classes, 13 percent did not mind it, and only 8 percent disliked it. Related studies showed that 79 percent of readers in a British public library and 88 percent of students using a junior high school library said they liked their fiction classified into genre areas (Ainley and Totterdell, 1982; Briggs, 1973). Other authors who have noted the overwhelming support of patrons for fiction categorization include Baker (1988), Spiller (1980), and Bordon (1909).

As might be expected, the potential for information overload increases as the size of the fiction collection grows. One major question then becomes: when does a collection grow large enough that narrowing devices like fiction categorization are needed to help patrons choose materials? Baker (1986a, 1988) found that patrons experienced overload in a library with a fiction collection of about 4,700 books but not in one with a collection of 2,500 books. Although browsers in the smaller libraries liked having fiction classified by genres, they did not feel as strong a need to have the works so classed because they were not as bewildered when making their selections.

Although this type of confusion also occurs in patrons seeking works of nonfiction, it is alleviated in part by the subject access provided in card catalogs. But in-depth "subject" access for fiction tends to be the exception, rather than the rule, in many public libraries. As Berman (1981) has noted, for years public libraries that were using conventional, LC-type cataloging typically failed to recognize common genre categories like spy fiction and suspense stories, gave fiction few if any subject tracings, and applied subject headings to fiction collections and anthologies but not to individual novels, films, or recordings. In recent years, groups like the American Library Association, the Library of Congress, and the Online Computer Library Center have taken a more active role in recommending that libraries routinely add fiction subject headings in the catalog.[13] It is unlikely, however, that this change will occur quickly. This is generally due to the fact that some public libraries are understandably reluctant to spend money to provide such access because many patrons who are seeking fiction bypass the catalog entirely and make their selections at the fiction shelves.

However, libraries can decrease overload and increase patron access fairly inexpensively if they take time to categorize their fiction collections. Library systems have often recognized this intuitively, a fact that explains, at least in part, why 94 percent of the large library systems in the United States (those serving populations of 100,000 or more people) have categorized at least some parts of their adult fiction collections (Harrell, 1985). Such categorization is particularly useful in increasing patron access to uncataloged collections of paperback fiction, because those collections usually are not organized in any fashion whatsoever, a nonarrangement that increases the patron's cost of using the works.

There are two major methods of categorizing fiction. Libraries that use the first label the spine of each title that falls within a particular genre but leave all items interfiled in a single alphabetical-by-author scheme. This type of labeling is the simplest way to subdivide a collection and does provide some selection guidance for patrons looking for titles of a particular kind. The second method, that of physical separation of genre titles, is more work initially because it requires that a library

1. label the spine of each title within a designated genre;

2. determine how much shelf space is needed for each genre area and where each genre will be located;

3. shift the shelves; and

4. update the catalog and the shelf list to reflect the new locations of works in each genre area.

Although physical subdivision requires more work than the mere labeling of spines, it is the practice recommended here because an overwhelming majority of patrons prefer to have different genres of fiction physically separated from each other (Baker, 1988). They often want books of only one type when they enter the library and find it easier to browse separate collections than to pick out books with relevant genre labels from among all the fiction titles (Baker, 1988; Baker and Shepherd, 1987; Spiller, 1980). This explains why one study found that, although both methods of subdivision caused the use of classed titles to rise, physical separation increased use substantially more than the simple labeling of genre fiction titles (Baker, 1988).

To date, there are no comprehensive research studies that indicate the best genre categories that public libraries can use to subdivide their fiction collections. However, the scattered research that has been done suggests four principles to keep in mind when deciding which categories to use.

The first principle is that public libraries should use headings that represent genres that are popular with their patrons. The *Gallup 1988 Annual Report on Book Buying* (Gallup, 1988) suggests that the most popular categories among book buyers are, in rank order, mystery-spy-suspense, romance, action-adventure-war, general best-sellers, historical fiction, science fiction, occult-supernatural, humor, and westerns.

The second principle is that public libraries should use genre headings that are in fairly common usage from library to library. This will help reduce the confusion of patrons who are moving from branch to branch within a single library system or from library system to library system. This principle has not always been followed. For example, Harrell (1985) found that the categories that large public libraries used to subdivide their collections varied greatly. A total of 26 different categories were listed by libraries serving populations of 100,000 or more; 15 of these were used by only one or two libraries. The most commonly used groupings were mystery, suspense, or spy stories; science fiction and/or fantasy; westerns; romances; short stories; historical fiction; horror; action, adventure or war stories; and classics.

Third, public libraries should choose genre headings that are easily understood by patrons. Not all of the headings recommended in various sources are. For example, one publication recommends the use of the heading "Bildungsroman" for novels in which the theme is the development of a character from youth to adulthood (American Library Association, 1990).

At least 11 of the current headings that are used in public libraries are consistent with these three principles. These include General fiction, Mystery fiction, Romance fiction, Science fiction, Fantasy fiction, Classic fiction, Horror fiction, Western fiction, Adventure fiction, Historical fiction, and Short stories.

A final principle is that large public libraries should consider using more subdivisions than smaller ones. The larger the collection, the more likely that patrons will experience information overload and need subdivision to help them narrow their selections to a manageable size. Some libraries have even split large collections of a particular category (e.g., mystery fiction) into subgenres (e.g., amateur detective stories and police procedurals).

Once the library has decided on appropriate subdivisions, it will need to find one or more bibliographies that indicate which genres its fiction titles might fall into. These can be located via indexes like *Library Literature* and *Bibliographic Index*. For example, the following four bibliographies are especially useful in categorizing adult fiction collections, which are the ones most commonly divided into genre areas:

a. Biagini, Mary K. *A Handbook of Contemporary Fiction for Public Libraries and School Libraries*. Metuchen, N.J.: Scarecrow Press, 1989.

This book list works within the following genres: romances, horror stories, spy stories, mystery and detective stories, science fiction and fantasy, westerns, historical fiction, "behind-the-headlines novels" (including adventures), and "trash-master novels" (those with glamorous characters, exotic settings, and lots of sex). Separate chapters define each genre and list titles by authors whose works are representative of that genre and who have achieved some prominence from World War II through 1988. The book also lists titles by 328 "high quality" American, British, and world authors.

b. Rosenberg, Betty, and Diana Tixier Herald. *Genreflecting: A Guide to Reading Interests in Genre Fiction*. 3d ed. Englewood, Colo.: Libraries Unlimited, 1991.

This book lists more than 1,500 authors in the following genres: westerns, thrillers, romances, science fiction, fantasy, and horror. Each chapter gives an overview of the genre and lists authors who are prolific, popular, or significant currently or in the history of the genre.

c. *Fiction Catalog*. New York: H. W. Wilson. Issued annually, with periodic cumulations.

This is a standard list of fiction titles recommended for inclusion in public libraries of all sizes. The index in the back lists many titles under standard genre headings—horror stories, adventures, fantasies, science fiction, and the like.

d. *Good Reading: A Guide for Serious Readers*. New York: R. R. Bowker. Issued irregularly.

This work is especially useful for identifying "classic fiction." Chapter 12 of the current edition lists 338 literary novels by American, British, and Continental writers from the 1800s to the present. But other chapters also can aid with categorization. Chapter 13 includes 85 anthologies of short stories by multiple or single authors; chapter 15, 70 science fiction novels and short story collections; and chapter 19, 64 mysteries.

These and similar works can be used to categorize items that are on the fiction shelves at the time of the initial screening, as well as items that are being returned from circulation.

Librarians will also need to categorize newly published works and those already owned works that are not listed in these bibliographies. They can do this by reading the description of each item (i.e., the blurb) on its inside cover and deciding whether to categorize it within a particular genre, considering both the definitions of each genre (given in the bibliographies) and the genre designations of other works by this author.

Physically labeling the works and shifting shelves are the next steps. As noted in chapter 6, the last should be done after reviewing research conducted by the Gallup Organization (1985) that shows that people who read one type of fiction tend to have common affinities and dislikes regarding other types of genre fiction. For example, people who read action-adventure stories are also quite likely to read mystery-suspense-spy stories and not at all likely to read horror stories. Libraries can use affinity tables, like the one shown in chapter 6, figure 6.5, to position genre areas that are preferred by readers of the same type in proximity to each other.

Specific, in-depth procedures for accomplishing the tasks associated with classifying a fiction collection into genre categories, marking the catalog and shelf list cards, and moving the collection are provided elsewhere (Baker, 1991) so will not be repeated here.

Reader, Viewer, or Listener Interest Categorization

As noted in chapter 6, many patrons find the Dewey Decimal System, the Alpha-Numeric System for Classification of Recordings (ANSCR), and other classification systems used by public libraries difficult to understand. They want libraries to place nonfiction items in separate, well-marked sections organized by broad subject instead, using the kinds of easily understandable reader interest categories that many bookstores prefer. For example, bookstores in the Waldenbooks chain use one or more variations on the categories shown in figure 10.1.

Note that reader interest categories are used in lieu of the call numbers assigned in standard classification systems. Thus, an ethnic cookbook may be placed under the category "Cookbooks" rather than the number 641.59. But interest categories do not replace standard subject headings and tracings, which are still assigned so that patrons who choose to do so can continue to access items via the catalog, rather than browsing among the interest categories.

Art	Home Care
Astrology/Occult	Humor
Bibles	Inspirational
Biography	Marriage/Sex
Business	Medical Care
Child Care	Music
Collectibles	Nature
Computers	Pets
Cooking	Photography
Crafts	Psychology
Diet	Reference
Dungeons and Dragons	Science
Field Guides	Social Sciences
Film	Sports
Fitness/Beauty	Travel
History	

Fig. 10.1. Adult reader interest categories used by Waldenbooks.

Reader interest categorization was first tried on a widespread basis by the Detroit (Michigan) Public Library (DPL) in the early 1940s (Rutzen, 1952). Because some patrons had difficulty locating works they would like in the large collection at the main library, DPL arranged a smaller collection of items by reader interest categories in an alcove near the circulation desk. Patron response was so favorable that DPL organized six new branch collections and 13 old ones entirely by reader interest categories between 1948 and the late 1950s. It also used such categories to organize subsets of the collections at other large branches in its system.

Although some public libraries in Great Britain and other countries have been using reader interest categories on a large scale for the last 15 years, few in the United States have followed suit. This is unfortunate because such categorization makes the arrangement of the collection more understandable and attractive to patrons of all ages in all types of libraries. For example, students using a paperback collection in a junior high school library and adults using a "popular" collection in a public library felt that organization by reader interest categories made it easier for them to find the types of books they liked (Langhorne, 1987; Webb, 1985). And arranging a collection of easy books, based on the reading interests of primary grade children, made the children more satisfied with their selections. It also helped to foster a sense of independence and self-worth among these small users, because it made them better able to choose books without help from librarians or teachers (Williams, 1973).

Because patrons can quickly and easily understand reader interest categories, their costs of using the collection may fall. This reduction may lead to increased use; indeed, libraries that have tried this practice have experienced increases in circulation of both nonfiction materials and the collection in general. For example, the circulation of nonfiction materials rose by 30 percent after they were displayed in reader interest categories in a British public library branch and by an average of 70 percent in six libraries of a South African library system (Venter, 1984; Sawbridge and Favret, 1982). Reported rises in overall circulation range from an 18 percent increase reported by one branch of the Multnomah County Library in Portland, Oregon, to an 84 percent increase over four years in a 6,500-book architecture collection (New Stock, 1989; Face-Out, 1988; Hubbard, 1967). And the Metropolitan Library System in Oklahoma City, Oklahoma, says that the more it arranges its books by popular subdivisions, the more use patrons make of them (Little, 1979).

Librarians have discovered, through trial and error, that collections of up to 30,000 items can be completely handled using a reader interest categorization system. This type of arrangement will be most useful, therefore, for any small or medium-sized collection, although it is especially appropriate for paperbacks, audiovisual materials (particularly videotapes, books-on-tape, and sound recordings), and materials that are housed in deposit collections, on bookmobiles, in minibranches, and in full-service branch libraries. One high school librarian, at the request of the English teachers in her building, has even regrouped a collection of biographies into nine interest categories: Women, Scientists, Artists, Musicians, Native Americans, Explorers, Sports, Empire Builders (e.g., Alexander the Great and Hitler), and Just People (Benezra, 1978).

Larger libraries that are interested in categorization of this sort will want to use one of two different approaches to dividing their collections. The first involves placing recent or popular works, or both, on the full spectrum of subjects in a browsing library and works that are more advanced, narrower in scope, or less used in the regular stacks. For example, some years ago the Phoenix Public Library located a "popular library" just inside the door of its main library near the circulation desk for the convenience of those who wanted to browse for good titles quickly and then be on their way. The popular library collection was organized by reader interest categories and contained "the best books on topics of general and popular interest for the reading public, [as well as new] books, best-sellers, paperbacks, popular magazines, and the rental collection" (Webb, 1985, 63). Phoenix placed all other materials in Dewey Decimal order within subject-oriented departments, which were staffed by specialists trained to give in-depth help to patrons with specific information needs.

This approach to subdividing a large collection into reader interest categories has a major advantage. A library can catalog all new works within the Dewey Decimal system, then place a reader interest label above the regular call number on those items that will be temporarily located in the popular library. When use of these items declines over time, the library can quickly remove the reader interest labels and shelve the items among the other nonfiction works in the regular stacks.

A few libraries have chosen to subdivide their collections in a different fashion, because they feel it would be confusing to place works on the same subjects in two different locations. These libraries have placed entire sections of the classification system — those that are considered to be generally popular or to contain materials for leisure use — in a browsing collection arranged by reader interest categories, even when these sections contain works that are older, narrower in scope, or less likely to be used for some other reason. Materials in all other subject areas are placed either in subject departments or in the regular stacks. This type of two-tier classification system was used to organize a collection of 140,000 volumes in the Willesden Green Library in England (Morson and Perry, 1982).

Libraries that have tried these two-tier approaches to categorizing their collections report varying degrees of success in terms of increases in user satisfaction and circulation. However, as Ainley and Totterdell (1982) note, most have felt that the benefits of using the system outweighed the costs and so have continued to use reader interest categories.

Libraries will need to consider a number of practical details if they choose to use reader interest categories. The first is choosing the categories. Generally, libraries will use one of three approaches to accomplish this. The first is determining which subject categories within its existing classification scheme are most used and designing interest category headings that reflect these. Libraries that have followed the product-analysis approach to collection evaluation recommended in this book will have already collected ample data that can help them accomplish this task.

A second approach is to use categorization schemes that others have developed. These can be found by browsing in the literature on the subject. One of the more useful is the 26-category scheme, shown in figure 10.2, that the American Booksellers Association and National Association of College Stores (ABA/NACS) developed for categorizing paperbacks.

Art	Literature
Biography	Medicine
Business	Music
Cooking	Nature
Crafts	Philosophy
Drama	Poetry
Education	Political Science
Fiction	Psychology
Games	Reference
History	Religion
Humor	Science
Juvenile	Sociology
Language	Travel

Taken from a list of approved subject headings given in *Paperbound Books in Print: Spring 1992* (1992).

Fig. 10.2. Reader interest categories used by the American Booksellers Association and the National Association of College Stores.

A third approach is to combine the first two methods—modifying an existing scheme to reflect local interests and requirements. For example, a library that is using the ABA/NACS scheme can add a category called "Spanish Books" to meet the needs of the large Spanish population that it serves.

The next step is marking materials with appropriate spine labels. Labels, custom designed to reflect the library's scheme, can be purchased fairly inexpensively from most library suppliers. These can easily be added to new materials that the library has purchased for its browsing collections.

But labels should also be added to already owned items that are being reclassified using a reader interest approach. As Milton (1986) notes, this type of reclassification is a major undertaking that will be easiest to accomplish if the library prepares a table of the sort shown in figure 10.3 to convert Dewey Decimal Classification numbers to each of the reader interest categories that will be used. These category labels should be assigned to the entire collection before any shifting of categories occurs.

The library will then need to estimate the amount of shelf space that will be required for each category and plan the layout of the new shelves.[14] The library can choose to house all interest categories separately from the fiction categories it has already set up or to group together or even integrate fiction and nonfiction categories that may have common readers. Figures 6.5 and 6.6 in chapter 6 list some of these affinities. For example, one library integrated Humor (827) and Cartoons (741.5) "into the *Humorous Novels* sequence, and true sea stories into the *Sea* category. Books about true crime were shelved next to the *Crime* section, *Occult* books next to *Horror Fiction* and books on the *Unknown* (from Atlantis to UFOs) next to the *Science Fiction* category" (Morson and Perry, 1982, 103).

Once the shifting has taken place, the library will want to mark each section with large signs that indicate the new categories. Each sign will ideally tell how the collection is organized within that category. Most categories (e.g., Philosophy) will lend themselves to organization by the author's last name. But others can benefit from a different treatment. For example, the "Computers" category may have subheadings for computer games, spreadsheets, and word processing packages.

Readers' Advisory and Reference Services

In times of limited funding, the internal promotion techniques discussed so far, which are designed to help more than one reader at a time, are particularly cost-effective because they help library users become more self-sufficient in finding titles that they might like to read. However, they are not a complete substitute for providing individual assistance to patrons who want or need it.

For this reason, most public libraries promote the collection, one work at a time, through reference and readers' advisory services. Such services link individual patrons with items that they might want to read, view, or listen to. For example, a librarian may recommend a book on origami for an artistic but bedridden hospital patient.

(Text continues on page 279.)

Category Name	Symbol (for marking book and catalog)	Main Dewey Allocations (*indicates that only part of the sequence is applicable or that books should be allocated to the most appropriate category)
Animal life & pets	ANI	156*, 500.9, 590*, 636, 638, 639
Archaeology & ancient history	ARC	560*, 573*, 930
Art, architecture & photography	ART	069*, 700-779*
Astronomy & space	AST	500.5, 520, 629.4, 999
Biography	BIO	920 (preferred unless better placed with subject)
Cars & cycles	MOT	338.7*, 629.2*, 796.6-7
Collecting & antiques	COL	069*, 090, 391*, 681.1, 684*, 688*, 700-769*, 790.1
Crafts	CRA	646*, 680*, 700-769*
Crime & police work	CRI	327.1*, 345, 363.2, 363.4, 364-365, 614.1*, 652.4*, 658.47*
Economics, business & management	ECO	003*, 330, 343-344*, 346*, 368, 380-384*, 650-653, 657-659
Electronics	ELE	001.5-6*, 621.37*, 621.38
Entertainment & performing	ENT	394.3*, 790-792*, 793.3, 808.5
Food & drink	FOO	394.1*, 637, 640-642*, 647*, 663-664
Government, law & politics	GOV	320, 335, 340-349*, 350-352.1
Great Britain, travel, geography & history	GRE	327*, 367.9*, 391*, 394*, 526*, 912*, 941-942*
Health, welfare & public services	HEA	178, 312*, 344*, 352.4-7, 360-363*, 610-619, 628*, 646.7*, 649.8
House maintenance & decorating	HOU	333.3*, 621.3*, 643-645, 648, 684*, 690*, 714*, 717*, 747
Indoor games	GAM	394.3*, 398.6*, 790-795*

Fig. 10.3. The relationship between the reader interest categories used by one library and the Dewey Decimal Classification scheme.

(Fig. 10.3 continues on page 278.)

Category Name	Symbol (for marking book and catalog)	Main Dewey Allocations (*indicates that only part of the sequence is applicable or that books should be allocated to the most appropriate category)
Literature & languages	LIT	010-029, 070-080, 098, 398.5-398.9*, 400, 800
Living & learning	LIV	131-131.3, 137.7, 150-155.9, 158, 170*, 300-307.7, 312*, 323*, 326, 362.6-8, 366*, 367*, 369*, 370*, 391.6, 395, 646.7*, 649
Local history	LOC	Any with local interest
Music	MUS	780
Philosophy	PHI	003*, 100-129*, 140-199*
Plant life & gardening	PLA	156*, 580*, 630-635*, 712*, 714-719*
Popular beliefs & the supernatural	BEL	001.9, 128.5-129.4, 133-135, 137.7*, 138-139, 147*, 149.3*, 292-299*, 366*, 390*
Quick reference	REF	As appropriate
Religion	REL	200-291, 292-299*, 377
Science & the earth	SCI	156*, 372*, 389, 500-519*, 526*, 530-550, 560-599*
Sports & outdoor activity	SPO	394.3*, 796-799*
Technology	TEC	001.5*, 601-609, 620-622*, 624, 627, 628*, 629.8, 630-631, 660-662, 665-699*, 710-711, 713, 714*, 717*
Transport	TRA	380.5, 385-388, 526*, 527-527.5, 621.33*, 623.8*, 625-625.7, 629-629.3*, 688.6*
Wars & warfare	WAR	343.1, 355-359, 363.3, 369*, 623-623.7, 623.8*, 794*, 904.7*, 940-999* (accounts of wars)
World travel, geography & history	WOR	324-325*, 327*, 367-9*, 391*, 526*, 647.9*, 901-912*, 929.8, 940-999*

N.B. Occasionally, these headings are amended if they do not fit on shelf guiding or are combined with other categories.

Reprinted with permission from Milton (1986, 16-17).

Although reference and readers' advisory services are similar, librarians performing a reference function generally link patrons with materials that will meet a specific information need. For example, a patron might request information about low-cost bicycle tours of Europe, establishing and maintaining an organic garden, or the life of Anne Boleyn. Generally, a reference librarian will use relevant indexes and the catalog to locate the titles of one or more suitable works.

Readers' advisers are trained to help patrons find fiction that they will enjoy. For example, a patron might ask for a well-written Regency romance, a novel with thoughtful or insightful characters, an action-packed adventure story with female protagonists, or a work by an author who "writes like Stephen King." Because few public libraries provide in-depth access to fiction in their catalogs (that is, access by some means other than author or title, such as character, setting, etc.), a readers' adviser generally uses personal knowledge of the collection and various fiction guides (e.g., *Fiction Catalog* or *Genreflecting*) to locate one or more works that will meet a patron's needs.[15]

Although public libraries have emphasized reference services for decades, they typically have not stressed readers' advisory services. For example, a 1972 survey of 150 public libraries in the United States showed that less than one-fifth had a fully designated position of readers' adviser (Reagan, 1973). However, the situation has improved somewhat since the mid-1980s, as librarians have realized the extent of confusion that patrons, especially browsers, feel when faced with numerous choices and have undertaken grass-roots efforts to promote such services. Readers' advisory advocates have persuaded various library associations to sponsor conference programs on this topic; have formed readers' advisory round tables at the local, regional, and national levels; and have written an increasing number of works—both how-to and research related—on the subject.

Both reference and readers' advisory services fall under a promotion category called personal selling. Personal selling can be especially effective in getting potential patrons to act. That is, if the librarian takes time to determine the needs of individual patrons and find sources that will meet these, the patrons will be more satisfied with and more likely to use the materials that have been found.

However, personal salespeople, that is, librarians, are most effective when they possess certain characteristics. The first is a strong service orientation—a strong personal desire to give the best service possible. This trait will help them devote their full energy and enthusiasm to helping patrons.

Second, they need to be friendly and approachable. Studies have shown that many users are reluctant to "bother" librarians with their questions. For example, Westbrook (1984) found that a majority of patrons in an academic library did not ask for help because the librarians appeared to be too busy to assist them, because they were unsure about the librarians' willingness to help, or because they felt librarians were definitely unwilling to help. One study by Kazlauskas (1976) showed that patrons felt the most approachable librarians were those who immediately acknowledged a patron's presence when the patron moved toward the reference desk—if not verbally then through establishing eye contact or "flashing their eyebrows." Receptive librarians also smile at patrons, use a friendly tone of voice, and use evaluative gestures, such as nodding to indicate they are listening to and absorbing patron requests (Crouch, 1981; Gothberg, 1976; Kazlauskas, 1976).

Third, the most successful and effective reference and readers' advisory librarians have good communication skills. Such skills help them to relate to the patron in an empathetic fashion and to conduct a comprehensive reference or readers' advisory interview to determine the exact nature of a patron's need.

Fourth, if librarians are serving a special target market (e.g., deaf persons, physically handicapped people, or recent immigrants), they should have the necessary training to help them understand the needs of this market. For example, youth services librarians who understand the developmental needs of children should be able to match a child's stated requirements with titles that will meet these.

Finally, librarians should have a good working knowledge of both the collection and ways in which they can access it. Research shows that librarians do not always use efficient search strategies or exploit the catalog and other access tools (e.g., from indexes like *Fiction Catalog* to pathfinders on certain subjects) as well as they might.[16]

Obviously, libraries can influence the effectiveness of their reference and readers' advisory librarians by selecting employees who have the traits noted. They can also encourage further development of these traits by providing a variety of continuing education and training programs. For example, Stephan and others (1988) showed that communication skills could be improved when they gave a three-day workshop for reference librarians in Maryland's public libraries. The workshop made librarians more aware of how they were handling reference questions; gave them intensive training in more appropriate behavior, particularly in conducting a comprehensive and clear reference interview; and provided them with ample opportunity to practice the techniques they had learned. The workshop is credited with improving reference accuracy rates from 55 percent to 77 percent. Two libraries that gave participating librarians additional feedback and coached them on their performance increased their accuracy rates to 95 percent.

Libraries should also take steps to help correct for the fact that not all patrons will ask for help. The simplest is to post signs in various stack locations and near the catalog that encourage patrons to ask for help when they have questions.

Libraries can also prominently display readers' advisory tools so that patrons who are having trouble finding fiction can use these items. For example, libraries can display *Genreflecting, Fiction Catalog*, or *A Handbook of Contemporary Fiction for Public Libraries and School Libraries* on special shelves at the beginning of the fiction stacks and Consumer Guide's *Rating the Movies*, and *Halliwell's Film Guide* next to the videocassette collection.

A few libraries are even developing or purchasing automated readers' advisory guides for their patrons to use. For example, the New Britain (Connecticut) Public Library designed its own internal computer program, dubbed "Byte into Books," which asks children questions about their sex, grade level, and reading preferences. The computer matches these responses to coded information (e.g., subject/genre, gender appeal, popularity, and reading level) on more than 500 books, both "high quality" and "popular" titles, that are of interest to children in grades one through eight. Then it prints a personalized book list for the child, complete with annotations and shelf locations. The staff note that children are borrowing a wider variety of materials than they did before the project began (Goodgion, 1986). The College of Education at Wichita State University has developed a similar tool, which can be purchased at a reasonable cost, to help students of all ages find fiction, while the Los Angeles County Public Library has put together a readers' advisory database of adult fiction (McKenna, 1987; Database, 1987).

What External Promotion Techniques Have Been Shown to Be Effective in Increasing Use or User Awareness of the Collection?

External promotion techniques are those used outside the library to entice potential users to come in and use library materials. Generally, the library promotes one or more aspects of the collection or a collection-related event, like an author visit, in local newspapers, on radio or television, through booktalks and other sales pitches to individuals or groups, or through some type of direct mail campaign to potential users in general or to a specific user group. Consider, for example, the following external promotion efforts conducted by three public libraries.

The Prince George (British Columbia) Public Library featured, at a local commerce trade show, a variety of sources that area businesses could use to obtain economic, marketing, or general business information (Tsunoda, 1985).

The Royal Oak (Michigan) Public Library challenged children and their parents who were participating in the summer reading program to an eight-day nonstop "Royal Readathon." Schools sent flyers publicizing the event home with children; the readathon was also featured in newspapers and on radio and television stations locally and in nearby Detroit. During the 192-hour program, 384 children, from ages three-and-a-half to 13, either read aloud to a parent or, for children too young to read alone, were read to by a parent in round-the-clock shifts of half-an-hour each (Balkema, 1991).

The Cuyahoga County (Ohio) Public Library (CCPL) featured its extensive collection of thematic story-telling and puppet-show kits in a campaign aimed at child care workers. CCPL mailed letters that described the collection to area day-care centers and nursery schools, then sent a librarian to interested organizations to train day-care providers in use of the kits. The library also mailed a quarterly newsletter that featured new kits and kits relevant to the season. These highly targeted promotion efforts have paid off. In one 11-month period, the library circulated over 2,100 kits that reached more than 70,400 children and care givers (Rome, 1989).

Unfortunately, there has been little rigorous research conducted to measure the extent to which external promotion techniques have increased awareness or use of the collection. This section of the chapter presents research on the most-studied of these, the booktalk, then gives suggestions for research for the other areas.

Booktalks and Talks Promoting Other Types of Materials

Many public libraries present, to a variety of clubs and organizations, talks on specific product items or lines that the group might find useful. For example, a library could promote its collection of materials on recycling at a meeting of a local environmental club and materials on time management to a group of business and professional women.

Although many articles address how to give booktalks, only a few report, in some detail, the exact effects of such talks on their audiences.[17] Although the research was primarily conducted in school libraries, it reveals several important points that public librarians may find of interest.

First, booktalks given to students have significantly increased the use of featured titles from the school library. For example, Bodart (1986a, 1986b) found that circulation of 14 titles to high school freshmen increased from 15 during the 1983-1984 school year, when they received no publicity, to 266 during the first five months of the 1984-1985 school year, when they were featured in booktalks presented to half of the freshman class. This represented a circulation increase of 1,773 percent.

Second, people who hear booktalks often share information about promoted titles with their friends. For example, in the Bodart study previously mentioned, this "grapevine effect" was associated with a 500 percent increase in circulation of featured titles among sophomores, juniors, and seniors: from a total of 18 circulations during the 1983-1984 school year to 90 during the first four months of 1984-1985.

Third, public librarians should not expect rises in the use of titles featured in their booktalks to be as dramatic as those experienced in school libraries. This is because it requires greater effort for public library patrons, who hear booktalks outside the library (e.g., at a meeting of the local historical society) to travel to the library to check out featured titles, than it does for students, who hear booktalks at school, to walk down the hall to check them out.

However, it is clear that public libraries can increase user awareness of library services, at least temporarily, by giving booktalks outside the library building. The Pikes Peak (Colorado) Library District recognized this when they persuaded four area bookstores to help sponsor a one-person classroom production that described the components of a mystery story, highlighted 12 children's mysteries and two mystery series, and promoted the collection in general. The library hired a local actor and storyteller to play the part of Inspector Penrose at 100-person presentations at each of 50 schools. The library received radio and television news coverage of this event and others during Children's Book Week and exposed 5,000 children to the idea that the public library had titles they might enjoy (Guthrie, 1986).

Fourth, single-presentation booktalks given at school do not appear to affect student attitudes toward reading in general (Bodart, 1986a, 1986b). This is not surprising because people's values and attitudes are unlikely to change after a single exposure to some stimulus.

It may, however, be possible for a library to encourage changes in individual use of libraries or attitudes toward reading by exposing people to library materials via a series of booktalks over a period of time. This may explain, at least in part, why Level (1982) managed to increase the library use of students with low reading abilities to 75 percent of the use of students with high reading abilities by giving a series of 12 15-minute booktalks to the former group.

Suggestions for Further Research on External Promotion Efforts

As noted previously, few studies have rigorously measured the extent to which other types of external promotion efforts have increased user awareness or use. However, a review of the statistics and anecdotal evidence reported by libraries that have tried external promotion efforts reveals some consistent patterns. Although these patterns are presented below, librarians should view these findings with great caution because broad generalizations based on scanty research are subject to many kinds of errors.

The first pattern is that public libraries, which compete with numerous profit-making and nonprofit organizations to capture consumer attention, seem to have the best chance of arousing a great deal of public interest when they

1. get well-known personalities to promote library materials. For example, in 1990 the American Library Association and the American Association of School Librarians jointly promoted the "Night of 1,000 Stars," a program that encouraged celebrities to visit the library and read to patrons. Literally thousands of library patrons around the country turned out to hear participants, who ranged from world-famous entertainers like Charlton Heston and Aretha Franklin to local celebrities like mayors and ministers, read aloud from their favorite titles in hundreds of libraries (Night, 1990).

2. use promotion materials that are creative enough or funny enough to capture consumer attention. For example, one public librarian interested 5,000 schoolchildren in the library's summer reading program by highlighting specific titles and popular literary characters like the spider in *Charlotte's Web* with a rap—an oral poem that combines talking and chanting with a rhythmic beat (Reid, 1988).

Second, the more publicity that occurs, the more likely it is that both use and awareness will increase. For example, the publicity blitz used by the Springfield (Massachusetts) City Library to promote its "Seussamania" festival (described earlier in this chapter) resulted in a 50 percent increase in circulation of children's materials during that festival (Youthreach, 1986). However, the increases in community awareness and use of many library collections will be smaller because most libraries, because of time constraints, do not engage in promotion campaigns on this large a scale.

Third, large-scale promotion efforts, even if they cost more to produce initially, may be the most cost-effective because of the number of households reached. For example, the Beverly Hills Public Library airs a 30-minute cable television show twice a week that promotes its collection indirectly, via interviews with authors like Gore Vidal and Ann Beattie as well as a variety of others involved in the book business—editors, illustrators, and publishers. The twice-weekly show reaches 140,000 households in Los Angeles. A similar program produced by the Denver Public Library reaches an estimated 81,000 people in and around the city (Dower, 1990).

Fourth, increases in awareness and use that have been generated by external promotion efforts may fall off rapidly unless a library is able to convince patrons who are trying out collection resources that the benefits of this use will outweigh the costs over the long term. One type of promotion effort that has a good chance of convincing patrons, over time, that the benefits of library service outweigh the costs is that directed toward existing patrons and potential patrons, rather than hard-core nonusers. As has been noted throughout this book, it is much easier for libraries to convince people who already read and use other library materials and who have developed the library habit of the benefits of using the collection.

But libraries can also convince patrons of the benefits of library services by carefully designing promotion efforts to meet the needs of a target market. Consider, for example, the various programs that public libraries have begun to meet the needs of patients exiting the hospital. The Toledo-Lucas County (Ohio) Library gives to all these patients a get-well card that says, "Sometimes recuperation means not being able to get out for awhile. If you have that problem, [we] would like to help. The library's Homebound Service can bring library materials directly to your home" (Catch, 1988, 27). The Council Bluffs (Iowa) Public Library distributes packets of materials about babies and reading to patients on hospital maternity wards. The packets include an article on choosing books for young children, a list of early childhood development activities, a brochure on library services, a bibliography on parenting and child development, and a list of "first reads" for babies (Herzog, 1989).

Conclusion

This chapter began by noting that libraries can increase the awareness or use of many kinds of works using various promotion devices. Promotion efforts will be most successful when marketing research has been conducted to show which promotion techniques will work and which won't. Many of the studies mentioned in this chapter were experimental studies in which a researcher consciously developed a hypothesis and tested it, measuring changes in user awareness or in use before and after a new promotion device was tried.

As Baker (1989) has noted, many librarians lack the time, resources, and special research skills needed to set up and evaluate rigorous research studies capable of determining whether significant changes in awareness or use are caused by a particular promotion technique. However, librarians should try to keep up with the findings of published research on the topic and communicate these findings to other staff involved in collection development efforts.

Librarians need to be aware of two final cautions regarding promotion efforts. First, librarians should avoid assuming that promotion techniques, when used alone, will cause awareness or use to increase on a permanent basis. There are at least two reasons for this:

1. Internal promotion efforts often shift awareness or use from non-promoted titles to promoted titles, rather than increasing the overall circulation. For example, Baker (1986a) discovered that prominently placed displays of fiction shifted circulation from the regular fiction stacks in two test libraries; however, the displays did not cause patrons to check out more fiction titles. This finding is not too surprising because the typical patron enters the library with a general idea about how many items he will borrow — an idea that is based on such factors as the amount of free time he will have to use library materials during the next few weeks.

2. External promotion efforts may increase awareness or use of the library. However, the increase will be temporary unless new users become convinced that the long-term benefits of using the library's collection outweigh the costs.

These findings suggest that libraries should not overemphasize promotion efforts at the expense of other tasks. Rather, as has been suggested throughout this book, they should develop integrated marketing schemes that involve analyzing the products in their collections, redesigning these collections to meet the needs of both existing patrons and the community in general, and promoting the materials in these collections to potential patrons.

A second caution is that promotion, the third step in a marketing-based collection management program, should not be the last. Rather, libraries should continually repeat the cycle of evaluation, selection, and promotion to obtain current information on what types of materials community residents require and will use.

Notes

[1]See, for example, Mueller (1965).

[2]See, for example, Taylor (1982), Bettman (1979), and Cohen (1977).

[3]See, for example, Bettman (1979).

[4]See, for example, Wright and Weitz (1977) and Wright (1974).

[5]See, for example, "Face-Out" (1988).

[6]See, for example, "Interiors" (1989).

[7]See, for example, Jones (1989).

[8]Everhart and others (1989) give more than 50 examples of thematic displays that can be used to promote books and other library materials and provide practical guidelines to constructing displays.

[9]Construction of these works is explained in some detail in Bronson (1982).

[10]See, for example, Langhorne (1987) and Tod (1983).

[11]See, for example, Golden (1983).

[12]See, for example, Spiller (1980) and Briggs (1973).

[13]See, for example, American Library Association (1990) and "Libraries" (1992).

[14]Milton (1986) gives instructions for performing this task.

[15]For a comprehensive look at readers' advisory services in public libraries, see Saricks and Brown (1989).

[16]For a more comprehensive review on this subject, see Baker and Lancaster (1991).

[17]Two recent titles that discuss practical aspects of presenting booktalks are Gillespie and Naden (1989) and Thomas (1989).

References

Ainley, Patricia, and Barry Totterdell. *Alternative Arrangement: New Approaches to Public Library Stock*. London: Association of Assistant Librarians, 1982.

American Library Association. *Guidelines on Subject Access to Individual Works of Fiction, Drama, Etc.* Chicago: American Library Association, 1990.

Baker, Sharon L. "The Display Phenomenon: An Exploration into Factors Causing the Increased Circulation of Displayed Books." *Library Quarterly* 56, no. 3 (July 1986a): 237-57.

_____. "Improving Business Services Through the Use of Focus Groups." *RQ* 30, no. 3 (Spring 1991): 377-85.

_____. "Overload, Browsers, and Selections." *Library and Information Science Research* 8, no. 4 (October-December 1986b): 315-29.

_____. "Problem Solving Through Experimental Research: The Need for Better Controls." *Library Trends* 38, no. 2 (Fall 1989): 204-14.

_____. "Will Fiction Classification Schemes Increase Use?" *RQ* 27, no. 3 (Spring 1988): 366-76.

Baker, Sharon L., and F. Wilfrid Lancaster. *Measurement and Evaluation of Library Services*. 2d ed. Arlington, Va.: Information Resources Press, 1991.

Baker, Sharon L., and Gay W. Shepherd. "Fiction Classification Schemes: The Principles Behind Them, and Their Success." *RQ* 27, no. 2 (Winter 1987): 245-51.

Balkema, Kathleen A. "Practically Speaking: Red Ribbons for Royal Readers." *School Library Journal* 37, no. 7 (July 1991): 30.

Benezra, Barbara. "A New Arrangement." *Ohio Media Spectrum* 30, no. 1 (January 1978): 69.

Berman, Sanford. "Reference, Readers and Fiction: New Approaches." *Reference Services in the 1980s*, nos. 1/2 (Fall-Winter 1981): 45-53.

Bettman, James R. *An Information Processing Theory of Consumer Choice*. Reading, Mass.: Addison-Wesley, 1979.

Bodart, Joni. "Book You!" *Voice of Youth Advocates* 9, no. 1 (April 1986a): 22-23.

_____. "Booktalks Do Work! The Effects of Booktalking on Attitude and Circulation." *Illinois Libraries* 68, no. 6 (June 1986b): 378-81.

Bordon, William Alanson. "On Classifying Fiction." *Library Journal* 34, no. 6 (June 1909): 264-65.

Briggs, Betty S. "A Case for Classified Fiction." *Library Journal* 98, no. 22 (15 December 1973): 3694.

Bronson, Que. *Books on Display*. Washington, D.C.: Metropolitan Washington Library Council, 1982.

" 'Catch 'Em in the Hospital' Approach." *Unabashed Librarian*, no. 68 (1988): 27.

Cohen, Sheldon. "Environmental Load and the Allocation of Attention." In *Advances in Environmental Research*, ed. Andrew Baum and Stuart Valins. Hillsdale, N.J.: Erlbaum, 1977.

Crouch, Richard K. C. "Interpersonal Communication in the Reference Interview." Ph.D. diss., University of Toronto, 1981.

"A Database for Older Fiction." *Library Hotline* 16, no. 28 (14 September 1987): 3.

Dower, Kim Freilich. "Tune in to Reading: Pushing Books Via Cable." *Library Journal* 115, no. 14 (1 September 1990): 171-72.

Dragon, Andrea C. "Marketing and the Public Library." *Public Library Quarterly* 4, no. 4 (Winter 1983): 37-46.

Engel, James F., David T. Kollatt, and Roger D. Blackwell. *Consumer Behavior*. 2d ed. New York: Holt, Rinehart & Winston, 1973.

Everhart, Nancy, Claire Hartz, and William Kreiger. *Library Displays*. Metuchen, N.J.: Scarecrow Press, 1989.

"Face-Out Book Shelving in Multnomah County." *Southeastern Library Services Regional Rag* 15, no. 5 (March-April, 1988): 7.

Gallup Organization. *The Gallup 1988 Annual Report on Book Buying*. Princeton, N.J.: Gallup Organization, 1988.

_____. *The Gallup 1985 Annual Report on Book Buying*. Princeton, N.J.: Gallup Organization, 1985.

Gillespie, John T., and Corrine J. Naden. *Seniorplots: A Book Talk Guide for Use with Readers Ages 15-18*. New York: R. R. Bowker, 1989.

Golden, Gary A. "Motivation to Select Books: A Study of Annotated and Unannotated Booklists in Public Libraries." Ph.D. diss., University of Illinois at Urbana-Champaign, 1983.

Goldhor, Herbert. "Experimental Effects on the Choice of Books Borrowed by Public Library Adult Patrons." *Library Quarterly* 51, no. 3 (July 1981): 253-68.

Goodgion, Laurel. "Byte Into Books." *School Library Journal* 32, no. 9 (May 1986): LC6-LC8.

Gothberg, Helen. "Immediacy: A Study of Communication Effect on the Reference Process." *Journal of Academic Librarianship* 2, no. 3 (July 1976): 126-29.

Guthrie, Donna W. "Youthreach: Inspector Penrose Clues Kids In." *American Libraries* 17, no. 4 (April 1986): 274-75.

Harrell, Gail. "The Classification and Organization of Adult Fiction in Large American Public Libraries." *Public Libraries* 24, no. 1 (Spring 1985): 13-14.

Herzog, Dianne. "Promoting Libraries and Reading in the Maternity Ward." *Iowa Library Quarterly* 26, no. 2 (1989): 6-8.

Hubbard, Lee. "A Boost for Browsing." *Library Journal* 92, no. 7 (1 April 1967): 1392.

"Interiors Showcase: Shelving and Display." *American Libraries* 20, no. 4 (April 1989): 350-51.

Jones, Margaret. "Shelf-Awareness: Getting a Fix on Fixtures." *Publishers Weekly* 236, no. 3 (21 July 1989): 18, 20-23.

Kazlauskas, Edward. "An Exploratory Study: A Kinesic Analysis of Academic Library Public Service Points." *Journal of Academic Librarianship* 2, no. 3 (July 1976): 130-34.

Langhorne, Mary Jo. "Marketing Books in the School Library." *School Library Journal* 33, no. 5 (January 1987): 31-33.

Level, June Saine. "Booktalk Power—A Locally Based Research Study." *School Library Media Quarterly* 10, no. 2 (Winter 1982): 154-55.

"Libraries." *Chronicle of Higher Education* 28, no. 19 (15 January 1992): A22.

Libretto, Ellen V. "Merchandising Collections and Services." In *New Directions for Young Adult Services*, ed. Ellen V. Libretto, 49-60. New York: R. R. Bowker, 1983.

Little, Paul. "The Effectiveness of Paperbacks." *Library Journal* 104, no. 20 (15 November 1979): 2411-16.

Long, Sarah P. "The Effect of Face-Front Display on the Circulation of Books in a Public Library." Master's project, University of North Carolina at Greensboro, Department of Library Science/Educational Technology, 1986. ERIC ED278415.

McKenna, Michael C. "Using Micros to Find Fiction: Issues and Answers." *School Library Media Quarterly* 15, no. 2 (Winter 1987): 92-95.

Mellon, Constance A. "Library Anxiety: A Grounded Theory and Its Development." *College and Research Libraries* 47, no. 2 (March 1986): 160-65.

Milton, Ian S. "Changing Faces: A Practical Guide to Reader Interest Categorisation and Library Facelifts." Wheathampstead, St. Albans, England: Branch and Mobile Libraries Group, 1986.

Morson, Ian, and Mike Perry. "Two-Tier and Total: Stock Arrangement in Brent." In *Alternative Arrangement: New Approaches to Public Library Stock*, ed. Patricia Ainley and Barry Totterdell, 101-18. London: Association of Assistant Librarians, 1982.

Mueller, Elizabeth. "Are New Books Read More Than Old Ones?" *Library Quarterly* 35, no. 3 (July 1965): 166-72.

"New Stock Layouts." *Library Association Record* 91, no. 3 (March 1989): 133.

"Night of 1,000 Stars: A Wellspring of Love." *American Libraries* 21, no. 6 (June 1990): 494.

Paperbound Books in Print: Spring 1992. New Providence, N.J.: R. R. Bowker, 1992.

Parrish, Nancy B. "The Effect of a Booklist on the Circulation of Fiction Books Which Have Not Been Borrowed from a Public Library in Four Years or Longer." Master's project, University of North Carolina at Greensboro, 1986. ERIC ED282564.

Reader, Den. "User Orientation in a Hertfordshire Branch." In *Alternative Arrangement: New Approaches to Public Library Stock*, ed. Patricia Ainley and Barry Totterdell, 34-46. London: Association of Assistant Librarians, 1982.

Reagan, Lee. "Status of Reader's Advisory Service." *RQ* 12, no. 3 (Spring 1973): 227-33.

Reid, Rob. "Practically Speaking: Rappin' Them into the Library." *School Library Journal* 34, no. 7 (March 1988): 134.

Rome, Linda. "On Assignment: Outreach for Preschoolers—Project LEAP." *Wilson Library Bulletin* 64, no. 2 (October 1989): 39-41.

Rutzen, Ruth. "Shelving for Readers." *Library Journal* 77, no. 6 (15 March 1952): 478-82.

Saricks, Joyce G., and Nancy Brown. *Readers' Advisory Service in the Public Library*. Chicago: American Library Association, 1989.

Sawbridge, Lynn, and Leo Favret. "The Mechanics and the Magic of Declassification." *Library Association Record* 84, no. 11 (November 1982): 383-84.

" 'Service of the Month' in Prince George's County." *Library Journal* 114, no. 8 (1 May 1989): 25.

Shaw, Ralph R. "The Influence of Sloping Shelves on Book Circulation." *Library Quarterly* 8, no. 4 (October 1938): 480-90.

Sherman, Steve. *ABC's of Library Promotion*. 2d ed. Metuchen, N.J.: Scarecrow Press, 1980.

Sivulich, Kenneth G. "How We Run the Queens Library Good (and Doubled Circulation in Seven Years)." *Library Journal* 114, no. 3 (15 February 1989): 123-27.

Spiller, David. "The Provision of Fiction for Public Libraries." *Journal of Librarianship* 12, no. 4 (October 1980): 238-65.

Stephan, Sandy, Ralph Gers, Lillie Seward, Nancy Bolin, and Jim Partridge. "Reference Breakthrough in Maryland." *Public Libraries* 27, no. 4 (Winter 1988): 202-3.

Taylor, Margaret Ann Thomas. "The Effect of Bibliographic Accessibility upon Physical Accessibility of Materials in a Public Library Setting." Ph.D. diss., University of Michigan, 1982.

Thomas, Rebecca L. *Primaryplots: A Book Talk Guide for Use with Readers Ages 4-8*. New York: R. R. Bowker, 1989.

Tod, Mary. "The Law of Slow Learning: Marketing at the Dallas Public Library." *Public Library Quarterly* 4, no. 2 (Summer 1983): 29-38.

Totterdell, Barry, and Jean Bird. *The Effective Library: Report of the Hillingdon Project on Public Library Effectiveness*. London: Library Association, 1976.

Tsunoda, Melanie. "Attract New Users—Set Up Shop at a Trade Show." *Canadian Library Journal* 42, no. 6 (December 1985): 369-72.

Tuggle, Ann Montgomery, and Dawn Hansen Heller. *Grand Schemes and Nitty-Gritty Details: Library PR That Works*. Littleton, Colo.: Libraries Unlimited, 1987.

Venter, Trude. " 'n Rangskikkingsmetode om die gebruik van nie-fiksie in openbare biblioteke te bevorder." *South African Journal for Librarianship and Information Science* 52, no. 4 (December 1984): 109-12.

Webb, Terry D. "Phoenix Public Library: Reorganization Based on a Hierarchy of User Types." In *Reorganization in the Public Library*, ed. Terry D. Webb, 52-66. Phoenix, Ariz.: Oryx Press, 1985.

Westbrook, Lynn. "Catalog Failure and Reference Service: A Preliminary Study." *RQ* 24, no. 1 (Fall 1984): 82-90.

Williams, Dianne T. McAfee. "A Study to Determine the Effectiveness of an Interest Grouping Classification for Primary Grade Children." Master's thesis, Western Michigan University, 1973.

Wood, Richard. "The Experimental Effects of Fiction Book Lists on Circulation in an Academic Library," *RQ* 24, no. 4 (Summer 1985): 427-32.

Wright, Peter. "The Harassed Decision Maker: Time Pressure, Distractions, and the Use of Evidence." *Journal of Applied Psychology* 59, no. 5 (1974): 555-61.

Wright, Peter, and Barton Weitz. "Time Horizon Effects on Product Evaluation Strategies." *Journal of Marketing Research* 14 (November 1977): 429-33.

"Youthreach: Seussamania in Geisel's Hometown." *American Libraries* 17, no. 6 (June 1986): 485.

Making Marketing Work: Creating a Marketing Mindset Throughout the Library

11

A major premise of this book is that, in today's tight economic times, when funding bodies are requiring that public libraries provide resources and services in the most cost-effective fashion possible, libraries that adopt a societal-marketing orientation will be better able to meet their goals than libraries that do not. This is because such an orientation is based on determining the needs and wants of community residents and then designing the library's collection and services to both satisfy these requirements and preserve or enhance the well-being of society.

But marketing activities are not cheap. It costs money for libraries to research their communities; to select roles that are in line with community needs; to scrutinize their collections and services in light of the variables of product, price, place, and promotion; and to adopt the type of integrated approach to collection management described in this book.

This raises the question: can public libraries afford to invest in marketing activities? Some libraries are trying to answer this question by experimenting with different marketing strategies at one or more test locations. For example, the County of Los Angeles Public Library system selected the East Los Angeles Library (ELAL) as a marketing test site and developed specialized marketing plans for that facility. ELAL revised its internal sign system, enhanced its collection of Spanish-language materials, installed special shelving for best-selling works, displayed Spanish and children's materials in creative fashions, and used bilingual advertising in community newspapers to promote its collections and services. During the months that these and other marketing strategies were implemented, the number of registered borrowers tripled and there were significant increases in walk-in count, in-house use, and circulation (Marketing, 1991).

Other libraries that have used the types of collection marketing techniques described in this book on a consistent and comprehensive basis are reporting availability rates much higher than that of the average public library. For example, Engel (1982) reported that the Baltimore County Public Library met user demands for 86 percent to 97 percent of specific known-title requests. Circulation per capita rates have risen significantly at these libraries as well. Because research has shown that there are no significant differences among the average number of items checked out by individual patrons at various public libraries, circulation per capita actually may be an indirect measure of the proportion of the service population that uses a library (D'Elia and Rodger, 1987). That is, librarians who use techniques to market their collections—making readily and easily available the titles and types of items that their patrons want—may be attracting a broader base. Librarians have been trying to build such a base for years because it may ultimately increase the levels of community support, monetary as well as nonmonetary, for library services.

Increases like these, in both use and effectiveness, are not uncommon among public libraries that have instituted carefully planned and thoughtfully coordinated marketing programs. This explains why public librarians across the nation are increasingly asking themselves whether they can afford to ignore marketing activities.

But marketing activities will be less successful if they are conducted in isolation. Indeed, as Drucker notes, "Marketing is so basic that it cannot be considered a separate function (i.e., a separate skill or work) within the business, on a par with others such as manufacturing or personnel. Marketing requires separate work, and a distinct group of activities. But it is, first, a central dimension of the entire business. It is the whole business seen from a point of view of its final result, that is, from the customer's point of view. Concern and responsibility for marketing, must, therefore, permeate all areas of the enterprise" (1974, 63).

Experienced librarians know that marketing efforts are most successful when public libraries gain support for them from all those who are involved, directly or indirectly, in providing library service: the board of trustees, top administrators, and every single member of the library staff. Yet it is more common for a marketing mindset to be adopted by a portion of the staff and implemented on a piecemeal basis, than it is for marketing to be an integral part of the philosophy of the typical public library.

This seems to result, at least in part, from the natural tendency of library administrators to play the role of manager when introducing change. As a number of authors have noted, managers generally tend to focus on the technical aspects of how work is accomplished, to improve operational practices that the library already has in place, and to master routine, as well as to solve the problems that arise on a day-to-day basis.[1] In short, a manager's main role is to improve the efficiency of library operations. This role works exceptionally well when any kind of technical or procedural change is being introduced and is thus appropriate in many library situations.

However, implementing a comprehensive marketing program of the type discussed in this book is a philosophical rather than a technical change. Major philosophical changes are best interwoven into the fabric of library operations, rather than imposed on top of them. This interweaving occurs most frequently when administrators assume the role of leader rather than manager.

Instead of focusing on the technical aspects of how library services and collections may be improved, a leader asks those with whom he works broad, philosophical questions about why the work should be done in certain ways. Rather than concentrating solely on improving efficiency and solving day-to-day operational problems, a leader tries to improve effectiveness by asking all those involved to anticipate problems and their solutions. In this process, the leader performs visionary tasks, using intuition, imagination, and foresight to predict events, measure the gravity of a problem, and facilitate effective contributions from employees.[2]

Leaders work to achieve a communal understanding of the issue at hand — an understanding that recognizes practical and philosophical details that should be addressed if the transformation is to be made. In other words, a leader tries to weave the diverse and colorful threads that exist within the library into a single tapestry of service that is rich and substantive because it contains important contributions from all. As Riggs (1988) has pointed out, when this has been done successfully, staff at all levels will bring greater confidence and enthusiasm to their positions. After all, each individual has helped enrich the tapestry by bringing his particular strengths and perspectives to it. Each has helped to set collective values and aspirations. Each has helped create a spirit of striving toward excellence that can energize everyone to move in a common direction.

But the leader also plays an important role in making sure that the marketing vision is actually implemented, that the marketing program is kept on track. As one author has noted, "Once the objectives of the campaign are established, an appropriate strategy for accomplishing them is selected, and a blend of tactical methods chosen, program control becomes all-important. It is very easy, during the day-to-day operations of a library to forget all of the hard work and determined planning that went on prior to the implementation of the plan. Problems and pressing duties tend to weaken the resolve of the librarian to be outward-looking" (Grunenwald, 1984, 30).

The question then becomes the following: What can a library leader do to encourage a truly collective effort to translate the marketing vision into reality? Management theorists suggest that a leader should work to establish a climate in which change can proceed smoothly, then follow an integrated, comprehensive approach to developing better collections and services.[3] Although this book as a whole has focused on marketing library collections, the approach suggested in this chapter is written from a more general view. It assumes that administrators will want to cultivate a marketing mindset for all types of library services, not just collection-related ones.

The approach recommended here is an idealized and broadly scaled one. It suggests that a library should

1. train staff members in basic marketing concepts, so each can fully participate in the marketing process;

2. devise a plan that will list marketing goals and objectives, then spell out practical activities to help translate the marketing vision into a reality;

3. provide sufficient resources to implement the plan;

4. evaluate the success of the plan and make changes as a result;

5. adopt other techniques to reinforce staff awareness of marketing concepts on a regular basis; and

6. be sensitive to issues relating to resistance to change.

This approach is based on the assumption that libraries that initially devote significant resources to weaving a strong marketing philosophy into the institution's consciousness will achieve full returns for their efforts in improved services and collections and, ultimately, in customer satisfaction. The reality, however, is that many public libraries will have to introduce marketing on a more limited basis. When this is the case, the library should focus initial efforts on training staff in marketing concepts and on designing and implementing a marketing plan on the largest scale it can afford. Other relevant activities— whether listed in this chapter, noted in other marketing works, or designed by library staff—should be phased in as time and resources permit.

Arranging for Initial Training in Marketing Concepts, as Needed

It is very important that library staff receive a good initial grounding in standard marketing concepts, because this information will form the warp and woof of the tapestry of service. That is, this information will provide the basis for shared communication on, goal setting about, and action toward any marketing activities. The library will, however, need to consider several basic questions before training is given. These include

1. Who will receive such training?

2. What concepts might be emphasized?

3. What type of training will be most effective?

Who Will Receive Training in Marketing Concepts?

All of those who work for or with the library can benefit from training in marketing concepts: professional and paraprofessional staff; technical services and public services staff; administrators, trustees, and regular employees. This is because inefficient or ineffective performance at any level can affect the quality of service a patron receives, his satisfaction level, and his overall perception of the library. The link is perhaps most noticeable in public service positions, because circulation staff, reference librarians, outreach specialists and similar employees market the library's wares, either one item at a time or en masse, directly to patrons. But less than optimum performance in behind-the-scenes tasks, like technical processing activities and reshelving, can also affect patron service and satisfaction levels. It is particularly important for supervisors and trustees to receive training in marketing concepts, because they play important roles in setting library policy and in allocating and managing both human and nonhuman resources.[4]

What Concepts Might Be Emphasized?

Many people in the library field have had little training in marketing issues. Unfortunately, this lack of training even applies to recent library school graduates. Weingand (1989) suggests this is because marketing is still taught as a peripheral concept in most library schools, rather than being fully integrated into the curriculum. Indeed, only 51 percent of the library schools accredited by the American Library Association employ, on a full- or part-time basis, a faculty member who states a specialization in marketing.[5] Because staff members lack training, they can confuse a number of marketing concepts. For example, when Vavrek (1988) asked rural librarians if they had participated in marketing activities, more than half said yes; further exploration revealed that these librarians often erroneously equated marketing with promotion of materials. Results of this and similar studies suggest that training programs should begin with the basics.

Ideally, training will be designed to help library employees and trustees answer the following questions in a fairly comprehensive manner:

1. What is marketing? How is the business term *marketing* related to the library term *service*?

2. What is a societal-marketing orientation?

3. What are the library's major products and services?

4. What do the concepts of product, price, place, and promotion mean in a marketing context?

5. How does the equation Satisfaction $-$ Cost > 0 relate to marketing?

6. What can each department in the library do to reduce the costs that patrons must bear to use collections and services?

Staff members who will assume immediate responsibility for carrying out more complex aspects of the marketing plan may need more advanced training. This group may include staff members who work at reference and readers' advisory desks, provide outreach services to one or more groups of patrons, manage branch libraries, evaluate and select resources, design promotional techniques, or supervise staff members with these duties.[6] Additional training for these staff members might focus on the following issues:

1. What is the rationale for conducting research on the community residents that the library serves?

2. What methods can the library use to collect information about community residents in general and their use of library services in particular?

3. What identifiable segments of the market is the library serving well? Not well?

4. What needs of particular market segments are not being met?

5. Are competitors meeting these unmet needs? If so, how?

6. Which target markets will the library concentrate its efforts on serving?

7. How will information on target markets be used to establish the library's mission, roles, goals, and objectives?

8. How can this be translated into an action plan to market the library's collections and services?

What Type of Training Will Be Most Effective?

Individuals can learn marketing concepts in a number of different ways. For example, they can read books and articles on the subject published by both the business and the library presses.[7] But printed matter may not address the specific concerns of a particular library. Moreover, reading is a rather passive form of learning that does not allow for discussion of concepts or for application to reinforce the ideas learned. Taking college courses on marketing and on marketing for nonprofit organizations may overcome these particular problems, but these courses may not focus specifically on marketing in a library context. Although programs at library conferences may be more focused, they may be too brief to present information in a comprehensive fashion. Another problem is that changes in motivational states are less likely to occur in response to programs of two hours or less.[8] Moreover, the cost of continuing education classes and library conferences may be prohibitive for all but the smallest libraries, because, ideally, all staff members and trustees should receive training in marketing concepts.

Many large and medium-sized public libraries will find it most cost-effective to contract with a consultant who has a comprehensive knowledge of marketing in general and of marketing public library services in particular, to present one or more in-house workshops on marketing. The one-day workshop or seminar is widely used to present marketing methods and techniques to profit and nonprofit organizations throughout the country. A study by Grunenwald and others (1990) has shown that such workshops can significantly

1. improve participant understanding of basic marketing concepts;

2. reduce the perception that marketing is simply hype and hustle; and

3. reduce the belief that marketing will not work in or is inappropriate for nonprofit organizations.

There are at least two other advantages of a library arranging for in-house marketing workshops. First, workshops can be tailored to meet the needs of a particular library and a particular group of individuals: paraprofessional versus professional staff; technical versus public services staff; employees versus trustees versus supervisors; people who need a basic understanding of marketing concepts to perform their jobs versus people who need a more comprehensive under-standing. Second, workshops can be scheduled in a flexible, staggered fashion, which is important if all staff members will attend.

Another issue related to training effectiveness is the extent to which the work-shop will be interactive. Employees who are new to marketing will learn better if a reasonable amount of structure is provided in the workshop. For example, the workshop instructor should give an initial lecture to introduce basic marketing concepts and definitions. But the instructor may also wish to provide oppor-tunities for structured, small group work, to allow employees to discuss from their own perspectives the marketing concepts to which they have been intro-duced. This strategy should be particularly effective near the end of the day when employees have received enough new information that they can begin to think about how they can apply it to their own jobs.[9] For example, the instructor might ask both public service and technical service employees what steps they could take in their own departments to reduce patron costs of using the collection.

Devising a Marketing Plan

Once training in marketing concepts has been completed, public libraries should develop plans to translate their marketing visions into reality. This is being done more by large institutions, like the County of Los Angeles Public Library, than by smaller ones.[10] However, all public libraries should consider writing coordinated marketing plans because these actually serve as patterns for the marketing tapestries that are being woven — patterns that reinforce a communal sense of direction and focus library resources in a thoughtful and consistent fashion. This focus is important because most libraries already, on a regular or irregular basis, conduct studies to determine user needs, establish outreach programs to entice potential patrons to use the library, promote individual collec-tions to various constituencies, and try to increase the efficiency of various tasks in an effort to improve services. In short, libraries already assign a number of resources, like staff, materials, and money, to marketing.

Ideally, these resources will be allocated in light of the library's long-term strategic plan. As discussed in chapter 3, a strategic planning process requires that a library decide what its major functions or roles will be, write a mission statement expressing this philosophy, and set long-term goals to guide the direction of the organization. A strategic planning process emphasizes creating short-term, measurable objectives to guide day-to-day activities, designing strategies to meet these objectives, and evaluating the success of these strategies.[11]

The problem is that librarians sometimes make decisions about which marketing tasks to accomplish on a fairly casual basis, without considering whether these tasks are in keeping with the library's strategic plan. For example, a library may set goals and objectives that emphasize providing reference and information services to businesses and students, then spend part of its small marketing budget on surveying adult reading interests and promoting materials to persons who are browsing for good books to read. Decisions like these usually result from a librarian's instinctive and commendable wish to respond to patron needs as these are identified. Nevertheless, the failure to concentrate existing and limited resources on planned communal goals can dilute the effectiveness of the marketing program.

Staff members can avoid this problem by reviewing, on an annual basis, the library's strategic planning document, determining critical elements in this that are related to marketing, then developing a formal marketing plan to supplement the strategic plan. Referring to this plan will allow staff members to allocate marketing resources consistently. Moreover, devising a new marketing plan every year allows the library to be fairly flexible in meeting new needs of its target markets, as these arise.

A plan of this nature ideally contains a number of different elements. It tells what collections and services will be the focus of marketing efforts. It describes new and existing target markets the library will concentrate on serving and the goals and objectives for reaching these. It lists specific marketing tasks, gives deadlines for accomplishing these, and estimates the resources that will be expended on each.[12] Figure 11.1 shows a short excerpt from the marketing plan the Pasadena (California) Public Library designed in the mid-1980s.

A library should consider involving as many staff members as possible in designing its marketing plan. This is because studies have generally shown that staff participation in goal setting can ease employee fears about making planned changes, increase individual motivation to work toward these changes, and increase management's understanding of the practical problems that might be involved in implementing the changes.[13]

However, it will be more difficult and more time consuming to reach consensus if the planning group is too large. One way to resolve this issue is to ask staff members in each department to review the strategic plan, then suggest target markets, programs, and tasks that their department might address. These ideas can then be presented to a centralized planning committee by one representative from each department.

Obviously, the comprehensiveness of the marketing plan will vary from library to library, depending on a number of different factors. These include

1. the number of service-oriented goals and objectives in the strategic plan;

2. the extent to which a library is serving a community where the target markets are changing or growing;

3. the amount of money that can be spent on marketing efforts;

4. the amount of staff time that can be devoted to marketing; and

5. the number of different staff members who will be involved in marketing efforts.

Libraries with few staff and resources may have marketing plans that are only a few pages in length. Large libraries that are planning many improvements in their services and collections may have plans of over 100 pages in length.

Most marketing plans of this sort do not spell out the names of the employees who will accomplish each marketing task. However, accountability can be encouraged at the departmental level by specifying who will be responsible for what task. Enthusiasm will run highest when employees are working on tasks that are best suited to their skills and interests.

(Text continues on page 306.)

GOALS

	I	II	III	IV	V
	1983-84	1984-85	1985-86	1986-87	1987-88

Goal #1

The Pasadena Public Library will develop a user-oriented library. Any barriers to use, including physical, language and cultural barriers, will be eliminated or minimized. In addition, library facilities, collections and services will be designed to be self-service as much as possible, since many library users do not ask for assistance in using the library. Emphasis will be placed on continual evaluation of accessibility of the buildings and collections and use by the public, with attention given to the needs of the handicapped.

Objective #1: Place a coordinated system of information and directional signs both outside and inside the central library and branches.

Action Items:

1. Place signs which indicate the location of central and branch facilities at strategic places and major intersections throughout the community.   x

2. Place uniform signs in front of each branch which are easily seen by passersby and which identify the building as a library.   x

3. Place uniform signs at each facility which indicate where the location of the parking lot is.   x

x = indicates project to begin

(Fig. 11.1 continues on page 302.)

Fig. 11.1. Excerpt from marketing plan of the Pasadena Public Library.

	I 1983-84	II 1984-85	III 1985-86	IV 1986-87	V 1987-88
4. Place uniform signs inside each branch which indicate juvenile and adult collections, restrooms, meeting rooms, location and visibility of special collections such as new books and displays, fire exits and fire extinguishers.		x			
5. Place signs at Central which indicate all of the above as well as special locations such as genealogy room, MCLS offices, children's historical room, microform and periodical center.					
a. Prepare comprehensive signage plan.	x				
b. Implement provisions of plan.		x			
6. Design and make available brochures and maps which show the location of materials and amenities, in other languages in addition to English. Assemble into packet for new library registrants.	x				

Objective #2: To provide library services and resources which take into account the information needs of special interest groups, foreign languages spoken by residents in the community, and changes and issues in the community which can be used as a guide to book selection and programming. In addition, the library will provide materials and information presenting all points of view on current and historical issues.

Action Items:

	I 1983-84	II 1984-85	III 1985-86	IV 1986-87	V 1987-88
1. Annual endorsement of Library Bill of Rights by Library Board.	x	x	x	x	x
2. Develop a book selection policy (See Goal #8, Objective #1).	x				

(Fig. 11.1 continues on page 303.)

	I 1983-84	II 1984-85	III 1985-86	IV 1986-87	V 1987-88
3. Although an indepth community analysis project will be completed every five years, an analysis of various statistics will be conducted annually by December in order to be aware of changes in the community.	x	x	x	x	x
Objective #3: Books will be arranged in the most convenient way for public use. Although the planned additional stack levels in the central library will allow for the arrangement of all adult circulating books in a single numerical order, individual departments will try as much as possible to interfile special collections and eliminate confusing shelving arrangements and broken runs of numbers.					
Action Items:					
1. Rearrange central stack area within existing space.	x	—	—	—	—
2. Complete construction of the second and third levels of stacks.	—	—	x	—	—
3. Rearrange reference collections after circulating material is moved to central stack area.	—	—	x	—	—
Objective #4: Expand services for those who cannot come to the library (i.e., the homebound, those in nursing homes and institutions).					
Action Items:					
1. Inventory and survey needs of those in institutions.	x	—	—	—	—

(Fig. 11.1 continues on page 304.)

	I 1983-84	II 1984-85	III 1985-86	IV 1986-87	V 1987-88
2. Coordinate volunteer activity to increase the number of people served at home or through institutions.		X	X	X	X
3. Provide accessibility to library services for homebound and those in institutions via cable TV.			X	X	X

Objective #5: Through responses to the market research survey and patron registration data, the library will identify those who do not use the library and will attempt to explain why. Although recognizing that many individuals or groups will never use the library, the library will identify potential users and plan programs, collections or other library activities of particular interest to these potential users of the library.

Action Items:

	I 1983-84	II 1984-85	III 1985-86	IV 1986-87	V 1987-88
1. Based on annual patron registration figures, nonusers will be identified and changes will be made to convert nonusers into users. (See Goal #2, Objective #5.)	X	X	X	X	X
2. Identify potential use and locations for minibranch service outlets and bookmobile service, as a means of reaching nonusers.	X				

Objective #6: Emphasis will be placed on improving staff skills in understanding and communicating with a variety of people and in being sensitive to their needs.

Action Items:

	I 1983-84	II 1984-85	III 1985-86	IV 1986-87	V 1987-88
1. Public service desks will be provided with a list of translators whom staff can call upon to assist foreign language patrons.	X				

(Fig. 11.1 continues on page 305.)

	I	II	III	IV	V
	1983-84	1984-85	1985-86	1986-87	1987-88
2. A staff development committee will be established which, in the first year, will work toward recommending specific training needs.	x				
3. Based on the above recommendations, implement a staff training program.		x	x	x	x

Objective #7: Patron use and hourly circulation figures, especially at the branches, will be studied to determine the best hours to provide library service. Staff schedules and hours of operation will be based on the needs of the community rather than the convenience of the staff. Varying hours of operation will be experimented with at the branches.

Action Items:

	I	II	III	IV	V
	1983-84	1984-85	1985-86	1986-87	1987-88
1. Operating hours will be evaluated and adjusted when appropriate on an annual basis.	x	x	x	x	x

Objective #8: Although the library cannot and should not develop indepth and comprehensive collections in many subject areas, emphasis will be placed on access to and rapid delivery of information from other libraries through local cooperative resource-sharing arrangements or interlibrary loan. (See Goal #6—cooperative ventures for action items.)

Reprinted with permission from Wood (1988).

Providing Sufficient Resources to Carry out the Marketing Plan

It will be easier for staff members to carry out the marketing plan if they are given adequate levels of resources, particularly staff time and money. Indeed, various studies have shown that the availability of resources is a major factor influencing both employee productivity and job satisfaction.[14] Failing to provide such resources can place an undue strain on employees and cause them, directly or indirectly, to resist marketing efforts.[15] Unfortunately, as Fine (1986) has noted, it is not uncommon for resources, particularly personnel resources, to be overextended just when a staff is experiencing the greatest stress of a planned change. This can happen if library administrators inadvertently make too many new demands, while failing to withdraw or limit old ones.

As McGinn (1988) has noted, most profit-oriented businesses have found that marketing is a time-consuming activity. Staff members take time to collect information about consumer needs, using various types of surveys like mail questionnaires, one-on-one interviews, and focus groups. They review these data and the products offered by their competitors, then design products to meet these needs and test them in the marketplace, repeating this process as required. At the same time, they develop pricing, distribution, and promotion strategies and test the efficacy of these.

Many profit-oriented businesses perform these tasks on a large scale, even though this consumes many personnel and monetary resources. After all, marketing activities essentially pay for themselves by increasing consumer sales and raising a company's profit margin.

But public libraries, like other nonprofit organizations, have often been hesitant to make large initial investments in marketing, because their budgets are already stretched thinly and they are reluctant to pass cost increases on to their patrons. As a result, many libraries choose to begin marketing on a smaller scale, one that emphasizes what McGinn (1988) calls "rudimentary" product development.[16] They often finance these efforts by reallocating money and staff time in their existing budget. For example, a library may drop one or more current but ineffective programs and channel the staff time and money saved into the marketing effort. Reallocation is easiest when the library has followed a strategic planning process that spells out which programs should receive funding priority and which, by their absence from the strategic plan, should not. Reallocating existing resources has a side benefit as well: the library's efficiency may be increased.

Nevertheless, limiting the initial investment in marketing activities to the small amount of funds that can be "raised" through budget reallocation may not be the best solution. This is because studies have shown that libraries that invest more money in marketing activities receive significantly more support from their funding bodies than libraries that do not. For example, Berger (1979) found higher levels of funding among public libraries that conduct marketing research and that plan and evaluate the success of their marketing efforts.

Studies like this suggest that public libraries should strive to introduce marketing on a larger scale whenever possible. It will be easiest for a library to intertwine a marketing philosophy throughout its operations if it hires a highly trained specialist to coordinate its marketing efforts. Ideally, the specialist should possess an in-depth knowledge of marketing techniques that will allow the library to anticipate, rather than simply react to, changes in the target markets. It can then put programs in place to meet these needs and increase institutional effectiveness over the long term. The St. Louis (Missouri) Public Library looked for someone with such expertise several years ago, when it placed the following advertisement seeking someone who could direct a systemwide marketing program: "Reporting to the director of development, the director of marketing formulates and maintains a marketing information system. Develops an annual marketing plan as well as a five-year marketing plan. Identifies and evaluates current situations and future trends that would have major marketing and public relations implications for the library. Develops and implements public relations programs designed to enhance the library's image, gain awareness and use of the library" (Classified, 1988, 11).

Libraries that cannot afford to hire a full- or part-time marketing expert should consider hiring a knowledgeable consultant or firm to help with marketing projects on an as-needed basis. For example, in 1986 the Queens Borough (New York) Public Library hired a nationally known polling firm to survey, via telephone, 2,000 library users and nonusers. The firm identified a number of specific problems on which the library could focus, including a generally low level of awareness of library services and low levels of use among low-income and Hispanic residents (Leerburger, 1989). Although marketing consultants do not come cheaply, the knowledge they bring can easily pay for itself.[17] It is particularly helpful to hire a consultant when setting up a systemwide marketing plan, because he may be able to quickly identify potential strengths and weaknesses in the library's approach.

Libraries with few discretionary funds may wish to recruit skilled volunteers to help with marketing activities. For example, one public library gathered a research team comprised of volunteers from area marketing firms and students from the Business Department at the University of Denver to survey parents and children about the types of facilities they needed in a children's room (Walters and Sandlian, 1991).[18] But using volunteers to aid with marketing efforts has its drawbacks. Some staff time still must be used to recruit volunteers, coordinate their efforts, and educate them about the library environment in general. Also, because volunteers have other commitments, they may not be as accountable for their actions as paid library staff. For these reasons, volunteers are best used for one-time projects, like setting up a marketing plan in a small library or conducting a single marketing study in a larger one.

In addition to providing personnel resources to carry out the marketing plan, the library should set aside some cash to cover marketing needs that are unrelated to staff time. For example, money may be needed to perform such tasks as printing marketing surveys, expanding particular sections of the collection, and advertising the library's wares.

Evaluating the Success of the Marketing Plan

Libraries that are interested in weaving a full and rich marketing tapestry should also take steps to evaluate the success of their marketing plans. Such evaluation can provide concrete information on whether the quality or quantity of services has increased as a result of marketing efforts. Changes made as a result of the findings help ensure that the library is providing high quality service designed to meet patron needs. But a good evaluation will have a cumulative effect as well, because the library that analyzes its mistakes can learn from these and build more successful marketing campaigns in the future.

A good evaluation plan will strive to answer two very basic questions. First, were the library's marketing objectives met? That is, did the marketing program improve services or collections to the target market(s)? Consider the case of a public library that is trying to increase high school students' knowledge and use of the reference collection by 15 percent. It might decide to survey students at the citywide high school at the beginning of the year to determine their levels of knowledge and use, then arrange for a reference librarian to visit each English class in the school to discuss reference materials of value to students. The librarian might discuss, in sophomore classes, resources that will aid them with homework in general; with junior classes, resources to help them complete an assigned term paper; and with senior classes, resources to aid with college and career choices. Several months later, the library can resurvey each group of students to determine how much their knowledge and use of the reference collection has increased.

A second question that the library will need to ask is the following: what were the strengths and weaknesses of a particular marketing strategy? The answer to this question will help the library determine which strategies should be repeated and which modified or dropped. For example, the library might discover that use of reference materials increased by 22 percent among juniors and by less than 10 percent among sophomores and seniors. It might conclude that tying marketing efforts to a class assignment is a strategy that should be repeated in the future, because this practice gave students more of an impetus to visit the public library.

Today, many public libraries lack comprehensive evaluation programs for a variety of reasons. One of the most common is a perceived lack of staff time.[19] It is likely, however, that those libraries experiencing the severest staff shortages will benefit most from evaluation. After all, evaluation has the potential to save staff time in the long run by making library operations more efficient and effective. Hiring an outside consultant to perform initial evaluations and to set in place an evaluation program is one way to resolve the difficulties here. Another is assigning evaluation responsibilities to a single staff member or, in larger libraries, one staff member per department.

A related problem is the lack of staff members who have an in-depth, specialized knowledge of evaluation techniques. In order for evaluation results to be both reliable and valid, staff members should be knowledgeable about the collection and analysis of marketing research data. Some professional staff members may have taken courses in evaluation techniques or in research methods when they were in library school. However, they may need to supplement these by taking continuing education classes or by reading some of the recently published books on evaluation or collection evaluation. These include works by Baker and Lancaster (1991), Bawden (1990), Hernon (1990), American Library Association (1989), Lancaster (1988), and Robbins and Zweizig (1988). Pickton's (1989) article also provides an overview of evaluation techniques that are commonly used by marketing and advertising specialists.

Another barrier to evaluation is fear. Staff members may be afraid that their abilities are being questioned, particularly if the evaluation uncovers flaws in the library's marketing scheme (Neenan, 1986; DuMont and DuMont, 1979). But a good evaluation program is a developmental activity rather than a judgmental one. Its main purpose is to collect factual data to identify strengths and weaknesses in the marketing strategies used. The former should be supported; the latter corrected in whatever manner is appropriate: modifying the marketing strategies used, training staff in more advanced marketing techniques, adding appropriate resources, or making other changes to improve service.

Fear can be lessened if those responsible for evaluation share information about how evaluation data will be collected, interpreted, and used to correct problems (Alkin, Stecher, and Geiger, 1982). In turn, staff can improve evaluation efforts by sharing their knowledge of services and patron needs, knowledge that may lead to more realistic suggestions for improvement and thus to increased utilization of evaluation results (Braskamp and Brown, 1980).

Another major barrier to evaluation of services is a lack of commitment to make changes based on the results. For example, Schlachter and Belli (1976) found in 78 percent of the California public libraries in which evaluations were performed, no changes were made. Some libraries may have had valid reasons for taking no action, such as the lack of immediate resources to solve the problem. However, the fact that so many libraries failed to make changes may also indicate that some evaluations were conducted on a pro forma basis rather than as a serious attempt to improve the quality of service. This pattern has been documented in settings other than libraries and may be overcome to some extent if the person who conducts the evaluation takes an active role in fostering the use of the information (Reisner and others, 1982; Braskamp and Brown, 1980).

Adopting Other Techniques to Reinforce Staff Awareness of Marketing Concepts on a Regular Basis

The awareness of staff, supervisors, and trustees about the importance of marketing will increase when a library trains its staff to understand basic marketing concepts and when it incorporates these concepts into the library's planning and evaluation processes. But a library will not be fully able to achieve its marketing vision unless it consistently reinforces the concepts learned.

Patrons naturally reinforce some marketing concepts by sharing their thanks, comments, and complaints with those who work on the reference or circulation desks. But employees who work behind the scenes do not receive direct feedback from patrons and so may not be able to refine, as quickly as public services personnel, their understanding of patron needs.[20]

Libraries can take a number of different steps to encourage staff members to interweave marketing concepts into their jobs. They can

1. provide continued training in marketing concepts, as needed;

2. hire replacement staff who have a marketing or service orientation;

3. schedule regular discussions of customer needs, services, and marketing concepts at meetings of the staff and board of trustees;

4. use positive motivators to stimulate marketing efforts among staff; and

5. build customer-service components into employee evaluation procedures.

Each is discussed below.

Providing Continued Training in Marketing Concepts, as Needed

In addition to the one-time marketing workshops mentioned earlier, public libraries ideally should arrange for continued training in marketing concepts. Two types of training are recommended: an introduction to basic marketing concepts for new staff and periodic training to reinforce and expand the marketing knowledge of existing staff members.

It is best to introduce basic marketing concepts to new staff during the employee's orientation sessions. This assumes that the library provides some type of orientation, an assumption which is, unfortunately, not always valid. The literature is replete with horror stories of librarians who were thrust onto the reference desk the first day they arrived, without knowing even such basic information as the location of the catalog (and the rest rooms!), the major collections within the building, or the procedures for filing reserve and interlibrary loan requests. Although little research has been done on this issue, the studies that exist show that library orientations tend to be brief and poorly planned affairs. For example, Stabler (1987) found that new staff members were introduced to their colleagues, then given short building tours and small amounts of very general information about the institution as a whole. Some new workers received the equivalent of one day of training and fewer than half of those in professional positions were trained for more than one week. Orientations like these often guarantee that customers will receive less than optimal service.

Thorough, well-planned orientations can decrease the apprehension and stress that new employees feel, increase the speed with which they learn their job, positively affect their job progress, and influence both how long they will stay with an organization and their degree of loyalty to it (Albsmeyer, 1986). This suggests that libraries that wish to produce a rich tapestry of excellent service, the kind a marketing mindset would dictate, should ensure that staff members receive adequate orientations. At the very least, new employees should receive information on the history and mission of the library, its organizational structure, the particulars of the jobs they were hired to perform, and the same type of training in marketing that other employees have had, including the relationship between marketing in general and the jobs they are filling. Customer-service personnel should also be given information about the library's major products, like the major collections that are offered, the benefits of using these products, and the systems and procedures that will allow patrons to obtain what they need. Obviously, the complexity of the job to be performed will dictate the length of the training program; this may range, on the average, from several days to several weeks.[21]

The library should also consider providing training in more sophisticated marketing concepts, once its staff members have fully grasped the basics. Such training will help staff members keep abreast of new developments in the field and develop expertise at particular tasks, like using census data in marketing research, conducting focus group sessions, and writing persuasive promotional materials. The Queens Borough (New York) Public Library, for example, had the regional sales manager of the local B. Dalton bookstore chain present a continuing-education program on merchandising collections (Sivulich, 1989).

Hiring Replacement Staff Who Have a Strong Marketing or Service Orientation

When a library needs to hire staff, whether for new or vacant positions, it should consider choosing personnel who exhibit a strong marketing or service orientation. This is because the characteristics of individual staff members can greatly affect user satisfaction, levels of use, and loyalty of patrons to the library in general. Staff members who lack such an orientation can, without meaning to, undermine the efforts that have been taken to attract patrons.

Consider, for example, the large body of literature, from libraries of all types, on marketing-related characteristics that patrons desire in public service librarians. One of these is friendliness or warmth. Gothberg (1976) verified this during a controlled experiment in a public library. She trained reference librarians to exhibit two different communication styles, using both verbal and nonverbal cues. Such actions as a friendly tone of voice, a listening attitude, and good eye contact characterized a caring style. The other style required the librarians to remain polite but to distance themselves from their patrons. As expected, library users were more satisfied when they dealt with the caring librarians. This was true even though patrons felt their queries were answered with equal competence by both types of librarians.

Another characteristic that patrons want in public service employees is approachability. For example, Westbrook (1984) found that 39 percent of the people who had questions did not ask for help because library staff members appeared too busy to assist them; another 18 percent felt the librarians might be unwilling to help them. A related study found that some staff members are significantly more approachable than others. These librarians immediately acknowledge a patron's presence when the patron moves toward them—if not verbally then through establishing immediate eye contact or "flashing their eyebrows." Receptive librarians also smile at patrons and use evaluative gestures, such as nodding, to indicate that they are interested in and are absorbing patron requests. In cases where patrons could choose between asking for help from a receptive and a nonreceptive staff member, patrons always approached the former. When users had a choice between two similarly receptive staff members, they approached standing librarians rather than seated ones 10 out of 11 times, because they perceived a seated librarian as one who was busy and would rather not be interrupted (Kazlauskas, 1976).

Patrons also want public service librarians to be assertive, to approach customers to see if they need help. In fact, this is rarely done; most librarians rely on patrons to initiate the reference query (Wilkinson, 1972). Although this is understandable in libraries that are very short-staffed, it is less so in libraries that have adequate levels of public service librarians on duty at any one time.

Discussing Customer Needs, Services, and Marketing at Regular Meetings of the Library Staff and Board of Trustees

Many libraries devote a majority of the time spent at departmental and librarywide staff meetings to discussing procedural changes, like modifications in how one requests sick leave or completes order cards. But staff meetings can also be used to reinforce various marketing concepts. For example, an administrator can take the opportunity to praise the employee who designed an especially effective book display, who took the time to lead a confused patron to the stack section he was seeking, or who redesigned his work station so that new books could be processed more quickly.

Staff meetings can also be used to give 10- or 15-minute continuing education talks that explain simple new marketing concepts or discuss how an already learned marketing concept can be applied. These may be particularly effective if such talks are designed by different staff members, both professional and nonprofessional, who can bring their own particular insights to a problem.

It is also important to discuss issues related to marketing at regular meetings of the board of trustees, because trustees are responsible for making the policy decisions that guide library operations. Although various authors have stressed the kinds of duties that trustees ideally perform, few researchers have examined in any detail the tasks that trustees perform during regular board meetings.

One exception to this is a study that analyzed in detail the contents of 80 different sets of minutes from a representative sample of Illinois public library trustees. Baker (1984) found little consideration of marketing-related issues at these board meetings. Discussions of community analysis and library service were held at only 6 percent of the meetings; of policy issues at only 7 percent; of public relations at only 4 percent; and of short- or long-term planning, at only 1 percent. Rather than concentrating their attention on these complex and substantive issues (issues that those surveyed admitted were important!), trustees tended to focus on performing simple tasks that had immediate and concrete results, like paying bills and making decisions about insurance coverage. Shavit (1986) drew a similar conclusion when discussing the politics of public librarianship.

Both Baker and Shavit also found that most of the agendas for board meetings were set by the head librarian rather than by the board. This suggests that many library directors were themselves focusing on easily performed, concrete tasks rather than on substantive issues related to services in general or marketing in particular. Obviously, this is a pattern that should be changed.

Using Positive Motivators to Stimulate Marketing Efforts

Library administrators should consider using a variety of motivational techniques to encourage employees to think in marketing terms. For example, supervisors may wish to discuss, early on, how each individual's job is critical to the success of the library's marketing program. This conversation will serve to reinforce the more general discussion of how departmental tasks affect the satisfaction levels of patrons who use the library, as well as let the employee know that the supervisor recognizes and values the job that the employee is performing.

Job enrichment can also be used to stimulate marketing activities. Job enrichment is the process of adding challenge to tasks that an employee considers routine in an effort to make the tasks more interesting. For example, the full-time shelver in a small library may become bored over time if her only duty is reshelving items that have been returned. However, she may become more highly motivated if the supervisor gives her complete responsibility for redesigning shelving procedures so that they are more efficient. Job enrichment practices can involve each employee in efforts to increase patron satisfaction and reduce patron costs. It can also encourage individual accountability for work performed and is thus capable of increasing productivity.

Coaching is another technique that can reinforce marketing concepts. In coaching, a supervisor assigns a particular task, like asking a technical services worker to come up with ways to increase productivity so that patrons won't have to wait as long for new books to be processed. The supervisor then monitors the employee's performance, coaching the employee by praising him for even small actions that lead to increased productivity. It is particularly effective to use the coaching technique immediately after presenting a workshop on a new concept, because this helps reinforce the ideas learned.[22]

Although praise is particularly critical when an employee is performing a new task, supervisors should not forget to praise, over the long term, each employee who applies marketing concepts correctly or who reveals a strong service orientation. This is because people have a natural desire for recurring recognition, a desire that consistent praise can meet effectively and inexpensively (Maslow, 1970). What's more, consistent praise has been found, in many settings, to improve performance significantly. For example, Goddard (1987) describes a series of studies that found that 87 percent of college students who had current work praised improved both the quality and quantity of future performances.

Building Customer-Service Components into Employee Evaluation Procedures

Library managers can also encourage a marketing orientation by building ratings on this aspect of performance into the performance appraisal and merit raise process. After all, "if a library manager primarily uses technical competence as criteria for distributing organizational rewards, then staff members will strive to become competent, efficient, consistent, and accurate. On the other hand, if managers begin to also recognize and reward those individuals who are willing to develop organizational systems that are accurate and responsive, consistent and compassionate, efficient and sensitive, then librarians might be more inclined to behave in a market-oriented manner toward patrons" (Dragon and Leisner, 1983, 37).

Supervisors can gather factual evidence about an employee's service orientation from personal observation of employee interaction with patrons, from patron letters, suggestions, and complaints, or from other staff members. For example, some years ago the Jones Library in Amherst, Massachusetts, asked staff members to assess their own performance and the performance of others with whom they worked, based on eight criteria that measured an employee's ability to relate to the public (Turner, 1978). Supervisors summarized and analyzed this information, then discussed possible improvements with each employee rated.

Being Sensitive to Issues Related to Resistance to Change

It will be easiest for the library to implement the changes discussed here if all employees, particularly the supervisors who assume important roles in leading them, are sensitive to the needs of those who are resistant to change. As Fine (1986) has pointed out, it is both natural and inevitable for employees to be nervous and to hesitate when they are faced with change. Indeed, Fine says that some resistance may even be positive because it slows the speed with which innovation might otherwise proceed and allows time for people to adjust to it.

The problem occurs when an administrator, frustrated by seeing someone resist change, overreacts and makes a statement that seems to attack the other person, rather than merely to question his behavior (Riggs, 1988). This practice can cause the natural and general uneasiness that many people experience when confronted with change to accelerate into more negative behaviors, including task avoidance, procrastination, and hostility (Baker, 1989).

Supervisors can avoid this acceleration by asking tactful questions designed to determine whether an employee has a valid reason for the resistance. For example, an employee may resist change if the library fails to provide enough resources to implement it effectively, causing the employee to feel stressed and overextended.

A more common reason for resistance is fear, particularly fear that the employee cannot successfully perform a new task. Supervisors can take a variety of steps to correct this problem, including providing sufficient training to reduce employee fears and assuring employees that mistakes made when learning new tasks are to be expected rather than condemned.

Employees can also resist changes that they feel are not needed. In one public library in Ohio, the staff resisted efforts to reintegrate the genre fiction collection into the general fiction collection. Management felt that one interfiled system would make it easier for the technical services staff to inventory the collection, because they would not have to look in three or four possible places for a particular book. However, the staff noted that patrons liked having mysteries and other genre areas separated from the regular collection and that inventories were conducted only once every 10 years. In this case, the employees perceived that the proposed change was not a valid one. Ultimately management agreed to let the collection remain separated by genre.

Questioning the reasons behind employee resistance should allow the supervisor and employee to determine and then address the real barriers to change rather than the surface resistance that may appear to be inflexibility and rigidity on the employee's part.

Conclusion

Public libraries are beginning to adopt the type of collection marketing scheme discussed throughout this book. That is, they are considering issues related to product, price, place, and promotion with an eye to increasing patron satisfaction and reducing patron costs of using the library. They are setting up programs to evaluate their collections and the immediate and long-term needs of community residents, are using marketing principles to redesign their collections to meet these needs, and are using effective promotional techniques. Finally, they are considering ways to weave a marketing mindset throughout the library.

The process described in this final chapter is one that libraries of all sizes can use to weave their own collection development tapestries. The sturdy warp threads, threads comprised of staff education about marketing concepts and of thoughtful planning and implementation of marketing activities, establish the basic pattern of collection development that each library will follow. Library leaders then assume the role of the shuttle by working to interlace employee ideas into this pattern. The result should be a tapestry that evolves over time into a strong and richly textured fabric of excellent service.

Notes

[1]See, for example, Riggs (1988), Bennis and Nanus (1985), and Burns (1978).

[2]For an in-depth review of the research on leadership, see Bass (1990).

[3]Damanpour and others (1989) provide an overview of the relationship between organization performance and the adoption of innovation over time.

[4]Stiles and others (1983) present a brief but thoughtful overview of the role the board can play in setting public relations policy. The model policy statement they include could readily be expanded to cover marketing activities in general.

[5]Percentage calculated from data listed in "Directory of the Association for Library and Information Science Education, 1990-1991" (1990-1991).

[6]The Scottsdale (Arizona) Public Library has even trained several of its most public relations minded staff members to specialize in dealing with patrons who have problems (Manley, 1983).

[7]Two excellent bibliographies of this literature are provided in Norman (1989) and Tucci (1988).

[8]See, for example, Griffore and Griffore (1983).

[9]Creth (1989) provides a good overview of general principles that trainers can use to design effective continuing education programs for library staff.

[10]See, for example, "Library's Marketing Department" (1990).

[11]Wood (1988) gives an excellent overview of the principles of strategic planning.

[12]Dalmon (1992) and Wood (1988) describe the design of effective marketing plans in some detail.

[13]See, for example, Baker (1989) and Damanpour and others (1989).

[14]See, for example, Goddard (1987) and Peters and others (1982).

[15]As Baker (1989) notes, failing to provide sufficient resources can inhibit any type of change that management proposes.

[16]A recent study found that libraries spend less than 2 percent of their budgets on marketing activities (Marketing, 1992).

[17]A national survey conducted in 1988 found that marketing consultants charged an average of $94.20 per hour for their services (Survey, 1988).

[18]Mueller-Alexander (1991) discusses the advantages and disadvantages of using volunteers, consultants, students, and other resources for marketing research.

[19]See, for example, Baker (1987).

[20]This may explain, at least in part, why the materials that public service librarians select are more likely to meet patron needs than those selected by their non-public-service counterparts. See, for example, Turow (1978) and Evans (1969).

[21]Information on orientation and other training programs offered by libraries around the nation can be obtained from the American Library Association Headquarters Library. Interested parties should request materials from the Staff Development Clearinghouse organized by the Library Administration and Management Association, Personnel Administration Section, Staff Development Committee.

[22]When Stephan and others (1988) conducted intensive workshops that emphasized how to conduct a proper reference interview, the accuracy rates of reference librarians rose from 55 percent to 77 percent. But accuracy rates increased to 95 percent in two libraries where follow-up coaching was used.

References

Albsmeyer, Betty. "Orientation of the New Library Employee." *The Unabashed Librarian*, no. 61 (1986): 25-27.

Alkin, Marvin C., Brian M. Stecher, and Frederica L. Geiger. *Title I Evaluation: Utility and Factors Affecting Use*. Northridge, Calif.: Educational Evaluation Associates, 1982.

American Library Association. *Guide to the Evaluation of Library Collections*. Chicago: American Library Association, 1989.

Baker, Sharon L. "Exploring the Use of *Output Measures for Public Libraries* in North Carolina Public Libraries." Iowa City: University of Iowa, School of Library and Information Science, 1987. ERIC ED288538.

_____. "Managing Resistance to Change." *Library Trends* 38, no. 1 (Summer 1989): 53-61.

_____. "A Survey of Illinois Public Library Trustees." *Illinois Library Statistical Report* 14 (August 1984): 1-60.

Baker, Sharon L., and F. Wilfrid Lancaster. *Measurement and Evaluation of Library Services*. 2d ed. Arlington, Va.: Information Resources Press, 1991.

Bass, Bernard M. *Bass and Stogdill's Handbook of Leadership: Theory, Research, and Managerial Applications*. 3d ed. New York: Free Press, 1990.

Bawden, David. *User-Oriented Evaluation of Information Systems and Services*. Brookfield, Vt.: Gower Publications, 1990.

Bennis, Warren, and Burt Nanus. *Leaders: The Strategies for Taking Charge*. New York: Harper and Row, 1985.

Berger, Patricia. "An Investigation of the Relationship Between Public Relations Activities and Budget Allocation in Public Libraries." *Information Processing and Management* 15, no. 4 (1979): 179-93.

Braskamp, Larry A., and Robert D. Brown. *Utilization of Evaluation Information*. San Francisco: Jossey-Bass, 1980.

Burns, James MacGregor. *Leadership*. New York: Harper & Row, 1978.

"Classified Advertising." *Library Hotline* 17 (7 March 1988): 11.

Creth, Sheila D. "Staff Development and Continuing Education." In *Personnel Administration in Libraries*, 2d ed., ed. Sheila Creth and Frederick Duda, 118-51. New York: Neal-Schuman, 1989.

Dalmon, Diane. "Planning for Progress." *Aslib Information* 20, no. 1 (January 1992): 24-26.

Damanpour, Fariborz, Kathryn A. Szabat, and William M. Evan. "The Relationship Between Types of Innovation and Organizational Performance." *Journal of Management Studies* 26, no. 6 (November 1989): 587-601.

D'Elia, George Patrick Michael, and Eleanor Jo Rodger. "Comparative Assessment of Patrons' Uses and Evaluations Across Public Libraries Within a System: A Replication." *Library and Information Science Research* 9, no. 1 (January 1987): 5-20.

"Directory of the Association for Library and Information Science Education, 1990-1991." *Journal of Education for Library and Information Science*, special edition (1990-1991): 9-35.

Dragon, Andrea C., and Tony Leisner. "The ABC's of Implementing Library Marketing." *Journal of Library Administration* 4, no. 4 (1983): 33-47.

Drucker, Peter. *Management: Tasks, Responsibilities, Practices*. New York: Harper & Row, 1974.

DuMont, Rosemary R., and Paul F. DuMont. "Measuring Library Effectiveness: A Review and an Assessment." In *Advances in Librarianship*, vol. 9, ed. Michael Harris, 103-41. New York: Academic Press, 1979.

Engel, Debra. "Putting the Public First: The Baltimore County Approach to Collection Development." *Catholic Library World* 54, no. 3 (October 1982): 122-26.

Evans, G. Edward. "The Influence of Book Selection Agents Upon Book Collection Usage in Academic Libraries." Ph.D. diss., University of Illinois, 1969.

Fine, Sara F. "Technological Innovation, Diffusion, and Resistance: A Historical Perspective." *Journal of Library Administration* 7, no. 1 (Spring 1986): 83-108.

Goddard, Robert W. "Well Done!" *Management World* 16, no. 6 (November/December 1987): 14-16.

Gothberg, Helen. "Immediacy: A Study of Communication Effect on the Reference Process." *Journal of Academic Librarianship* 2, no. 3 (July 1976): 126-29.

Griffore, Robert J., and Gaile D. Griffore. "Some Effects of Study Skills and Adjustment Skills Workshops on College Students." *NASPA Journal* 20, no. 3 (Winter 1983): 34-41.

Grunenwald, Joseph P. "Steps to Take: Marketing the Rural Library." *Rural Libraries* 4, no. 2 (1984): 21-35.

Grunenwald, Joseph P., Linda A. Felicetti, and Karen L. Stewart. "The Effects of Marketing Seminars on the Attitudes of Librarians." *Public Library Quarterly* 10, no. 2 (1990): 3-10.

Hernon, Peter. *Evaluation and Library Decision Making*. Norwood, N.J.: Ablex, 1990.

Kazlauskas, Edward. "An Exploratory Study: A Kinesic Analysis of Academic Library Public Service Points." *Journal of Academic Librarianship* 2, no. 3 (July 1976): 130-34.

Lancaster, F. W. *If You Want to Evaluate Your Library....* Champaign: University of Illinois, Graduate School of Library and Information Science, 1988.

Leerburger, Benedict A. *Promoting and Marketing the Library*. Rev. ed. Boston: G. K. Hall, 1989.

"Library's Marketing Department." *Library Administrator's Digest* 25, no. 9 (November 1990): 66.

Manley, Will. "Facing the Public." *Wilson Library Bulletin* 57, no. 10 (June 1983): 846-47.

"Marketing: It Works!" *Library Administrator's Digest* 26, no. 8 (October 1991): 58.

"Marketing the Library." *Library Administrator's Digest* 27, no. 1 (January 1992): 3.

Maslow, Abraham H. *Motivation and Personality*. 2d ed. New York: Harper & Row, 1970.

McGinn, Howard F. "Libraries and Marketing: New Worlds – Old Worlds." *North Carolina Libraries* 46, no. 3 (Fall 1988): 126-31.

Mueller-Alexander, Jeanette M. "Alternative Sources for Marketing Research for Libraries." *Special Libraries* 82, no. 3 (Summer 1991): 159-64.

Neenan, Peter A. "Impact Evaluation: Context and Function." *RQ* 25, no. 3 (Spring 1986): 305-9.

Norman, O. Gene. "Marketing Library and Information Services: An Annotated Guide to Recent Trends and Developments." *Reference Services Review* 17, no. 1 (Spring 1989): 43-64.

Peters, L. H., C. D. Fisher, and E. J. O'Connor. "The Moderating Effect of Situational Control of Performance Variance on the Relationship Between Individual Differences and Performance." *Personnel Psychology* 35, no. 3 (Autumn 1982): 609-21.

Pickton, David. "Evaluating a Campaign Programme: Will It Work, Is It Working, Has It Worked ... Why?" In *Planned Public Relations for Libraries: A PPRG Handbook*, ed. Margaret Kinnell, 88-109. London: Taylor Graham, 1989.

Reisner, Elizabeth R., Marvin C. Alkin, Robert F. Boruch, Robert L. Linn, and Jason Millman. *Assessment of the Title I Evaluation and Reporting System*. Washington, D.C.: U.S. Department of Education, 1982.

Riggs, Donald E. "Leadership Versus Management in Technical Services." In *Library Management and Technical Services: The Changing Role of Technical Services in Library Organizations*, ed. Jennifer Cargill, 27-39. New York: Haworth Press, 1988.

Robbins, Jane, and Douglas L. Zweizig. *Are We There Yet? Evaluating Library Collections, Reference Services, Programs and Personnel*. Madison: University of Wisconsin-Madison, School of Library and Information Studies, 1988.

Schlachter, Gail, and Donna Belli. "Program Evaluation – An Alternative to Divine Guidance." *California Librarian* 37, no. 4 (October 1976): 26-31.

Shavit, David. *The Politics of Public Librarianship*. Westport, Conn.: Greenwood Press, 1986.

Sivulich, Kenneth G. "How We Run the Queens Library Good (and Doubled Circulation in Seven Years)." *Library Journal* 114, no. 3 (15 February 1989): 123-27.

Stabler, Karen Y. "Introductory Training of Academic Reference Librarians: A Survey." *RQ* 26, no. 3 (Spring 1987): 363-69.

Stephan, Sandy, Ralph Gers, Lillie Seward, Nancy Bolin, and Jim Partridge. "Reference Breakthrough in Maryland." *Public Libraries* 27, no. 4 (Winter 1988): 202-3.

Stiles, Florence Frette, Janet R. Bean, and Virginia Beckler. "Public Relations for the Public Library." In *Persuasive Public Relations for Libraries*, ed. Kathleen Kelly Rummel and Esther Perica, 47-59. Chicago: American Library Association, 1983.

Survey of Consulting Rates and Business Practices. 1988/1989 ed. San Jose, Calif.: Professional and Technical Consultants Association, 1988.

Tucci, Valerie K. "Information Marketing for Libraries." In *Annual Review of Information Science and Technology*, vol. 23, ed. Martha E. Williams, 59-82. New York: Elsevier Science, 1988.

Turner, Anne M. "Why Do Department Heads Take Longer Coffee Breaks? A Public Library Evaluates Itself." *American Libraries* 9, no. 4 (April 1978): 213-15.

Turow, Joseph. "The Impact of Differing Orientations of Librarians on the Process of Children's Book Selection: A Case Study of Library Tensions." *Library Quarterly* 48, no. 3 (July 1978): 276-92.

Vavrek, Bernard. "The Public Library at Crisis: Is Marketing the Answer?" *North Carolina Libraries* 46, no. 3 (Fall 1988): 142-47.

Walters, Suzanne, and Pamela Sandlian. "A Room of Their Own: Planning the New Denver Children's Library." *School Library Journal* 37, no. 2 (February 1991): 26-29.

Weingand, Darlene E. "Educating Staff for Public Relations." In *Planned Public Relations for Libraries: A PPRG Handbook*, ed. Margaret Kinnell, 3-8. London: Taylor Graham, 1989.

Westbrook, Lynn. "Catalog Failure and Reference Service: A Preliminary Study." *RQ* 24, no. 1 (Fall 1984): 82-90.

Wilkinson, Billy R. *Reference Services for Undergraduate Students: Four Case Studies*. Metuchen, N.J.: Scarecrow Press, 1972.

Wood, Elizabeth J. *Strategic Marketing for Libraries: A Handbook*. Westport, Conn.: Greenwood Press, 1988.

Index